Stress-testing the Banking System

Stress tests are used in risk management by banks in order to determine how certain crisis scenarios would affect the value of their portfolios, and by public authorities for financial stability purposes. Until the first half of 2007, interest in stress-testing was largely restricted to practitioners. Since then, the global financial system has been hit by deep turbulences, including the fallout from sub-prime mortgage lending. Many observers have pointed out that the severity of the crisis has been largely due to its unexpected nature and have claimed that a more extensive use of stress-testing methodologies would have helped to alleviate the repercussions of the crisis. This book analyses the theoretical underpinnings, as well as the practical aspects, of applying such methodologies. Building on the experience gained by the economists of many national and international financial authorities, it provides an updated toolkit for both practitioners and academics.

Mario Quagliariello is a senior economist in the Regulation and Supervisory Policies Department of the Bank of Italy. He has been the representative of the Bank of Italy in a number of international working groups dealing with financial stability issues and has published several articles in international and Italian journals. He has a PhD in economics from the University of York.

Stress-testing the Banking System

Methodologies and Applications

Edited by

Mario Quagliariello

CAMBRIDGE UNIVERSITY PRESS
Cambridge, New York, Melbourne, Madrid, Cape Town, Singapore, São Paulo, Delhi

Cambridge University Press
The Edinburgh Building, Cambridge CB2 8RU, UK

Published in the United States of America by Cambridge University Press, New York

www.cambridge.org
Information on this title: www.cambridge.org/9780521767309

First published 2009

Printed in the United Kingdom at the University Press, Cambridge

A catalogue record for this publication is available from the British Library

Library of Congress Cataloguing in Publication data
Stress-testing the banking system : methodologies and applications / edited by Mario Quagliariello.
  p.   cm.
ISBN 978-0-521-76730-9
1. Banks and banking.   2. Banks and banking – Risk management.   3. Bank failures – Prevention.
4. Financial crises.   I. Quagliariello, Mario.   II. Title.
HG1601.S687   2009
332.1068′1–dc22
2009010745

ISBN 978-0-521-76730-9 hardback

Contents

Figures

Tables

Boxes

Contributors

Editor

Mario Quagliariello is a senior economist in the Regulation and Supervisory Policies Department of the Bank of Italy. He has been the representative of Banca d'Italia in a number of international working groups dealing with financial stability issues and has published several articles in international and Italian journals. His interests concern macro-prudential analysis and stress tests, Basel 2 Capital Accord and procyclicality, the economics of financial regulation. He has a Ph.D. in economics from the University of York (UK).

Contributors

Patrizia Baudino joined the Financial Stability Board (FSB) in 2007. She is seconded from the European Central Bank (ECB), which she joined in 2002 after completing her Ph.D. at Princeton University. At the FSB, as well as at the ECB, she works on financial stability issues.

Michael Boss is a member of the Financial Stability Analysis Division at the Oesterreichische Nationalbank (OeNB), where his main working area is quantitative financial stability analysis

and stress-testing. In cooperation with colleagues from the OeNB's Research Department and academia, he initiated and co-headed the project 'Systemic Risk Monitor', which is presented in this book. He regularly participates in missions of the International Monetary Fund (IMF) to Central and Eastern European countries as an expert on financial stability analysis. Prior to joining the OeNB in 1999 he was a research assistant at the Vienna Institute for Advanced Studies.

Francesco Cannata is Head of the Regulatory Impact Assessment Unit in the Regulation and Supervisory Policies Department of the Bank of Italy. He holds an M.Sc. in finance from the Cass Business School (UK) and a Ph.D. in finance from University 'Tor Vergata', Rome (Italy). His main interests are the economics of financial regulation, Basel 2 and credit risk.

Mike Carhill is Director in the Risk Analysis Division (RAD) of the Office of the Comptroller of the Currency since September 2003. RAD employs quantitative risk modelling experts who specialise in one of about one dozen lines of business to advise bank examiners, bankers and policymakers on the state-of-the-art in risk management information systems. He holds a Ph.D. in monetary theory from Washington University.

Olli Castrén has worked for the ECB since 1999. In his current job as principal expert in the Financial Stability Division, he coordinates the analysis of the euro area banking sector and also many of the briefing notes to the ECB executive board members. From 1999–2004, he worked as Senior Economist in the Directorate General Economics of the Bank. Prior to joining ECB, he worked at the Bank of Finland and Bank of England, and finished his Ph.D. in 1998 (Warwick University, UK).

Mathias Drehmann currently works as an economist at the Bank for International Settlements. After finishing a Ph.D. from the University of Bonn, he worked for the Bank of England and briefly for the European Central Bank. His main expertise lies in measuring financial stability as well as credit and liquidity risk modelling.

John Fell is Head of the Financial Stability Division of the ECB and editor of the ECB's *Financial Stability Review*. He is also Chairman of the Task Force on Macro Stress-Testing of the Banking Supervision Committee (ECB). He previously worked as an advisor on capital market issues in the Monetary Policy Directorate of the ECB, at the European Monetary Institute and the Central Bank of Ireland. He holds postgraduate degrees in economics (University College of

Dublin) and in finance (Dublin City University).

Adam Głogowski works as an economist at the National Bank of Poland. His main areas of responsibility include the development of stress-testing methodologies for the Polish banking system as well as contributing to the Financial Stability Report. He holds a Master's degree in economics from the Warsaw School of Economics.

Takashi Isogai is Deputy Head of the International Affairs Section of the Financial Systems and Bank Examination Department at the Bank of Japan. He received an M.A. in information engineering from Shinshu University (Japan). His main expertise lies in credit and market risk model analysis, software development in related fields and computer science.

Gerald Krenn joined the Oesterreichische Nationalbank in 1997 as part of the banking inspections team with a focus on internal market risk models. He is now working with the Financial Stability Analysis Division as a specialist for quantitative methods of financial stability analysis and stress-testing. He holds a Ph.D. in computer science from Technical University Vienna, where he was a research assistant prior to joining the Nationalbank.

Ulrich Krüger joined the Deutsche Bundesbank in 1999 and started to work for the Banking Supervision Department in 2002. He is a senior economist and carries out quantitative research related to Basel 2 and credit risk. He was involved in the Quantitative Impact Studies organised by the Basel Committee between 2001 and 2006. Before joining Deutsche Bundesbank he completed a Ph.D. in mathematics.

Sebastiano Laviola is Head of the International Cooperation Division in the Regulation and Supervisory Policies Department of the Bank of Italy. He is the Chairman of the Working Group on Macroprudential Analysis of the Banking Supervision Committee (ECB) and of the Subgroup on Operational Networks of the Committee of European Banking Supervisors.

Franka Liedorp is Policy Advisor with De Nederlandsche Bank. She works in the Quantitative Risk Management Section, focusing on a new solvency framework for insurance companies. Before that, she worked in the Supervisory Strategy Section, on a range of strategic topics, including the analysis of interbank contagion, internationalisation of banks and the risk of reinsurance.

Juri Marcucci holds a Ph.D. in economics from the University of California, San Diego. He works in the Research Department of the Bank of Italy, which he joined in 2004. He has been a lecturer at the University of Bologna since 2003. His research interests are in financial econometrics, forecasting and applied econometrics. His work has appeared in several journals.

Clément Martin joined the Banque de France in 2006, and is currently an

economist in the Banking Studies Division of the French Banking Commission. He graduated from ENSAE, obtained a Master's degree in economics from the University of Paris–Dauphine and a Master's degree in international relations from the University of Paris–Assas.

Marina Moretti is Deputy Chief of the Financial Sector Policy Division in the IMF's Monetary and Capital Markets Department. She is currently seconded to the secretariat of the Financial Stability Board in Basel. Prior to joining the IMF in 1999, she served as Financial Economist at the World Bank and at the Organisation for Economic Co-operation and Development (OECD).

Marc Pröpper works as a senior policy advisor for De Nederlandsche Bank. Areas of his work include the Financial Assessment Framework for pension funds in the Netherlands, the future solvency and supervisory standard for insurance companies and stress-testing. Marc graduated as a physicist from the University of Utrecht and worked for several years on ALM and risk management for a large financial conglomerate. He regularly publishes articles on insurance and pensions.

Claus Puhr worked as a research assistant at the University of Applied Science Wiener Neustadt before he joined the Financial Stability Analysis Division of the Oesterreichische Nationalbank in 2005 to support the implementation of the 'Systemic Risk Monitor' presented in this book. He has also spent time at the Bank of England to help develop a similar quantitative systemic risk assessment model.

Steffen Sorensen is Senior Consultant at Barrie and Hibbert. Prior to joining Barrie and Hibbert he finished a Ph.D. at the University of York in financial econometrics and worked as an economist in the monetary analysis and financial stability areas of the European Central Bank and the Bank of England.

Stéphanie Stolz is an economist in the Financial Sector Policy Division in the IMF's Monetary and Capital Markets Department. Prior to joining the IMF in 2006, she served as an economist in the Micro and Macro Prudential Analysis Division of the Deutsche Bundesbank's Banking and Financial Supervision Department and at the Kiel Institute for the World Economy.

Marco Stringa works as a senior economist in the Monetary Analysis Department of the Bank of England. His professional interests span most aspects of financial markets. He studied at the Universities of Warwick and Bologna, and holds the CFA qualification.

Martin Summer is Head of the Economic Studies Division at the Oesterreichische Nationalbank (OeNB). Before joining the OeNB in 2000 he worked as a lecturer at the Universities of Vienna, Birmingham and Regensburg. He also worked as a visiting researcher at the Bank of England and the Financial Markets Group of the London School of Economics in 2004. His research

interests are banking regulation and systemic risk, financial stability and financial economics.

Mark Swinburne is Assistant Director, and Chief of the Financial Sector Policy Division in the IMF's Monetary and Capital Markets Department. Current responsibilities include oversight and development of the Financial Sector Assessment Program, including quantitative assessment methodologies such as stress-testing. Prior to joining the IMF in 1994, he held senior advisor and senior manager positions in the Reserve Bank of New Zealand.

Muriel Tiesset is Deputy Head of Banking Studies Division of the French Banking Commission, specifically in charge of the stress-testing and risk measurement team. After graduating from ENSAE, she joined the Banque de France in 1998 and was initially appointed in the Economics Department, in charge of forecasting and monetary policy analysis. She also obtained a Master's degree in economics from the London School of Economics and spent one year on secondment at the Bank of England, in the Financial Stability Department.

Vincenzo Tola joined the Banking Supervision Department of the Bank of Italy in 2005. He has a Master's degree in quantitative risk management from the University of Palermo (Italy) and a Ph.D. in economics from the Università Politecnica delle Marche (Italy). His main interests are credit risk modelling, financial markets, decisions and games theory.

Maurizio Trapanese is a senior economist in the Regulation and Supervisory Policies Department of the Bank of Italy. He holds an M.Sc. in economics from the University of Warwick (UK). His main interests are financial stability, macroprudential analysis and crisis management. He chairs the Crisis Management Task Force of the Committee of European Banking Supervisors.

Nico Valckx has worked for the ECB since 2002. His responsibilities in the Financial Stability Division include monitoring large banks and analysis of financial stability issues. He worked for two years as Advisor in the ECB office in Washington DC and previously was Secretary of the ESCB Working Group on Banking Developments. Prior to joining ECB, he worked for the Bank of Finland, De Nederlandsche Bank and, as a research associate, for the Belgian Fund for Scientific Research. He finished his Ph.D. in 2000 (Antwerp University, Belgium).

Iman van Lelyveld is Senior Policy Advisor with De Nederlandsche Bank and Chairman of the Basel Committee Research Task Force on stress-testing. In addition, he holds an appointment as Associate Professor at Radboud University. He has published widely on risk management, both from an individual institutional as well as from a systemic point of view.

Foreword

Past and recent events have shown the disruptive power of financial crises. The direct costs of the crises on the financial system – however measured – are high; indirect effects to the entire economic system may be dramatic and long-lasting.

Looking at the experience of the past century, one remains astonished by the recurring tendency of the financial system to accumulate risk and leverage over a number of years, to then suddenly change sentiment and discard risk sharply and indiscriminately. While markets, asset types, players involved and the triggering event differ from one episode to the next, risk accumulation cycles tend to be similar. Crises have also shown that risks and vulnerabilities for the financial system do not stem only from endogenous developments but – probably much more frequently – are the consequence of changes in the macroeconomic and financial environment.

While these recurrences do not make crises more predictable, they have stimulated public authorities to search for ways of reducing the likelihood and impact of crisis events. One of the main lessons drawn from past turbulences is that it is important to complement the supervision of individual institutions with a constant monitoring of conditions of the system as a whole.

Reducing the impact of financial instability entails the development of a comprehensive kit of tools, ranging from forecasting techniques to preventive policy measures, to effective management and resolution devices. The first line is obviously trying to prevent the crisis from breaking out. The identification of risk sources and the prediction of potential threats are therefore crucial elements of any financial stability toolbox.

In that respect, macroeconomic stress tests are increasingly considered as the basic, indispensable tool of any systematic effort to reduce the likelihood and impact of crisis events. Stress-testing *per se* is not new – it is just an evolution of more primitive 'what if' thinking – but it has become much more structured and sophisticated in recent times. Testing the resilience of the financial system to a situation of stress – along with the smooth working of financial stability arrangements – is a top priority for the authorities responsible for safeguarding financial stability.

This book provides the reader with a systematic presentation of the latest developments in the field of stress-testing, taking advantage of the experience of colleagues from leading financial supervisory authorities and central banks. The first part of the volume introduces the reader to the main methodological aspects of stress-testing and explains the theoretical underpinning of different tools. The second part gives a comprehensive and updated overview of stress-testing approaches in various countries.

Given the difficulty in identifying the next crisis, the design of extreme but plausible stress tests is of great value: if understood and used correctly, they may strengthen the awareness of policy-makers on new risk factors as well as on the resilience of major institutions, markets and infrastructures under stress conditions. While technical aspects are certainly essential for ensuring the reliability and practical usefulness of such simulations, human judgment – as pointed out in many chapters – is also a central component of stress-testing. Therefore, the exchange of experiences among experts of various countries can help improve methodologies and develop a common language for checking the robustness of different approaches and interpreting the outcome of the simulations.

Notwithstanding the undeniable advances of the methodologies and applications, it is fair to say that the framework has not yet reached a steady state. Almost all contributors very openly claim that the challenges for stress-testing are still significant and there is room for further developments.

As Governor Draghi argued in the aftermath of the sub-prime crisis, 'every crisis leaves policy-makers shaken by the poorness of their forecasting ability. While it is sometimes possible to see the risk factors clearly, it is nevertheless impossible to predict the precise moment that the market will choose to trigger the crisis, the exact forms this will take or the links decisive for its propagation.' Indeed, every crisis is a lesson for the authorities and an incentive to enrich the toolkit at their disposal. Any progress in stress-testing methodologies does represent a valuable step in this direction.

Giovanni Carosio
Bank of Italy, Deputy Director General

Acknowledgements

The seeds of this book were planted some years ago, when I was a young economist at the Bank of Italy and involved in the technical team responsible for developing new stress-testing methodologies for the incoming Italian Financial Sector Assessment Program (FSAP). I owe many more debts that I can possibly acknowledge, but I wish to thank Maurizio Trapanese, who initiated me to macroprudential analysis, and Sebastiano Laviola, who encouraged me to work on stress tests.

The project of a book on macroeconomic stress tests has become reality because so many colleagues and friends from either the Bank of Italy or other prominent financial institutions have enthusiastically agreed to contribute to it. I am obviously very indebted to all the contributors, but I am particularly grateful to Michael Boss, Mathias Drehmann, Gerald Krenn, Sebastiano Laviola, Juri Marcucci, Claus Puhr, Steffen Sorensen, Marco Stringa, Martin Summer and Maurizio Trapanese, who agreed to write their chapters when the 'probability of default' of the project was terribly high.

I am also indebted to Francesco Cannata and Juri Marcucci for their continuous encouragement, help and suggestions. Francesco has bravely read the whole manuscript, providing comments that greatly enhanced the fine-tuning of the book.

At the various stages of the project, many people have provided generous advice on the structure of the book and the contents of some chapters. I would like to thank Corrado Ciavattini, Chiara Guerzoni, Francesca Lotti, Luciana Mancinelli and two anonymous referees for their hints. Claudio Medico and his uncanny ability to find typos helped me in the final revision of the book.

Last but not least, I wish to thank Chris Harrison, publishing director with Cambridge University Press, for his invaluable suggestions during the entire process that eventually led to this book, and Philip Good, Joanna Breeze and Jennifer Miles Davis for their help and patient support.

Introduction

Mario Quagliariello[*]

'Excuse me!
Ladies and gentlemen,
forgive me for appearing alone.
I am the Prologue'.

R. Leoncavallo, I Pagliacci, 1892

Stress tests are quantitative tools used by banking supervisors and central banks for assessing the soundness of financial systems in the event of extreme, but still plausible, shocks (macroeconomic stress tests). They are also an important management instrument for banks since they provide financial institutions with useful indications on the reliability of the internal systems designed for the measurement of risks (microeconomic or prudential stress tests). Under the new Basel Accord on banks' capital adequacy the presence of sound stress-testing methodologies is a prerequisite for the adoption of the advanced methods for the quantification of minimum capital requirements.

Until the first half of 2007, interest in stress-testing had been circumscribed to practitioners, i.e., risk managers, central bankers and financial supervisors. Since then, the global financial system has been hit by deep turbulences and all major economies have been affected by high volatility in financial markets, deterioration of the value of portfolios, widespread repricing of risk and severe liquidity drying up. It has been pointed out that the severity of the crisis has been largely due to its unexpected nature and that a more extensive and rigorous use of stress-testing methodologies would have probably helped to alleviate the intensity and repercussions of the turmoil. In such a context, stress tests have become a key issue in policy discussions and a regular subject for newspapers' columnists.

---

[*] Bank of Italy. The opinions expressed herein are those of the author and do not necessarily reflect those of the Bank of Italy.

Just some examples show the importance of these issues in such a debate.

Stress-tests are particularly useful for risk monitoring and assessment as they make it possible to quantify the likely impact of shocks, which helps to rank risks by their importance and allows assessment and surveillance to be more focused. Moreover, stress-tests can help provide early warning signals and thus contribute to the forward-looking dimension of financial stability monitoring and assessment. (L. Papademos, Conference on 'Simulating financial instability: stress-testing and financial crisis simulation exercises', European Central Bank, Frankfurt am Main, 2007).

Supervisors need to sharpen incentives for regulated institutions to improve risk management and stress testing practices and the adequacy of their capital and liquidity buffers. [They] need to sharpen firms' focus on tail risks and enhance stress testing regimes in order to identify and mitigate the build-up of excessive risk exposures and concentration risks. (Financial Stability Forum, Interim Report to the G7 Finance Ministers and Central Bank Governors, 2008).

The regulator should conduct system-wide stress tests of those scenarios most likely to produce systemic stress – such as a 40 per cent drop in house prices. Fears of a meltdown in global house prices were not rare before the crisis. These tests will probably underestimate spillover effects, but the information gleaned from them could help regulators estimate these effects and consider mitigating action. (J. Eatwell and A. Persaud, *Financial Times*, 25 August, 2008).

Indeed, in 2009 US supervisory agencies have carried out a comprehensive stress-testing exercise for determining the financial health of the major banks and defining their capital needs. Notwithstanding the importance of the topic, books covering the different facets of macroeconomic stress-testing are missing so far. While many articles have been published on specific issues and some textbooks deal with prudential stress tests, a systematic survey of methodologies and applications of macroeconomic stress-testing is not available. This book aims at filling this gap, by providing practitioners and academics with a comprehensive and updated discussion of the theoretical underpinnings as well as the practical aspects of the implementation of such exercises. Prudential stress tests carried out by banks are not analysed in the book, even though it is not always practicable (and sensible) to distinguish them from macroeconomic stress tests.

The book builds on the experience gained by the economists of many national and international financial authorities in their day-to-day surveillance activity. All the contributors have an extensive expertise in financial stability issues and stress-testing methodologies. Obviously, due to space constraints, some potentially interesting applications may have been omitted. Nevertheless, the book – while not exhaustive – is wide-ranging and includes outstanding presentations of the most significant approaches as well as an inner description of the state-of-the-art in this field.

While tailored for an expert readership, the book has the ambition to remain accessible to other readers, thanks to its plain language, clear explanation of the different issues and recurrent use of examples. Readers can either pick specific chapters of interest or easily move from simple to more complex topics as they progress through the text.

The book is organised in two parts. The first part (Chapters 1–7) introduces the fundamentals of macroeconomic stress-testing; the second part (Chapters 8–16) reviews some of the most significant applications and experiences.

Chapter 1 introduces the concept of financial stability and serves the purpose of setting the stage for the whole book. While Chapter 2 illustrates the basic definitions and examines the main components of these exercises, Chapter 3 reviews the most significant statistical and econometric techniques that can be used for stress-testing banking risks and offers a rich menu to disentangle the empirical issues arising from the development and implementation of such techniques. Chapters 4 and 5 conclude the description of the methodologies, discussing scenario calibration and risk integration.

Chapter 6 illustrates the information needed for carrying out macroeconomic stress tests; after a general overview of the data needs for running any stress test, it concentrates on credit risk. The first part of the book ends with a discussion on the possible uses of stress tests (Chapter 7); in particular, it describes how the output of such exercises can be employed to communicate with the public, identify weaknesses in the financial system that authorities can address in normal times and inform the policy response at times of stress.

The second part of the volume illustrates several applications. Chapters 8, 9 and 11 deal with selected national experiences on stress tests for specific banking risks, namely credit risk in Italy, market risk in the United States and interbank risk in the Netherlands, whereas Chapters 10 and 12 describe the approaches developed in the United Kingdom and Austria respectively for integrating different types of risk. Chapter 13 analyses the methodologies developed in France and shows how macroeconomic stress tests can be linked to microprudential supervision.

Chapter 14 presents the experience of the EU new member states, analysing the peculiarities of the financial systems of these countries and highlighting the challenges for the development of appropriate stress-testing methodologies where data typically deserve special attention. Chapter 15 turns to the issue of stress-testing in a cross-border dimension, examining the challenges in terms of modelling strategies and data availability in the European Union. Finally, Chapter 16 focuses on the experience with stress-testing gained in the Financial Sector Assessment Programs (FSAPs) by the International Monetary Fund, a leading authority in this field.

Part I

Fundamentals

1 A framework for assessing financial stability

Maurizio Trapanese[*]

1.1 Introduction

In recent years, policy-makers and banking supervisory authorities reinforced their efforts aimed at ensuring financial stability, considering it as a relevant policy objective, autonomous with respect to both monetary and microeconomic stability (see Schinasi, 2003). Many central banks regularly publish reports in which they disclose their assessment of the factors that may threaten financial stability. Ad hoc fora have been established in order to discuss the implications for financial stability of globalisation, financial innovation and macroeconomic fluctuations. Major financial institutions also devote a large part of their activity to the analysis of the vulnerabilities of financial systems.

However, as pointed out by Schinasi (2005), 'compared with the analysis of monetary and macroeconomic stability, the analysis of financial stability is still in its infancy. As anyone who has tried to define financial stability knows, there is as yet no widely accepted model or analytical framework for assessing or measuring it.'

The definition of financial stability itself is difficult to provide. Padoa-Schioppa (2003) considers financial stability as: 'a condition whereby the financial system is able to withstand shocks without giving way to cumulative processes, which impair the allocation of savings to investment opportunities and the processing of payments in the economy'. Financial stability does not necessarily imply that all components of the financial system operate at or near peak at all times, but a stable financial system has the ability to limit and resolve existing imbalances (Schinasi, 2005).[1]

---

[*] Bank of Italy. The opinions expressed herein are those of the author and do not necessarily reflect those of the Bank of Italy.
[1] For a survey of possible definitions, see Houben *et al.* (2004).

Financial instabilities have the potential to jeopardise the correct functioning of one or more components of the financial system, which – in turn – can have a substantial impact on the real economy and imply 'second-round effects' to the financial system. The extent of the impact greatly depends on the underlying vulnerabilities in the financial system and on the possibility that this is able to absorb or withstand the shock and continue to perform its key functions. Another key factor, which is likely to have substantial consequences on the behaviour of public authorities, is the speed of propagation of the instability within the financial system (Hoggarth and Saporta, 2001).

Because of the multifaceted nature of financial stability, the main challenge for policy-makers is the definition of an effective framework for assessing the state of health of the financial system. Such an assessment is a composite and, to some extent, iterative process; it is the result of quantitative measures and qualitative intuition. It relies on predefined rules and some degree of discretionary judgment.

It is worth underlining that the goal of the assessment is not necessarily to prevent problems from materialising; rather it is to protect the stability of the financial system and, at the same time, minimise the potential harmful economic impacts of the crises. In other words, the efficient functioning of the financial system requires that authorities, while not pursuing a zero-failure regime, try to prevent potential weaknesses from becoming systemic.

For the purposes of this chapter a systemic crisis can be defined as an event that leads to the failure of a relevant number of financial institutions, or has a substantial impact on the functioning of financial markets or infrastructures, thereby undermining the main functions of a financial system and having an impact on the real economy. Systemic crises imply two key elements: shocks and contagion channels. Shocks can be idiosyncratic or systemic depending on whether they affect a single financial institution, the price of a single asset or a relevant part of the financial system. The contagion channel is the mechanism through which shocks are transmitted from one financial institution or market to the other.

The goal of public authorities is to build a framework through which the likelihood that such a crisis occurs and the severity of its impact on the real economy can be identified as early as possible. Any analytical framework for assessing financial stability does not define *ex-ante* quantitative benchmarks for qualifying instabilities as systemic, but it assumes that *ex-ante* the public authorities are aware of the potential channels through which a systemic crisis may appear. In that respect, stress tests provide a very powerful and eclectic tool for carrying out such an assessment.

This chapter provides a brief overview of these issues and sets the stage for the following parts of the volume. It is organised as follows. Section 1.2 sketches the main building blocks of a framework for financial stability in modern economies; section 1.3 introduces the tools that can be used to carry out the assessment and section 1.4 offers some inputs from a policy perspective.

1.2 Building the framework

Financial stability analysis aims at understanding whether the financial system is exposed to shocks and quantifying the possible repercussions of a crisis should the shock occur. Therefore, any framework for assessing financial stability should focus on three main elements: the risks and vulnerabilities that make the financial system weak, the shock that can trigger those vulnerabilities and the propagation mechanisms that amplify the impact of the crisis.

This requires systematic monitoring of individual parts of the financial system as well as the real economy (households, firms, the public sector). The analysis should also consider cross-sector and cross-border linkages, because imbalances are often caused by a combination of weaknesses from different sources.

While it is clear that both the shock that triggers the crisis and the contagion channels that propagate it across intermediaries and markets play a role in determining financial instability, the significance of each of these elements is disputed. As an example, in the study of the pattern of financial instability episodes, Davis (1999) distinguishes between primary shocks or 'displacements', which act as propagation mechanisms of financial fragility, and secondary shocks, which actually trigger the episode of financial instability. Since the aim of any framework for assessing financial stability is to detect early signals of distress, the focus is on the propagation mechanisms, that is, on the leading indicators of the crises. According to Borio (2003), 'the triggering shock is, in fact, the least interesting aspect of the story' and it would be detected too late to be a leading indicator.

Therefore, the crucial point in defining and making operational a framework for financial stability is the analysis of potential sources of fragility. This analysis should be as comprehensive as possible, trying to include all the underlying factors that can have an impact on the functioning of the system. The assessment should ideally end up with a categorisation of the existing vulnerabilities according to their intensity, scope and potential threat to financial stability and the definition of the policy responses that are deemed adequate.

A useful contribution to the design of such a framework could derive from the distinction of financial vulnerabilities according to their impact on the main elements of the financial system, namely financial institutions, financial markets and market infrastructures. A special focus should be assigned to the analysis of the contagion channels across borders and sectors. Indeed, both those elements have gained relevance, given the increased pace of financial integration in the global financial system. In addition, as highlighted by the 2007–8 financial crisis, the vulnerability of the financial system increases when shocks hit portfolios that are not liquid, hedged or diversified enough; furthermore, the interaction among different types of risks may magnify the impact of any shock. All these factors should thus be taken into account when ranking different risks.

In the assessment, one should ideally distinguish the risks that may arise within the financial system and those that may originate outside the financial system – for example from the real economy – and still have an impact on the functioning of the financial system itself. These different sources of risk have important consequences in terms of the choice of the more adequate policy responses: endogenous vulnerabilities can be offset by preventive policies in terms of regulation and supervision and their effects can be alleviated by appropriate crisis management tools; conversely, the impact of external imbalances on the financial system can only be mitigated by the policy responses of the authorities.

As far as the triggering event is concerned, it is up to the analyst to determine the most plausible shocks and identify the institutions that are more likely to be affected. The following chapters show that this is not an easy task and therefore the assessment should be based on statistical methods and human judgment.

Finally, the interconnections across markets and intermediaries increase the probability that the shocks are transmitted among the major components of the financial system, thus exacerbating the crisis. Because of this propagation mechanism, an idiosyncratic shock at, for example, one or a few banks may result in a systemic crisis where many institutions or markets are in turn affected through their linkages with these banks.

Two main channels exist through which such contagion risks can occur, namely the exposure channel and the information channel. The former refers to the knock-on effects on other institutions or markets through real exposures (via wholesale payment systems or the interbank market). The latter refers to contagious actions by depositors/investors (through deposit with-drawals, asset sales) who are imperfectly informed about the shocks hitting the financial system. Hence, the risk of bank runs and systemic crises are inter-linked with the public's confidence in the stability of the financial system.

1.3 The use of macroprudential analysis for assessing financial stability

Macroprudential analysis is the tool that public authorities use for assessing financial stability. According to the IMF (2001), macroprudential analysis is 'a methodological tool that helps to quantify and qualify the soundness and vulnerabilities of financial systems'. The perspective of macroprudential analysis is clearly focused on overall financial stability, whereas (traditional) microprudential analysis concentrates on single financial institutions. Indeed, the main goal of such a tool is to reduce the likelihood of the failure of significant parts of the financial system and the relative costs; the failure of individual intermediaries is a matter of indifference if it does not have systemic effects on financial markets.

The importance of macro-prudential analysis for assessing financial stability is witnessed by the speech that Andrew Crockett (2000) made before the Eleventh International Conference of Banking Supervisors:

Where will the journey take us? In sketching the challenges ahead in the 21st century, as befits today's theme, I would like to share with you some personal reflections on a possible future direction. I shall argue that in order to build most productively on past achievements in the pursuit of financial stability, we should strive for a better marriage between the microprudential and macroprudential dimensions of the task. We should, in other words, consolidate a shift in perspective that is already taking place, complementing the microprudential perspective with increased awareness of, and attention to, the macroprudential facet.

Macroprudential analysis clearly requires the systematic use of a huge set of information in order to capture early signals of fragility in the financial system as a whole.[2] The integrated use of micro and macroeconomic information, the development of stress-testing exercises and the analysis of the structural and institutional framework are increasingly regarded as useful tools to identify the determinants of financial instability.

---

[2] Evans *et al.* (2000).

Therefore, the analysis is based on a continuous process of information gathering, technical analysis and on-going monitoring of the main developments that may threaten the health of the financial system. Public authorities can benefit from the timely collection of information required for the assessment of the resilience of the financial system to adverse shocks and they try to draw a better picture at an early stage of the source of vulnerability they deal with.

The first bit of information is typically provided by statistical indicators. They should cover the different components of the financial system. Additional information may be also derived for the functioning of the payments systems and infrastructure. Financial fragility indicators could give useful insight in order to evaluate the financial position of households and firms. Finally macroeconomic variables can provide supplementary information and underline possible imbalances outside the financial system.[3]

Turning to a more forward-looking perspective, early warning systems play an important role in weighting the importance of different variables for financial stability, and in anticipating financial instabilities both within and across classes of financial institutions and within and across the various markets. Stress tests are the natural evolution of the early warning system, since they depict an overall picture of the resilience of some parts of the economy under extreme conditions.

The framework should be as comprehensive and analytical as possible. Along with the knowledge of the economic and financial conditions of institutions, markets and financial infrastructure, it is also relevant to take into account the regulatory, supervisory and surveillance mechanisms.

1.4 Looking for instability

The most intuitive way to identify possible sources of instability is to split up the financial system in terms of its main functions: (1) the facilitating role in the mechanism for the executions of payments; (2) the contribution to align the savings and investment decisions of the economic agents; and (3) the management and efficient allocation of financial risk among market participants.

Each component of the financial system plays one or more roles and contributes to the smooth exercise of these functions and, as a consequence, is subject to specific risks.

---

[3] Imbalances can be defined as 'endogenous accumulations of factors that increase the risk of instability and crisis' (Ferguson *et al.*, 2007).

Households are typically lenders, while firms and the public sector tend to borrow financial resources in order to finance their investments and purchases. In recent years, non-financial sectors have become increasingly exposed to financial risk as the result of rising debt/leverage levels, an increase in the weight of risky assets in their portfolios and greater use of financial markets (Ferguson *et al.*, 2007).

Financial resources can flow from lenders to borrowers either directly or indirectly. While in direct finance, markets for financial instruments are the means for exchanging funds, in indirect finance, funds are traded through financial intermediaries. In any financial transaction, infrastructures ensure the smooth flow of funds and effective exchange of financial instruments.

Financial integration and the consolidation process that has taken place mainly in the banking sector are factors that have contributed to deepen financial markets and to better manage risks. In this way the resilience to systemic risk of financial markets has been enhanced.

However, at the same time, the development of complex financial instruments and the greater interlinkages among financial institutions and markets have increased the impact of the shocks should they materialise.

1.4.1 Financial institutions

Financial stability implies that the financial system is able to withstand adverse developments in the real economy or even internally originated shocks and it is able to perform its key functions in conditions of normality. Since financial institutions play a central part in financial stability functions, this section deals primarily with the assessment of the stability conditions of such institutions.

Crisis episodes may arise in financial institutions in several ways. In some cases, problems may initially arise at a single institution and subsequently spread to other parts of the financial system; in other circumstances several institutions may be affected simultaneously because of similar exposures.

As mentioned before, a crisis affecting a weak financial institution is determined by the shock and the contagion mechanisms. As to the shock, it can be considered systemic if it is related to a systemically relevant institution. From a theoretical point of view, those institutions can be defined as the firms whose failure would most likely have effects on the smooth functioning of the financial system and consequences on other financial institutions or markets.

As to the contagion mechanism a crucial element is the assessment of the cross-border dimension. In this regard, two types of contagion can be distinguished: (1) idiosyncratic shocks can lead to direct contagion through (cross-border) balance sheet linkages across intermediaries; and (2) widespread or systematic shocks can cause indirect contagion through (cross-border) common exposures (European Central Bank, 2004).

The main linkages for direct cross-border contagion are related to cross-border interbank links in money markets and cross-border ownership links. Common shocks to foreign economies and global financial markets can affect banks' exposures through changes in credit quality, market valuations and funding costs.

The main linkages for indirect cross-border contagion are typically the result of cross-border credit exposures (lending to non-monetary financial institutions, international syndicated lending and credit risk transfer exposures), market risk exposures (holdings of securities and off-balance sheet positions), common cross-border funding (financing through market instruments), cross-border settlement risk and the use of common settlement systems (operational risk).

The cross-border relevance of these linkages could be related to either their absolute size (the cross-border exposure in terms of total banking sector assets) or to their relative size (the cross-border component of a particular balance sheet item).

The assessment of financial stability should therefore include the analysis of these factors. In that respect, a first step is the examination of indicators such as sectoral balance sheet data, measures of counterparty risk, measures of liquidity and asset quality, open foreign exchange positions and exposures within individual sectors with special attention to measures of concentration.[4]

1.4.2 Financial markets and infrastructures

Financial markets are a second source of endogenous risk, not only because they offer alternative sources of finance to non-financial sectors but also because they systemically link financial institutions and more directly savers and investors. Financial markets are also vulnerable to contagion. Financial infrastructures are a third important endogenous source of risk, in part because they link market participants but also because they provide the operational framework in which financial institutions and markets operate.

Financial markets play a crucial function in a modern financial system, since they contribute to the efficiency of the price formation mechanism and have an important role in the redistribution of risks among participants.

---

[4] Beck *et al.* (2002).

Banks and financial firms participate in the markets to meet their funding needs and to manage the risks coming from the structure of their balance sheets; markets are also participated in by non-financial firms and government bodies. The household sector is also an indirect user of some markets, particularly those that offer longer term saving opportunities.

Financial markets may face difficulties in different ways: (1) a disruption of the infrastructures may render markets no more able to perform their core functions; (2) a loss of confidence may limit the involvement of intermediaries and impact on the formation of prices; and (3) a failure of a key market player or a sudden change in the risk attitude of market participants can have even wider effects and reduce market liquidity conditions.

Financial market disruption can have both direct and indirect effects on the economy. The disruption of markets may reduce the ability of economic agents to raise funds and change their saving and investment decisions. Changing conditions in the price formation would impact the allocation of resources in the real economy. As to the indirect effects, disruption of markets may also impact on financial institutions themselves and reduce intermediaries' incomes from trading activities. Resulting weaker profits and capital levels may have an ultimate effect to undermine the resilience of the financial system to adverse shocks.

An important factor to be taken into account refers to the speed through which the shock is spread across markets. Short-term markets are likely to be more important than markets for long-term funding, as disruption could quickly lead to bank illiquidity. Another crucial element is the available degree of substitution for both markets and products. Interconnections between markets also need to be considered. Many markets are linked to each other by arbitrage/hedging activities, and disruption to one would quickly affect the others.

1.4.3 The impact on the real economy

A financial stability framework should finally include the assessment of the direct or indirect effects of the crisis on the real economy. According to some authors, what really matters is the impact of financial instability on consumption and investment. However, it is a shared understanding that the identification of such effects is really difficult.

As the following chapters point out, the challenges in assessing and estimating the likelihoods of events with low probability and high associated costs are both methodological and practical. The possible real impact of a crisis might be investigated using simulation exercises, sensitivity analyses or stress-testing. Such difficulties can become of crucial importance during a crisis situation when time is tight and available information is likely to be incomplete and uncertain.

However, there are two important elements to be explicitly addressed: the financial losses incurred by economic agents and their limited access to financial services. In the case of a shock hitting a financial institution, losses include those incurred by creditors, shareholders and counterparties; in the case of financial markets, households and non-financial corporations are vulnerable to the extent that they hold financial instruments, either directly or indirectly.

Financial services can become unavailable and this can cause adverse real effects limiting the range of saving, investment and consumption options available to economic agents. This may come at a significant welfare loss. Alternative suppliers may be available, but often only at higher costs. Disturbances in the retail part of the financial infrastructure may constrain the possibilities for non-financial corporations and households to transact.

1.5 Conclusions

The analysis of financial stability aims at providing public authorities with a common understanding of the functioning of the financial system and with an analytical tool which allows them to identify *ex-ante* possible fragilities and, *ex-post*, assess the systemic nature of a crisis. It is to be intended as a precondition to develop appropriate policies that need to be implemented to limit the adverse effects of a potential shock and to prevent the building up of spill-over effects.

Therefore, the development of an adequate framework for assessing financial stability allows public authorities to have timely warning of possible vulnerabilities, identify their repercussions on the financial system and provide prompt policy responses. Such an assessment – based on a combination of statistical data, quantitative methods and human judgment – takes into account the functions the financial system plays and its key components. The ultimate goal is to either establish appropriate preventive measures or design prompt policy responses should a crisis emerge.

An increasingly important component of the financial stability toolkit is the cooperation among authorities of different countries. Indeed, the globalisation and integration of the financial systems often require coordinated assessment and responses of several national authorities. Structures and arrangements that ensure information sharing should be strengthened: well functioning networks of national supervisors and central banks may, for example, improve the dialogue in normal times and help develop a common language for financial stability assessment. In that respect, one of the tasks of the networks may be to carry out stress test exercises in order to compare the different approaches, share the results of the simulations and reach a common understanding of possible weaknesses in the financial system.

REFERENCES

Beck, T., A. Demirguc-Kunt and R. Levine (2002), 'Bank Concentration and Crises', *NBER Working Paper*, 9,921.

Borio, C. (2003), 'Towards a Macroprudential Framework for Financial Supervision and Regulation', *BIS Working Paper*, 128.

Borio, C. and P. Lowe (2002), 'Asset Prices, Financial and Monetary Stability: Exploring the Nexus', *BIS Working Paper*, 114.

Crockett, A. (2000), Welcoming Address, 11th International Conference of Banking Supervisors, Basel.

Davis E. P. (1999), 'Financial Data Needs for Macroprudential Surveillance – What are the Key Indicators of Risks to Domestic Financial Stability?', in Bank of England – Centre for Central Banking Studies, *Handbooks in Central Banking*, Lecture Series, 2.

European Central Bank (2004), 'Cross-border Bank Contagion Risk in Europe', *Financial Stability Review*, December.

Evans, O., A. M. Leone, M. Gill and P. Hilbers (2000), 'Macroprudential Indicators of Financial System Soundness', *IMF Occasional Papers*, 192.

Ferguson, R. W., P. Hartmann, F. Panetta and R. Portes (2007), *International Financial Stability*, CEPR.

Hoggarth, G. and V. Saporta (2001), 'Costs of Banking System Instability: Some Empirical Evidence', *Bank of England Financial Stability Review*, June.

Houben, A., J. Kakes and G. J. Schinasi (2004), 'A Framework for Safeguarding Financial Stability', *IMF Working Paper*, 101.

International Monetary Fund (2001), Macroprudential Analysis: Selected Aspects Background Paper, Washington DC.

Padoa-Schioppa, T. (2003), Central Bank and Financial Stability, Remarks at the Bank of Indonesia, Jakarta.

Schinasi, G. J. (2003), 'Responsibility of Central Banks for Stability in Financial Markets', *IMF Working Paper*, 121.

   (2005), 'Preserving Financial Stability', *International Monetary Fund Economic Issues*, 36.

   (2006), *Safeguarding Financial Stability. Theory and Practice*, International Monetary Fund.

2 Macroeconomic stress-testing: definitions and main components

Mario Quagliariello[*]

2.1 Introduction

As described in Chapter 1, the financial sector is particularly prone to fragility, contagion and, thus, systemic crises. In general, the episodes of instability are the consequence of the existing weaknesses, while the external shock simply ignites the crisis: the more fragile the financial system, the more severe the effects of a crisis.

Therefore, it is important to evaluate the linkages between the conditions of the macroeconomy and the stability of the financial system. The first step in such assessment is the evaluation of the current state of health of the financial system. This is typically done using both aggregated microdata and macroeconomic indicators, called financial soundness (or macroprudential) indicators by practitioners.[1] The second step is the assessment of the resilience of the system, i.e., its ability to absorb potential exogenous shocks. This analysis is typically carried out through stress tests. Since credit institutions are the backbone of the financial system in most countries, the scrutiny focuses very often on the banking sector.

This chapter provides a general overview of stress-testing, introducing the main concepts and describing the most relevant components. In Chapter 3, the quantitative methodologies for stress-testing the main banking risks are analysed.

[*] Bank of Italy. The opinions expressed herein are those of the author and do not necessarily reflect those of the Bank of Italy. The author is indebted to Patrizia Baudino, Francesco Cannata, Luciana Mancinelli and Marina Moretti for valuable comments on a draft version.
[1] Financial soundness indicators are indicators of the current financial health and soundness of the financial institutions in a country, and of their corporate and household counterparts. They embrace both aggregated individual institution data and indicators that are representative of the markets in which the financial institutions operate (IMF, 2006).

2.2 Objectives of stress-testing: the micro and macro perspectives

Stress-testing techniques have been applied at the individual level by large, internationally active banks since the early 1990s. They are generally used in the context of banks' risk management in order to complement the estimates derived by internal models. With respect to standard value-at-risk (VaR) techniques, they are able to assess the impact of arbitrary extreme events.

A strong incentive to develop such techniques has been provided by prudential regulation. Since 1996, banks and investment firms have been required to develop stress tests as part of their internal models for the calculation of capital requirements for market risk.[2]

More recently, the new Capital Accord and the EU Capital Requirements Directive (CRD) have required intermediaries to use stress-testing techniques for other risks as well, in order to assess their ability to keep adequate capital resources in stress situations.[3] In the new prudential regime, stress tests address two distinct needs. First, they allow banks to determine whether and to what extent the estimation of the risk parameters depends on the economic conditions prevailing in the period of time used for the estimation. In other words, they can be used for assessing the degree of cyclicality of the capital requirements implied by the estimation process. Banks with more cyclical capital requirements are expected to hold higher capital buffers. Second, they can be employed in order to quantify the amount of extra capital that banks may need in extreme, but plausible, market conditions (see Box 2.1).

In addition to being applied at the level of individual financial institutions' portfolios (micro level), stress-testing techniques have more recently assumed an important role as a component of the toolkit available to public authorities in financial stability analysis (macro level). In the context of the Financial Sector Assessment Program (FSAP), the IMF and World Bank (2005) have increasingly used macroeconomic stress tests; likewise, central banks and supervisory authorities in industrialised countries have recently developed econometric models combining micro and macro data for the assessment of

---

[2] In 1996, the Basel Capital Accord was amended in order to incorporate market risks. This is known as market risk amendment. Basel Committee on Banking Supervision (2006).

[3] The Capital Requirements Directive, which implements the Basel Accord in the European Union, comprises Directive 2006/48/EC and Directive 2006/49/EC.

Box 2.1 Stress tests in Basel 2

The new Capital Accord (Basel 2) requires banks to perform stress tests for credit risk, liquidity risk in relation to the value of collateral and market risk. Supervisors are also asked to ensure that institutions conduct 'rigorous and forward-looking stress testing' to identify factors that 'could adversely affect the bank'.

Banks that plan to adopt the internal rating-based approaches for credit risk have to develop adequate stress-testing methodologies. Indeed, the presence of such methodologies is a prerequisite for supervisory validation. Furthermore, the new framework requires all intermediaries to carry out stress tests – including those for credit risk – when assessing the adequacy of their internal economic capital in the framework of Pillar II provisions (internal capital adequacy assessment process, ICAAP).

More precisely, the discipline envisages that: 'A credit institution shall have in place sound stress-testing processes for use in the assessment of its capital adequacy. Stress-testing shall involve identifying possible events or future changes in economic conditions that could have unfavourable effects on a credit institution's credit exposures and assessment of the credit institution's ability to withstand such changes' (Directive 2006/48/EC). It also asks banks to regularly perform a credit risk stress test to assess the effect of certain specific conditions on its total capital requirements for credit risk. The test to be employed shall be one chosen by the credit institution, subject to supervisory review.

Finally, with reference to the supervisory review and evaluation process (SREP) under Pillar II, the new framework envisages that competent authorities will consider, among other things, the results of the stress test carried out by the banks applying an internal ratings-based approach.

---

threats to systemic stability.[4] Since 2001, nearly all G-10 countries have used these large-scale simulations to assess the soundness of their financial systems. In the euro area, most national central banks have adopted stress tests as a tool for assessing the robustness of their financial systems (European Central Bank (ECB), 2006).

The implementation of macroeconomic stress-testing programs such as those underlying the IMF–World Bank FSAP has undoubtedly encouraged the development of comprehensive frameworks for assessing the resilience of financial systems to adverse disturbances. Also, running stress tests entailed indirect benefits for the authorities; in particular, it triggered an assessment of the amount and nature of the data required for the purpose of ongoing financial stability surveillance, thus contributing to capacity building (Čihák, 2004).

---

[4] The FSAP is a joint IMF and World Bank initiative introduced in 1999. It aims at enhancing the efforts to promote the soundness of financial systems in member countries. Under the program, the IMF and World Bank seek to identify the strengths and vulnerabilities of each country's financial system, to determine how key sources of risk are managed, to ascertain assistance needs and to help prioritise policy action. See Chapter 16 for a survey of the IMF experience.

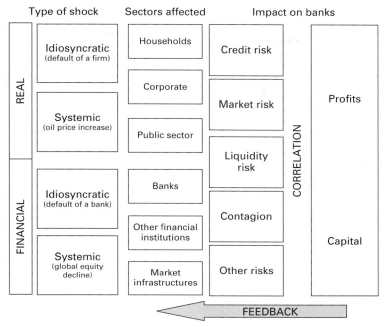

Figure 2.1   Overview of macroeconomic stress-testing

The main goal of macroeconomic stress tests is to identify structural vulnerabilities in the financial system and to assess its resilience to shocks. In this respect, aggregate stress tests can usefully enrich the financial stability toolbox, mostly because they provide forward-looking information on the impact of possible extreme events. Furthermore, this kind of simulation allows consideration of the interconnections across economic sectors, capturing major risk sources for intermediaries, disentangling interactions across different risks.

Figure 2.1 provides a stylised example of how shocks propagate through the economy (Haldane *et al.*, 2007). The initial shock, which can be either real or financial depending on the economic sector hit in the first instance, causes the underlying vulnerabilities in the economy to crystallise. In some circumstances, the shock stems from problems at specific firms (idiosyncratic shock); in others, it derives from macroeconomic imbalances or difficulties that affect the financial system as a whole (systemic shock).[5]

---

[5] Another possible distinction is between risks to the financial system (i.e., the trigger events that might cause a crisis) and the underlying vulnerabilities that will determine the impact of the shock should it materialise.

Regardless of the nature of the shock, its impact is transmitted – directly or indirectly – to the financial sector. While credit, market and liquidity risks are the major sources of losses when shocks materialise, they do not exhaust the whole set of possible repercussions of the crisis; in fact, potential contagion across institutions may entail some domino effects in the financial system, which also jeopardise those financial institutions that were not immediately affected by the shock. Furthermore, the correlation across different risk types may put intermediaries under further pressure, deepening aggregate losses and, in turn, exacerbating the impact on profit and capital levels. Also, feedback effects from the financial system to the real economy may emerge, should intermediaries be materially impaired by the adverse scenario and reduce credit supply to the rest of the economy.

2.3 Stress tests: definitions

The different objectives of stress tests are reflected in the working definitions of this tool. According to the Committee on the Global Financial System (2005),

stress-testing is a risk management tool used to evaluate the potential impact on a firm of a specific event and/or movement in a set of financial variables. Accordingly, stress-testing is used as an adjunct to statistical models such as value-at-risk (VaR), and increasingly it is viewed as a complement, rather than as a supplement, to these statistical measures.

The focus here is clearly on the microeconomic perspective.

Conversely, the IMF (see Sundararajan *et al.*, 2002) considers stress-testing from a macroeconomic point of view and defines it as,

a key element of macroprudential analysis that helps to monitor and anticipate potential vulnerabilities in the financial system. It adds a dynamic element to the analysis of financial soundness indicators – that is, the sensitivity, or probability distribution, of financial soundness indicators outcomes in response to a variety of (macroeconomic) shocks and scenarios.

Stress tests help public authorities to anticipate the evolution of the financial system and support policy decisions and more effective communication with market participants. Indeed,

by anticipating the potential impact of specified events on selected financial soundness indicators, stress tests also help to focus on financial system vulnerabilities arising from particular banking system, macroeconomic, and sectoral shocks.

Embracing the latter perspective, throughout the volume, a macroeconomic (or system-wide) stress test is defined as a way to measure the risk exposure of a relevant set of institutions to stress events.

In more practical terms, stress tests comprise a range of techniques aimed at quantifying the sensitivity of a portfolio to a range of 'extreme but plausible' events. In other words, the main outcome of a stress test is an estimate of the change in value of the portfolio when large variations in a set of financial variables (or risk factors) are assumed. In some cases, such an estimate may be a relatively accurate prediction of how risk exposures may change in value under stress conditions; more often, stress test results are only a rough approximation of what happens to a given portfolio in unfavourable conditions. As pointed out by Jones *et al.* (2004), stress-testing is not a precise tool 'that can be used with scientific accuracy', rather it is an art, which requires quantitative techniques, human judgment and a series of discretionary assumptions.

When setting up the framework for stress-testing exercises, it is necessary to identify the kind of risks that have to be considered and the range of factors to be included. In the first place, stress tests can be used to analyse either the impact of changes in a single risk factor (e.g., a decline of equity prices) or the effect of a multivariate scenario, where simultaneous changes in several risk factors are combined (e.g., a fall in gross domestic product (GDP) together with a decline of equity prices and a rise of interest rates). These typologies of simulation are defined sensitivity analyses and scenario analyses respectively (Figure 2.2).

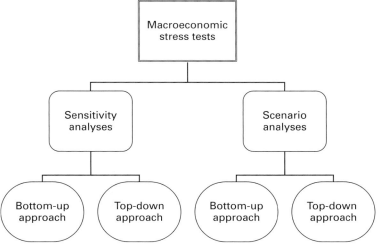

Figure 2.2   Approaches to macroeconomic stress tests

Macroeconomic stress tests derive from microeconomic simulations but entail specific methodological problems. In particular, a major challenge is to determine the most appropriate way for quantifying the aggregate impact of the shock on intermediaries' portfolios. In that respect, two solutions are available for obtaining system-wide results. A first option is that authorities define the macroeconomic shock (or a set of shocks), let the intermediaries evaluate its impact on their balance sheets and then aggregate the bank-level outcomes in order to get the overall effect. This kind of approach to stress-testing is usually called bottom-up. An alternative way for system-wide stress tests is the top-down approach, where the authorities themselves (typically, central banks or supervisory authorities) apply the shock – either to individual bank data or to an aggregated banking system portfolio – and analyse its effect on the banking system as a whole.[6]

The bottom-up methodologies tend to be more tailor-made, since each bank will reflect the shock on its own portfolio more accurately. Also, the datasets used in the simulations are generally richer and the possibility to break the impact of a given shock into several sub-portfolios makes the results more realistic. Since single institutions have a comparative advantage in terms of data availability, the use of their own data and internal models helps optimise the information flows and enhances the quality of the results (IMF and World Bank, 2005). However, the cross-section comparability of bottom-up stress tests may be seriously impaired since each intermediary will likely employ different methodologies and modelling assumptions, making the aggregation less meaningful. Also, the aggregation of individual results, if done at all, cannot take into account the possible interdependencies across institutions. From a more practical perspective, the direct involvement of banks in this kind of simulation is rather costly, especially for the intermediaries, which precludes frequent running of such exercises. In addition, while banks' internal models can be easily adapted to run sensitivity tests, they are generally much less well-suited for scenario analyses.

Conversely, the top-down approach enhances the comparability of results, but it is often less accurate – especially when carried out on aggregated system-wide data. Authorities may indeed apply top-down approaches, working on institution-level data in order to avoid possible loss of information arising from the aggregation, and analyse the dispersion of the results around the average figures (Čihák, 2004).

---

[6] Needless to say, the boundary between bottom-up simulations and stress tests carried out by financial institutions for internal risk management and capital allocation purposes cannot be clearly defined.

The level of detail that top-down stress tests may pursue depends critically on data availability by national authorities.[7] Reliance on detailed off-site supervisory data allows, in turn, the use of the more sophisticated modelling approaches.

To sum up, in defining the most adequate framework for stress-testing, there is a clear trade-off between simple but highly stylised exercises on the one hand, and complex but more realistic ones on the other. Sensitivity analyses and aggregated top-down techniques are relatively simpler but their accuracy tends to be lower. By contrast, scenario simulations and bank-by-bank exercises are more complex and costly but they allow more reliable estimates of how healthy the banking system is.

Part II will show that the different approaches are not mutually exclusive, rather they are complementary. Indeed, given the advantages and disadvantages of each of them, it is very common to employ a wide range of tools and assumptions. Cross-checks, benchmarking procedures and comparisons between the outcomes of different approaches are crucial in guaranteeing consistent results and reliable policy conclusions. An appropriate cost–benefit analysis should help authorities in tailoring stress-testing exercises.

2.4 The ingredients for macroeconomic stress-testing

Macroeconomic stress-testing is a complex multi-step process that can be seen as the interaction of different skills: it is 'part investigative, part diagnostic, part numerical, and part interpretative' (Jones *et al.*, 2004). The process requires therefore several ingredients (Figure 2.3).

First of all, the set of intermediaries most relevant for financial stability is to be selected and data needs recognised. Second, the major risks to the financial system and the underlying vulnerabilities are to be identified in order to focus on real pressure points. Furthermore, some assumptions are to be made on the severity and plausibility of the shocks and – as far as scenario analyses are concerned – on how shocks are translated into consistent scenarios. Another relevant step is the choice and the development of the statistical methodologies that allow mapping of how the changing macroeconomic environment will affect banks' portfolios. Finally, the outcomes of the simulations are to be assessed in order to get guidance for possible policy reactions. The availability and quality of such ingredients ensure the success of the entire stress-testing process.

---

[7] See Chapter 6.

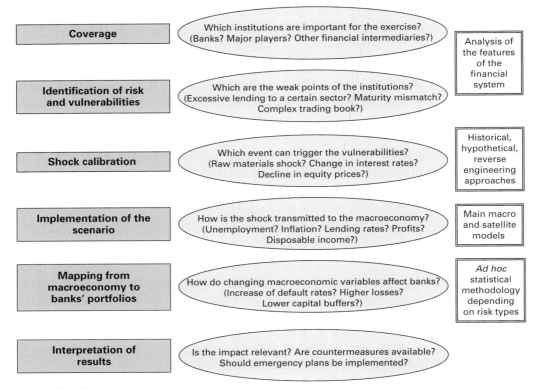

Figure 2.3   Main components of stress-testing procedures

2.4.1 Coverage

The process of stress-testing begins with the selection of the intermediaries. While considering the whole financial system of a country would allow a comprehensive simulation of the effects of the stress scenario, this approach may be extremely burdensome. In most countries, it is advisable to select a group of core institutions that are considered particularly important for the stability of the financial system and are likely to be affected by common risk factors. As a rule of thumb, the coverage of the simulation exercise should be great enough to represent a significant portion of the financial system, but it should not be so broad as to make the exercise impracticable (see Chapter 16). Therefore, the number of institutions to be considered and their market share can be used for identifying possible cut-off points (Čihák, 2004).

The ideal coverage also depends on the approach that authorities are willing to use: while aggregated top-down exercises can be conducted involving a large number of intermediaries (virtually the whole financial sector) since they are generally less challenging in terms of data needs and computational capacity, bank-by-bank and bottom-up stress tests should be confined to a narrower set of institutions.

As far as the categories of intermediaries are concerned, stress tests very often focus on banks, which are the most significant financial institutions in many countries and whose role in the payment systems is a potential source of contagion (the 2007–8 market turmoil is a clear example of this). However, this can be very country-specific. As an example, in those jurisdictions where non-bank intermediaries – such as insurance companies and financial con-glomerates – hold a large share of financial intermediation, the scope of stress tests might need to be extended. Covering foreign-owned institutions in stress tests raises additional issues that are significant for countries where these institutions play a prominent role.[8]

2.4.2 Identification of major risks

The next step in the stress-testing process is the discussion of the potential risks that may endanger the financial system and exposures to those risks. Along with the selection of the intermediaries, this part of the stress-testing process allows the tailoring of the simulation to the specific country, deter-mining the weakest points of its banking system, making the whole process more effective and avoiding the misuse of time and resources (Jones *et al.*, 2004).

Knowing the characteristics of the banking system, the kinds of business the intermediaries carry out, the features of financial regulation and the broader macroeconomic environment, allow the concentration of the simulation exercises on specific risk factors which are more likely to affect banks or whose impact is potentially more harmful for the stability of the system. The number of risk drivers should ideally be selected in such a way as to guarantee the inclusion of all the parameters that are likely to affect the value of the aggregate portfolio under examination. While the analysis of a wide range of sources of vulnerabilities may enhance the predictive power of the simulation and the accuracy of the outcomes, it also entails increased design-ing, computational and reporting costs (Sorge, 2004).

---

[8] For more details, see Chapter 14, which describes stress tests in the European Union (EU) new member states.

As examples, when banks are mainly active in the domestic loan markets, the analyst should focus on credit risk and those factors – such as interest rates, unemployment, real estate prices, etc. – that may have negative repercussions on that business; for large internationally active banks, foreign risk factors – oil and other raw materials prices, exchange rates, etc. – are far more important, while for small open banking systems the risk of contagion from other countries needs to be captured adequately. In some circumstances, however, other risk sources may be important. For instance, exchange rate risk may be relevant in small countries, as is exchange rate-indexed credit risk in dollarised countries. Liquidity risk may be relevant in a domestically focused system if there is significant wholesale funding from abroad, or lack of deposit insurance at home. Liquidity risk and contagion risk are also clearly major ones for larger and complex intermediaries. Since the number of potentially relevant channels through which a crisis propagates may be very large, stress testing is subject to some feasibility constraints (ECB, 2006).

2.4.3 Shock calibration

Once the major risks have been identified, it is necessary to investigate the events that trigger the shock and determine the level above which the magnitude of the shock leads to the materialisation of the risk, i.e., to a stress scenario. Indeed, 'setting the hurdle too low or too high might make the whole exercise meaningless' (Sorge, 2004). While it is generally not necessary to attach exact figures to the probability of scenarios, they still need to be somewhat plausible (Breuer and Krenn, 1999).[9]

The choice of extreme but plausible events is frequently based on a discretionary assessment by the analysts, which tends – however – to be the result of fiercely debated discussions, both within the authorities and with the banks. Macroeconomic and financial data can certainly help perform this activity, but the final decision on the range of exogenous shocks to be considered rests with the analyst.[10] Indeed, since the goal of the exercise is to understand what happens to the financial system in the case of rare (or never occurred) events, the scenarios designed tend to be beyond the normal range of experience (Jones *et al.*, 2004).

---

[9] See also Chapter 4.
[10] Discussing the interaction between supervisors and banks, Berkowitz (2000) points out that 'regulators may be able to identify 'bad' stress tests ... Certifying a stress test as sound would require the two parties to agree on the assignment of probabilities to unusual (or unheard of) events.' However, assigning such a probability is all but a straightforward task.

For any stress test, appealing shocks are those that are severe enough to produce significant turbulence in the system and hit sizeable parts of institutions' portfolios. When the shock is severe, but the resulting losses are limited, the impact on the financial system will be small or negligible, thus requiring a review of the risk assessment. For this reason, the implementation of stress tests tends to be an iterative process 'since some originally identified risks may lead to relatively small impacts, while some risks originally assessed as small may lead to large impacts if there are substantial exposures' (Čihák, 2004).

Roughly speaking, a stress scenario is merely a conjecture on the potential future developments of the economy. In designing a stress test, it is thus important to determine whether such conjecture should be based on historical events, assuming that past shocks may happen again, or rather on hypothetical shocks, that is, on extreme but plausible changes in the external environment regardless of the historical experience.

While historical scenarios are easier to implement and somewhat more tangible, hypothetical scenarios may be the only available option when structural breaks in the financial system – such as deregulation, consolidation, the change of the currency, etc. – make the past history no longer informative.[11] In fact, the calibration of a shock corresponding to an event that could occur once every 100 years is reasonable only if the external environment is expected to be stable over the same time horizon (Oyama, 2007). Nevertheless, the use of historical episodes often helps define the magnitude of hypothetical shocks. Therefore, hybrid solutions, i.e., hypothetical scenarios which are informed by historical market movements but not necessarily linked to a specific event, are frequently adopted (Committee on the Global Financial System, 2005). Also, what has been done in peer financial systems may be used as a reference for calibrating the shocks.

Table 2.1 lists some examples of historical scenarios that are frequently used in stress-testing.[12]

This approach for determining possible adverse scenarios is also referred to as worst case selection. Another, though less common, way to proceed to shock calibration is the threshold approach, which consists of determining the largest shock that would still leave the system above a certain threshold of, say, profits or capital – or indeed the shock that would wipe out banks' profits and/or capital (Van den End *et al.*, 2006). This 'catastrophic scenario' approach

---

[11] Indeed, the set up of historical scenarios is based on the assumption that future crises will be similar to past ones. 'The use of historical data would not make sense without this assumption' (Breuer and Krenn, 1999).

[12] An interesting reference is Matz (2007).

Table 2.1 Some examples of historical scenarios and crisis triggers

1973	First oil crisis – increase of oil prices by OPEC
1979	Second oil crisis – cut of Iranian oil supply
1987	Black Monday – stock market crash in the US
1991	Gulf war – oil price increase
1992	European Monetary System crisis – speculation against weaker currencies
1995	Tequila crisis – Mexican current account deficit
1997	East Asian crisis – US dollar peg cutting
1998	LTCM – LTCM collapse
2001	September 11 – terrorist attacks in the US
2007–08	Sub-prime mortgages crisis – rise in home foreclosures

can be useful for benchmarking purposes and should not be ruled out *a priori* from the financial stability surveillance toolkit.

A scenario offers an internally consistent representation of the impact of the simultaneous change in a group of risk factors. This raises the issue of the plausibility of the shock, i.e., of the probability that can be attached to the joint movement of the risk factors. The results of stress tests might be disregarded by the decision-makers if the scenarios upon which they are based are considered highly implausible (Breuer and Krenn, 2000). When sufficiently long time series of data are available (e.g., for market risk) and modelling techniques are relatively simple (e.g., for a single factor sensitivity analysis), an option is to derive the probability of the scenario looking at the past patterns of volatility and correlation. As an example, it is possible to estimate the joint empirical distribution of past deviations from trend of the selected variables and assess the probability of tail deviations.[13] However, in other circumstances, particularly in the case of multi-factor stress tests, it is more difficult to model an empirical distribution and the validity of the assumptions relies – again – on analysts' judgment. A combination of historical and hypothetical scenarios is a pragmatic way for assessing the plausibility of the different shocks more easily and for interpreting the outcomes more intuitively. As an example, historical events can be used for benchmarking the assumptions underlying hypothetical scenarios.

Finally, the timeframe over which the stress test is to be run plays a crucial role in the calibration of the scenario. Time horizon should be defined taking into account the type of risk under examination as well as the maturity and liquidity of the underlying portfolios. More specifically, the suitability of the

---

[13] However, this sort of analysis is rarely done for sensitivity tests.

time horizon should be determined depending on whether changes in the portfolio under analysis take a longer time to realise or not as well as on the realism of the *ceteris paribus* assumption regarding market participants and authorities' behaviour under stress conditions. For instance, while market risk should be monitored over short time horizons (e.g., daily, weekly) since it tends to change rapidly as a consequence of a shock, credit risk may be assessed by assuming longer timeframes (e.g., one or more years), since shocks are slowly transmitted to the banking books and intermediaries cannot adjust their credit policies as quickly as they do for trading activities. This has important implications for the conduct of macro tests that look at different sources of risks; indeed, in that case, the choice of an adequate timeframe is not straightforward.[14]

2.4.4 Implementing the scenario

While stress scenarios are by design simplified representations of the economy, it is still imperative that their implementation allows for coherent movements in key variables and risk factors (Haldane *et al.*, 2007). In that respect, structural macroeconometric models are the most appropriate tools for understanding how the economic system behaves when the assumed shock materialises. Indeed, these models are typically developed for forecasting the evolution of key macroeconomic indicators, providing a coherent description of the financial and non-financial sectors. Once the risk factors have been identified and the shocks affecting such factors properly calibrated, the model uses such information as an input and returns – as outputs – the values of the macroeconomic variables under stress conditions.

Since the assessment of financial stability is based on the analysis of a wide range of risk factors, an ideal model should be able to capture the relevant contagious mechanisms in the financial system. In practice, macroeconometric models very rarely incorporate these features and it is unlikely that a single model is able to satisfactorily handle all of them (Bardsen *et al.*, 2006); quite often, the level of aggregation is not suitable for the purpose of macroeconomic stress-testing since some sectors (e.g., households) or variables (e.g., corporate defaults), which may be of interest to the analyst, are neglected by the model.

In these cases, some additional components are needed in order to fully understand the consequences of the shock. Typically, satellite models, which

[14] See Chapter 3.

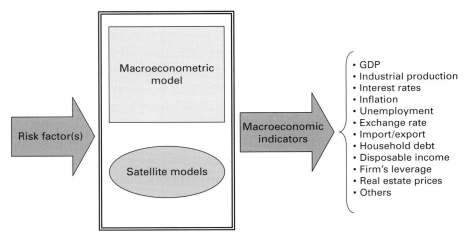

Figure 2.4   From risk factors to key macroeconomic variables

are reduced-form econometric equations that explain in more detail the beha-viour of a specific sector (or of a relevant part of it), are used (Figure 2.4). As an example, they may integrate the main model with a set of equations that facilitate the analysis and forecasting of corporate and household balance sheets and the implications on the financial exposures of the relationships already considered in the model (Benito *et al.*, 2001). Simpler reduced-form models can also be used when fully fledged macroeconometric models are not available, at the cost of more limited internal consistency.

However, the presence of a macroeconometric model does not reduce the need for expert judgment. Indeed, the design of the scenario entails a series of decisions that are crucial for the validity of the exercise and the reliability of the results. First of all, the interpretation of the shocked variables depends on the assumption of the baseline scenario. This may be a simple no-change scenario based on the last available data or a more forward looking one, based on the most recent forecasts. Furthermore, it should be assessed whether and to what extent the *ceteris paribus* assumption is valid or, rather, if some variables – beyond those that are directly stressed – are expected to react (and how) as a consequence of the shock.

From a more technical perspective, most macroeconomic models are valid tools for forecasting the evolution of the economy in normal situations; indeed they are based on the hypothesis of linear relationships across macroeconomic and financial variables, which is unlikely to be valid in extreme market conditions, when non-linearities can be substantial. Moreover, such models generally do not assume any structural change in the macroeconomy either in the past or in the future (Oyama, 2007).

Another essential choice is the inclusion of feedback effects. The expression 'feedback effects' is generally used for describing different phenomena that can affect the results of the stress-testing process.

First, they can underlie some second-round impact, i.e., the possible domino effects from the institutions that are directly affected by the shock to other intermediaries and, possibly, to market infrastructures and the entire financial system. For example, the default of a bank, which is particularly active in the interbank market, may lead to the failure of other banks. From this point of view, the term stands for contagion (the 2007–8 financial crisis offers some good examples of such phenomena).

In other instances, the expression refers to the possibility that the different players react to the stress scenario adjusting their behaviour, thus exacerbating/alleviating the impact of the shock. Indeed, when the time horizon of the scenario is sufficiently long or the magnitude of the shock considerable, it is unrealistic to assume that no behavioural response will take place. For example, banks may modify their credit policies in crisis times; also, it is sensible to assume that public authorities, like central banks, intervene to alleviate the repercussion of the stress scenario.

Finally, feedback effects can be synonymous for procyclicality, i.e., the mechanisms through which the instability of the financial system is transmitted to the non-financial sectors, deepening, in turn, financial problems. An illustrative example is represented by credit crunch episodes that may follow financial crises.

All these effects are important for stress-testing. Neglecting these kinds of reactions may determine a loss of information for the analyst and render the interpretation of the outcomes of the exercise less comprehensive. On the other hand, the response of market participants to extreme shocks may be difficult to model and forecast, also due to the lack of relevant data.

2.4.5 From scenarios to the map of bank losses

Once the scenario has been run, the stressed figures of the key macroeconomic variables are used for determining the impact of the shock on banks. This generally requires *ad hoc* statistical methodologies that help quantify the link between macroeconomic variables and banking variables, typically some indicators of default, losses or value adjustments.

The choice of the most suitable approach largely depends on the risk that is under analysis and the main objectives of the simulation as well as data availability. For instance, while the use of reduced form regression methods is very common for credit risk, VaR related approaches are generally used for market risk. In principle, the modelling strategy should also include the analysis of how different risks interact in crisis times, since it is not very sensible to assume independence across risks. However, the methodologies for the integration of different risks are still at an embryonic stage and represent one of the main challenges ahead. Chapter 5 deals with these issues.

2.4.6 Interpreting results

As a final step, the resulting figures for bank losses under stress conditions are to be compared to some synthetic indicators of financial soundness in order to assess the capacity of the banking system to withstand the given shocks. To this purpose, it is very common to compare the magnitude of losses with pre-tax profits of banks (i.e., the income that is available for absorbing the extra losses arising from the stress scenario) and the level of regulatory capital above the minimum requirements (i.e., the buffer against losses that go beyond banks' income).

Even if macroeconomic stress tests aim at assessing the aggregate impact of the shock, the interpretation of their results requires a clear understanding of

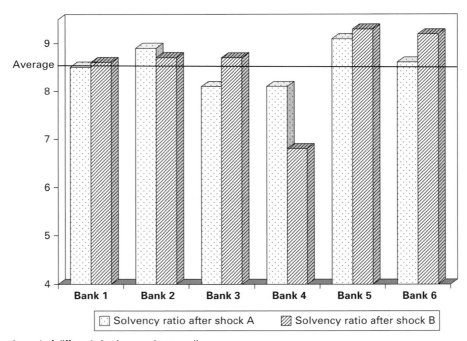

Figure 2.5   Impact of different shocks on solvency ratios

the actual distribution of losses.[15] Indeed, looking just at either aggregate or average figures may hide important pieces of information on the consequences of the shock event. As pointed out by Drehmann (2008), two different scenarios may end up with similar average capital adequacy ratios, even though in one case all banks remain solvent whereas in the other a major intermediary is no longer able to meet minimum requirements.

In the example illustrated in Figure 2.5, two different shocks produce equal average solvency ratios, but different distributions across banks; in particular, while all banks remain above the regulatory minimum under shock A, bank 4's solvency ratio falls below 8 per cent under shock B.

Therefore, average figures weighted by the size of the affected institutions associated with some measure of dispersion – such as minimum and maximum losses or interquantile ranges – provide the most complete picture of the robustness of the banking system. Unfortunately, this can only be done if the actual tests are run bank-by-bank; measures of dispersion are not available when working with aggregated data.

The interpretation of stress test results and particularly their use for policy decision-making are discussed in more detail in Chapter 7.

REFERENCES

Bardsen, G., K.G. Lindquist and D.P. Tsomocos (2006), 'Evaluation of Macroeconomic Models for Financial Stability Analysis', *Norwegian University of Science and Technology Working Paper*, 4.

Basel Committee on Banking Supervision (2006), *International Convergence of Capital Measurement and Capital Standards: a Revised Framework*, Basel.

Benito, A., J. Whitley and G. Young (2001), 'Analysing Corporate and Household Sector Balance Sheets', *Bank of England Financial Stability Review*, December.

Berkowitz, J. (2000), 'A Coherent Framework for Stress Testing', *Journal of Risk*, 2, 2.

Blaschke, W., M. T. Jones, G. Majnoni and S. Martinez Peria (2001), 'Stress Testing of Financial Systems: an Overview of Issues, Methodologies, and FSAP Experiences', *IMF Working Paper*, 88.

Breuer, T. and G. Krenn (1999), *Guidelines on Market Risk. Stress Testing*, 5, OeNB.
(2000), *Identifying Stress Test Scenarios*, OeNB.

Bunn, P., A. Cunningham and M. Drehmann (2005), 'Stress Testing as a Tool for Assessing Systemic Risk', *Bank of England Financial Stability Review*, June.

Čihák, M. (2004), 'Stress Testing: a Review of Key Concepts', *CNB International Research and Policy Note*, 2.

---

[15] Needless to say, this can be done only if firm-level data are available.

Committee on the Global Financial System (2000), *Stress Testing by Large Financial Institutions: Current Practice and Aggregation Issues*, Basel.

(2005), *Stress Testing at Major Financial Institutions: Survey Results and Practice*, Basel.

Drehmann, M. (2008), *Stress Tests: Objectives, Reality, Limitations and Possibilities*, ECB.

European Central Bank (2006), 'Country-level Macro Stress-testing Practices', *Financial Stability Review*, June.

Haldane, A., S. Hall and S. Pezzini (2007), 'A New Approach to Assessing Risks to Financial Stability', *Bank of England Financial Stability Paper*, 2.

International Monetary Fund (2006), *Financial Soundness Indicators Compilation Guide*, Washington DC.

International Monetary Fund and the World Bank (2005), *Financial Sector Assessment: A Handbook*, Washington DC.

Jones, M. T., P. Hilbers and G. Slack (2004), 'Stress Testing Financial Systems: What to Do When the Governor Calls', *IMF Working Papers*, 127.

Matz, L. (2007), 'Scenario Analysis and Stress Testing', in Matz, L. and Neu, P. (eds.), *Liquidity Risk: Measurement and Management*, Wiley Finance.

Oyama, T. (2007), 'Plausibility of Stress Scenarios', *IMF–DNB 2nd Expert Forum on Advanced Techniques on Stress Testing: Applications for Supervisors*, Amsterdam, 23–4 October.

Sorge, M. (2004), 'Stress-testing Financial Systems: an Overview of Current Methodologies', *BIS Working Paper*, 165.

Sundararajan, V., C. Enoch, A. San José, P. Hilbers, R. Krueger, M. Moretti and G. Slack (2002), 'Financial Soundness Indicators: Analytical Aspects and Country Practices', *IMF Occasional Paper*, 212.

Van den End, J. W., M. Hoeberichts and M. Tabbae (2006), *Modelling Scenario Analysis and Macro Stress-testing*, DNB mimeo.

3   Macroeconomic stress-testing banks: a survey of methodologies

Mathias Drehmann[*]

3.1 Introduction

As discussed in previous chapters, macroeconomic stress tests have become an essential component of authorities' toolsets to analyse financial stability. This chapter reviews current methodologies of top-down macro stress tests focusing on banks. Figure 3.1 summarises the model structure of macro stress tests.

As Summer (2007) points out, this structure is essentially rooted in the quantitative risk management framework (McNeil *et al.*, 2005), which also underpins banks' risk management models.

From a modelling perspective the starting point of the quantitative risk management framework is risk exposures. In the context of macro stress tests this could be the total risk exposures of the banking system in a country. It is assumed that the value of these exposures at a future date T is driven by a set of exogenous systematic risk factors such as interest rates or gross domestic product (GDP). The main part of the stress-testing model embodies the data-generating process which captures the interdependence of different risk factors between each other and across time. Finally, by modelling the impact of systematic risk drivers on exposures at time T the model allows the calculation of risk measures such as value-at-risk (VaR) or profitability. Once the model is in place, different stress test scenarios can be run.

Before discussing this modular stress testing structure in more detail, it is worth noting that, as any other model, stress tests can only capture reality in a stylised fashion. Model-builders therefore have to make choices on what is essential, what can be represented in a reduced form fashion and what can be ignored. To do this, it is necessary to understand the ultimate objectives of the model.

[*] Bank for International Settlements (BIS). The views expressed in this chapter are those of the author and not necessarily those of the BIS.

Figure 3.1 Schematic structure of current macro stress-testing models

Drehmann (2008) shows that different objectives can lead to different model requirements. If the main goal is decision-making, model accuracy and forecast performance are essential. While these characteristics are important they may not be overriding priorities for communication, which is often the main objective for central banks. This objective requires primarily that the model is transparent and suitable for storytelling. Unfortunately, transparency, the suitability for storytelling, model accuracy, forecast performance and other priorities cannot always be achieved equally well within the same model. For example, it is well known that simple models such as auto-regressive specifications may even outperform the true model with respect to forecast performance (Clements and Hendry, 1998). However, auto-regressive specifications are not granular enough for policy evaluation or communication. Understanding these trade-offs for different model specification is not easy, even though it is essential when building stress-testing models. It is also important to have objectives in mind when discussing different models used for the building blocks shown in Figure 3.1.

The chapter is organised as follows. Section 3.2 starts with exposures and explores how different models identify different systematic risk drivers. Risk measures are discussed in section 3.3 and the data generating process in section 3.4. Section 3.5 discusses the challenges arising from modelling risks endogenously. Section 3.6 describes the efforts made so far to model the whole financial system in an integrated framework and concludes the chapter.

3.2 Exposures to risk

Which exposures deserve attention is the first question any modeller has to address. In principle, macro stress tests aim at capturing the financial system in its entirety. Practically, however, most practitioners concentrate on banks and particularly on credit risk. This risk category therefore forms a large part of the discussion below. Some stress tests have also taken account of market risk – and especially interest rate risk in the banking book – and counter party credit risk in the interbank market.

In this chapter, the discussion starts with credit risk models, which can be divided into models using aggregate and accounting data, market data or firm and household default data. Then market and counterparty credit risks are briefly discussed.

Before doing so, it is worth mentioning two general issues. First, within risk classes most supervisory authorities and central banks focus on domestic rather than international exposures. This is driven by data availability and a desire to keep focused. However, a key issue in modelling both domestic and international exposures jointly is that this increases the complexity of the model of the data-generating process. Second, macro stress tests generally do not take into account off-balance sheet exposures. Again, this is mostly driven by data limitations, even though off-balance sheet commitments can have important implications for systemic risk as has been seen in the most recent turmoil. But even under more normal conditions it has been shown that the draw down of committed credit lines – an important part of off-balance sheet exposures – increases when firms approach default (Jimenez et al., 2007a). Notwithstanding their importance, this chapter takes exposures to be on-balance sheet (unless otherwise stated) in line with the current state of macro stress-testing practices.

3.2.1 Credit risk

Models based on aggregate and accounting data

Early models use time series at the aggregate level to assess the impact of macro factors on measures of credit risk. For example Blaschke et al. (2001) suggest linking the aggregate ratio of non-performing loans over total assets to nominal interest rates, inflation, GDP and changes in the terms of trade. Kalirai and Schleicher (2002) undertake such an exercise for Austria. Similarly, Bunn et al. (2005) estimate the impact of aggregate default rates and measures of loss given default of aggregate write-offs for corporate, mortgage and unsecured lending in the UK. Aggregate default rates in turn are driven by standard macroeconomic factors like GDP, unemployment or interest rates but also by a set of variables normally not included in macro models such as income gearing or loan to value ratios. Pesola (2007) argues that loan losses should be driven by unexpected shocks and their impact should be worse if the system is in a more fragile state. Hence, financial fragility, measured by aggregate indebtedness, and unexpected shocks to income and the interest rate should interact in a multiplicative fashion. Pesola finds strong evidence for this argument using aggregate data on loan losses for a panel of ten European countries.

A key problem of using aggregate time series is that such an approach implicitly assumes that the quality of credit exposures of all banks in the system is the same, even though some banks may pursue riskier strategies or have better risk management approaches.[1] Other models therefore rely on panel data econometrics to link banks' accounting variables to macroeconomic factors. An early study in this regard is Pain (2003), who finds that loan loss provisions of UK banks are affected by real GDP growth, interest rates and aggregate lending. The composition of banks' portfolios is also an important explanatory factor. Van den End *et al.* (2006) use a two-stage approach. First they assess the impact of real GDP and the term spread on aggregate default rates. Using a panel of Dutch banks, they then assess the impact of defaults and macroeconomic factors (interest rates, GDP for the Netherlands and the EU) on the ratio of loan loss provisions over total assets.[2] Bank-specific characteristics are not explicitly identified but accounted for by fixed effects. Quagliariello (2007a) uses a large panel of Italian banks. He finds that both bank-specific (e.g., cost to income ratio, total assets, credit growth, capital asset ratio) and macro factors (GDP, the stock market, interest rates and spreads) impact significantly on loan loss provisions and the flow of new debt. The impact of recessionary conditions can be deep and long lasting. Interestingly, Quagliariello estimates both static and dynamic models. Dynamic models generally improve model fit. However, there is an issue whether they are ideal for macro stress tests with a focus on communication. If lagged dependent variables have a large impact on results, such a model may not reveal much about the transmission mechanism from shock to impact, which is essential for storytelling. Indeed, Quagliariello takes his results as support for income smoothing, which is related to accounting issues rather than fundamental credit risk losses.

Data for aggregate default series is often limited, which can imply large estimation errors when using parametric econometric techniques. Therefore, Segoviano and Padilla (2007) suggest a stress-testing model based on a minimum cross entropy approach. This allows them to recover robust estimates of conditional probabilities of default (PDs) for loan groups in various sectors and/or risk-rating classes. Given it is non-parametric, non-linearities are also picked up by the estimation method. In addition, Segoviano and Padilla

---

[1] Differences across banks may occur because aggregate time series may be available for specific sub-portfolios (e.g., corporate and household) and exposures of banks to these sectors are known.

[2] Van den End *et al.* (2006) also look at sub-portfolios by distinguishing credit exposures to the Netherlands and the rest of the world. Default rates for the latter are based on bond data and US variables are used as macro factors.

recover the portfolio loss distribution using only aggregate time series such as non-performing loans. Again this method is based on a minimum cross entropy approach and does not rely on any assumptions regarding the underlying default correlation structure among loans. They implement their model for Denmark and show that for various lag lengths GDP, the interest rate, foreign exchange rates and the ratio of private sector credit to GDP are important explanatory variables of PDs. In a second step, the portfolio loss distribution is simulated and expected and unexpected losses are calculated for three stress test scenarios.

Models based on market data

While early macro stress tests use aggregate national time series, credit risk models implemented by banks use firm-specific information. The classic, structural approach is based on Merton's (1974) seminal idea that equity is nothing else than a call option on the underlying assets with debt as the strike price. By inverting the option pricing formula, the asset value and the parameters governing its stochastic process can be recovered from observable information and hence the probability of default over a specific horizon can be calculated (Box 3.1).

Box 3.1 A simple Merton model for credit risk

In his initial work Merton (1974) assumed that the value of assets of a firm follows a stochastic process. He also assumed that the firm is financed by equity and debt. The latter is a single zero coupon bond and the company's default can only occur at the time T when the bond matures. Merton's insight was that in this setup equity is nothing else than a call option on the underlying assets with the face value of the bond as the strike price, i.e., similar to a call option, equity holders' payoff is either zero, if the firm defaults, or the remaining asset value of the firm once debt holders are paid off (Figure 3.2).

From an empirical perspective it is unfortunate that the asset value, its drift and volatility cannot be observed. However, using the well-known option pricing formula, it is possible to recover these variables from observable data either by maximum likelihood (Duan, 2000) or by using theoretical restrictions implied by the Merton model (Hull, 2000). Once they are known the distribution of future asset values at time T can be easily calculated. Hence, it is also possible to calculate the probability of default, i.e., the likelihood that the asset value falls below the default barrier (which in Merton's case is the face value of the bond) at time T. Sometimes PDs are also expressed as the distance to default (DD). This is the number of standard deviations the asset value is above the default barrier, taking account of the trend. The intuition behind the simplest Merton credit risk model is best explained graphically as shown in Figure 3.2.

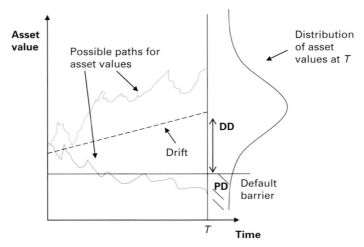

Figure 3.2   A graphical representation of Merton's model

Several macro stress tests have used this approach. Drehmann (2005) implements a very simple Merton model for corporate credit risk and identifies macroeconomic factors as systematic risk drivers. He finds a significant non-linear impact of macro factors on credit risk. A key paper in this area is by Pesaran *et al.* (2006) who develop a credit risk model for a sample of globally active firms. The authors map changes of equity prices to changes in ratings (including a default category). They then use panel econometric techniques to recover systematic risk drivers for equity returns.[3] Their preferred specification includes inflation, interest rates, the stock index and exchange rates. Interestingly GDP seems not to be significant. The innovation of the paper is the way they model the interaction of systematic risk drivers across countries, which will be discussed in section 3.4.1. This allows them to assess the impact of changes in foreign risk factors on national firms, which can be important. For a euro area stress test, Castren *et al.* (2008) follow Pesaran *et al.* in the way they model the data generation process of systematic risk factors. Rather than using firm-specific data to model the default process, they link the median sectoral PD as estimated by Moody's KMV to macro-economic variables.[4]

Instead of relying on equity return data, Gupton *et al.* (1997) suggest to draw on another source of market data. They use ratings transition matrixes

---

[3] They implement a mean group estimator which allows for heterogeneous slope coefficients across firms.
[4] See Chapter 6.

to derive loss distributions for credit portfolios. This approach does not only take into account defaults but can also assess the change in the credit quality of exposures. However, Gupton *et al.* (1997) do not explicitly identify observable factors driving the default correlations of borrowers. Neither do De Bandt and Oung (2004) who use data from the loan register in France and link the probability of rating transitions to observable macro factors. This allows the authors to undertake macroeconomic stress tests with this model.

Models based on firm and household default data

An important drawback for Merton-type models is that they rely on market prices. Those are not available for non-listed companies and households, which constitute large parts of banks' portfolios.

There is also a debate in the literature about model robustness because of several empirical problems. When implementing a simple Merton model it is for example assumed that interest rates remain constant and liabilities are equivalent to a zero coupon bond with a maturity equal to the horizon of interest. Even though the literature has suggested ways to address these issues, Jarrow *et al.* (2003) argue that empirical evidence strongly rejects Merton type models. An alternative method is therefore to use a so-called reduced form approach. Early papers follow Beaver (1966) and Altman (1968) and use only accounting items like leverage as explanatory variables for defaults. Wilson (1997a, b) uses a probit model and identifies not only firm-specific but also macroeconomic factors as systematic risk drivers. Several papers apply his model setup in a stress-testing context (Boss, 2002; Sorge and Virolainen, 2006). More recent models, such as Shumway (2001) or Hillegeist *et al.* (2003), use hazard rate models with time-dependent macro and firm-specific covariates to predict PDs.

Generally, the stress-testing literature focuses on forecasting PDs for a one-year horizon. But it has been recognised that the choice of forecast horizon can change empirical findings. For example, the conditional probability of default for the second year is generally not the same as for the first year, even if the predictor variables remain constant. In recognition of this, Duffie *et al.* (2007) estimate the term structure of hazard rates based on a mean reverting time series process for macro and firm-specific variables. Alternatively, Campbell *et al.* (2008) directly estimate probabilities of defaults at various horizons in the future, conditional on survival up to that period.

Drehmann *et al.* (2006) undertake a similar study using a large data set of corporate defaults in the UK. However, they focus on the importance of non-linearities more deeply. Following Jordà (2005), they argue that standard linear models used as econometric specifications can be seen as first order Taylor series approximation of the true model. If interest lies in studying the impact of small shocks around the equilibrium of the process, then using standard models may produce adequate forecasts even if the impact on PDs of systematic risk drivers is non-linear. However, stress tests do not consider small shocks, and the actual impact may be far from linear. In their paper they show that allowing for non-linearities leads to substantially different predictions of portfolio losses in severe macroeconomic stress scenarios.[5]

The recent literature has also shown that default correlations cannot be fully explained by observable factors alone. Das *et al.* (2007) therefore include an unobservable factor which leads to significantly fatter tails of the loan loss distribution. In this spirit, Jimenez and Mencia (2007) aggregate loan-specific defaults into default frequencies for ten corporate and two household sectors in Spain. They show that default frequencies exhibit strong serial dependence and are influenced by GDP and interest rates up to four lags.[6] Latent factors cause fatter tails in the loss distribution because they are important drivers for cross-sectoral contagion.

Loss given default

Stress-testing models for credit risk which do not explicitly model write-offs or non-performing loans have to make assumptions about loss given default (LGD) to assess the full impact of defaults on banks' balance sheets. LGD is often assumed to be constant. More sophisticated approaches draw LGDs from a beta distribution calibrated to historical data (e.g., Pesaran *et al.*, 2006, or Jimenez and Mencia, 2007). This can lead to fatter tails of the loss distribution, but does not capture the link between macroeconomic factors and LGDs. There is for example strong evidence that recovery rates are lower in recessions than during booms (Altman *et al.*, 2005).[7] In addition, Altman *et al.* find that higher aggregate defaults also depress average annual recovery rates. However, Acharya *et al.* (2007) show that this is due to omitted variables and the significance vanishes once industry-specific conditions are taken into account. Their findings support Schleifer and Vishny's (1992) fire sale hypothesis, i.e., recovery rates are lower if the industry is in distress,

---

[5] The authors also present an innovative method to derive quarterly PDs series for firms from annual default rates.

[6] An extended version of the model also considers the impact of interest rate spreads, the gross value added per sector and the unemployment rate.

[7] The recovery rate equals one minus LGD.

non-defaulted companies in this industry are short of cash and assets are highly industry-specific. Bruche and Gonzalez-Aguado (2008) use a latent, unobserved factor model to capture the dynamic join distribution of default probabilities and recovery rates in the US. In terms of forecast performance, they find that this model outperforms models based on observable macro factors.

A summary

Having discussed so many different approaches begs the question what is best. No clear answer can be provided as this depends on data availability and the objective of the stress tests. Nonetheless, some issues are worth considering. Using aggregate data leads to models which are relatively compact and can therefore be more transparent. The latter can be very useful if the objective is communication. However, their forecast performance may be very limited. Further, models basing the credit risk analysis on aggregate time series or accounting measures generally focus on expected losses, even though model-ling unexpected losses is important to assess the very severe tails of the loss distribution.[8] That said, if unexpected losses are primarily driven by random errors, this may not be very satisfactory either.

Many credit risk models using firm-specific default data discussed above identify macro and firm-specific factors as systematic risk factors. While macro factors are informative about the level, firm-specific factors help to better predict the cross-sectional distribution of default risk (Carling *et al.*, 2007). Therefore, it would seem best to consider both. But it is unclear how firm-specific factors change during stress. Some of them – such as size – are likely to be unaffected, while others – such as profitability or leverage – certainly vary. Nonetheless, even stress tests using such a credit risk model generally assume that firm-specific factors remain constant, which seems the only possible approach but raises difficult questions.

It also seems the case that models identifying latent factors as systematic risk factors improve model fit. These models may be useful from a risk management perspective, but using unobservable factors limits their potential to illustrate the transmission from shock to impact and hence is less suitable if communication is the objective. The literature on LGD also raises further questions for stress-testers, which are somehow representative for credit risk modelling in general. Several papers (e.g., Acharya *et al.*, 2007, Carey and Gordy, 2007) show that contract and firm-specific characteristics may be the

---

[8] See also Chapter 6.

most important determinants for loss given default. An all encompassing model should take these issues into account. However, the desire to incorporate every contractual detail would inevitably lead to an enormous model with millions of underlying data points and hundreds of equations. Such a model would likely have limited forecast performance and would be rather intractable.

3.2.2 Market risk

Interest rate risk in the banking book

After credit risk, interest rate risk in the banking book is the second most important risk faced by commercial banks (IFRI–CRO, 2007).[9] However, few stress-testing models have incorporated this risk into their analysis. Bunn *et al.* (2005) capture net-interest income in a reduced form fashion, using aggregate time series data for the UK. They only find real GDP to be a significant factor. Following Flannery and James (1984), De Bandt and Oung (2004) use a dynamic panel approach and show that the nominal growth rate of lending, the spread and volatility of interest rates significantly impact on net-interest income. Other studies using accounting data on net-interest income find, however, little evidence that macro factors are important (English, 2002).

One of the simplest ways to capture interest rate risk is gap analysis. In this approach, assets, liabilities and off-balance sheet items are allocated to time buckets according to their repricing characteristics. Net-positions are then revalued with the appropriate yield curve. By now, the literature has identified several problems with standard and more sophisticated gap analysis (Staikouras, 2006). From the perspective of integrated risk management, a key problem is that these interest rate risk models implicitly assume that shocks to the risk-free yield curve have no impact on the credit quality of assets even though they are a key driver of PDs as seen in section 3.2.1. This is not an issue for Boss *et al.* (2006), who model default and interest rate risk in an integrated fashion as they explicitly condition on the underlying systematic factors of both risks. Nonetheless, their approach is in the spirit of gap analysis as they revalue the interest rate sensitive net-position in each bucket conditional on the stress scenario.[10] Because of the netting procedure, this may still

---

[9] See Chapters 9 and 10.
[10] In their paper they take account of assets, liabilities and off-balance sheet items for four maturity buckets and six currencies.

fail to consider non-linearities and, consequently, underestimate the impact of interest rate risk.[11]

Drehmann *et al.* (2008) derive a bottom-up model integrating credit and interest rate risk. Their analysis highlights that modelling the whole banking book including assets, liabilities and interest sensitive off-balance sheet items in a coherent fashion is critical. The interaction of interest rates and default probabilities tends to create non-linear effects that are difficult to capture outside a comprehensive model of overall economic risk.[12]

Market risk in the trading book

Stress tests are heavily used by financial firms for risk management purposes of the trading book. Frequently run stress test scenarios are for example 9/11 or the Long-Term Capital Management (LTCM) crisis (CGFS, 2005).[13] For such a historical stress test it can be the case that all market risk factors are stressed in line with previously observed price changes during the stress period.[14] Alternatively, hypothetical stress tests are constructed by changing only a few risk factors. The impact on all other assets held in the portfolio can then be determined by simple correlations, copulas or factor models.

The results of stress test scenarios in the trading book are very portfolio dependent as a severe price drop can be beneficial for banks with short positions and detrimental for others with long positions. Portfolio-specific information is changing continuously and public authorities generally do not have access to this information. Therefore, market risk in the trading book is often not assessed. An exception is the Austrian Central Bank, even though the portfolio information they observe is coarser than the ones used by private banks.[15] Nonetheless, they not only model interest rate risk but also foreign exchange, and domestic as well as international equity price risk. In essence they follow standard risk management methods (McNeil *et al.*, 2005) and revalue losses and profits of the portfolio in line with simulated market risk factor changes (see section 3.4.2).

---

[11] An important non-linearity arises because of prepayment risk. Further, some short-term customer deposit rates track the risk-free rate plus a negative spread. Hence, for large falls in the risk-free term structure, banks may not be able to lower deposit rates in line with the risk-free rate because they are bounded by zero.

[12] The model is extensively described in Chapter 4.

[13] See Chapter 2 for other examples of scenarios.

[14] Historical stress tests generally require some manipulation as well. For example, modellers have to decide whether to use relative or absolute changes of the respective systematic risk factors considered in the stress. Further, they have to come up with ways to model new financial products.

[15] See Chapter 12.

3.2.3 Counterparty credit risk

Once a bank is insolvent because of credit or market risk exposures counter-party credit risk in the interbank market crystallises.[16] This has been modelled e.g., by Elsinger *et al.* (2006). The surprising conclusion of their study is that counterparty credit risk is of second order importance for financial stability. Results for pure contagion models seem to support this view (Upper, 2007). For model-builders these results suggest that for a first order approximation it is not necessary to model counterparty credit risk. And it may be useful to concentrate modelling efforts on other areas. That said, counterparty credit risk models are relatively straightforward to incorporate. Once the matrix of interbank exposures is known (or derived by maximum entropy from data on banks' balance sheets as commonly done), a clearing mechanism *à la* Eisenberg and Noe (2001) is simple to implement.

3.3 The risk measure

Public authorities measure the vulnerability of the financial sector by looking either at losses, capital adequacy or profitability of the banking sector based on the exposures captured by the model. Other measures are the number of defaults or possible lender of last resort injections to recapitalise the banking system (for an overview of different measures, see Čihák, 2007).[17] Against this background, several issues deserve attention.

The first is whether to use a risk measure based on a mark-to-market perspective or an accounting perspective. Whereas the mark-to-market per-spective provides a long-term view of banks' health based on economic fundamentals, an accounting perspective assesses whether there could be future regulatory or liquidity constraints (e.g., when there are significant losses in the short run but sufficient profits in the long run so that the bank is fundamentally sound but capital adequacy is threatened over a one-year horizon).[18] The choice of perspective should be aligned with the accounting standards in the country. This is obvious for private banks. But it should also

---

[16] See Chapter 11 for an application.

[17] The ultimate variable of interest from a welfare perspective is the real economy and hence GDP. Stress tests have not successfully tackled this problem because of formidable technical challenges. As will become apparent in section 3.5.3, current models which capture feedback from the financial sector to the real economy are of highly reduced form.

[18] For a detailed discussion on this issue see Drehmann *et al.* (2008).

be the case for macro stress tests to enhance communication efforts and to ensure comparability of results of private and public players.

Second, a key question is over which time horizon the stress test should be run. Some guiding principles are given by the regulatory framework which specifies a ten-day horizon for market risk and a one-year horizon for credit risk. Early macro stress tests also used a one-year horizon but it has been acknowledged that the emergence of severe credit risk losses takes time to trickle through the system. By now, central bank practitioners therefore often use a three-year horizon. However, Drehmann *et al.* (2008) show for one stress test scenario that, while credit risk losses take three years to fully impact on banks' balance sheets, the maximum loss occurs after less than two years, if interest rate risk and net-interest income is modelled appropriately.

As mentioned in Chapter 2, the choice of the time horizon implies a trade-off between the time a vulnerability needs to crystallise and the realism of the modelled behavioural responses by market participants and policy-makers in times of stress. This question is linked to the problem of endogeneity of risk, which will be discussed in section 3.5. But the horizon is also important to assess the key systematic risk drivers which should be captured by the model. It is for example obvious that for a ten-day horizon macroeconomic factors will not play an important role as they fluctuate at a much lower frequency. Overall, there is no golden rule for the optimal horizon to consider in a stress test. And again, this question has to be decided by the ultimate objective of the stress-testing exercise.

Third, macro stress tests often normalise losses by capital to assess whether the banking system is robust or not. This is problematic for two reasons. First, banks generally make positive profits which act as the first buffer against any losses. Hence, the risk of the stress scenario is possibly overestimated, if profits are not stress-tested as well (which is rarely the case). Second, banks set capital against all risks including market, credit, operational, business and reputational risk. All these risks impact on profits and losses, but are normally not stress-tested, even though they may also crystallise in severe scenarios. Hence, the buffer indicated by capital may be too large.

Finally, a key problem for macro stress tests is that representing the financial system with aggregate variables may be misleading. Take for example average capital adequacy for a banking system. As shown in the previous chapter, two different stress tests may result in average capital adequacy ratios which are well above minimum requirements, even though in one case all banks are solvent while in the other a major player defaults. From a financial stability perspective these scenarios are clearly different. Stating all individual results, on the other hand, may not be very useful either. First, this may be resisted because of confidentiality agreements. But second, even presenting interquartile ranges or anonymous minima and maxima may distort the message. For overall financial stability, it is not just the capital adequacy but the size of the affected institution which is key. A failure of a very small player can be generally absorbed by the financial system while a large player can create financial instability leading to severe losses for the real economy.

3.4 The model of the data generating process

The risk measure and time horizon are important determinants in choosing an appropriate model for the data-generating process. But most crucial are the underlying systematic risk factors identified in the first stage. As seen in section 3.2 some models only identify macroeconomic risk factors and/or firm-specific factors, some market risk factors and some both. The discussion in this section follows this split. The data-generating process of firm-specific risk factors is not discussed as models generally assume these factors to remain constant during the stress period.[19]

3.4.1 Macroeconomic risk factors

The simplest way to model the data-generating process of macroeconomic factors is to use independent autoregressive processes for each factor (e.g., Wilson, 1997a, b; Duffie *et al.*, 2007). From a stress-testing perspective this is not ideal. By design, such an approach does not capture the interdependence of systematic risk factors between each other. This is crucial if the aim is to implement hypothetical stress test scenarios. An alternative is to use vector autoregression (VAR) macro models (Boss *et al.*, 2006). VARs capture the data-generating process in a reduced form fashion without imposing much theoretical structure.[20]

---

[19] Latent factors are also not discussed explicitly. They are either modelled as autoregressive (AR) process or they can be included in the vector autoregression model (VAR).

[20] Macroeconomic VARs were introduced by Sims (1980). In a univariate setting, an autoregression is a single linear equation model where the variable is explained by its own lags. A VAR is an n-equation, n-variable model where each variable is explained by its own lags and the lags and current values of all other variables. Initially, VARs did not impose any structure on the model. Later 'structural' VARs impose restrictions on the distribution of residuals to identify shocks and better understand their transmission through the system.

Given their widespread use, they are computationally simple to implement with most standard econometric packages. As long as not too many systematic risk factors are identified in the first stage, it is therefore very easy to model the data-generating process using a VAR approach. This can also be done if the set of systematic macro risk factors is broader than the standard variables such as GDP, inflation and interest rates.

VAR models can also be used to capture the interdependencies of national and international macroeconomic variables. However, standard methods are not applicable in this case because of a lack of degree of freedoms. Pesaran *et al.* (2004) address this problem by proposing a global VAR model (GVAR). Within a GVAR, each country is modelled as a standard VAR model augmented by a set of contemporaneous and lagged 'foreign' factors, constructed as weighted averages of the other countries' variables. Under fairly general conditions, foreign variables are weakly exogenous within each country-specific VAR. Hence, the VARs can be estimated individually and then combined to generate mutually consistent forecasts for the set of countries or even the whole global economy. As the model integrates both national and international macroeconomic risk factors, it has become popular with stress-testers. For example, Pesaran *et al.* (2006) use it for a credit risk stress test of a portfolio of globally active firms. And Castren *et al.* (2008) use a GVAR in the context of stress-testing credit risk for European companies.

While the Dutch Central Bank also considers national and international macroeconomic risk factors it uses a structural macroeconomic model (Van den End *et al.*, 2006).[21] However, most central banks' structural macro models capture only their respective national economy. Modern dynamic stochastic general equilibrium models (DSGE) start from first principles, i.e., the model is based on optimising representative agents, competitive markets and rational expectations. Model parameters are then estimated in a consistent fashion with parametric or Bayesian econometrics. Such a model is for example used by Jokivuolle *et al.* (2007) to run stress tests for the Finnish banking sector.[22] More and more, DSGE models replace first generation macro models. The latter use economic theory to derive a coherent system of equations which are then estimated in a piecewise fashion. Following the change in methodology for the inflation forecast in the UK, Haldane *et al.* (2007) use a DSGE model, while Bunn *et al.* (2005) rely on the previous first generation macro model.

---

[21] They use NIGEM, a well-known commercially available international macro model.

[22] Interestingly, Jokivuolle *et al.* (2007) are able to stochastically simulate the DSGE model which other authors such as Haldane *et al.* (2007) found difficult. This allows them to derive the entire probability distribution of future loan losses.

The remaining model structure of both stress tests is, however, identical. The ultimate variables of interest are aggregate write-offs. In an intermediate step, these papers use earlier work of the Bank of England analysing the relationship between macroeconomic variables and aggregate defaults, which shows that aggregate default rates are not only driven by standard macroeconomic factors but also by a set of variables not included in the main Bank of England macro model (e.g., income gearing, debt levels or loan to value ratios). Other stress-testing models face similar problems (see Norges Bank, 2007). Therefore these approaches need additional satellite macro models to capture the interactions of general macro factors and these systematic risk drivers. While this improves the explanatory power of the credit risk module, the increased complexity is likely to decrease robustness of the overall model as estimation errors will add up along the model chain.

Different macro models have different benefits in terms of forecast performance, computational simplicity and speed, tractability and ability to tell stories. This means that modellers have to find the right trade-offs.[23] If communication is the main objective for a stress test, using structural macroeconomic models to forecast the impact of shocks on credit risk may be very good as they illustrate the key macroeconomic transmission channels. However, DSGE models are often computationally very cumbersome. For example, it may not be straightforward to undertake simple stress tests such as a 40 per cent drop in house prices as the model requires that only deep parameters (e.g., preferences or productivity) are shocked. This may lead to reduced form VAR models which are flexible, computationally simple and easy to implement. However, given their reduced form nature they are less useful in understanding and illustrating the economic reasoning behind the paths of macroeconomic factors during the stress test scenario.

3.4.2 Market risk factors

Models of the data generating process of market factors are always reduced form. The simplest possible approach is to take return series of all systematic market risk factors, estimate the covariance matrix and simulate the model by assuming returns follow a multi-variate normal or t distribution. But these distributional assumptions are arbitrary and do not fully characterise the distribution of market returns.

---

[23] For a further discussion about macro models for financial stability and trade-offs involved see Bardsen *et al.* (2006).

The dependency structure is also more complex than can be captured by correlations. Boss *et al.* (2006) therefore uses a grouped *t* copula to capture the interdependence of systematic market risk factors.[24] In a first stage, they estimate a host of different models to describe marginal distributions of innovations in the individual factors.[25] All marginal models are then tested statistically for the adequacy of the distribution forecast. Based on these tests, the authors find that the marginal distributions of innovations of 30-day returns are best described by a model where the bulk of the distribution is estimated by a kernel and the top and bottom 10 per cent are estimated via extreme value methods (for the latter, see McNeil *et al.*, 2005).

3.4.3 Macroeconomic and market risk factors

If models identify both market and macro factors as systematic risk drivers, modellers usually deal with the problem that these factors are observed at different frequencies. When modelled separately, the data-generating process is often captured on a daily or weekly frequency for market and on a quarterly basis for macroeconomic factors. For modelling both risks jointly a consistent time frame has to be chosen. A simple method frequently used in the industry is to scale up market factor changes by the square root of time (e.g., to get quarterly returns from daily data). Boss *et al.* (2006) use quarterly macro-economic time series and find that 60-day returns for market factors are best forecasted by iteratively forecasting market factor changes based on 30-day returns. Rosenberg and Schuermann (2006) integrate market, credit and operational risk. To derive annual economic capital they simulate a path of 252 days of market factor changes and 12 months for credit factors. Aggregation is then achieved in a top-down fashion. In comparison to simply adding up the individual VaRs they show that integrating them using either a variance–covariance approach or a copula leads to better results.

Rosenberg and Schuermann's methodology will only lead to correct results for integrating market and credit risk, if systematic factors driving market risk exposures and systematic factors driving credit risk exposures are separable. However, in practice positions can depend on both market and credit factors.

---

[24] For details, see Chapter 5.

[25] Analysed models differ in two ways. First, whether innovations in log-returns are described by normal distributions, *t* distributions, Garch (1,1) models with normally and *t* distributed errors as well as the kernel and extreme value distribution as described in the main text. Second, they assess whether it is best to forecast 60 days by using 60-day returns or iteratively using 1, 5, 10, 20 or 30-day returns. In total they assess 30 models for the DGP of market factors.

In this case Breuer *et al.* (2007) have shown theoretically as well as empirically that the level of economic capital measuring market and credit risk jointly can be lower or higher than the sum of economic capital if risks are considered separately.[26] This is an important result as it goes against standard intuition which would suggest that there are diversification benefits between the banking and the trading book. It also underlines the importance of modelling the data-generating process of systematic risk factors in an integrated and consistent fashion.

The most important market risk factor, interest rates, but also equity returns or exchange rates, are often captured by structural and reduced form macro models (see section 3.4.1). These models are therefore often sufficient to analyse credit and interest rate risk in a coherent way (Drehmann *et al.*, 2008; Alessandri and Drehmann, 2009). Boss *et al.* (2006) achieve a coherent bottom-up model integrating the data-generating process for both credit and market factors by using a grouped *t* copula, which captures the interdependencies of innovations in market factor changes (see section 3.4.2) and innovations in a reduced form macro VAR representing the data-generating process of macro credit risk factors.

Following the macroeconomic forecasting literature, Fiori and Iannotti (2008) propose a factor augmented vector autoregressive approach (FAVAR). This allows us to understand the dynamic interactions of a large set of factors as well as their impact on exposures. Fiori and Iannotti for example consider around a hundred time series for Italy. Some of them are classical market factors such as equity prices for various sub-sectors, Fama and French factors, volatility measures or interest rates. But they also include macro factors. By additionally considering aggregate default rates of eight industrial sectors they already incorporate measures of credit risk. The FAVAR methodology then reduces this large dataset by a principal component analysis into a manageable set of unobserved factors. In their analysis the authors identify four factors which approximate equity, credit, volatility and macroeconomic risk. In a second step, a VAR model is estimated which captures the interactions of these unobserved factors between themselves as well as an observable monetary policy variable.[27] This allows for undertaking a classical impulse response analysis.

---

[26] The intuition behind Breuer *et al.* (2007) can be clarified with a simple example, albeit in a context of options. Take a simple European call option and assume that a historical price series does not exist. Also assume that the volatility does not change. Given non-linear interactions, it seems obvious that the expected shortfall if both interest rates and equity prices are simulated simultaneously is not necessarily the sum of (a) expected short fall if interest rates are held constant and equity prices are simulated and (b) the expected short fall if interest rates are simulated and equity prices not.

[27] Conceptually, other observable variables such as oil prices could be included as well.

3.5 Methodological challenges

Any stress-testing modeller will meet important challenges. Most of them are well understood but, because of their complexity, limited progress has been made. Figure 3.3 extends the schematic representation of stress tests from Figure 3.1 to indicate where these challenges lie along the modelling chain.

As will be discussed in Chapter 6, data problems are an overarching issue. From a modelling perspective the second big issue is to capture the endogeneity of risk, because once risk is endogenous, it is well-known that standard risk management models break down (e.g., Danielsson, 2002). Endogenous risk is essentially due to behavioural reactions by agents in the economy including the policy-maker. This is also true for macro feedbacks and liquidity risk. Developing models which are able to capture the endogeneity of risk is possibly the most important challenge stress tests currently face.

Making progress on modelling endogenous risk appropriately for macro stress tests would also have wider benefits. All models underpinning the current regulatory framework (Basel 2) are based on the quantitative risk management framework. Hence, they may break down because they are unable to capture endogenous risk. This problem is most acute in stress situations which are the main interest for the regulator. Lessons learned for developing macro stress tests could therefore help to enhance stress-testing capabilities at banks and over time risk management practices in general. These potential benefits from macro stress tests partly underpin the bottom-up stress-testing exercises run by

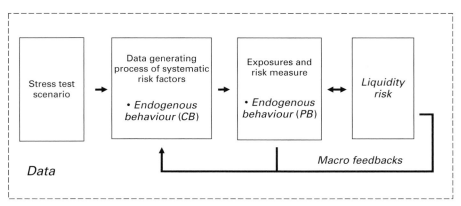

Figure 3.3   Challenges for stress-testing models
Note: Words in italics indicate challenges for stress-testing models. CB/PB stands for central and private banks respectively.

national central banks as part of an IMF Financial Sector Assessment Programme (see IMF and World Bank, 2003).

3.5.1 Endogenous behaviour

As shown in Figure 3.1, stress tests are a chain from an exogenous shock via the modelled data-generating process to the impact on banks' balance sheets. Exogenous behavioural responses are important at several stages (Figure 3.3).

In standard stress tests exposures only change because of defaults and/or the market value changes. Implicitly, banks are sitting on their initial portfolio allocation during the stress event without trying to hedge losses or re-align their portfolio. Over a one to three-year horizon, this is clearly unrealistic. Most modellers are aware of this problem but so far have not really addressed it. An ideal model would consider full portfolio optimisation in each period. This has been done by the operations research literature discussing stochastic programming models for dynamic asset and liability management. But even the latest papers can only undertake this modelling exercise for tradable assets funded with a simple cash account (Jobst *et al.*, 2006). When analysing credit and interest rate risk, Drehmann *et al.* (2008) therefore use a simple rule of thumb. They assume that banks as well as depositors are passive, i.e., that they continue to invest in the same assets with the same risk characteristics as before.[28] Clearly, rules of thumb are not ideal. However, it is a first step in modelling endogenous behaviour because it forces model users to think about this issue.

De Bandt and Oung (2004) follow a different strategy. Rather than building a structural model, they establish a relationship between the demand and supply for credit and the state of the economy. Hence, balance sheet adjustments by banks are accounted for in a reduced form fashion. Several other papers have taken a reduced form approach as well. Jimenez and Mencia (2007) show that the total number of loans in each sector is driven by lagged observations and observable macro factors as well as a latent factor. Exposure sizes of each loan are then independently drawn from an inverse Gaussian or inverse Gamma distribution where the mean is affected by the same macroeconomic shocks as the macro VAR model (which is used as a model of the data-generating process). The authors demonstrate that unexpected losses in

---

[28] Drehmann *et al.* (2008) also have to make an assumption about the re-investment of profits. The modelling framework is generally flexible enough to look also at rules of thumb where balance sheets are increasing or portfolio re-alignment occurs. Alessandri and Drehmann (2009) base a full economic capital model on the same set-up.

the stress scenario rise significantly once exposures are modelled dynamically. Out of sample tests show good forecast performance of the model. However, much explanatory power is driven by lagged dependent variables and unobservable latent factors. It remains unclear how useful such a specification is for communication purposes aiming to explain the transmission mechanism from shock to impact.

To assess risk taking behaviour of banks, Jimenez *et al.* (2007b) and Ioannidou *et al.* (2007) explore unique datasets for Spain and Bolivia respectively. In particular, they show that a decrease in the monetary policy stance before loan origination leads to a deterioration in lending standards and a shift towards more risky loans. Quagliariello (2007b) empirically analyses investment decisions by banks in Italy. He finds that the allocation between loans and risk free assets is significantly determined by firm-specific and macro factors. In times of severe stress banks' ability to accurately forecast returns is limited and herding behaviour tends to emerge. All these papers point to important endogenous behavioural adjustments by banks in the light of stress scenarios.

When discussing endogenous behaviour, it is crucial to consider the policy-makers as well. If the model of the systematic risk drivers is reduced form, then the (average past) central bank policy response is already embedded in the data-generating process. To clarify this, we could assume that the events of 2007–8 are run as a historical stress test scenario using the observed changes in market prices. The latter are, however, a result of the stress event as well as central banks' liquidity interventions. Hence, by re-running this scenario a similar central bank reaction is implicitly assumed. Market participants may reasonably expect this in the future if a similar scenario would unfold again. However, if this stress test is run by a central banker aiming to explore the robustness of the system with and without policy interventions, this is obviously a problem.

Reduced form macro models representing the data-generating process share a similar problem as past interest rate decisions are embedded in the data-generation process. If a structural macro model is used to capture the dependence of macro factors, most stress tests do not model the behaviour explicitly but rely on an estimated Taylor rule, i.e., they assume that the central bank mechanically sets interest rates to minimise deviations in inflation and output. It is well-known that this assumption imposes problems in generating severe stress scenarios. For example, a severe shock to the housing market would lead to a reduction of the interest rate, which dampens the impact of the initial shock on banks' balance sheets as interest rates are an important driver for corporate and household defaults. Without additional shocks to inflation, it is therefore very hard to generate consistent scenarios where interest rates rise while house prices fall, even though this was the case for example in the early 1990s recession in the UK, which was a stress event for banks.

No easy answers can be provided on modelling endogenous behaviour. However, it is already important to be aware of the problem. A simple step seems to be to explore rules of thumb for both policy-makers and banks. Further research on reduced form models seems also very important to understand empirical regularities better.

3.5.2 Liquidity risk

Liquidity risk crystallises because of an endogenous behavioural response by agents. In the classic paper on liquidity risk by Diamond and Dybvig (1983), agents run because other agents run. It is not only funding liquidity risk but also market liquidity risk which can affect the overall stability of the financial system. Markets may be illiquid because of informational frictions as is the case in the classical markets for lemons (Akerloff, 1970). And market liquidity more broadly may dry up because of behavioural responses by agents when they for example withdraw their money from weak performing funds (Vayanos, 2004) or if there is a negative feedback loop between funding and market liquidity risk (see for example Gromb and Vayanos, 2002, and Brunnermeier and Pedersen, 2009).[29]

Market participants would argue that such spirals have happened, for example during the LTCM crisis or more recently during the turmoil in 2007–8. Rather than aiming to embed these spirals into the model themselves, market practitioners use these events as historical stress tests. If these scenarios are indeed representative of market liquidity dry-ups and the main objective of the stress test is to assess the robustness of capital, this may be a valid strategy. That said, such an approach cannot reveal much about the underlying transmission mechanism and hence it is less well suited for macro stress tests.

Therefore, and because banks are generally illiquid before they are insolvent, some macro stress tests aim to incorporate liquidity risk (Jenkinson,

[29] The intuition behind these spirals is as follows. Assume a severe drop in asset prices which induces higher margin calls. If the funding liquidity of PBs is constrained, higher margin calls can only be satisfied by selling assets. This lowers asset prices further if many PBs have to raise cash because of a lack of market liquidity. In turn this raises margin calls, leading to increased funding liquidity demands and so forth. While such a spiral is theoretically understood it is very hard to model empirically. For a survey on asset market feedbacks see Shim and von Peter (2007).

2007). However, making empirical progress on this question remains difficult. First, to measure liquidity risk, not only assets but also liabilities and off-balance sheet items and their respective maturities have to be considered. This expands the universe of necessary data considerably. Banks' own approaches rely on vast amounts of confidential data which are changing continuously and rapidly, especially during stress. This limits their use from a macro stress-testing perspective. Second, data on behavioural responses by depositors and counterparties in the interbank market are essentially not available. Therefore, liquidity stress tests used by banks are based on rules of thumb rather than on empirical relationships. Using bidding data from open market operations, Drehmann and Nikolaou (2009) is so far the only study that measures funding liquidity risk with data available to central banks. The authors are able to capture the recent turmoil but data restrictions imply that they can measure liquidity risk only over a one-week horizon. It remains unclear how their approach could be incorporated into a model with a much longer horizon. The more general problem is that the link between shocks and solvency, modelled by current stress tests, and liquidity is even less clear.

3.5.3 Macro feedbacks

There is strong evidence that system-wide solvency and liquidity crises in the banking system lead to significant costs in terms of loss of GDP (e.g., Hoggarth *et al.*, 2002). But so far, linking the real and the financial sector has proven to be difficult. Christiano *et al.* (2007) for example build on the financial accelerator literature (Bernanke *et al.*, 1999) and include an aggregate banking/financial sector in a DSGE macro model. They find that this sector is a source of shocks which can account for a significant portion of business cycle fluctuations. But the sector is also an important amplification mechanism.

While this is an interesting macro model, it is of limited use for macro stress tests. As has been vehemently argued by Goodhart in many publications (e.g., Goodhart *et al.*, 2006a, b) and should also be clear from the discussion on risk measures above, it is important to model heterogeneous actors within the financial system. Considering an aggregate financial sector will mask many of the important relationships. For example, different banks may have different preferences. Hence, they may take different risks and the most risky ones are likely to fail first. Further, aggregate (funding) liquidity conditions are set by the central bank. As long as it does not make any massive policy mistakes, the level of aggregate liquidity is not so much of an issue even in crises. But the distribution of liquidity across institutions certainly is, as an institution short of liquidity will fail. Given interbank markets, such a failure may induce contagion to other banks – i.e., counterparty credit risk – with different ramifications for the real economy depending on how many and which banks fail.

The only successful approaches so far are reduced form models, which are different in nature than the standard stress-testing model set-up depicted in Figure 3.1.

These models are generally VARs and based on the idea of linking the standard set of macro factors with risk measures of the financial system. For the UK, Hoggarth *et al.* (2005) develop a macro VAR model which includes write-offs by banks as a risk measure. They find little evidence of feedbacks. Not so Marcucci and Quagliariello (2008), who use a VAR approach to assess the interdependencies of default rates, the output gap, inflation, the interest rate and the exchange rate in Italy. To test for the importance of feedbacks they also use a specification which includes proxies for bank capital and the credit supply. Other papers use larger scale VAR models. Aspachs *et al.* (2006) use a cross-country approach and proxy financial sector risk by bank defaults and bank profitability. Jacobsen *et al.* (2005) do not explicitly model banks but set up a panel VAR modelling macro factors and the likelihood of default for Swedish companies. They find that macro feedbacks can have important implications and that sometimes monetary policy and financial stability objectives can conflict. De Graeve *et al.* (2007) follow the approach of Jacobson *et al.* (2005) but use PDs for the German banks directly. They show that a negative monetary policy shock impacts significantly on the robustness of the banking sector, but only once the feedback from bank PDs back to the macro economy is allowed for.

3.6 The new frontier: an integrated approach to macroeconomic stress-testing

So far all stress-testing models essentially follow the set-up depicted in Figure 3.1, except the highly reduced form models discussed to capture macro feedbacks back to the real economy. The only exception taking a system-wide perspective is the work stream by Goodhart *et al.* (2004, 2005, 2006a, b).[30] The authors theoretically derive general equilibrium models with incomplete markets where agents are heterogeneous and default can occur. As stressed by Goodhart *et al.*, both of these features are essential when aiming to

[30] Their theoretical model to assess financial stability is based on Tsomocos (2003a, b).

model financial stability. The model by Goodhart *et al.* goes well beyond the standard stress-testing models as all agents, in all markets, in all states of the world are fully optimising over quantities, prices and defaults. The model is therefore able to incorporate endogenous behavioural responses.

Modelling defaults in a general equilibrium framework is one of the key challenges for their set up. In the classic Arrow–Debreu model it is implicitly assumed that all agents honour their obligations, and thus there is no possibility of default. Hence, Goodhart *et al.* follow Shubik and Wilson (1977) and treat default as the repayment rate which is endogenously chosen by agents. In this sense defaults are partial and voluntary. Even though Tsomocos and Zicchino (2005) show that there is an equivalence between a general equilibrium model with incomplete markets and endogenous default and a model where default probabilities are exogenous, this model structure makes it already hard to communicate with senior central bank management or banks as they see default as an exogenous event. Communication is also not fostered by the complexity and intractability of the model.

Ultimately, calibrating and finding computational solutions for the model are the major difficulties. So far this has only been tried for the UK (e.g., Goodhart *et al.*, 2006b) and Colombia (Saade *et al.*, 2007). In both cases, it was only possible to implement a highly stylised model world with three different banks, two time periods and two states of the world (stress and no stress).[31] Even in this case, calibration proves difficult. As Saade *et al.* (2007) explain, some parameters such as policy variables are observed, some can be calibrated using econometric methods (e.g., the income elasticity) and others such as the likelihood of the occurrence of the stressed state in the next period are arbitrarily imposed. Using this simple model, Saade *et al.* try to replicate data for Columbia during banking crises in 1997–9. Prediction errors for some model variables such as the volume of mortgage loans are small. For others, such as GDP, projections are far off true developments.

An alternative is therefore to extend the model set-up in Figure 3.1 to the model depicted in Figure 3.3. This is the aim of the Bank of England (Jenkinson, 2007). As a starting point it takes the structure of the standard Bank of England stress-testing model (Bunn *et al.*, 2005 and Haldane *et al.*, 2007) which covers the macroeconomy, credit risk and banks' net-interest income. Following the Bank of Austria's model (Boss *et al.*, 2006 and Chapter 12), the basic structure is extended to include market risk exposures of banks and

---

[31] In the model there is a one-to-one relationship between a class of households and a bank. Hence, there are also three different types of households.

counter party credit risk. Additionally, interest rate risk is modelled structurally along the lines of Alessandri and Drehmann (2009). The aim is to also cover macro feedbacks as well as market and funding liquidity risk. Because of a lack of data, robust estimates for the latter may not be possible and hence these channels may be very much based on rules of thumb. Nonetheless, the model breaks important new ground and will certainly highlight interesting channels. First model results suggest for example that the distribution of systemic risk, if measured as the aggregate loss distribution of the banking system, may be bi-model (Jenkinson, 2007).[32]

Such a model may be the only possible solution to deal with the limitations of current stress tests. However, an important drawback for this approach is that it does not break with the modular structure inherent in all current stress-testing models. This implies that there will be most likely empirical as well as theoretical inconsistencies across modules.[33] Given piece-wise estimation it is also likely that model errors add up with important implications for the robustness of the model. There is also a clear danger that such a model will become so complex and non-transparent that only a few highly specialised economists will be able to understand the dynamics of the model if parameters are changed. Lack of model robustness and high degree of complexity may ultimately limit its usefulness for external communication, which is an important consideration as this is the main objective of financial stability analysis for a non-supervisor central bank. That said, engaging in a model-building process is already an important step in deepening the understanding of financial stability and its system dynamics. Limitations of these models will certainly remain. But an overall financial stability model can already provide useful inputs into the policy debate and help communication efforts, as long as these limitations are made transparent and model results are presented carefully.

REFERENCES

Acharya, V. V., S. T. Bharath and A. Srinivasan (2007), 'Does Industry-wide Distress Affect Defaulted Firms? Evidence from Creditor Recoveries', *Journal of Financial Economics*, 85 (3), 787–821.

Akerlof, G. E. (1970), 'The Market for "Lemons": Quality Uncertainty and the Market Mechanism', *Quarterly Journal of Economics*, 84 (3), 488–500.

---

[32] It should be pointed out that this result relies on an extreme assumption for market risk.

[33] An easy-to-make mistake would for example be to treat interest rates as I(1) variable in one module but I(0) in another.

Alessandri, P. and M. Drehmann (2009), *An Economic Capital Model Integrating Credit and Interest Rate Risk in the Banking Book*, ECB Working Papers, 1041.

Altman, E. I. (1968), 'Financial Ratios, Discriminant Analysis, and the Prediction of Corporate Bankruptcy', *Journal of Finance*, 23.

Altman, E., A. Resti and A. Sironi (2005), *Recovery Risk*, Risk Books.

Aspachs, O., C. Goodhart, M. Segoviano, D. Tsomocos and L. Zicchino (2006), 'Searching for a Metric for Financial Stability', Financial Markets Group *(FMG) Special Paper*, 167.

Bardsen, A., K. G. Lindquist and D. Tsomocos (2006), 'Evaluation of Macroeconomic Models for Financial Stability Analysis', *Norges Bank Working Paper*, 1.

Beaver, B. (1966), 'Financial Ratios as Predictors of Failure', *Empirical Research in Accounting: Selected Studies*, Supplement to *Journal of Accounting Research*, Autumn.

Bernanke, B. S., M. Gertler and S. Gilchrist (1999), 'The Financial Accelerator in a Quantitative Business Cycle Framework', in J. B. Taylor and M. Woodford (eds.), *Handbook of Macroeconomics*, 1.

Blaschke, W., M. T. Jones, G. Majnoni and S. M. Peria (2001), 'Stress Testing of Financial Systems: an Overview of Issues, Methodologies and FSAP Experiences', *IMF Working paper*, 1.

Boss, M. (2002), 'A Macroeconomic Credit Risk Model for Stress Testing the Austrian Credit Portfolio', Oesterreichische National bank *(OeNB) Financial Stability Report*, 4 October.

Boss, M., G. Krenn, C. Puhr and M. Summer (2006), 'Systemic Risk Monitor: a Model for Systemic Risk Analysis and Stress Testing for Austria', *OeNB Financial Stability Report*, 11, 83–95.

Breuer, T., M. Jandacka, K. Rheinberger and M. Summer (2007), *Inter-risk Diversification Effects of Integrated Market and Credit Risk Analysis*, OeNB mimeo.

Bruche, M. and C. Gonzales-Aguado (2008), *Recovery Rates, Default Probabilities and the Credit Cycle*, Centro de Estndios Monetarioy Financieros (CEMFI) mimeo.

Brunnermeier, M. K. and L. H. Pedersen (2009), *Market Liquidity and Funding Liquidity*, the Review of Financial Studies, forthcoming.

Bunn, P., M. Drehmann and A. Cunningham (2005), 'Stress Testing as a Tool for Assessing Systemic Risk', *Bank of England Financial Stability Review*, June.

Campbell, J. Y., J. Hilscher and J. Szilagyi (2008), 'In Search of Distress Risk', *Journal of Finance*, 63 (6), 2899–939.

Carey, M. and M. Gordy (2007), *The Bank as Grim Reaper: Debt Composition and Recoveries on Defaulted Debt*, Federal Reserve Boards, mimeo.

Carling, K., T. Jacobson, J. Lindé and K. Roszbach (2007), 'Corporate Credit Risk Modelling and the Macroeconomy', *Journal of Banking and Finance*, 31 (3), 845–68.

Castren, O., S. Dees and F. Zaher (2008), 'Global Macro-financial Shocks and Corporate Sector Expected Default Frequencies in the Euro Area', *European Central Bank (ECB) Working Paper*, 875.

Christiano, L., R. Motto and M. Rostagno (2007), *Financial Factors in Business Cycles*, ECB mimeo.

Čihák, M. (2007), 'Introduction to Applied Stress Testing' *IMF Working Paper*, 07/59.

Clements, M. P. and D. F. Hendry (1998), *Forecasting Economic Time Series*, Cambridge University Press.

Committee on the Global Financial System (2005), *Stress Testing at Major Financial Institutions: Survey Results and Practice*, CGFS publication No. 24.

Danielsson, J. (2002), 'The Emperor has No Clothes: Limits to Risk Modelling', *Journal of Banking and Finance*, 7, 1273–96.

Das, S., D. Duffie, N. Kapadia and L. Saita (2007), 'Common Failings: How Corporate Defaults are Correlated', *Journal of Finance*, 62, 93–117.

De Bandt, O. and V. Oung (2004), 'Assessment of "stress tests" Conducted on the French Banking System', *Banque de France Financial Stability Review*, 5, November.

De Graeve, F., T. Kick and M. Koetter (2007), *Monetary Policy and Financial (in) Stability: an Integrated Micro-macro Approach*, mimeo.

Diamond, D. and P. Dybvig (1983), 'Bank Runs, Deposit Insurance, and Liquidity', *Journal of Political Economy*, 91, 401–19.

Drehmann, M. (2005), *A Market Based Stress Test for the Corporate Credit Exposures of UK Banks*, mimeo.

(2008), 'Stress Tests: Objectives, Challenges and Modelling Choices', *Riksbank Economic Review*, June.

Drehmann, M. and N. Nikolaou (2009), *Funding Liquidity Risk: Definition and Measurement*, ECB Working Papers, 1024.

Drehmann, M., A. Patton and S. Sorensen (2006), *Corporate Defaults and Macroeconomic Shocks: Non-linearities and Uncertainty*, Bank of England mimeo.

Drehmann, M., M. Stringa and S. Sorensen (2008), 'The Integrated Impact of Credit and Interest Rate Risk on Banks: an Economic Value and Capital Adequacy Perspective', *Bank of England Working Paper*, 339.

Duan, J. C. (1994), 'Maximum Likelihood Estimation using the Price Data of the Derivative Contract', *Mathematical Finance*, 4, 155–67.

(2000), 'Maximum Likelihood Estimation using the Price Data of the Derivative Contract', *Mathematical Finance*, 10, 461–2.

Duffie, D., L. Saita and K. Wang (2007), 'Multi-period Corporate Default Prediction with Stochastic Covariates', *Journal of Financial Economics*, 83.

Eisenberg, L. and T. H. Noe (2001), 'Systemic Risk in Financial Systems', *Management Science*, 47 (2), 236–49.

Elsinger, H., A. Lehar and M. Summer (2006), 'Risk Assessment for Banking Systems', *Management Science*, 52 (9), 1301–41.

English, W. B. (2002), 'Interest Rate Risk and Bank Net Interest Margins', Bank for International Settlements (*BIS*) *Quarterly Review*, December, 67–82.

Fiori, R. and S. Iannotti (2008), *Channels for Interactions of Market and Credit Risk: a FAVAR Approach*, Bank of Italy mimeo.

Flannery, M. J. and C. M. James (1984), 'The Effect of Interest Rate Changes on the Common Stock Returns of Financial Institutions', *Journal of Finance*, 39 (4), 1141–53.

Goodhart, C. A. E., P. Sunirand and D. P. Tsomocos (2004), 'A Model to Analyse Financial Fragility: Applications', *Journal of Financial Stability*, 1 (1), 1–30.

(2005), 'A Risk Assessment Model for Banks', *Annals of Finance*, 1, 197–224.

(2006a), 'A Model to Analyse Financial Fragility', *Economic Theory*, 27, 107–42.

(2006b), 'A Time Series Analysis of Financial Fragility in the UK Banking System', *Annals of Finance*, 2(1), 1–21.

Gromb, D. and D. Vayanos (2002), 'Equilibrium and Welfare in Markets with Financially Constrained Arbitrageurs', *Journal of Financial Economics*, 66, 361–407.

Gupton, G., C. Finger and M. Bhatia (1997), *Creditmetrics: Technical Document*, The RiskMetrics Group.

Gupton, G. and R. M. Stein (2002), *Losscalc: Model for Prediction Loss Given Default*, Moody's KMV.

Haldane, A., S. Hall and S. Pezzini (2007), 'A New Approach to Assessing Risks to Financial Stability', *Bank of England Financial Stability Paper*, 2.

Hillegeist, S. A., E. A. Keating, D. P. Cram and K. G. Lundstedt (2003), 'Assessing the Probability of Bankruptcy', *Review of Accounting Studies*, 9.

Hoggarth, G., R. Reis and V. Saporta (2002), 'Costs of Banking System Instability: some Empirical Evidence', *Journal of Banking and Finance*, 26 (5), 825–55.

Hoggarth, G., S. Sorensen and L. Zicchino (2005), 'Stress Tests of UK Banks using a VAR Approach', *Bank of England Working Paper*, 282.

Hull, J. (2000), *Options, Futures and Other Derivatives*, Prentice Hall.

IFRI–CRO Forum (2007), *Survey on Economic Capital Practice and Applications*, Institute of the Chief Risk Officers (CRO) and International Financial Risk Institute (IFRI).

International Monetary Fund and World Bank (2003), *Analytical Tools of the Financial Sector Assessment Programme*, Washington D C.

Ioannidou, V., S. Ongena and J. Peydro-Alcalde (2007), *Monetary Policy and Sub-prime Lending: a Tall Tale from the Low Federal Funds Rates, Hazardous Loans and Reduced Loan Spreads*, ECB mimeo.

Jacobson, T., J. Linde and K. Roszbach (2005), 'Exploring Interactions between Real Activity and the Financial Stance', *Journal of Financial Stability*, 1 (3), 308–41.

Jarrow, R., D. R. Deventer and X. Wang (2003), 'A Robust Test of Merton's Structural Model for Credit Risk', *Journal of Risk*, 6 (1), 39–58.

Jenkinson, N. (2007), 'The Bank of England's Approach to Top-down Systemic Stress Testing', *ECB Conference on Simulating Financial Instability*.

Jimenez, G. and J. Mencia (2007), 'Modelling the Distribution of Credit Losses with Observable and Latent Factors', *Bank of Spain Working Paper*, 709.

Jimenez, G., J. A. Lopez and J. Saurina (2007a), 'Empirical Analysis of Corporate Credit Lines', *Federal Reserve San Francisco Working Paper*, 14.

Jimenez, G., S. Ongena, J. Peydro-Alcalde and J. Saurina (2007b) 'Hazardous Time for Monetary Policy: what can Twenty Three Million Bank Loans Say about the Effects of Monetary Policy on Credit Risk', Centre for Economic Policy Research (*CEPR*) *Working Paper*, 6514.

Jobst, N. J., M. Gautam and S. A. Zenios (2006), 'Integrating Market and Credit Risk: a Simulation and Optimisation Perspective', *Journal of Banking and Finance*, 30, 717–42.

Jokivuolle, E., J. Kilponen and T. Kuusi (2007), 'GDP at Risk in a DSGE Model: an Application to Banking Sector Stress Testing', *Bank of Finland Working Papers*, 26.

Jordà, O. (2005), 'Estimation and Inference of Impulse Responses by Local Projections', *American Economic Review*, 95 (1), 161–82.

Kalirai, H. and M. Schleicher (2002), 'Macroeconomic Stress Testing: Preliminary Evidence from Austria', *OeNB Financial Stability Report*, 3.

Marcucci, J. and M. Quagliariello (2008), 'Is Bank Portfolio Riskiness Procyclical? Evidence from Italy using a Vector Autoregression', *Journal of International Financial Market, Institutions & Money*, 18, 46–63.

McNeil, A., R. Frey and P. Embrechts (2005), *Quantitative Risk Management: Concepts, Techniques and Tools*, Princeton University Press.

Merton, R. C. (1974), 'On the Pricing of Corporate Debt: the Risk Structure of Interest Rates', *Journal of Finance*, 29, 449–70.

Norges Bank (2007), *Financial Stability*, December.

Pain, D. (2003), 'The Provisioning Experience of the Major UK Banks: a Small Panel Investigation', *Bank of England Working Paper*, 177.

Pesaran, M. H., T. Schuerman and S. Weiner (2004), 'Modelling Regional Interdependencies using a Global Error-correcting Macroeconometric Model', *Journal of Business and Economic Statistics*, 22 (2), 129–62.

Pesaran, M. H., T. Schuerman, B. J. Treutler and S. M. Weiner (2006), 'Macroeconomic Dynamics and Credit Risk: a Global Perspective', *Journal of Money Credit and Banking*, 38 (5), 1,211–62.

Pesola, J. (2007), 'Financial Fragility, Macroeconomic Shocks and Banks' Loan Losses: Evidence from Europe', *Bank of Finland Working Paper*, 15.

Quagliariello, M. (2007a), 'Banks' Riskiness over the Business Cycle: a Panel Analysis on Italian Intermediaries', *Applied Financial Economics*, 17, 2.

(2007b), 'Macroeconomic Uncertainty and Banks' Lending Decisions: the Case of Italy', *Bank of Italy Working Paper*, 615.

Rosenberg, J. V. and T. Schuermann (2006), 'A General Approach to Integrated Risk Management with Skewed, Fat-tailed Risks', *Journal of Financial Economics*, 79 (3), 569–614.

Saade, A., D. Osorio and S. Estrada (2007), 'An Equilibrium Approach to Financial Stability Analysis: the Columbian Case', *Annals of Finance*, 3, 75–105.

Schleifer, A. and R. Vishny (1992), 'Liquidation Values and Debt Capacity: a Market Equilibrium Approach', *Journal of Finance*, 47, 1,343–66.

Segoviano, M. and P. Padilla (2007), 'Portfolio Credit Risk and Macroeconomic Shocks: Applications to Stress Testing under Data-restricted Environments', *IMF Working Paper*, 06/283.

Shim, I. and G. von Peter (2007), 'Distress Selling and Asset Market Feedback: a Survey', *BIS Working Paper*, 229.

Shubik, M. and C. Wilson (1977), 'The Optimal Bankruptcy Rule in a Trading Economy using Fiat Money', *Journal of Economics*, 37, 337–54.

Shumway, T. (2001), 'Forecasting Bankruptcy More Accurately: a Simple Hazard Rate Model', *Journal of Business*, 74.

Sims, C. A. (1980), 'Macroeconomics and Reality', *Econometrica*, 48, (1) 1–48.

Sorge, M. and K. Virolainen (2006), 'A Comparative Analysis of Macro-stress Testing with Application to Finland', *Journal of Financial Stability*, 2, 113–51.

Staikouras, S. K. (2006), 'Financial Intermediaries and Interest Rate Risk: II', *Financial Markets, Institutions and Instruments*, 15 (5), 225–72.

Summer, M. (2007), 'Modelling Instability of Banking Systems and the Problem of Macro Stress Testing', *ECB Conference on Simulating Financial Instability*.

Tsomocos, D. P. (2003a), 'Equilibrium Analysis, Banking and Financial Instability', *Journal of Mathematical Economics*, 39 (5–6), 619–55.

(2003b), 'Equilibrium Analysis, Banking, Contagion and Financial Fragility', *Bank of England Working Paper*, 175.

Tsomocos, D. P. and L. Zicchino (2005), 'On Modelling Endogenous Default', *Financial Markets Group Discussion Paper*, 548.

Upper, C. (2007), 'Using Counterfactual Simulations to Assess the Danger of Contagion in Interbank Markets', *BIS Working Paper*, 234.

Van den End, W., M. Hoeberrichts and M. Tabbae (2006), 'Modelling Scenario Analysis and Macro Stress-testing', De Nederlandsche Bank (*DNB*) *Working Paper*, 119.

Vayanos, D. (2004), *Flight to Quality, Flight to Liquidity, and the Pricing of Risk*, mimeo.

Wilson, T. C. (1997a), 'Portfolio Credit Risk (I)', *Risk*, September.

(1997b), 'Portfolio Credit Risk (II)', *Risk*, October.

4 Scenario design and calibration

Takashi Isogai*

4.1 Introduction

In Chapter 2 identification of major risks and shock calibration in stress scenario-building has been described in the context of macro stress-testing. It has been mentioned that the choice of stress events is frequently based on a discretionary assessment of the analyst. Pros and cons of some scenario calibration approaches including historical, hypothetical and worst-off have been discussed, and the plausibility issue of a stress scenario has been raised.

In this chapter, the discussion regarding the plausibility issue will be extended in more detail, clarifying objectivity of stress-testing and introducing both practical and technical approaches for building extreme but plausible stress scenarios. The purpose of this chapter is to describe difficulties in defining what is a 'plausible' stress scenario, and to present a way forward to establishing objectivity in calibration.

In conducting a stress test, some degree of objectivity is required in scenario-building as well as in the design of the test, so as to have constructive discussions based on the result of the test. Extreme but plausible scenario calibration in stress-testing is critically important from that point of view. However, it seems that there is not an established measure or rationale to evaluate the plausibility of a stress scenario. The threshold of an extreme but plausible scenario seems to depend on a risk manager's judgment, for want of any established definition at the moment. From that point of view, discussions on practical solutions to plausibility issues may provide some intuition and hints for further exploration. The following discussions mainly focus on stress-testing at a firm level, but they are also applicable to macro stress-testing run by national authorities.

* Bank of Japan. The opinions expressed herein are those of the author and do not necessarily reflect those of the Bank of Japan.

4.2 Objectivity and plausibility of stress tests

In any type of scenario (historical, hypothetical or a hybrid of the two), scenario selection is subjective by its nature, especially in choosing risk factors and determining severity of shocks. However, objectivity is an essential criterion in evaluating a stress test and its results. No valuable information can be obtained from a stress test that lacks objectivity. In this section, objectivity of stress-testing is first discussed, followed by the discussion about extreme but plausible stress scenarios from a viewpoint of scenario calibration. Finally, some practical principles that help build extreme but plausible scenarios are introduced.

4.2.1 What is objectivity of stress tests?

The value at risk (VaR) method is widely used as a standard risk monitoring tool for both market and credit portfolios. Stress-testing is used for the risk management of portfolios as a supplementary tool, which aims at providing information about risks that fall outside those typically captured by VaR. Stress-testing also plays an important role to notify bank management about latent risks that they are unaware of, which can be an early warning sign of unexpected risk materialisation. It is often said that the VaR method has some serious shortcomings. VaR requires estimation of the extreme tail of a return distribution, while the number of extreme observations for the estimation is not always sufficient. The scarcity of extreme data may make the estimation less reliable. However, these tail events are of greater interest from a viewpoint of risk management. Stress-testing is expected to help focus specifically on those stress events.

It should be noted that some conditions are to be satisfied in order for stress-testing to be a useful supplementary tool in risk management. Most importantly, objectivity should be well established in any type of stress-testing. Stress-testing as a risk management tool for individual financial institutions is expected to invoke various discussions on risk control between risk managers and bank management, as well as between banks and regulators. Both in a micro and a macro stress test, objectivity is an essential criterion in evaluating the test and its result. There are two types of objectivity for a stress test: one is the objectivity of the model and the other is the magnitude of shocks to be considered.

The former type of objectivity is relatively easy to understand; that is how the model is constructed and what its background is. The second type of objectivity is more difficult to be established due to limited common understanding. Even if a bank succeeds in building an excellent model to gauge market or credit risk, that would not be enough to establish objectivity of stress-testing. A set of risk factors that are assumed to be stressed in a scenario should be appropriately chosen; the size of the shock should be carefully examined in order to build extreme but plausible stress scenarios. This is also true for macro stress-testing conducted by regulatory authorities, in which econometric models are frequently used.

4.2.2 How severe should stress scenarios be?

In VaR estimation, a confidence interval needs to be determined in advance. The level, for example 99 per cent or even higher, is determined according to the risk appetite of the institution as well as the amount of its economic capital. Similarly, there is a need to determine the size of shocks, i.e., severity of the scenarios assumed at the beginning of stress-testing. There is the same problem in macro stress-testing, when setting an initial shock in any econometric model. The outcome of stress-testing is largely dependent on the initial settings; therefore, the size of shocks should be carefully examined. The key-phrase that has been frequently used in scenario-building is extreme but plausible. However, as mentioned in Chapter 2, it is highly difficult to establish a clear standard of plausibility or to identify the threshold level at which plausibility of a stress scenario can be assured; therefore, the choice of the scenario inevitably depends on risk managers' or bank executives' discretionary assessment.

This subjective aspect can be a significant drawback of stress-testing. For example, less severe scenarios might be intentionally chosen in stress-testing to obtain less unfavourable results, where there are no criteria for scenario specification. Such manipulation would be meaningless and even harmful with a distorted image of the bank's risk profile. It would be difficult to get any clear message from stress-testing without clear understanding of the appropriate size of the shock or likelihood of the stress scenario. Although there is no general rule or guidance in setting the size of shock or the severity of stress at an appropriate level, it is desirable to apply some objective criteria in specifying stress scenarios and to account for those criteria in interpreting the result of stress-testing. In that sense, if a probability can be assigned to a stress scenario, it will help both risk managers and bank executives to evaluate stress scenarios and their results.

In this context, the most frequently used measurement scale to indicate the probability of a stress scenario is the 'once in n years event' type of expression. In stress-testing, scenarios often consider events expressed in terms of 'once in a hundred/thousand years event', implying that the event is extreme but still imaginable. Such a measurement scale seems to be objective and assign probability to a stress scenario, but there is still the fundamental problem of how to set the probability level. In other words the 'once in n years event' scale should be carefully examined to know how the n years is computed. Otherwise, such a scale can be significantly mis-leading. It should be also noted that it is difficult to know the actual frequency of events occurring based on historical time series, since such long time-series data are very rarely available for many risk factors. The potential problem of the 'once in n years event' scale will be discussed in more detail in section 4.3.1.

Advanced statistical methods, some of which will be mentioned later in section 4.3.2, may be of some help in defining plausibility of a stress scenario; however, such methods also have potential problems. For instance, in many statistical approaches, parameters are estimated from historical data, and this parameterisation has the same problem as VaR methods. They are more or less 'backward-looking' in their nature. Another issue with these statistical approaches is that they are based on some type of parametric assumption; e.g., 'risk factors follow normal distribution', which is fre-quently used in building market and credit risk models, although such an assumption is not always assured. In addition, it should be noted that such models generally do not assume possible structural changes of economy especially in the future.

Taking these problems into consideration, there is a need to find practical solutions to the objectivity issue of stress-testing.

4.2.3 Practical principles for plausible scenario-building

In this section, some practical principles that can be used as a guide in judging scenario plausibility are proposed. It should be noted that plausibility relates to both qualitative and quantitative aspects of stress scenarios. The qualitative requirement is a sensible choice of risk factors, whereas the quantitative requirement is fine-tuning the degree of stress to be considered. In this context, the following points need to be considered. These principles are listed mainly for stress-testing at financial firms, but the concepts are also applicable to macro stress-testing at a national level.

A range of severity levels

It is very difficult to identify the exact degree of severity of a stress scenario due to the subjective nature of risk perception within the same institution; a significant gap may exist between risk managers, bank executive managers and regulatory authorities.[1] For example, a scenario that sounds extreme but plausible for a risk manager may not sound the same to a bank executive manager, since the risk perception is largely dependent on one's subjective judgment. A simple but important practical solution for the problem is to run multiple scenarios with different degrees of severity in a stress test, based on the same risk model. An extreme but plausible scenario can possibly be found for everyone, though not matched, from a set of the same type of scenarios with different degrees of severity. Discussions about risk tolerance will be prompted by such perception gaps, if any. Although this cannot be a fundamental solution, a range of severity levels of the same type of stress scenario should always be considered in scenario-building. It would be better for bank executives to join the scenario-building process for closer communication with risk managers.

Consistency with the purpose of stress-testing

A stress scenario needs to be assessed within the context of how the test is used. There is no predefined way for the application of a stress test. However, stress scenarios need to be designed in line with the use of the test so that the information derived from it will be meaningful enough. For instance, if concentration of credit portfolio on a specific industry is of interest, risk factors that affect that industry need to be appropriately chosen and stressed.

Enough coverage of risk factors considered in a stress scenario

If the scenario relates to more than one risk factor in a risk model used for stress-testing, all the relevant risk factors should be included in a stress scenario. In scenario-building, the choice of risk factors is generally subjective

---

[1] With regard to severity of stress scenarios, UK Financial Services Authority (FSA) (2006) stated as follows: 'We were struck by how mild the firm-wide stress events were at some of the firms we visited. On the evidence of our review, few firms were seeking out scenarios such as those that might require a dividend cut, generate an annual loss, or result in shortfalls against capital requirements while still remaining plausible'.

and based on an expert judgment; however, various linkages between multiple risk factors should be carefully considered.[2] In this context, correlation between risk factors is an issue to be addressed, although it is highly technical to discuss the relationship between risk factors during a stress period, which may not necessarily be the same as that in normal condition.[3] A flexible setting of correlation is apparently a merit of stress-testing.

Adequate consideration of technical limitations of models and data used in risk management

Stress-testing is used as a supplementary tool for portfolio risk management. In general, any model has technical problems to some extent, and data on which such a model is based may also have some limitations. The characteristics and drawbacks of the model and data should be fully understood by the analyst, and stress scenarios can also be built so as to provide information about hidden risks that cannot be captured by the usual risk measurement tool. A risk factor that has not been incorporated in the model can be adopted in a hypothetical stress scenario, although the stress test cannot be conducted using the model as is.

Relevance to individual portfolios and effects on bank management

The analyst needs to choose stress scenarios from thousands of possible options in which many risk factors are combined with multiple degrees of severity. It is important to focus on stress scenarios that are relevant to the market or credit portfolio of the financial institution, e.g., in terms of exposure to specific industries, type of credit instruments and correlation structures.[4] Therefore, stress scenarios do not necessarily have to be equally detailed among financial institutions. Stress-testing should be informative enough for bank executive managers when they evaluate the impact of an extreme event and make any decision in light of their risk appetite. In this regard, the effect of a stress test on bank management can be a non-numerical indicator of stress-testing plausibility.

---

[2] Bonti *et al.* (2006) present a framework for implementing stress scenarios in a multifactor credit portfolio model, in which a small number of key systematic factors are stressed and other systematic factors are impacted through correlations to the stressed factors. The method aimed at stressing sector concentration through a truncation of the distribution of the risk factors, but the discussions about the joint distribution of systematic factors and their dependency structure are meaningful from a scenario-building perspective.

[3] See Chapter 5.

[4] In macro stress-testing conducted by national authorities, scenario specifications can reflect an aggregated position of financial industry and macro economic condition.

Forward-looking scenario-building

While historical scenarios are a good measure of both objectivity and credibility, they do not provide much value-added as a supplementary tool to VaR analyses, since they do not include the possibility of inexperienced events. Therefore, even if historical data are employed in scenario-building, some forward-looking aspects should be included in stress scenarios.

Consistency with economic conditions

Consistency with current and near-future economic conditions is another issue to be addressed in scenario-building. If scenarios that are scarcely imaginable from current economic conditions are assumed, stress test results would sound unimaginable. This may seem counterintuitive, since stress tests target 'extreme' scenarios, which are far from the current economic conditions. However, what is important is to focus on a plausible (logically imaginable) direction of economic developments from a very wide range of probability.

4.3 Technical discussion on the plausibility of stress scenarios

As mentioned earlier, it would be beneficial to have numerical criteria for an 'extreme but plausible' risk, i.e., severity of shocks assumed in a stress scenario. In this regard, the most frequently used criterion is a 'once in n years event' type of measurement scale that can assign probability to a stress scenario as a percentile of a particular statistical distribution. Although this method is straightforward and useful in comparing severity between multiple scenarios, it is important to be careful when relying on this measurement scale in scenario-building.

4.3.1 Potential problems of 'once in n years event' scale

The expression 'once in a hundred years event' is quite often used to express the severity of an extreme event when building a stress scenario. The frequency of an event is regarded as a threshold level of corresponding risk. This type of probabilistic scale is based on a specific parametric assumption for the statistical distribution of the risk factor as well as stability of an economic structure without any serious structural change.

In many cases, for both risk measurement and stress-testing, the distribution of a risk factor is assumed to be normal distribution; parameters are estimated from sample data to derive a percentile value for the stress event. The approximation by normal distribution is quite useful, since it is easily applicable to many situations. However, such an assumption may not always be appropriate. Assuming non-normal distributions with fat tails might result in much higher probability, say 'once in fifty or thirty years', which leads to an underestimation of the stress event risk. It is apparent that the problem comes not from the definition of 'once in n years event' probabilistic scale but from the parametric assumption of the risk factor distribution. A similar tail problem exists, for example, in VaR risk measurement based on historical data. In many market and credit risk models (both single or multi-factor), each risk factor is usually assumed to be normally distributed. It is not easy to change the normality assumption when the fundamental logic of the model heavily depends on it. Data should be examined more carefully in order to see if the normal distribution approximation is appropriate, since stress tests focus more on effects of tail events, i.e., 'extreme' values of the risk factors.[5]

4.3.2 Advanced approaches for scenario calibration

There are few approaches for addressing the plausibility issue of a stress scenario, proposing some new concepts of objective criteria of plausibility. As mentioned earlier in Chapter 2, Breuer and Krenn (1999, 2001) proposed a methodology for explicitly measuring the plausibility of stress scenarios in the context of a multi-factor model. They proposed a sensible way to search 'the worst-off stress scenario' with the maximum loss of some given portfolio in some domain of given plausibility, maximising severity of stress scenarios.

In the standard worst-off scenario approaches that are widely used in stress-testing, the most adverse shocks over a certain time horizon are combined for a number of risk factors; however, this approach tends to ignore correlations between risk factors and yield implausible scenarios. In order to overcome this problem, Breuer and Krenn took the joint distribution of multiple risk factors, and searched algorithmically for a set of factor changes

---

[5] When fitting sample data on normal distribution, one can rely on the central limit theorem: distribution of the sample mean can be approximated by normal distribution regardless of parent population, if the number of data is large enough. If all the sample data are used for fitting, then, the distribution is constructed to fit the central observations best, since most observations are central. Therefore, extreme observations may be ill-suited to the estimated distribution.

that resulted in the worst loss at a given threshold. They define stress scenarios as simultaneous relative changes of multiple risk factors from the current condition to the stressed condition, and then calculate a distance between the current and the stressed condition, which is translated into a numerical plausibility based on a multivariate distribution assumption of risk factors. In Breuer *et al.* (2008), Mahalanobis distance has been proposed as a measure of plausibility of stress scenarios.[6] The approach ensures that no harmful scenarios are missed, does not analyse scenarios which are too implausible and allows for a portfolio-specific identification of key risk factors (Breuer *et al.*, 2008).

That method seems to contribute to enhancing the objectivity of a stress scenario, although it also has its limitations: the method assumes elliptical distribution as multiple risk factor distributions. A family of elliptical distributions, that include not just normal distributions but also *t* distributions and some others, has good statistical properties for risk modelling. That means that it may not be applicable to non-elliptically distributed risk factors. This distributional assumption seems to be less restrictive than normal distribution approximation, but it should be carefully examined if such an assumption can be acceptable in view of the property of individual risk factors.

Another approach for systematic scenario-building that focuses more directly on the 'fat tails' feature of underlying risk factor distribution is an extreme value theory (EVT) based method, which can estimate an extreme quantile of the distribution from historical data. CGFS (2005) and MAS (2003) stated the nature of the theory and its possible application to a stress-testing framework in the context of market risk stress-testing:

VaR models for market risk, especially those that use variance–covariance methods, assume that the probability distribution of portfolio changes is well approximated by a normal distribution. However, it has been found that actual returns distributions display a higher level of probability for extreme events than that supposed by the normal distribution. This is the reason why the actual distributions are said to have fat tails. EVT is a theory that models these fat tails. (MAS, 2003)

As mentioned above, EVT deals with 'fat tail' problems under non-normality. It has been applied to the extension of existing VaR methods, since it is useful for assessing risk for highly unusual events.[7] The theory tells

---

[6] Mahalanobis distance is based on correlations between two sets of risk factors. It can also be defined as a dissimilarity measure between two groups of the same distribution with a covariance matrix. For more details about the approach, see Breuer *et al.* (2008).

[7] Longin (1999) developed an EVT-based VaR for market risk measurement. McNeil (1999) and McNeil and Frey (2000) also discussed an application of EVT to risk management.

what the asymptotic distribution of extreme values should look like regardless of the original distribution, given certain conditions. More precisely, the asymptotic distribution of extreme values converges to general extreme value (GEV) distribution.[8] It is analogous to central limit theorem, but applies to the extremes of observations. The theory can also be applied to estimate the conditional distribution of the excess beyond a very high threshold.[9] It would be useful in modelling the behaviour of such excess values for dealing with tails in both VaR estimation and stress scenario calibration. In this case, the asymptotic distribution of excess values over the threshold is called generalised pareto distribution (GPD).[10]

What is important here is that EVT does not require any parametric assumption, e.g., normality, with regard to the parent population. EVT enables one to focus just on the tail of the distribution based on sample historical data; the main interest is to estimate the extreme quartiles. It is also possible to estimate probability of an extreme event that has never been experienced from the estimated tail distribution. Those properties of EVT are suitable for stress scenario specification, since there is no need to estimate the entire figure of risk factor density distributions in stress-testing.

It should be noted, however, that EVT is not the final solution; the many conditions required to apply the theory and scarcity of extreme data are still a major problem even in EVT-based methods of scenario calibration. Things would be more complex if correlation between multiple risk factors in a stress scenario were taken into account in application of the theory to a multi-dimensional distribution problem.[11] In addition, EVT, as well as other statistical methods, has the significant drawback that the risk factors may not behave as they did in the past. Those methods assume that there is no structural change over the entire period.

4.4 Conclusions

Objectivity and credibility are critical for valid stress-testing. However, there is no general guideline to identify plausible and sensible scenarios. In scenario

---

[8] The maximum values over the sequence of n-size blocks, e.g., n-days or n-years, are fit to GEV to estimate the parameter of the distribution. The model is called block maxima, or BM.

[9] The model is called as peak over threshold, or POT.

[10] GEV and GPD distributions are closely related; both of the two asymptotic distributions share the same shape parameter, which determines the shape or thickness of the tail of parent distribution.

[11] For more details, see McNeil *et al.* (2005).

calibration, it is difficult to establish a clear standard of plausibility or to identify the threshold level at which plausibility of stress scenarios can be assured. Advanced statistical methods can be of some help, but many of them are still at an experimental stage. As things stand now, it is advisable to be not too prescriptive in addressing this issue.

A way forward may be to develop practical principles that can be used as a guide in building plausible and sensible stress scenarios. Most importantly, multiple stress scenarios of the same risk factors but with different degrees of those risks should always be considered when building a scenario to cover differences in risk perception that reflect a person's subjective judgment. It will be better for both risk managers and bank executives to have close communication and share a common view of the plausibility of stress scenarios. Some other points raised in this chapter, including awareness of the technical limitations of risk models and data, as well as forward-looking scenario-building, are also relevant for meaningful stress-testing. Further discussion on practical solutions for plausibility issues and research on technical problems will give intuition and hints in enhancing the role of stress-testing as a supplemental tool for portfolio risk management.

REFERENCES

Aragones, J. R., C. Blanco and K. Dowd (2001) 'Incorporating Stress Tests into Market Risk Modelling', *Derivatives Quarterly*, 7, 3.

Bonti, G., M. Kalkbrener, C. Lotz and G. Stahl (2006), 'Credit Risk Concentrations under Stress', *Journal of Credit Risk*, 3.

Breuer, T. and G. Krenn (1999), *Stress Testing Guidelines on Market Risk*, 5, Oesterreichische Nationalbank (OeNB).

    (2001), 'What is a Plausible Stress Scenario?', *Computational Intelligence: Methods and Applications*, January, 215–21.

Breuer, T., M. Jandacka, K. Rheinberger and M. Summer (2008), *Inter-risk Diversification Effects of Integrated Market and Credit Risk Analysis*, OeNB, mimeo.

Čihák, M. (2000), 'Stress Testing: a Review of Key Concepts', *CNB International Research and Policy Note*, April.

Coles, S. (2001), *An Introduction to Statistical Modelling of Extreme Values*, Springer-Verlag.

Committee on the Global Financial System (CGFS) (2000), *Stress Testing by Large Financial Institutions: Current Practice and Aggregation Issues*, CGFS.

    (2005), *Stress Testing at Major Financial Institutions: Survey Results and Practice*, CGFS.

Embrechts, P., C. Klüppelberg and T. Mikosch (1997), *Modelling Extreme Events for Insurance and Finance*, Springer-Verlag.

Kupiec, P. H. (1998), 'Stress Testing in a Value at Risk Framework', *Journal of Derivatives*, Autumn.

(2000), 'Stress Test and Risk Capital', *Journal of Risk*, Summer.

Longin, F. (1999), 'Stress Testing: a Method Based on Extreme Value Theory', *BSI Gamma Foundation Working Paper*.

MAS (2003), 'Technical Paper on Credit Stress-Testing', *MAS Information Paper*, 1.

McNeil, A. J. (1999), *Extreme Value Theory for Risk Managers*, Risk Books.

McNeil, A. J. and R. Frey (2000), 'Estimation of Tail-Related Risk Measures for Heteroscedastic Financial Time Series: an Extreme Value Approach', *Journal of Empirical Finance*, 7.

McNeil, A. J., R. Frey and P. Embrechts (2005), *Quantitative Risk Management*, Princeton University Press.

Pritsker, M. (1997), 'Evaluating Value at Risk Methodologies: Accuracy versus Computational Time', *Journal of Financial Services Research*, 12.

Sorge, M. (2004), 'Stress Testing Financial Systems: an Overview of Current Methodologies', *BIS Working Paper*, 165.

UK Financial Services Authority (FSA) (2005), 'Stress Testing', *Discussion Paper*, 2, May.

(2006), *Stress Testing Thematic Review*, letter to chief executives at ten large banking firms, October.

5 Risk aggregation and economic capital

Vincenzo Tola[*]

5.1 Introduction

Risk aggregation represents one of the major challenges for stress tests. It is also a topic where the interconnections between macro stress-testing and banks' risk management practices are clear, particularly when bottom-up approaches are used for stress-testing the banking system.

In recent times, banks have been giving greater emphasis on the management of risk on an integrated firm-wide basis and, also, have been making efforts to aggregate different risk types through quantitative risk models (Basel Committee on Banking Supervision, 2003). Such trends have been influenced by and, simultaneously, have influenced the supervisory practices. The improvements of the techniques for risk aggregation have also led to significant advances in the methodologies for prudential and macroeconomic stress-testing, providing tools for assessing the joint impact of several risks.

Indeed, the development of more sophisticated risk management approaches ensures both a better measurement and control of risks and, most of all, a deeper understanding of the relations among them. An integrated risk management system favours a better estimate of the overall risk undertaken and supports the research of sound measures of risk aggregation, such as economic capital.

Risk aggregation is the process of merging different risk types into a single metric. It represents a preparatory procedure to assess the economic capital. Economic capital is the capital that shareholders should invest in the bank in order to limit the probability of default to a given confidence level over a specified time horizon. In this sense, the economic capital is a key tool to understand and quantify the overall risk undertaken by banks, useful to

* Bank of Italy. The opinions expressed herein are those of the author and do not necessarily reflect those of the Bank of Italy.

support the capital adequacy and the value-based management (McNeil *et al.*, 2005). Therefore, economic capital represents the measure that summarises all the information about the overall degree of risk undertaken by banks. Stress-testing exercises on economic capital represent a tool that helps to better appreciate the capital adequacy profile of specific institutions as well as of the banking system as a whole.

The chapter proceeds as follows. In sections 5.2 and 5.3 we introduce some basic definitions and provide a brief overview of the main works on financial risk aggregation. Section 5.4 offers an overview of the copula functions. Section 5.5 is divided into three subsections. In the first, we focus on some issues related to methodological choices preparatory to a sound economic capital assessment. We discuss, in particular, the choices of risk metrics, time horizon and confidence level. In the second, after illustrating naive methods to estimate economic capital, we report a theoretical framework of an economic capital model using copula functions to aggregate different risk types. In the third, we discuss experimental results descending from our simulation analysis. In particular, we talk about the sensitivity of the economic capital to different copulas and marginal distribution specifications. Section 5.6 concludes the chapter.

5.2 Some basic definitions

From a methodological point of view, the risk aggregation problem consists of joining the marginal loss distributions, concerning different risk types, in a joint distribution. The problem becomes more complex since the distributional shape of each risk type varies considerably. As a matter of fact, while market risk marginal distribution can be generally approximated by a Gaussian distribution, credit and most of all operational risks are characterised by more skewed and leptokurtic loss distributions. Another complication comes from the change of the distributional shape according to the time scale. For example, while the empirical distribution of financial returns measured on a daily basis is leptokurtic, the distribution of yearly returns becomes much closer to the Gaussian distribution.

A more intricate technical difficulty arises from the modelling of dependence structures among different risk types. In fact, while some risk types are characterised and measured more easily than others, much less is known about the relationships among them. In this sense, the current methodological challenge for a sound integrated risk management system is to deal with the issue of correlation and dependence.

In the world of elliptical distributions, linear correlation is a natural and good measure of dependence.[1] Nevertheless, in the non-elliptical world, the meaningfulness and strength of a linear correlation argument breaks down, so that the use of linear correlation may lead to significant mistakes.

Although contemporary risk management tends to use correlation to describe dependence among risks, the shapes of empirical loss distributions for credit and operational risk, typical skews and leptokurtics, should dishearten the use of linear correlation (Embrechts *et al.*, 2002).

Since economic capital is very sensitive to the measure of dependence among different risk categories, a deeper understanding of dependence among different risk types is needed to better assess it.

Before performing the aggregation, banks have to define the values of some parameters. In particular, they have to choose a common time horizon and confidence level for all different risk types. Then, in order to assess economic capital, banks have to choose the aggregate measures of risk. The goodness of the assessment of the economic capital depends on the reliability of the parameter estimates. These issues will be briefly discussed in section 5.5.

The most relevant challenge in risk aggregation is obtaining the simultaneous distribution of all risk types, i.e., determining the joint distribution of risks. In the literature, we can distinguish two kinds of approach that are able to combine marginal risk distributions into a joint distribution.

The first, the commonly named base-level approach, is driven by the idea that there are few common risk factors that have more influence on the different risk types. The dynamic of economic risk factors induces, by means of different non-linear loss functions, manifold loss distributions related to the different risk types. The structure of dependence of risk factors can be described by means of either a correlation matrix or a copula specification. Therefore, the marginal loss distributions are indirectly correlated through the relationship among the risk factors.

The second is the top-level approach. Under this method, the marginal loss distributions are derived from single independent models, which are developed for each risk type. The marginal losses are merged into a joint distribution by means of a copula function or correlation matrix.

In this chapter, we show how marginal loss distributions can be aggregated through a copula function and how economic capital can be assessed. This

---

[1] Elliptical distributions represent the most used distributions in quantitative risk management. They support both the use of value-at-risk (VaR) as a measure of risk, and the mean–variance approach to risk management and portfolio optimisation. See Embrechts *et al.*, 2002 for details.

technique, that is framed into the top-level risk aggregation approach, is becoming a best practice in the banking industry. The comparison of the outcomes from different copulas and marginal distribution specifications shows the sensitivity of economic capital to the choice of both elements. This analysis highlights important indications and warnings, especially from a supervisory authority's point of view.

5.3 Related literature

One of the first works that uses a base-level aggregation approach for risk aggregation is the one by Alexander and Pezier (2003). The authors introduce a method for risk aggregation based on a risk factor model to characterise the joint distribution of market and credit risk. They link the profit and loss distribution of different business units to six common factors by means of a linear regression model. These risk factors are modelled by a Gaussian multivariate distribution, using the tail correlations. Each set of correlated realisations is weighted, using the betas for each risk factor, and summed to obtain a realisation for the total profit and loss.

However, most of the contributions on risk aggregation employ the top-level approach. Kuritzkes *et al.* (2003) address the problem of risk aggregation in a financial conglomerate environment, which includes banking and insurance businesses. The authors suggest a method that aggregates risks at three successive levels: first, stand alone risks are aggregated within a single risk factor model; second, risks are aggregated across different risk factors within a single business line; finally, risks are aggregated across different business lines. The aggregation to overall economic capital is done assuming that all risks are normally jointly distributed. The economic capital is assessed using the variance/covariance formula *à la* Markowitz.

Ward and Lee (2002) determine the economic capital using a Gaussian copula to aggregate risk types. Some of the marginal distributions are analytically computed (credit risk is assumed to follow a beta distribution), and some by simulation (mortality risk for life insurance).

Rosenberg and Schuermann (2006) implement a method to aggregate market, credit and operational risk distributions into an overall risk distribution using a t copula and empirical marginal distributions. Comparing this technique with the simple sum of the different risks and the multi-variate Gaussian joint model they find that the first approach overestimates risks by more than 40 per cent and the latter underestimates risks by a similar amount.

Aas *et al.* (2005) develop a model for total risk by means of sub-models for each separate risk and the relationship among them. In their framework, they use the base-level aggregation approach for combining market, ownership and credit risk, and a top-level aggregation method for linking operational and business risk to the others. First, they describe the risk factors that influence market and ownership risk on a daily resolution, using the multi-variate constant conditional correlation GARCH (1,1) model, with the Student *t* distribution as a conditional distribution for the market and ownership risk factors.[2] Therefore, they describe the dependence structure between the credit risk factor and the market and ownership risk factors on a yearly resolution. Finally, operational and business risk, modelled by means of log-normality distributions, are linked to the other ones at the loss distribution.

5.4 Copulas

Copula function is a statistical tool that helps us understand the dependence topic in a deeper way. Copula function was introduced by Sklar (1959) at the end of the 1950s, and nowadays covers a large spectrum of applications in the area of risk management.[3] The basic idea underlying the concept of copula is that every joint distribution for a random vector of risk types implicitly contains both information about the marginal distributions of individual risk types and information about their dependence structure. The copula function allows us to isolate the description of the dependence structure. Therefore, copula, meaning 'coupling', couples the marginal distributions together to form a joint distribution. The dependence relationship is entirely determined by the copula function, while scaling and shape are led by the marginal distributions.

Sklar's theorem contains this idea:

Let $X = (X_1,\ldots,X_n)$ be an n-dimensional random vector and let F be a joint distribution function with continuous margins $F_1,\ldots,F_n$. Then, there exists a unique copula $C: [0,1]^n \rightarrow [0,1]$ such that

$$F(x_1, \ldots, x_n) = C(F_1(x_1), \ldots, F_n(x_n)) \tag{1}$$

---

[2] Ownership risk is associated only with negative movements in the financial assets of a life insurance company.

[3] For a complete treatise on copula function we refer to Nelsen, 1999. Typical applications of copula functions to risk management include the modelling of default dependence (see for instance Frey *et al.*, 2001), the pricing of credit derivatives (see for instance Cherubini *et al.*, 2004) and the description of the structure of dependence among different risk types.

Conversely, if C is a copula and $F_1,...,F_n$ are distribution functions, then the function F given by equation (1) is a joint distribution function with margins $F_1,...,F_n$.

We can extract a unique copula C from a multi-variate distribution function F with continuous margins $F_1,...,F_n$ by calculating

$$C(u_1, \ldots, u_n) = F\left(F_1^{-1}(u_1), \ldots, F_n^{-1}(u_n)\right) \tag{2}$$

where $u_i \in [0,1]$ and $F_1^{-1}(u_1), \ldots, F_n^{-1}(u_n)$ are inverses of $F_1,...,F_n$. We call C the copula of F or of any random vector with distribution function F.

5.4.1 The Gaussian copula

If X has a multivariate standard normal distribution with correlation matrix R, then the copula of X is called the Gaussian copula and it is described by

$$C_R^{Ga}(u_1, \ldots, u_n) = \Phi_R\left(\phi^{-1}(u_1), \ldots, \phi^{-1}(u_n)\right) \tag{3}$$

where Φ_R denotes the joint distribution function of X, R is the linear correlation matrix of X and ϕ is the distribution function of univariate standard normal. For $n = 2$ the expression (3) becomes:

$$C_R^{Ga}(u_1, u_2) = \int_{-\infty}^{\phi^{-1}(u_1)} \int_{-\infty}^{\phi^{-1}(u_2)} \frac{1}{2\pi\left(1 - R_{12}^2\right)^{1/2}} e^{\left\{-\frac{\left(s^2 - 2R_{12}st + t^2\right)}{2\left(1 - R_{12}^2\right)}\right\}} ds\,dt \tag{4}$$

The Gaussian copula is asymptotically independent in both tails. This means that, regardless of the level of correlation we choose, the extreme events, far enough into the tails, appear to occur independently in each margin.

5.4.2 The *t* copula

The t copula represents the dependence structure implicit in a multi-variate t distribution. The t copula is conceptually very similar to the Gaussian copula. Nevertheless, with respect to the Gaussian one, the t copula better captures the phenomenon of dependent extreme values, which is often observed in financial data (see Demarta and McNeil, 2005). A n-dimensional random vector X with multi-variate t Student distribution with v degrees of freedom, mean vector μ and covariance matrix $\dfrac{\nu}{\nu-2}\Sigma$ (for $v > 2$ and Σ the positive–definite dispersion matrix) can be represented in the following way

$$X \stackrel{d}{=} \mu + \sqrt{W}Z \tag{5}$$

where $\mu \in \Re^n$, $Z \sim N_n\,(0,\,\Sigma)$ and W is independent from Z and satisfies $\nu/W \sim \chi_\nu^2$. The t copula with v degrees of freedom of the random vector X can be represented in the following way

$$C_{\nu,R}^t(u_1,\ldots,u_n) = t_{\nu,R}\big(t_\nu^{-1}(u_1),\ldots,t_\nu^{-1}(u_n)\big) \tag{6}$$

where R is the correlation matrix implied by the dispersion matrix Σ, such as $R_{ij} = \dfrac{\Sigma_{ij}}{\sqrt{\Sigma_{ii}\Sigma_{jj}}}$, $t_{v,R}$ is the joint distribution function of the vector X and t_ν^{-1} denotes the quantile function of a standard uni-variate t_ν distribution.

For $n = 2$ the expression (6) becomes:

$$C_{\nu,R}^t(u_1,u_2) = \int_{-\infty}^{t_\nu^{-1}(u_1)} \int_{-\infty}^{t_\nu^{-1}(u_2)} \frac{1}{2\pi(1-R_{12}^2)^{1/2}}$$
$$\left\{1 + \frac{(s^2 - 2R_{12}st + t^2)}{\nu(1-R_{12}^2)}\right\}^{-(\nu+2)/2} ds\,dt \tag{7}$$

The copula of the bi-variate t distribution shows an asymptotical tail dependence both from the upper and the lower tail. This dependence increases as the correlation rises and decreases when the degrees of freedom go up (see Demarta and McNeil, 2005 for details).

5.4.3 Meta t distribution

As reported above, given a t copula, $C_{\nu,R}^t$, for an n-dimensional random vector X with uni-variate t marginal distributions with the same degree of freedom v, from the Sklar's theorem it follows that the multi-variate joint distribution is given by a t distribution with v degrees of freedom. Instead, if we combine any other set of uni-variate distribution functions using the t copula, we obtain a multi-variate joint distribution function, named meta-t_v distribution (see Demarta and McNeil, 2005 for details). For example, a meta-t_v distribution is obtained when $F_1,\ldots,F_n$ are uni-variate standard normal distributions and the copula function is a t copula, $C_{\nu,R}^t$.

5.5 Copulas in an economic capital model

5.5.1 Risk measurement

The notion of economic capital is deeply linked to the concept of the joint distribution of losses. A consistent aggregation of the marginal risk distributions into a joint distribution represents a preparatory process to a sound economic capital assessment. Coherent risk aggregation and good estimates of economic capital require that banks define appropriate: (1) risk metrics; (2) time horizons and (3) risk appetites.

As for the risk metrics, it is worthwhile to underline that sensitivity measures, like duration for bond portfolio and Greeks for derivate portfolios, are not very useful for the evaluation of the capital adequacy. In fact, these sensitivity measures, which typically take the form of a derivative, are able to identify changes in the portfolio value, given a change in one of the underlying risk factors. Besides, sensitivity measures create problems in aggregation of risk (see for details McNeil *et al.*, 2005).

Recently, new risk measures based on the loss distribution have become popular across academics and practitioners. These risk metrics are statistical quantities extracted from a loss distribution. Examples of these measures are the expected loss, the standard deviation of the loss distribution, the VaR and the expected shortfall. Since the estimation of losses is the main goal of risk management and stress-testing, it is natural to base a risk measure on loss distribution. In fact, the loss distribution is able to reflect important economic phenomena like netting and diversification effect. Besides, loss distributions can be compared across different risk types. Further, the loss distribution-based measures can be easily used in the stress-testing of economic capital framework. For these reasons loss-based risk measures are frequently used in economic capital assessment. Among the different statistical quantities, risk managers and supervisory authorities focus their attention on the tail of the loss distribution, which is associated with the highest loss levels. Therefore, VaR and expected shortfall, risk measures based on loss distribution's tail, are preferred.

There is a certain consensus among academics and risk managers on the set of properties a reasonable risk measure should satisfy. Such a set of properties is given by the axioms of coherence proposed by Artzner *et al.* (1999). Using economic reasoning, the authors call a risk measure coherent if it is monotonous, positively homogeneous, translation invariant and subadditive.

While it can be shown that, in the case of an elliptical distribution (for example, Gaussian and t Student distributions), the VaR is a coherent risk measure, this does not hold in general, since the VaR fails to be subadditive. In particular, in case of highly skewed and leptokurtic distributions, there is a high probability that the subadditivity axiom is not satisfied (McNeil et al., 2005 and Embrechts et al., 2002). Intuitively, the non-subadditivity of the VaR means that, given two marginal loss distributions, the VaR associated to the aggregated loss distribution is not necessarily lower than the sum of the two VaRs related to the marginal loss distributions. This occurrence is in contrast with the economic idea that there should be a diversification benefit associated with merging portfolios. In other words, it is not certain that the aggregation of VaRs related to different risk types allows obtaining a bound for the overall risk of the bank. Another drawback of VaR is that it does not give information about the severity of the stress losses. On the contrary, expected shortfall is not affected by such disadvantages (Acerbi and Tasche, 2002). For these reasons, the use of the expected shortfall as a risk measure should be preferred.

As far as the time horizon is concerned, all the marginal distributions have to be rescaled on a yearly basis since economic capital is usually measured on an annual timeframe.

Finally, banks have to decide the confidence level, that is the probability level below which losses do not exceed their risk-taking capacity. Such confidence level represents the banks' risk appetite and it is directly linked to their probabilities of default. The higher the confidence level chosen by the bank, the lesser its willingness to take risks not covered by capital and, thus, its probability of default.

5.5.2 Theoretical framework

Once the choices of parameters have been made, banks have to assess their economic capital (ECAP). From a methodological point of view, the simplest method to determine economic capital is to sum the values of the n standalone economic capitals:

$$ECAP_\alpha(L) = \sum_{i=1}^{n} ECAP_\alpha(L_i) \tag{8}$$

where L represents the total loss distributions, L_i represents the loss marginal distribution related to the i-th risk type and α is the confidence level.

This approach tends to overestimate the value of capital that is required at the aggregate level, because it implicitly presumes that the different risk types are perfectly correlated. In other words, this approach assumes that the worst-case scenarios for each risk type occur simultaneously, ignoring the possibility of the diversification effect.

An alternative approach, which is instead capable of taking into account the diversification benefits, is the variance/covariance method, based on Markowitz's theory. The major advantage related to this technique is the simplicity of computing the economic capital, by means of the following closed form solution:

$$ECAP_\alpha(L) = \sqrt{\sum_{i,j=1}^{n} \rho_{ij} ECAP_\alpha(L_i) ECAP_\alpha(L_j)} \tag{9}$$

where ρ_{ij} is the correlation coefficient between the i-th and j-th risk types.

However, this approach relies on the strong assumption that the joint loss across the different risk types is characterised by a multi-variate normal distribution and this implies that the uni-variate marginal loss distributions are characterised by a Gaussian distribution. Such hypothesis does not seem to be coherent with the empirical evidence, which suggests that marginal loss distributions are characterised by heavier tails than the Gaussian distribution and several of them by high skewness (see, for instance, the works of Mandelbrot, 1963 and Glasserman *et al.*, 2002 for market risk; Crouhy *et al.*, 2002 for credit risk; Chernobai and Rachev, 2006 for operational risk).[4] The implication is that if we model the joint behaviour of different risk types through a multi-variate Gaussian distribution, we might underestimate the actual overall risk.

A more general approach is clearly the one based on the copula functions. Copula is particularly useful in those areas of risk management where the marginal behaviour of individual risk factors is better known than their dependence structure. In order to obtain a multi-variate joint loss distribution, the marginal distributions are modelled separately and coupled together with a selected copula function. Since in the copula approach, in general, there is not a closed-form solution for the economic capital, the risks aggregation and the related economic capital assessment process have developed by using

---

[4] The empirical evidence indicates that market risk distribution is nearly symmetric, while credit risk distribution is quite left-skewed and operational risk distribution is much more left-skewed.

simulation algorithms. Therefore, banks need to generate many loss scenarios in order to obtain the overall loss distribution. Each scenario represents a vector of losses, the elements of which correspond to a joint realisation of the losses related to the different risk types. In order to generate a scenario, we need to know the marginal distributions and the copula function that describes the structure of dependence among the different risk types. In the following, we briefly outline the algorithm that can be used to generate loss scenarios from a t Student copula:[5]

(1) generate a correlated random vector X, n-dimensional, using a given correlation matrix;

(2) compute the cumulate t_ν distribution $T = t_\nu\left(X\sqrt{\frac{\nu}{\chi(\nu)}}\right)$;

(3) compute the single losses inverting the marginal distributions in T: $L_i = t_\nu^{-1}(T_i)$;

(4) calculate the scenario loss summing the marginal losses: $L = \sum_{i=1}^{n} L_i$.

This process yields an overall loss related to a single scenario. Iterating the algorithm many times, an overall simulated loss probability density function f_L can be found. We can then calculate economic capital using the chosen risk metric m and the confidence interval α:

$$ECAP = m_\alpha(f_L) \tag{10}$$

5.5.3 An experiment

As already mentioned, in order to build a joint loss distribution we need to know the individual risk marginal distributions and inter-risk correlations. Furthermore, we have to specify a copula function that models the structure of dependence among the different risk types. The most natural and popular copula is the Gaussian copula. Nevertheless, in recent financial applications, the t Student copula has been greatly used because it can capture tail dependence (see, for instance, Frey $et\ al.$, 2001; Demarta and McNeil, 2005; Rosenberg and Shuermann, 2006; Morone $et\ al.$, 2007; and Kole $et\ al.$, 2007).

In the following, we calculate the economic capital of a commercial bank when the multi-variate distributions change. We use three distributions belonging to the family of elliptical distributions (Gaussian copula with

---

[5] The algorithm to aggregate different risk types using a Gaussian copula is very similar to the t copula one: the correlated random vector X has to be mapped to a vector of uniform variates by using a standard uni-variate normal distribution; finally, by using the inverse of the cumulative standard normal distributions, the single losses will be found.

standard normal margins, t_3 copula with Student t margins with three degrees of freedom and t_{20} copula with Student t margins with twenty degrees of freedom) and a non-elliptical distribution (meta t_3 copula with normal standard marginal distributions). In the experiment, the choice of copula functions is not based on statistical fit tests, such as Kolmogorov–Smirnov and Anderson–Darling tests, but it is only driven by economic reasoning.[6] We can think of Gaussian and t_3 copulas as two good benchmarks: the first can be used to perform the losses aggregation under very idealised conditions; the second can be used to perform the losses aggregation in a very turbulent phase of the economic cycle.[7] The t_{20} copula represents a sound compromise between idealised and stressed market situations.[8] Finally, we use the meta t_3 copula with normal standard marginal distributions because it represents a model that some banks have been applying.

Before illustrating the results in terms of economic capital we try to catch a simple geometrical intuition looking at, in a plane, the different shapes of bi-variate random vectors generated by the four chosen distributions. For each of them, one hundred thousand simulated bi-variate random vectors (X_1, X_2) are displayed in Figure 5.1.[9]

Comparing the shapes of the bivariate distributions we can observe that the meta t_3 copula with normal standard marginal distributions (panel b) is able to capture loss levels with the same order of magnitude as the Gaussian ones (panel a). Nevertheless, the meta t_3 copula model is better suited to model phenomena in which the extreme and simultaneous losses happen more frequently.[10] By contrast, the joint distributions with marginal distributions endowed with fatter tails (panels c and d) are better able to model much higher levels of losses related to unfavourable events.

Following the intuition given by Figure 5.1, we performed a simulation based on the input data reported in Morone *et al.* (2007), to quantify economic capital induced by the four joint distributions.[11]

---

[6] For an interesting discussion about statistic tests for the fit of copulas see Kole *et al.*, 2007.

[7] We can think of a Gaussian distribution like a t Student distribution with $v = \infty$.

[8] A t Student distribution converges to a Gaussian distribution as the degrees of freedom increase. A t distribution with twenty degrees of freedom tends to a good approximation of a Gaussian distribution.

[9] The linear correlation coefficient has been set to 0.7.

[10] As a matter of fact, if we applied the meta t_3 copula function with normal standard margins to a credit risk model problem, based on the latent variable approach, we could observe that it has a much greater tendency to generate simultaneous extreme values than the Gaussian copula function.

[11] The authors consider nine risk types belonging to the macrocategories of credit ('performing loans' and 'defaulted loans'), market ('banking book', 'trading book', 'equity' and 'property'), operating ('business' and 'operational') and 'insurance'. The correlation matrix used is the linear correlations implicit in rank correlation stressed at 99 per cent confidence levels. Since the correlation matrix is not positive

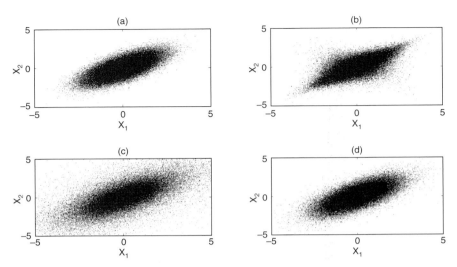

Figure 5.1   Simulations of bi-variate random vectors from different distributions

Note: One hundred thousand simulations of bi-variate random vector (X_1, X_2) from different distributions: (a) Gaussian copula with standard normal margins; (b) t_3 copula with normal standard marginal disteibutions; (c) t_3 copula with Student t margins with three degrees of freedom; (d) t_{20} copula with Student t margins with twenty degrees of freedom. The linear correlation coefficient has been set to 0.7.

In order to determine the four loss distributions, we simulated one hundred thousand loss scenarios. In the left side of Figure 5.2 we display the overall loss distributions induced by the four chosen models. The figure shows that if we relax the Gaussian hypothesis, both for the copula and for the margins, and we employ a t Student distribution, the overall loss probability density function is characterised by fatter tails. Besides, the joint distribution is very sensitive to the change in margins. As a matter of fact, the loss distribution induced by the t_3 copula is very different from that of the the meta t_3. This huge difference is only due to a different functional specification of the marginal distributions.

This phenomenon is more evident if we look at the right side of Figure 5.2, in which we have plotted the ratio of percentiles (from 80th to 100th) between t_3 and meta t_3 copulas. We observe that for the highest percentiles, the ratio's curve shows a sudden rise. The meaning is that economic capital values are dramatically different, especially for the terminal side of the tail of the loss distribution, on which risk managers and supervisory authorities pay special attention.

semi-definite, in order to match the 'invalid' correlation matrix we have used the spectral decomposition method, as detailed in Jäkel, 2002.

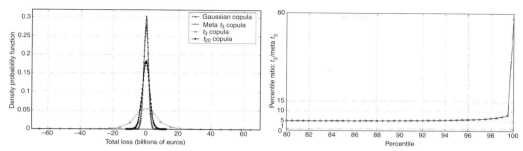

Figure 5.2   Comparison from different loss density probability functions and ratio of percentiles (from 80th to 100th) between t_3 and meta t_3 copulas

Note: On the left side of the figure are plotted the total loss density probability functions generated to: Gaussian copula, meta t_3 copula, t_{20} copula and t_3 copula. On the right side, the ratio of percentiles (from 80th to 100th) between t_3 and meta t_3 copula is displayed.

In order to test the robustness of these results we performed a Monte Carlo simulation repeating the one hundred thousand scenarios fifty times for each chosen copula model. We computed some risk measures induced by the simulation experiment: the expected loss, the diversified VaR, the unexpected loss and the expected shortfall.

For each of these risk measures we computed some descriptive statistics. The outcomes show that the tail risk measures gradually increase moving from the Gaussian copula model to the t_3 copula one (Table 5.1). This result is not very surprising, since the Gaussian copula, not providing for tail dependence, does not capture the event of joint losses.

Table 5.2 compares the four resulting average outcomes in terms of undiversified and diversified total economic capital measured through VaR at a 99.96 per cent confidence level.[12] From a diversification effect point of view, the meta t_3 copula function seems to yield the most conservative outcome, generating a diversification effect of 12 per cent, considerably lower than that of the Gaussian approach (22 per cent) and the t_3 and t_{20} model's (both 24 per cent). Intuitively, this effect can be appreciated if we look again at Figure 5.1: the sharp-pointed shape of the cloud of points generated by the meta t_3 copula gives the idea that the stressed losses are quite mutually dependent.

The diversification effect can be more easily appreciated looking at the left side of Figure 5.3, where we have plotted, for each model considered,

---

[12] Even if our results here are discussed in terms of VaR, they remain valid also in terms of expected shortfall. Besides, especially if we consider the meta t_3 distribution, expected shortfalls such as risk measure should be recommended, because the meta t_3 distribution does not belong to the elliptical distribution family.

Table 5.1 Descriptive statistics of some risk measures computed in the Monte Carlo simulation. The confidence level, the number of scenarios and replications have been respectively set to 99.96 per cent, 100,000 and 50.

Risk measure	Min	Max	Median	Mean	St. dev
Expected loss: Gaussian copula	−0.00722	0.01075	0.00029	0.00037	0.00423
Expected loss: meta t_3 copula	−0.00777	0.00964	−0.00101	0.00017	0.00386
Expected loss: t_3 copula	−0.08376	0.04118	−0.00760	−0.01047	0.02956
Expected loss: t_{20} copula	−0.01484	0.01325	0.00005	0.00053	0.00583
Diversified VaR: Gaussian copula	4.70646	5.00423	4.85775	4.85813	0.05597
Diversified VaR: meta t_3 copula	5.26092	5.63828	5.47573	5.47373	0.08699
Diversified VaR: t_3 copula	69.56372	87.65576	77.91633	77.99309	4.30492
Diversified VaR: t_{20} copula	8.30686	8.87062	8.58379	8.57384	0.13338
Unexpected loss: Gaussian copula	4.70338	5.00374	4.85794	4.85776	0.05617
Unexpected loss: meta t_3 copula	5.25584	5.64379	5.47486	5.47390	0.08752
Unexpected loss: t_3 copula	69.56711	87.71062	77.94632	78.00357	4.30563
Unexpected loss: t_{20} copula	8.32170	8.86974	8.58402	8.57330	0.13199
Expected shortfall: Gaussian copula	5.03490	5.55079	5.24097	5.23982	0.08882
Expected shortfall: meta t_3 copula	5.77307	6.19295	5.97513	5.97974	0.10645
Expected shortfall: t_3 copula	97.80667	138.73497	113.81303	115.03838	9.84042
Expected shortfall: t_{20} copula	9.06515	9.92615	9.42656	9.42587	0.20210

Table 5.2 Comparison among undiversified and diversified economic capitals at the 99.96 per cent level of confidence

Copula	VaR undiversified		VaR diversified		Ratio	
	Mean	St. dev	Mean	St. dev	Mean	St. dev
Gaussian	6.2228	0.0448	4.8581	0.0560	78.07%	0.80%
meta t_3	6.2191	0.0588	5.4737	0.0870	88.02%	1.23%
t_3	102.3910	3.7466	77.9932	4.3049	76.17%	3.05%
t_{20}	11.2197	0.0894	8.5738	0.1334	76.42%	1.00%

the undiversified and diversified density distributions in the case of a specific sample randomly chosen out of the fifty that were simulated. On the right side of Figure 5.3 we compare, as the model changes, the diversified and undiversified economic capital values in each of the fifty simulated samples.

What stands out from our results is that economic capital is quite sensitive both to the copula specifications used to model the dependence among different risks types and to the hypotheses we make on the marginal distributions. If we leave the Gaussian hypothesis on marginal distributions and go towards fatter tail distributions we obtain much greater economic

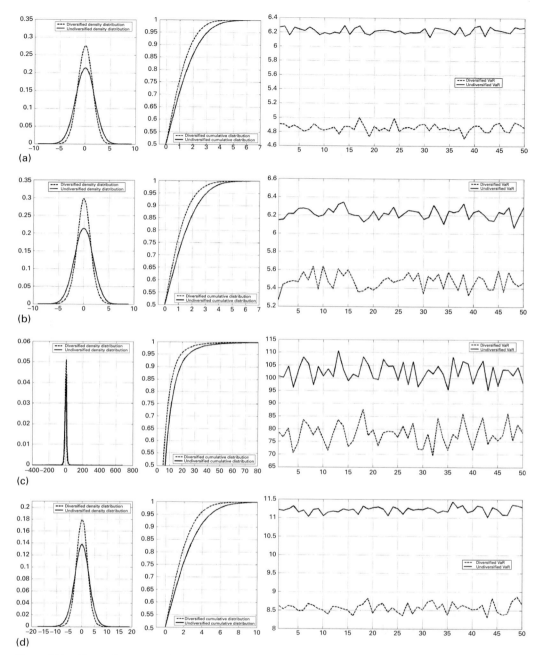

Figure 5.3 Comparison across diversified and undiversified loss density distributions and across economic capital values

Note: The left figures show, for each model considered, the undiversified and diversified density distributions in the case of a specific sample randomly chosen out of the fifty that were simulated. The right figures show the comparison between diversified and undiversified value-at-risk (VaR). Panel (a) shows the graphs under Gaussian copula; panel (b) shows the graphs under meta t_3 copula; panel (c) shows the graphs under t_3 copula; panel (d) shows the graphs under meta t_{20} copula.

capital values. Besides, using a meta t_3 copula with a Gaussian marginal distributions model, the increase of economic capital linked to a lower diversification effect seems to be secondary with respect to the decrease of economic capital value induced by the choice of the Gaussian specifications. It is important that risk managers and overall supervisory authorities are aware of this.

5.6 Conclusions

In this chapter we have discussed the issue of risk aggregation for economic capital assessment. After introducing two kinds of approach used to create a joint risk distribution (base-level and top-level approach), we analysed a top-level approach based on the copula function. This methodology is becoming best practice in the banking industry.

The results of the simulation, while not purporting to indicate the 'right' copula model, may help us to understand the relationships among the choices of the copula, the marginal distributions and economic capital.

Sound economic capital models have to be consistent with the actual data and the goodness of a model should be judged in terms of adherence to the internal data. Therefore, a validation process based on goodness of fit tests should be ideally carried out. Nevertheless, sometimes the scarcity of internal data can make the copula calibration and the choice of the distributions difficult, and this represents a major weakness of copulas. Therefore, whenever possible, the empirical marginal distributions should be used.

We have shown a non-elliptical loss distribution (the meta t_3 copula with standard normal margins) that could be used for economic capital assessment. This model has an interesting economic property: its geometrical characteristics ensure quite a low diversification effect. This, from a supervisory authority point of view, could be appreciated since a lower diversification effect translates into a higher level of capital charge. Besides, the choice of a copula function endowed with very fat tails (t_3) can reassure the supervisory authorities. Nevertheless, we stress that if in an economic capital model we couple the t_3 copula with Gaussian marginal distributions, we will obtain economic capital values with the same order of magnitude as those obtained through a Gaussian copula model, and this does not represent a prudent outcome. It follows that, in order to perform stress tests on economic capital, meta t_3 distribution is not a suitable model. In other words, to obtain stress outcomes, the use of a very fat tail distribution (t_3) is not sufficient. A sound stress test model requires both a copula function able to capture tails' dependence and marginal distributions endowed with fat tails.

The overall loss distribution is very sensitive to the shifting of marginal distributions. As a matter of fact, if we abandon the Gaussian hypothesis for the margins and adopt fatter tail distributions, the economic capital value changes considerably. Therefore, the calibration of the copula and the choice of marginal distributions play a crucial role in the building of a sound economic capital model.

REFERENCES

Aas, K., K. X. Dimakos and A. Øksendal (2005), *Risk Capital Aggregation*, Norwegian Computing Centre.

Acerbi, C. and D. Tasche (2002), 'On the Coherence of Expected Shortfall', *Journal of Banking and Finance*, 26, 1487–503.

Alexander, C. and J. Pezier (2003), 'On the Aggregation of Firm-wide Market and Credit Risks', *ISMA Centre Discussion Papers in Finance*, 13.

Artzner, P., F. Delbaen, J. M. Eber and D. Heath (1999), 'Coherent Measures of Risk', *Mathematical Finance*, 9 (3), 203–28.

Basel Committee on Banking Supervision (2003), *Trends in Risk Integration and Aggregation*, Basel.

Chernobai, A. and S. T. Rachev (2006), 'Applying Robust Methods to Operational Risk Modelling', *Journal of Operational Risk*, 1 (1), 27–41.

Cherubini, U., E. Luciano and W. Vecchiato (2004), *Copula Methods in Finance*, Wiley.

Crouhy, M., D. Galai and R. Mark (2002), 'A Comparative Analysis of Current Credit Risk Models', *Journal of Banking and Finance*, 24, 59–117.

Demarta, S. and A. McNeil (2005), 'The t Copula and Related Copulas', *International Statistical Review*, 73 (1), 111–29.

Embrechts, P., A. J. McNeil and D. Straumann (2002), 'Correlation and Dependency in Risk Management: Properties and Pitfalls', in M. A. H. Dempster (ed.), *Risk Management: Value at Risk and Beyond*, Cambridge University Press.

Frey, R., A. McNeil and M. A. Nyfeler (2001), 'Copulas and Credit Models', *Risk*, 10, 111–14.

Glasserman, P., P. Heidelberger and P. Shahabuddin (2002), 'Portfolio Value-at-Risk with Heavy-tailed Risk Factors', *Mathematical Finance*, 12, 239–70.

Jäkel, P. (2002), *Monte Carlo Methods in Finance*, John Wiley & Sons.

Kole, E., K. Koedijk and M. Verbeek (2007), 'Selecting Copulas for Risk Management', *Journal of Banking and Finance*, 31, 2405–23.

Kuritzkes, A., T. Schuermann and S. M. Weiner (2003), 'Risk Measurement, Risk Management and Capital Adequacy of Financial Conglomerates', in R. Herring and R. Litan (eds.), *Brookings-Wharton Papers in Financial Services*, Brooking Institution Press 141–94.

Mandelbrot, B. (1963), 'The Variation of Certain Speculative Prices', *Journal of Business*, 36, 394–419.

McNeil, A. J., R. Frey and P. Embrechts (2005), *Quantitative Risk Management*, Princeton University Press.

Morone, M., A. Cornaglia and G. Mignola (2007), *Economic Capital Assessment via Copulas: Aggregation and Allocation of Different Risk Types*, mimeo.

Nelsen, R. B. (1999), *An Introduction to Copulas, Lecture Notes in Statistics*, 139, Springer Verlag.

Rosenberg, J. V. and T. Schuermann (2006), 'A General Approach to Integrated Risk Management with Skewed, Fat-tailed Risks', *Journal of Financial Economics*, 79, 569–614.

Sklar, A. (1959), 'Fonctions de Répartition à n Dimensions et Leurs Marges', *Publications de l'Institut de Statistique de L'Université de Paris*, 8, 229–31.

Ward, L. and D. Lee (2002), 'Practical Application of Risk-adjusted Return on Capital Framework', Casualty Actuarial Society (CAS) *Forum Dynamic Financial Analysis Discussion Paper*.

6 Data needs for stress-testing

Francesco Cannata[*] and Ulrich Krüger[**]

6.1 Introduction

As in the case of any other economic application, stress tests depend heavily on data. The aim of this chapter is to provide an overview of what the main information needs are for stress-testing purposes.

In Chapter 2 of this book, it is pointed out that stress tests can be carried out at the level of individual institutions, groups of institutions or the financial system as a whole. They may be used by central banks and supervisory authorities to assess the stability of the financial system or by individual banks in order to design appropriate capital planning and/or identify weaknesses in their risk management systems. In all cases it is necessary to identify the types of data needed for the exercise.

As discussed in the following sections, information needs can vary significantly and depend on several factors, such as the complexity of the simulation, the technical skills available at the institutions and the type of risk which is to be investigated. First, the distinction between sensitivity analyses, based primarily on an isolated change in an input variable, and scenario analyses, which are based on more complex interactions of risk variables and can potentially capture different types of risk, can matter significantly. Second, data inputs depend on whether the simulation is based on historical experience or hypothetical assumptions. In the latter case, data should be combined with expert judgment. Third, the choice of focusing on credit, market, interbank or liquidity risks can lead to substantial differences in the inputs to be used and, consequently, on the complexity and the operational burden of the entire exercise.

[*] Bank of Italy.
[**] Deutsche Bundesbank.
   The opinions expressed herein are those of the authors and do not necessarily reflect those of the respective institutions. Sections 6.2 and 6.4 have been prepared by F. Cannata, section 6.5 by U. Krüger and sections 6.1 and 6.3 by both authors.

The chapter is organised as follows. Section 6.2 provides a broad discussion on the data needed for stress-testing, with special emphasis on the theoretical circumstances leading to financial instability; section 6.3 contains an overview of information needs by risk type, while section 6.4 focuses on credit risk, which is the most relevant source of risk for banks; section 6.5 illustrates a template as a possible example of data organisation for stress-testing purposes.

6.2 Overview of the information needed for stress-testing

Data needs generally reflect the objective for which stress tests are designed. As discussed in previous chapters, the aim of macro stress tests is to assess the resilience of the banking system to severe, unlikely but plausible scenarios. However, what might change is the theoretical model used to measure financial (in)stability.[1]

In a framework where a direct relationship between debt and financial fragility is defined (Fisher, 1933; Kindleberger, 1978; Minsky, 1977), the links between debt, financial instability and financial crises are considered as a consequence of the excessive borrowing that can occur in financial markets in a boom phase of the business cycle. Financial fragility, driven by a cyclical upturn and an increase in credit supply, translates into an increase in debt finance, a shift from long to short-term debt, a boost of speculative activity in asset markets and a weakening of the financial conditions of intermediaries. In such a context, it is mainly flow-of-funds data and financial accounts that are analysed, given the importance of corporate or household debt accumulation relative to assets.

According to monetarists (Friedman and Schwarz, 1963), the reputation of banks plays a crucial role in triggering a financial crisis, i.e., the failure of a financial institution is likely to reduce public confidence in the banking system's ability to convert deposits into currency, thereby producing contagion phenomena and possibly bank runs. In this case, it is mainly monetary aggregates that are examined, as leading indicators of financial instability.

In a world *à la* Diamond and Dybvig (1983), bank runs are the consequence of the maturity mismatch between institutions' assets and liabilities and imperfect information in the loan market; therefore, there might be an incentive for panic runs even in the event of a solvent institution, owing to imperfect information on bank assets, the inability of the intermediary to

---

[1] Quagliariello (2005).

sell or cash illiquid assets at par, and the 'first come first served' process for meeting the claims. In such a scenario, micro data on banks' conditions – such as capital ratios, interest rate margins, returns on assets or equity, interbank claims – may signal changes in the soundness of the financial system under investigation. However, market indicators of bank riskiness (such as credit default swaps, spreads between interbank claims and treasury bills or the behaviour of bank share prices in relation to those of other market participants) and the behaviour of different categories of depositor may also provide valuable information.

Finally, where financial crises are explained by the existence of asymmetric information, adverse selection and agency costs in the credit market (Mishkin, 1991), the dynamics of capital ratios and leverage of borrowers might be the main factors to be investigated.

Notwithstanding such theoretical scenarios, episodes of financial instability have been driven in practice by a wide variety of factors, which often show a large degree of interaction. As reviewed by Davis (1999), who has summarised the features of selected individual financial crises occurring between 1933 and 1998, such drivers include debt accumulation, asset price booms, risk concentration, financial innovation, declining capital adequacy of financial institutions and unexpected or sharp changes in monetary conditions. In some cases these features occurred separately, and in other cases as a combination, leading to different degrees of intensity of the stressed situations.

Therefore, as a starting point for building a reference dataset for stress-testing purposes, a wide range of information has to be considered, so as to be able to simulate the impact of any predefined macro shock on the financial system.

First of all, macroeconomic data (e.g., gross domestic product (GDP) growth, oil price) allow us to measure the dynamics of the economic cycle; flow-of-funds information can help keep track of the pattern of corporate and household financial positions (i.e., indebtedness), which represent a key element in the transmission mechanism from the real economy to the financial system. Prices can provide highly frequent and timely information on the reaction of monetary and financial markets to changes in the economic environment. Monetary aggregates and/or interest rates represent an essential link between policy actions and banks' behaviour.

Generally speaking, knowledge of the macroeconomic environment – based on the above data – can provide an overall idea of the performance of the financial system under analysis and indicate potential sources of shocks. 'Understanding the macroeconomic picture aids the understanding of what is *normal* for an economy with respect to its own history and in comparison with other countries.'[2] From the viewpoint of data availability, the majority of these data types can be used for the design of the scenario and are usually easily available in well-known databases, therefore not representing a major data challenge.

On the contrary, a greater challenge is posed by banking data, which provide the micro dimension of financial stability and can be used in a stress-testing exercise for measuring the impact of the simulated scenario on the financial system. As discussed in detail later in the chapter, type, nature and frequency of such information depend on a wide range of factors, such as the structure of the financial system and the institutional framework of monetary and supervisory bodies in the jurisdiction.

Last but not least, like any quantitative exercise, stress tests can also be successfully supported by qualitative factors, which are not easily captured by dataset and/or quantitative algorithms but can provide valuable information (e.g., changes in financial regulation, technological innovation). As an example, discussions with supervisors and regulators and private sector analysts as well as market participants can easily reveal likely sources of vulnerability in a financial system, even if in some cases the information can be anecdotal in nature and not easy to interpret.

A valuable data source for stress-testing, which includes many of the aforementioned types of information, is the Financial Soundness Indicators (FSI) dataset compiled by the International Monetary Fund (IMF). As widely described by the IMF (2004) and World Bank (2005), FSIs are indicators – mainly based on aggregated data (country by country) – of the current financial health and soundness of the financial institutions in a given country, as well as of their corporate and household counterparts, and include indicators that are representative of the markets in which the financial institutions operate.

There are two groups of FSIs: 'core' and 'encouraged'. The 'core' set of indicators consist mainly of balance sheet measures, covering the main risk profile of financial institutions (capital adequacy, asset quality, earnings and profitability, liquidity and exposure to foreign exchange (FX) risk). By contrast, the 'encouraged' set of FSIs includes a wide variety of indicators, ranging from indebtedness of the corporate and household sectors to liquidity in the securities market, from the performance of the real estate market to the size and relative importance of non-banking financial institutions in the financial

---

[2] International Monetary Fund (2004).

market. Therefore, FSIs can be easily employed in a stress test both in the measurement of the transmission effects from the macro shock to the financial system (for example, via corporates and households) as well as in the assessment of the final impact on the simulated stress. A major advantage in using such a database is clearly the greater – though not complete – comparability of the indicators across jurisdictions, a fact which potentially turns out to be extremely valuable in macro stress tests covering more than one jurisdiction (see Chapter 15).

More generally, the selection of data must also follow a pragmatic approach, assessing the costs of gathering the information *vis à vis* the benefits of designing a more realistic simulation; in practice, a wide range of databases is available, including those derived from data sources of national and international organisations as well as commercial databases.[3] Availability of information at a centralised level and/or via single institutions, frequency and length of time series, consistency over time, comparability of data to be used in aggregate exercises (i.e., covering different jurisdictions), confidentiality restrictions and lack of risk data (for example, duration or default measures in countries where risk management systems are less sophisticated) are only some of the issues that must be addressed at a very early stage of the exercise.

Finally, standard rules governing any applied exercise also need to be carefully taken into consideration: how to select a reasonable number of indicators, how to combine variables and how (and to what extent) to incorporate qualitative information.

6.3 Data needs by risk type

The practical use of different groups of information for macro stress tests depends – besides the above-mentioned rules on data selection and processing – on the specificities of the exercise, i.e., primarily on the risk sources identified as most relevant for a given financial system. As widely discussed in the second part of the book, there is a significant range of diversity across countries from this point of view.

Credit risk is likely to pose significant challenges from a data point of view: first of all, because of the features that characterise this risk *vis à vis* other types of risk (e.g., market risk) for which the frequency of data and

---

[3] For a discussion of the features and pros/cons of the most popular data sources, see Annex C in World Bank (2005).

probability distribution of losses make measurement much easier; and second, because of the recently issued Basel 2 rules, where a more analytical framework for measuring the main components of credit risk is embedded (see section 6.4).

Given their key role in the assessment of financial stability as well as of conditions of individual institutions, supervisory and monetary authorities usually have a comprehensive information set, both at a micro level and on an aggregated basis. Indeed, the actual availability strongly depends on the surveillance framework existing in each country: since supervisory agencies collect – either via reporting or with on-site visits – data on credit risk at the micro level (i.e., for each supervised entity) and central banks rely on system-wide information, synergies can be successfully exploited in those jurisdictions where the two functions collapse.

Three main data sources are usually available: (1) supervisory reports; (2) credit registers; (3) company account registers:[4]

(1) in most countries the bulk of information that banking supervisors can rely on for their activity is included in the periodic reports that supervised institutions are required to transmit to them. The degree of articulation of such reports varies significantly across countries and strongly depends on the reliance that a given supervisory framework puts on off-site versus on-site analysis. In general, all the main risk profiles – supported by predefined reporting formats and information coding instructions – are covered, such as banking risks, capital adequacy and profitability; credit-risk-driven information usually represents a large portion of such datasets;

(2) in several countries, credit registers are established in order to provide intermediaries with a powerful credit risk management tool, since they record the transactions of each bank borrower against the banking system. Most banking supervisors tend to exploit such information to carry out off-site monitoring of credit risk. Since they usually contain the entire population of loans granted by financial institutions exceeding certain materiality thresholds, they enable meaningful indicators (both at micro and macro level) to be constructed for the analysis of the performance of the banking system.[5] As discussed by Trucharte (2004),

---

[4] Quagliariello (2005).

[5] As examples, in Germany and Italy raw data contained in the Central Credit Register managed by the central banks, i.e., Bundesbank and Bank of Italy, include a wide range of exposure types above a predefined threshold as well as additional information needed to identify borrowers (name, sector of activity, geographical area). Additionally, the Italian Credit Register includes information on bad debts irrespective of their size whereas in Germany additional details on the creditworthiness of the borrower such as the probability of default and the risk-weighted assets are collected.

the methodologies introduced by the Basel 2 framework to measure credit risk makes the information provided by credit registers even more useful;

(3) in most countries there usually exist databases containing financial statements of companies. Their main value added is the wide coverage, the processing of data (i.e., building ratios and/or reclassification of published balance sheets and profit and loss (P&L) accounts) as well as comparability across firms.

The same information set also represents the starting point for stress-testing credit risk on a portfolio basis, i.e., looking at the concentration of a pool of exposures with regard to single names, industrial sectors and/or geographic areas. In such a context, the breakdown of exposures by these dimensions, the default probabilities assigned to them as well as the cross-correlations are essential data inputs. As an example, intersector correlations may be determined on the basis of some indices, such as the Industry Classification Benchmark provided by FTSE Group and Dow Jones Indexes.

As regards market risk, a wide spectrum of time series on financial prices are available (exchange rates, equities, bonds and interest rates). Databases are widely known and exploited (among others, Bloomberg, Thomson Datastream and Bondware) and high-frequency prices are usually of good quality and easily comparable. Unlike credit risk, the key issue is not the availability and access to data but their interpretation, in light of accounting rules and market dynamics; from the latter point of view, the experience of the financial turmoil occurring in 2007–8 has highlighted the lower reliability on market prices in stressed conditions, particularly for less liquid financial instruments.

A risk type where data collection and processing can be extremely resource-consuming is interbank risk, which is part of the stress-testing framework used in some countries (see, for instance, Chapters 11 and 12). The common idea is to design the flow of interbank connections among institutions, for example, the 'network model' developed by Austrian financial authorities in their stress-testing exercise (see Chapter 12); for these purposes, a mixed combination of data stemming from supervisory reports and the payment system can be used, even though these simulations tend to be challenged by the lack of cross-border data. As an alternative, a simulation approach can also be used, given the high number of transactions to be tracked.

As far as liquidity risk is concerned, most of the stress tests are usually based on scenarios which are either market-related (for example, simulating emerging market or country crises, failure of a clearing or settlement system or a systemic shock with disruption in financial markets) or firm-specific (such as deposit withdrawals driven by reputation risk or the default of a major counterparty). Unlike other risk types, the range of scenarios is far more varied; given that the measurement of liquidity risk usually cannot rely on long time series, hypothetical scenarios are used more than historical ones, i.e., building on the experience and the judgment of market participants and risk managers. Starting points for the scenario design are the cumulative cash ladders for balance sheet items, i.e., computing the expected cash inflows and outflows; in addition, existing off-balance sheet commitments also need to be incorporated. Finally, this type of exercise also requires other input factors, such as the probability of repayment, the ability to roll over, time horizons for liquidation or the probability of draw-downs of uncommitted credit lines sold.

6.4 A focus on credit risk

6.4.1 Different models for credit risk

As discussed in Chapter 3, the assessment by financial authorities of the impact of macro factors on credit risk can usually be made using different models, with which different data challenges are associated.

A first option is to use models based on aggregate time series of accounting data for a given financial system, for example, focusing on the impact of a macro shock on aggregate default rates and/or ratio of non-performing loans to total assets. Such a solution clearly implies the same impact for all institutions in the system, thereby not accounting for any dispersion of results across institutions. This last issue can be investigated using a panel analysis, provided that bank-level data are available, so as to explicitly consider the impact of bank-specific information as well.

A second possibility is to rely on market-based data on corporates (building on the well-known framework *à la* Merton), which implies the existence of a deep and liquid equity market from which meaningful prices and other indicators (such as volatilities) can be derived; obviously, the number of listed firms is a key driver in assessing the scope and reliability of such a methodology, *de facto* leaving out all non-financial firms which are not listed in the stock exchange.[6] This can represent a major shortcoming for those countries where small and medium-sized firms do represent the bulk of the economic structure.

---

[6] For details of Merton's framework see Chapter 3.

Finally, a third family of models typically used for assessing credit risk of non-listed companies is based on a 'discrete-variable' approach, which builds on the wide stream of literature starting from the statistical models used by Beaver (1966) and Altman (1968) up to the more recent tools based on hazard rates.

Notwithstanding the type of model which is in use, it is also important to define what type of intermediaries is to be examined. Indeed, the scope of stress-testing might depend on the structure of the financial system, i.e., looking at the role of banks and other non-banking financial intermediaries. On the one hand, if the volume of business intermediated by non-banking financial companies is large, the ambition of carrying out a thorough analysis would suggest including such intermediaries in the exercise; on the other hand, the costs associated with such an option must be carefully assessed, especially in terms of the different statistical sources from which these data can be derived and possible difficulties in interpreting the aggregated results, given the specificities of non-banking financial intermediaries *vis à vis* banks. The same holds for cross-border issues, i.e., focusing only on domestic exposures rather than extending the analysis to international flows.

6.4.2 Building on the Basel 2 framework

As already mentioned, the measurement of credit risk has been significantly strengthened by the Basel 2 rules, which were introduced internationally in 2004 and entered into force in major countries in 2007 and 2008.[7]

Building on the basic concepts of the theory of finance as well as on the best practices of major international players, the Basel Committee on Banking Supervision (BCBS) developed a regulation where credit risk can be measured in different ways. On the one hand, the simplest method offered to institutions (Standardised Approach) requires them to classify the banking book exposures of their balance sheet in accordance with regulatory asset classes, characterised by different risk dynamics, and to rely on ratings assigned by specialised agencies to single borrowers. On the other hand, under the more sophisticated method (Internal Ratings Based – IRB), banks are required to provide their own estimates of the parameters into which a credit loss can be decomposed (probability of default – PD, loss given default – LGD, exposure

---

[7] The Basel Committee on Banking Supervision issued the final version of the new capital framework in 2004, followed by a second comprehensive version in 2006; at the European level the two recasted Directives (2006/48 and 2006/49) were finalised in June 2006.

at default – EAD, maturity – M) and to derive – via a predefined algorithm (based on the Asymptotic Single Risk Factor model developed by Gordy, 2003) – the capital requirements to cover the unexpected component of credit loss.

Focusing on the IRB approach, the analytical framework followed in the capital adequacy discipline builds on the distinction between expected loss (EL) and unexpected loss (UL): the former represents the components of loss which are statistically expected and therefore can be covered with provisions and write-offs, i.e., representing a significant cost component of lending business; the latter relates to potentially large losses that occur rather seldom and are therefore covered with capital.

As explained in BCBS (2005), EL in currency amounts can be written as the following:

$$EL = PD * EAD * LGD \tag{1}$$

or, if expressed as a percentage of the EAD, as the following:

$$EL = PD * LGD \tag{2}$$

where:

PD is the probability of default per rating grade, which describes the average percentage of obligors of that grade which are expected to default in the course of one year;

LGD represents the percentage of exposure which the bank might lose if the borrower defaults. These losses are usually shown as a percentage of the exposure and depend, among others, on the type and amount of collateral as well as on the type of borrower and the expected proceeds from the workout of the assets;

EAD is an estimate of the amount outstanding (drawn amounts plus likely future draw-downs of yet undrawn lines) if the borrower defaults.

From a data point of view, PD is the key variable, because it must always be estimated by banks.[8] It also represents the major input for portfolio models (i.e., where correlation among borrowers is explicitly modelled). The estimate of PD is usually based on balance sheet information as well as on behavioural information, i.e., related to the dynamics of the relationship

---

[8] The IRB methodology offers two distinct approaches: in the Foundation IRB approach PD is the only risk parameter banks must estimate on their own, in the Advanced IRB approach they also have to provide LGD, EAD and M.

between the bank and individual customers; as discussed above, the latter piece of information is typically contained in banks' archives and credit registers.

For the estimation of LGD the reference dataset usually captures a wider variety of inputs, ranging from geographical and sectoral information to data related to the recovery channel used for different types of exposure. Given that LGD has a linear impact on capital requirements (unlike PD), its estimation also deserves special attention with regard to the monitoring of data quality. As far as EAD is concerned, data limitations may also represent an important issue for the treatment of off-balance sheet items. Both the literature and stylised facts show that off-balance sheet exposures can substantially change the risk profile of an institution, especially in a stressed situation, when borrowers tend to rely on the granted credit line more than in normal circumstances; indeed, prudential rules also devote specific attention to modelling these exposures and apply adequate treatment in terms of risk-weights. Again, a careful cost–benefit analysis should enable a full assessment to be made of the impact of including or neglecting this type of exposure.

Another significant piece of information for simulating the impact of a given shock on regulatory capital requirements is represented by banks' provisions: their amount relative to loans is likely to have a significant effect on the final amount of capital an institution is required to hold for prudential purposes.[9]

As already mentioned, another side of credit risk is represented by concentration risk, which is addressed by the regulatory regime on large exposures as well as by the Pillar II process of the new prudential framework. In particular, data on economic capital (i.e., including correlations among obligors) might serve as a valuable basis for a stress test on capital-at-risk estimated by banks, notwithstanding the amount of regulatory capital which they are required to hold for prudential purposes. For example, one possibility would be to generalise the IRB approach to a multi-factor credit portfolio model by taking into account a richer correlation structure; the idea is to replace the systematic risk factor in Gordy's model with a wider set of systematic factors describing dependencies of borrowers on certain economies and/or types of industry and thus modelling more accurately their impact on the asset-value or other drivers of the ability-to-pay variable. The stress scenario is then modelled as a set of constraints on the systematic risk factors.

---

[9] In particular, the IRB framework requires institutions to compare the expected loss with provisions. If the difference between EL and provisions is positive, then banks can compute such a difference in the regulatory capital (Tier 2); in the opposite case, the difference must be deducted.

In practice, data needs also depend on the type of exercise under construction. Sensitivity analyses aim to assess how regulatory capital levels (or alternatively portfolio values) change if risk factors change by a certain percentage. A possible way to determine potential changes is to plug in the modified quantities, for example PDs, into the Basel 2 risk-weight function; such sensitivity analyses require the distribution of exposures across the relevant risk parameter as an input. In cases where portfolio characteristics can be described not only in terms of PDs but also on the basis of migration matrixes, effects of a downturn on portfolio loss distributions including capital-at-risk figures can be determined.

6.5 A possible tool for organising data

In this section we present a data template which can serve as a valuable example of how data on credit risk can be organised for stress-testing purposes. This tool had been originally designed by the working groups within the BCBS in charge of the analysis of the impact of the Basel 2 rules on the average level of minimum required capital.[10] Given that it does represent a common framework across major countries, it can be used as a starting point for sensitivity analyses as well as for more complex stress-testing exercises.

In the Quantitative Impact Studies (QIS) template, data on IRB credit risk are collected in a very granular way. For this reason, assumptions on how macroeconomic fluctuations would translate into changes in the risk characteristics of banks' exposures can be easily used to simulate the impact on aggregated figures such as expected losses, regulatory capital and solvency ratios. As explained in section 6.4, a thorough assessment of credit risk requires the estimation of both the expected and unexpected component of loss (EL and UL). In contrast to many simulation-based stress tests of credit risk, the QIS templates explicitly allow for an assessment of how the UL component of loss changes in a stress scenario.

---

[10] From 2001 to 2006, Quantitative Impact Studies (QIS) were carried out by the Basel Committee to define the Basel 2 rules regarding calibration of the Pillar I capital requirements. Specifically, the final policy decisions were taken on the risk-weights under the Standardised Approach for the different exposure classes as well as on the risk-weight functions designed for the IRB approaches. The QIS process helped the Basel Committee to ensure that the goal to keep at international level the level of minimum required capital versus Basel 1 broadly unchanged on average while setting incentives to adopt the more sophisticated approaches to measure risks could be achieved.

The following more in-depth illustration of the QIS templates starts with the most granular type of information captured, i.e., the risk parameters, and proceeds with remarks on the general structure in which information is arranged.

As regards risk parameters, exposures must be classified by PD and LGD buckets.[11] This 'two-dimensional' framework presents clear advantages.

First, the risk-weighted assets can be computed individually for each cell of a PD–LGD matrix, i.e., for the borrowers sharing a very similar risk-profile in terms of PD and LGD. Compared to a computation which simply relies on average risk-parameters, this yields more precise results as it takes account of the non-linear shape of the risk-weight functions and considers that the distribution of exposures across LGD buckets may be different for different values of PDs.

Secondly, potential correlations between PD and LGD are captured. For stress tests this is clearly advantageous as the impact of a downturn on well-rated borrowers is likely to be different from that on borrowers with a bad rating before the downturn occurs. Identifying correlations between risk parameters can be particularly useful for a precise quantification of changes in portfolio credit risk which result from an economic downturn. Furthermore, it is possible to indirectly overcome one of the strongest limitations in Gordy's framework (independence between PD and LGD).

Finally, the assignment of exposures to buckets of PD and LGD is efficiently combined with the collection of data on the maturity of exposures; the exposure-weighted average of maturities has been considered as a second entry in the matrix of the PD and LGD buckets. The computation of the exact amount of risk-weighted assets is possible on the basis of this matrix because the risk-weight functions are linear in the maturities for fixed values of PD and LGD.

Following the Basel 2 rules, all exposures are assigned to regulatory classes, which are associated – *ceteris paribus* – to different risk-weights (for example,

---

[11] The QIS templates well reflect the key role of LGD in the computation of the IRB regulatory capital charge. Banks are required to consider a potential economic downturn when estimating LGDs. This requirement is particularly important for defaulted assets as the systematic risk component of the recovery rates needs to be considered. The Basel 2 rules explicitly ask institutions to provide two different assessments of the LGD: one reflecting the current stage in the economic cycle and a second LGD which takes account of those years in the economic cycle which showed the highest loss rates for the respective facilities. In the computation of risk-weighted assets, these two different LGDs (often referred to as expected LGD and downturn LGD) yield a capital charge proportional to the difference of the two LGD values. In this regard the Basel 2 capital requirements already capture scenarios of a potential downturn which may result in higher realised loss rates than those estimated at the reporting date.

to corporates, small and medium-sized enterprises (SMEs) and retail customers). From the perspective of risk assessment, the assignment of exposures to regulatory classes reflects the fact that banks usually apply different rating systems and estimation methodologies for different classes of loans, building on different loss behaviours. From the view point of stress-testing, the segmentation by class can be very important, as in periods of a macroeconomic downturn the impact of a shock in risk parameters (i.e., PDs) on minimum required capital for large corporates, small and medium enterprises and retail customers might well be different. The QIS templates also collect information on more innovative types of lending, for example, asset-backed securities. Securitised assets are captured along the line of the regulatory approaches which the bank uses to compute the capital charge.[12] In this way, an assessment of the volume of the securitisation activities of banks – both on the originator's as well as on the investor's side – and on the risk profile of these activities is possible.

Besides this categorisation, exposure types are considered. The QIS template distinguishes between drawn exposures, undrawn exposures, exposures subject to counterparty credit risk and off-balance sheet exposures within each exposure class.[13]

While the undrawn exposure panel is primarily reserved for the reporting of commitments, the panel devoted to other off-balance sheet exposures mainly comprises guarantees. This differentiation is crucial for assessing credit risk as the inherent risk profile of the exposure types may be fundamentally different. For example, in assigning credit conversion factors (CCFs) to a commitment, a bank has to consider that borrowers under stress tend to withdraw committed lines to a larger extent than in normal times. Even if the lines are unconditionally cancellable, the question is crucial as to whether a deterioration in the creditworthiness can be recognised early enough by the risk management of the bank in order to cancel the commitment. The risk profile of the commitment may also depend on covenants in the credit contract. QIS templates can allow for a supervisory assessment of how estimates of CCFs affect regulatory capital charges. In this way, potential assumptions on how CCFs might change during times of an economic downturn can be evaluated.[14]

---

[12] These are the Ratings Based Approach, Supervisory Formula Approach and Internal Assessment Approach.

[13] For this category a breakdown between repo-style transactions and over the counter (OTC) derivatives is additionally considered.

[14] Two other exposure types for which EAD estimation methodologies turned out to be drivers of regulatory capital charges are the OTC derivatives and repo-style transactions. When revising the

The QIS template also devotes attention to guarantees and collaterals (credit risk mitigation). It distinguishes between secured exposures, i.e., exposures for which either guarantees or credit protection are available, collateralised exposures as well as exposures to which the 'double default' treatment applies. On this basis, the effects of different scenarios concerning a decline in collateral values or downgrades of guarantees can be easily examined.

As described above the QIS template reflects the clear split between EL and UL recognised in the IRB framework. The two components of loss are shown as separate information. By the separate treatment of EL and UL an assessment is possible whether a sufficient level of provisions has been built against EL and to what extent a shortfall or excess contributes to the change in minimum required capital at a bank level.[15]

The design of the data template used for the QIS followed the principle that, to the maximum extent possible, all formulae are implemented so that the risk-weighted assets in accordance with the Basel 2 framework are computed automatically (once the exposures have been assigned to the selected buckets of risk parameters). Consequently, any changes applied to the inputs directly link into the risk-weight functions resulting in the minimum required capital levels.[16] For purposes of stress-testing, these flexible features could prove to be very useful as they easily enable a simulation to be made of a wide spectrum of scenario analyses, for example, by imposing add-ons on risk parameters (see Box 6.1) and changing the distribution of exposures across PD/LGD buckets.

After the detailed explanations of the structure of the QIS templates, the final part of this section discusses how the impact of a stress scenario on aggregated capital figures can be fully assessed.

Trading Book relevant parts of the Basel 2 framework the Basel Committee decided to admit more sophisticated techniques for EAD estimation. In particular, EAD estimates based on the Expected Positive Exposure (EPE) is now recognised as an eligible method besides the more traditional methodologies which are based on replacement costs and add-on. Banks were offered two alternative ways to report repurchase agreements (repos) which are usually characterised by huge nominal exposure amounts and – simultaneously – a high level of collateralisation. They could either report the nominal exposure amounts reflecting collateral in the LGD or, alternatively, the reduced exposure amount, often referred to as E*, which results from the comprehensive approach to credit risk mitigation.

[15] Aggregating EL from the very granular level of PD buckets yields EL on portfolio and entire bank level which is compared with provisions.

[16] Equally, any specifications on the side of supervisors, such as LGD values (e.g., a 45 per cent LGD is assigned to uncollateralised exposures under the Foundation IRB approach) or required CCFs for certain types of exposures, are implemented. For example, if the user of the QIS template intends to change the assumptions concerning the asset correlations, they only need to change those cells in the template defining the asset correlations for the respective exposure class. All formulae including the asset correlations would then be adjusted without any further action on the side of the user.

Box 6.1 An example using Quantitative Impact Studies (QIS) data

This box describes an example of how data collected through the QIS template can be used to compute the impact of a system-wide shock on the probabilities of default (PDs).[17] The example is based on the two-dimensional assignment of exposure data to buckets of the risk parameters PD and loss given default (LGD). Two scenarios have been tested using QIS5 data of a sample of German and Italian banks (reference date between June and September 2005).

In scenario A (moderate stress), an add-on of 30 per cent has been applied to all PDs assigned to borrowers from the corporate, sovereign and interbank sectors. In terms of rating buckets as used by rating agencies and the corresponding default rates, this add-on would approximately describe a downgrade of all borrowers by one rating notch. The add-on applied to retail customers has been assumed to be lower under this scenario: an add-on of 15 per cent has been used in order to reflect the fact that the impact of an economic downturn on the PDs will not be as severe as for corporates. In scenario B (strong stress), a downgrade of all obligors by two rating notches, which could roughly be modelled by imposing add-ons of approximately 60 per cent to original PDs, has been considered. For the reason already described above, a 15 per cent add-on for retail borrowers has been applied.

Both scenarios have a significant impact on banks' capital ratios. Scenario A caused an average decrease in capital ratios of 0.7 percentage point, the capital ratios dropped by another 0.7 percentage point under scenario B (i.e., the ratios dropped by 1.4 percentage points under scenario B compared to the 'baseline scenario' PDs). Nevertheless, capital ratios remained well above the Pillar I minimum requirements.

For banks using the advanced Internal Ratings Based (IRB) approach these scenarios can be easily enhanced to capture an increase in the LGD as well, as is likely to be the case in an economic downturn.

In a Basel 2 framework the impact on minimum required capital (MRC) is the most clear and straightforward way to assess the effects on banks of a simulated shock. The QIS templates reflect this by providing the automatic computation of MRC in a stress scenario. In this regard, the distinction between the impact on a specific exposure class *vis à vis* a bank level might matter. While certain rules are likely to show major effects on specific types of lending, the overall impact at institution/system level might be small due to the fact that the relative size of that specific type of business is small for a bank or a certain group of institutions. Focusing on MRC, this interrelation can be captured by the concepts 'change in MRC on exposure class level', 'size' of the exposure class in terms of MRC and 'contribution' of the exposure class to the change in MRC at a bank level.

[17] Deutsche Bundesbank (2006).

Let MRC$^{\text{Basel 2, PF}}$ denote the MRC for a certain exposure class under normal circumstances (where PF stands for portfolio), i.e., before a financial stress scenario is considered. Similarly, let MRC$^{\text{Stress, PF}}$ be the level of MRC after a shock has been applied to certain input parameters – for example, the PDs of the respective exposure class. Furthermore, let Contr$^{\text{Stress, PF}}$ denote the change in the entire bank level which has to be attributed to the exposure class PF. Then the following relation holds:

$$Contr^{Stress,\, PF} = \left(\frac{MRC^{Stress,\, PF}}{MRC^{Basel\, 2,\, PF}} - 1 \right) \cdot \frac{MRC^{Basel\, 2,\, PF}}{MRC^{Basel\, 2}}$$

(3)

$$= \%\Delta MRC^{Stress,\, PF} \cdot size^{PF}$$

While the first factor on the right-hand side describes the percentage change in MRC for the exposure class PF, i.e., the 'isolated effect' of the stress scenario for PF, the whole expression quantifies the impact of the stress scenario at a bank level. For this reason, the portfolio change needs to be multiplied by the size of the exposure class (second factor on the right-hand side).

Finally, the information on the amount of actual regulatory capital requested in the QIS template – which represents the numerator of the solvency ratio – enables us to assess whether single banks and/or a banking system do have sufficient capital buffers in place to absorb shocks to the credit risk exposures of a bank, which are measured by a reduction in banks' net worth due to losses and/or rating downgrades in the case of an economic downturn. Within scenario analyses, capital ratios before and after a given stress can be analysed.

REFERENCES

Altman, E. (1968), 'Financial Ratios, Discriminant Analysis and the Prediction of Corporate Bankruptcy', *Journal of Finance*, 23.

Basel Committee on Banking Supervision (2005), *An Explanatory Note on the Basel II IRB Risk Weight Functions*, Basel.

(2006), *Results of the Fifth Quantitative Impact Study (QIS5)*, Basel.

Beaver, B. (1966), 'Financial Ratios as Predictors of Failure', *Empirical Research in Accounting: Selected Studies*, Supplement to *Journal of Accounting Research*, Autumn.

Davis, E. P. (1999), 'Financial Data Needs for Macroprudential Surveillance. What are the Key Indicators of Risks to Domestic Financial Stability?', *Bank of England Handbooks in Central Banking, Lecture Series*, 2.

Deutsche Bundesbank (2006), *Financial Stability Review*, November.

Diamond, P. and P. Dybvig (1983), 'Bank Runs, Deposit Insurance and Liquidity', *Journal of Political Economy*, 91, 401–19.

Fisher, I. (1933), 'The Debt Deflation Theory of Great Depression', *Econometrica*, 1, 337–57.

Friedman, M. and A. J. Schwartz (1963), *A Monetary History of the United States 1867–1960*, Princeton University Press.

Gordy, M. (2003), 'A Risk-factor Model Foundation for Ratings Based Capital Rules', *Journal of Financial Intermediation*, 12 (3), 199–233.

International Monetary Fund (2004), *Financial Soundness Indicators Compilation Guide*, Washington DC.

Kindleberger, C. (1978), *Manias, Panics and Crashes. A History of Financial Crises*, Basic Books.

Minsky, H. (1977), 'A Theory of Systemic Fragility', in E. Altman and A. Sametz (eds.), *Financial Crises*, Wiley.

Mishkin, F. (1991), 'Asymmetric Information and Financial Crises: a Historical Perspective', in R. Hubbard (ed.), *Financial Markets and Financial Crises*, University of Chicago Press.

Quagliariello, M. (2005), 'Assessing Financial Stability at the Bank of Italy: Data Sources and Methodologies', *IFC Bulletin*, 23.

Segoviano Basurto, M. and P. Padilla (2006), 'Portfolio Credit Risk and Macroeconomic Shocks: Applications to Stress Testing under Data-restricted Environments', *IMF Working Paper*, 283.

Trucharte, C. (2004), 'A Review of Credit Registers and their Use for Basel II', *FSI Award 2004 Winning Paper*, Financial Stability Institute.

World Bank (2005), *Financial Sector Assessment – A Handbook*, Washington DC.

7 Use of macro stress tests in policy-making

Patrizia Baudino[*]

7.1 Introduction

Over the past decade, authorities have increasingly employed stress tests for policy-making, and the use of stress tests for policy decisions continues to be explored and extended. There are two broad approaches to using stress tests by policy-makers: on the one hand, encouragement of individual institutions to use stress tests, and, on the other, the study and application of macro stress-test models by authorities themselves.

Before turning to the main focus of this book, i.e., macro stress tests, we briefly review the use of stress tests by individual institutions. Authorities have increasingly recommended the use of stress tests by financial firms and have embedded stress tests in prudential regulation for banks. For many countries, this is enshrined in the so-called Basel 2 framework, a compilation of guidance on regulatory practices that banking supervisory authorities of major countries have committed to adopt (Basel Committee on Banking Supervision (BCBS), 2006 and 2009). Basel 2 has been recently finalised and is expected to replace the earlier and simpler regulatory framework known as Basel 1. An aspect in the shift from Basel 1 to Basel 2 that is relevant to the use of stress-testing was the acknowledgement of the need to respond to the increasing complexity of banks' activities and, especially for the most advanced banks, the sophistication of their internal risk management.[1] In this light, the recommendation to firms to use stress tests was introduced in Basel 2. This policy reflects the view that stronger and better managed individual financial institutions are a precondition for a strong financial system. Therefore their correct use of stress tests has important policy

---

[*] Financial Stability Board (FSB). The views expressed in this chapter are those of the author and not necessarily those of the FSB or of FSB members.

[1] Financial institutions have also used stress tests prior to the Basel 2 guidance, especially the most sophisticated ones (see, e.g., Committee on the Global Financial System, 2005).

implications.[2] Although individual institutions are the first to stand to gain from improved risk management practices, systemic benefits ensue as well. In terms of the success of this policy in enhancing financial stability, it is also clear that this remains work in progress, as the 2007–8 market turmoil, which revealed weak stress-testing practices even at large financial institutions in major financial centres, has shown.[3] As a result, policy-makers need to continue calling on institutions to ensure that their risk management systems, including stress tests, are aligned to the nature and complexity of the risks they face (e.g., Kohn, 2008).

But the focus of this book is on macro stress tests, which are the natural candidates for thinking about stress-testing for policy-making. The book also deals with macro stress tests for the banking sector only, reflecting the importance of banks as financial intermediaries, as well as the availability of supervisory banking data.[4] In countries with more traditional, bank-based financial systems, the lack of precision required by this approximation is probably small. More market-based financial systems may be more difficult to reduce to a bank-based model, and further analysis will be needed to produce appropriate stress test frameworks for them too. In an ideal setting, macro stress tests should cover not only the banking system, but other parts of the financial system, and possibly the entire economy, including links with foreign counterparties. But it is clear that modelling techniques have not developed enough to meet these high standards, not only for stress-testing, but in economic theory in general, although progress documented in other chapters of this book is proof of on-going efforts to extend the scope of the analysis and reduce the need for modelling simplifications. The question for policy-making is to what extent these inevitable simplifications impact on the realism of the results of macro stress tests, and of the accuracy of the policy decisions based on them. Correctly identifying the purpose of macro stress tests, as explained below, will help sharpen the interpretation of the results, so that restricting the analysis to the banking sector will not risk misdirecting the ensuing policy decisions.

To set the stage for the following discussion, it is important to put forward two key 'instructions to users' when considering what macro stress tests can

---

[2] For instance, the recommendation by the Financial Stability Forum (FSF) that hedge funds' counterparties strengthen their stress tests also highlights the systemic benefits that derive from stress-testing at individual institutions, including non-banks (FSF, 2007).

[3] For an overview of how financial institutions' risk management practices fared during the 2007–8 market turmoil, see the 2008 report by the Senior Supervisors Group (SSG).

[4] See Chapter 6.

offer to policy-makers. First, macro stress tests are a technique, and have no intrinsic policy content. The policy relevance of macro stress tests arises from the fact that, based on their results, authorities may decide that action is needed. And the necessary action may be taken by the public sector or by the private sector. This is a simple but important point, as several deficiencies have been identified in macro stress tests, possibly because of some misconception of what macro stress tests are.

Second, policy-makers should not treat macro stress tests as a 'black-box' from which they receive an output to be taken unconditionally. Rather, they should first clearly define the policy question they want to address. In other words, they should decide *ex-ante* in light of which perceived vulnerabilities they want to analyse the resilience of the financial or banking sector.[5] In this regard, a useful starting point is to identify imbalances in the macroeconomy that could affect the financial system, or vulnerabilities in the financial system itself that policy-makers think could have material consequences if put under stress. This hands-on approach is likely to be useful to correctly interpret the results of macro stress tests when making a policy decision.

With these simple qualifications in mind, we can turn to a review of the main limitations and benefits of macro stress tests for policy-making. As discussed in section 7.2, among the limitations, some depend on the need to develop more suitable modelling techniques, while others are more fundamental, and depend on the properties of macro stress tests. But notwithstanding these limitations, it is clear that there are important benefits to be gained by including macro stress tests among the tools used by policy-makers. On-going refinements promise to respond to existing limitations. For instance, a number of firms has recently found that their stress tests may have been based on an estimation of correlations that overestimated the economic benefits of diversification in stressed markets, and has responded by planning to refine their estimation and their stress-test models accordingly (SSG, 2008). And more broadly the official community has recommended upgrading stress tests in response to failures in firms' practices that emerged during the 2007–8 market turmoil (FSF, 2008). These actions point to the intention also in the regulatory community to improve stress tests rather than to replace them with other techniques or renege on a quantitative approach.

---

[5] There are also examples of macro stress tests that focus on parts of the economy other than the financial sector. See, for instance, for the household sector, Danmarks Nationalbank (2007), and for the corporate sector, Misina *et al.* (2007).

7.2 Use of macro stress tests for policy-making: limitations and benefits

In several countries, the use of macro stress-testing was spurred by the work of the International Monetary Fund (IMF) as part of its Financial Sector Assessment Program (FSAP), starting in the late 1990s (see Chapter 16). Since then, not only has the IMF been refining its approach, but over time and in some cases independently of IMF FSAPs, many central banks have been working on methodologies for macro stress tests and have started to regularly publish their results in their financial stability publications. These include Banco Central do Brasil (2008), Banco de Espana (2008), Bank of Canada (2008), Bank of Japan (2008), Bank of England (2008), Danmarks Nationalbank (2008), Sveriges Riksbank (2008) and Swiss National Bank (2008). This list is clearly not exhaustive but it shows the wide dispersion in terms of geographical location, size and national institutional arrangements among countries whose central banks conduct macro stress tests.

Starting from simple sensitivity analysis with a single source of risk, and highly stylised financial sectors, national and international authorities have engaged in the design of more robust and comprehensive modelling techniques. As mentioned in Chapters 2 and 3, models for macro stress-testing are under continuous refinement, overcoming simplifications in the object of analysis that were necessary in the early stages. This is done by extending the scope of the analysis to cover diverse sources of risk, interrelation across risks and across geographical regions, by covering more parts of the financial system or of the national economy. This process of refinement is important to strengthen the usefulness of macro stress tests for policy-making, and its continuation is to be conducted by modellers and encouraged by the official community.

With the improvements on the modelling front well in train, the next logical step is to decide how to use the results of these models in forming decisions on policy action. Documentation on how this step has been undertaken by national authorities is sparse (as an exception, see e.g., Jenkinson, 2007). To some extent, this simply reflects the multi-dimensionality of policy-making, which requires taking into account several sources of information, some of which are in a qualitative format, before deciding on and implementing a policy choice. And for confidentiality constraints, and possibly to avoid moral hazard in those cases where authorities decide to intervene to avoid a systemic failure in the financial system, authorities may be reluctant to publish their views on the policy implications of adverse macro stress test results, even when the stress test was run on the banking or financial sector as a whole rather than on individual financial firms.[6]

But this paucity of evidence may also reflect awareness in the official community of some structural weaknesses in macro stress tests, rather than in the specific modelling techniques, that call for caution in employing their results too mechanically.

In this regard, a key point is the choice of scenario.[7] At the cost of over-simplifying, the value of the output of a macro stress test is only as good as its input, which, in contrast to other types of model, is subject to a high degree of discretion in the choice of initial conditions used to build a scenario. Even in those cases where commendable efforts have been made to link the financial sector shocks to broader developments in the macroeconomy, and hence realism has been added to the type of shocks that are taken into account, it remains a fact that the selection of the initial scenario is largely an external input into the model.[8]

When using macro stress tests for policy-making, it is the responsibility of the policy-maker to identify conditions that are capable of putting stress on the vulnerabilities in the financial system and that are meaningful in terms of policy action. This is clearly no easy task, as choices need to be made both in terms of the type of shock in the macroeconomy or within the financial system that is assumed to put the existing vulnerabilities under stress and in the calibration of the size of these shocks. For instance, credit risk has traditionally been the focus of attention for firms and supervisory authorities, but the structural changes of the financial system towards a larger share of financial transactions through markets requires more attention to liquidity risk, as recently done by the BCBS (2008). Moreover, models should ideally cover various types of risk jointly, but in practice this has rarely been done.[9] Similarly, the key vulnerabilities in the financial system need to be identified, so that their resilience under stress can be tested. But key vulnerabilities can change over time, and authorities running macro stress tests need to constantly monitor the build-up of imbalances in the financial system. Recent examples that have caught regulators' attentions have been, for instance, exposures to hedge funds

---

[6] An important recent exception is the publication of stress test results and policy implications for nineteen individual US banks (Board of Governors of the Federal Reserve System, 2009). This is, however, a step taken as a response to a financial crisis (see Section 7.3).

[7] See also Chapter 4.

[8] See, e.g., European Central Bank (ECB, 2007) and references therein.

[9] This results from the modelling complexities of treating more than one type of shock at the same time. For a discussion of this point, see Chapters 2, 3 and 5.

(see, e.g., FSF, 2007) or the increasing complexity of exposures involving securitisation. But to prove the difficulty in identifying the key vulnerabilities in the financial system is enough to consider the lack of focus on the off-balance sheet positions of banks in the form of conduits and special investment vehicles (SIVs) over the past few years. Missing key vulnerabilities also weakens authorities' ability to identify the type of shocks that can affect them, such as, to complete the example on conduits and SIVs, the 2007–8 disruption in the asset-backed commercial paper market. An additional point that complicates the design of scenarios is the identification of the links across parties within the financial system. These links can become a channel for contagion at times of stress, and are therefore key to the build-up of those systemic vulnerabilities that call for policy-makers' attention. Yet, the nature of the contagion links across financial institutions can change over time, and policy-makers need to constantly update their models. For instance, following the academic literature *à la* Allen and Gale (2000), contagion has been modelled as originating via counterparty risk, while more recently there has been considerable interest in contagion arising from prices for financial assets and common exposures (e.g., Cifuentes *et al.*, 2005). With the more extensive use of valuation methodologies such as mark-to-market, it is likely that contagion will need to be increasingly modelled on the basis of asset prices.

As a result, the first issue for the policy-maker willing to use macro stress tests needs to be the choice of a valid set of scenarios which are, as traditionally defined, 'extreme but plausible', but also that are in line with the existing vulnerabilities of the financial system at each point in time. The regular analysis of systemic vulnerabilities, in the form of imbalances building up in the financial system, and of potential shocks originating outside of the financial system but capable of affecting it, is likely to represent the best source for the identification of correct stress scenarios. In this light, the use of historical scenarios may be less useful for policy-makers, although it remains important for regular risk management practices.

A second feature of stress tests that has a bearing on their use for policy-making is the time horizon over which to simulate the stress factors as they propagate through the economy. Because of the modelling complexities involved even in the simplest macro stress tests, the longer the time horizon over which the model is expected to describe the adjustments in the economy, the more the inevitable simplifications in it will have the potential to produce an outcome that is different from what would happen in reality. This limitation suggests that policy-makers should give more weight to the first-round effects, coming from the immediate impact of the shock on the financial system, and less so to higher order effects produced by allowing the initial shock to propagate through the system.[10] Moreover, it is difficult to model interactions across various risks and heterogeneous agents, and the financial system can become an amplifier of financial stress, making it endogenous to the financial system (Borio, 2007; Allen and Carletti, 2008). As a result, the measurement of the first-order impact is likely to remain more accurate even as modelling techniques continue to improve.[11]

Notwithstanding these 'health warnings', it is important to recognise the benefits of including macro stress tests among the tools used by policy-makers. The first advantage is that macro stress tests are better at measuring the impact of stress conditions on the financial system than available alternatives, such as value-at-risk (VaR), exclusively qualitative analysis, or models originally designed for macroeconomic forecasting.[12]

A second advantage is that, by imposing the use of modelling and quantitative techniques, macro stress tests require a careful delineation of a framework for financial stability as soon as the scope of the analysis is widened from a highly stylised representation of the banking sector or other sectors in the national economy and more complex scenarios are adopted. Such a framework is necessary to conceptually link the various parts of the system under analysis and to give internal consistency to the potentially different methodologies that national authorities may have developed to assess the resilience of the various parts of the system. There is a lively debate in the official and academic communities about how to create such a framework and the role of macro stress tests in it, and this conceptual work is on-going in the various institutions that conduct financial stability analysis (e.g., Schinasi, 2006, ECB, 2005, Haldane *et al.*, 2007, IMF and World Bank, 2005, Andersson, 2008, De Bandt *et al.*, 2008). For instance, De Bandt *et al.* (2008) mention at least three different ways in which such a framework could be built: the contingent claims analysis, based on option theory;

---

[10] The term second-order effects usually implies that economic agents adjust their behaviour to the new conditions in their operating environment. Due to the difficulties in modelling these reaction functions, they have rarely been included in macro stress tests. Some adjustments in the financial system however operate automatically if the shock is allowed to propagate itself through the system and may be easier to include. For instance, an initial slowdown in economic growth, which makes households' default rates on their loans increase, affects banks' profitability and capital ratios. But as capital ratios fall, banks must restrict lending on account of regulatory requirements.

[11] For instance, Goodhart *et al.* (2006) introduce heterogeneity among agents in their model, an important step in the way to add realism to the results of macro stress tests.

[12] VaR models (or their newest format, i.e., expected loss) suffer from the key limitation that they cannot be employed to model materially disruptive shocks that would fall outside the shape of the probability distribution adopted to compute the VaR. Models for economic forecasting aim to capture the central, most-likely outcome, and are inadequate to measure the extreme events that are of interest in financial stability analysis.

the semi-structural framework, which emphasises contagion links across institutions; and structural modelling, which attempts to include heterogeneity across agents and endogenous default probabilities. Others, e.g., Schinasi (2006), view the modelling limitations in macro stress tests – in particular the risk that a partial equilibrium analysis for the financial sector would fail to properly account for the dynamic adjustment in other sectors and second-round effects; the higher uncertainty attached to estimates of the impact of extreme and rare shocks; the existence of non-linear and sometimes unexpected links across parts of the economy – as a first hurdle before macro stress tests can be usefully incorporated in a financial stability framework. Goodhart (2006) lists the conceptual challenges of creating a framework for financial stability, in addition to the specific limitations of macro stress-test models. All of these limitations are well known and are discussed in other parts of the book in more detail (Chapter 3), but it can be safely argued that macro stress tests can contribute to the formulation of analytical frameworks for financial stability by imposing the rigor of quantitative models, especially by requiring careful modelling and calibration of links across agents and sectors.

An additional and related benefit of the use of macro stress tests derives from the fact that, with the analytical framework still under development, the practice of macro stress-testing has usually preceded the formulation of the theories of financial stability. In this light, the introduction of macro stress-testing practices has been beneficial as a commitment device to undertake financial stability analysis, especially in countries that did not yet have a tradition of conducting such analysis but started using macro stress-testing for guiding their policy work. This is clearly one of the benefits of the numerous FSAP missions conducted by the IMF, as they have contributed to create awareness and preparation for financial stability analysis by promoting the use of macro stress tests by policy-makers.

Finally, a crucial benefit of the use of macro stress tests for policy-making is that the results of macro stress tests, by making more visible the potential costs of persisting vulnerabilities in the financial system, are likely to encourage national authorities to correct the imbalances emerged in the analysis.

7.3 How macro stress tests have been used for policy-making

Keeping in mind the limitations but also the benefits outlined above, we can now see how macro stress tests have actually been used for policy-making. There are at least three such ways: first, to communicate with the public, including financial institutions; second, to identify information gaps, and third, to identify weaknesses in the financial system and, if needed, to decide on the suitable policy response. Finally, in some country-specific cases, the results of macro stress tests can also be beneficial to the design of standards for capital and liquidity requirements (Haldane *et al.*, 2007), but as this use relates more closely to regulatory issues, it is not discussed further in this chapter.

In order to improve communication with the public on risks and vulnerabilities, the results of macro stress tests have been reported in various financial stability publications, mainly by central banks and some international institutions, making them easily accessible to all interested parties.[13] The value-added of macro stress tests versus those conducted by individual market participants lies in the aggregate view of risks impinging on the financial sector the former adopt. This is both because authorities can use detailed information on conditions in the economy as a whole, and because, when using individual firms' supervisory reports, they can also form a more precise view of the weaknesses in the financial sector. Results of macro stress tests are particularly useful to individual financial firms, who can use this information to complement their own firm-level stress-testing. Reading these results can therefore allow them to cross-check their own findings. In addition, by communicating scenarios used for macro stress tests, authorities provide firms with a benchmark of the type of shocks to be considered for sufficiently conservative stress tests. Provided that authorities can correctly identify the main weaknesses and sources of risk affecting the financial system, the communication of macro stress test results based on relevant scenarios could strengthen authorities' message to financial firms about the need for changes in market practices. This message in particular can be addressed to regulated financial institutions – a sort of moral suasion that can usefully substitute for more heavy-handed policies. More broadly, sharing the results of macro stress tests allows authorities to communicate more clearly to the public the potential costs of imbalances in the financial system and to prepare the public for the potential need to undertake tighter policies.

At the same time, authorities need to be aware that the communication of existing vulnerabilities to shocks can have a self-fulfilling effect, by

[13] In almost all cases, these publications report the outcome of aggregate, sector-level macro stress tests. Institution-by-institution results are highly confidential, and a few authorities report such results, typically in an anonymous format (Sveriges Riksbank, 2008). But authorities can enrich the information content of macro stress tests run on aggregate sectors by providing information on the measure of dispersion of the results, if institution-level data are available to the authorities and have been used to run the macro stress tests.

prompting market participants to react suddenly and in large numbers to the publication of macro stress tests results. To avoid this, authorities need to make clear that macro stress tests represent a worst case outcome type of exercise, and that scenarios should be interpreted in a probabilistic sense, even when the probability distribution of various scenarios is set *ex-ante* by the policy-maker. This type of concern has possibly been less pressing in the first decade of use of macro stress tests, given the very benign global macroeconomic and financial environment, and the results of these exercises, showing the national financial or banking systems were expected to be resilient to the assumed stress scenarios.[14] But going forward, as models become more sophisticated and in preparation for communication of macro stress test results also at times of adverse general economic conditions, authorities will have to strike a careful balance between being informative and effective in their communication of potential risks, and avoid generating panics.

Turning to the second way of using the results of macro stress tests, because macro stress tests require that enough data be available to quantify exposures of all relevant parties, and that all relevant components of the system be clearly identified, including links among them, running these tests helps to inform authorities of the areas over which information is not available and where disclosure and transparency is to be increased. Adopting a stress-testing mindset can allow authorities to identify gaps in the availability and reliability of information available in normal conditions and at times of stress.

Finally, the ultimate goal of macro stress tests is its use for making decisions on policy actions, both in normal times, when vulnerabilities can be identified but are not yet under strain, and at times of stress, when imbalances in the financial system come under severe market pressure. It is difficult to say to what extent authorities may already be using the results of their macro stress tests for their policy decisions, as the process of policy-making is confidential. But policy changes following the findings in FSAP macro stress tests probably come closest to an example of this type of use. Nevertheless, it is clear that the operationalisation of the policy implications of macro stress tests should not be mechanical, as stress tests should be only one of the tools to be used by authorities in their decision-making. But as

---

[14] Institution-specific results may have at times been less positive, but as they have generally been considered confidential and have usually not been published, they have not posed the same challenges in terms of communication policies.

macro stress tests can be embedded in an analytical framework and are based on numerical models, they can make a substantial contribution to the clarity and rigour of policy-making on financial stability. At a minimum, macro stress tests can be used to get a sense of the size and direction of the various sources of risk identified within the financial system, especially in relation to first-round effects, as already discussed, and help prioritise the areas to be addressed by policy action. As models become more reliable and realistic, they should help authorities rank the various sources of risk and vulnerabilities based on their potential impact on the economy. Ultimately, macro stress tests could be used to calibrate the quantitative response by the authorities, although this is admittedly a goal that will take long to achieve.

Authorities can also use stress-testing models to conduct crisis simulation exercises. These simulations of crisis conditions have been employed by authorities to test their preparedness to deal with financial stress.[15] One way to employ macro stress tests for these exercises is to reverse-engineer macro stress tests in order to identify the size of initial shocks that would be capable of putting the existing vulnerabilities in the financial system under stress. When material weaknesses are identified via such exercises, authorities can use this information to change relevant guidance or regulation, or supervisory authorities can use it to guide regulated financial institutions to change related risky market practices. Authorities can also react to the findings by addressing imbalances in the financial system with non-supervisory policy measures.

Finally, authorities can use macro stress tests at times of stress, and the results of these exercises can help them speed up the identification of areas for policy action, if needed. This is important given the constraints on time availability for taking policy decisions in such circumstances. In addition, these results can facilitate exchange of information and cooperation with other institutions, nationally and internationally, and with the markets, if the results are published. The clarity of the results of macro stress tests can greatly contribute to the efficiency of such information exchange.[16]

---

[15] For crisis management exercises, see, for related work in the European Union, e.g., Committee of European Banking Supervisors (2005), or European Commission (2008).

[16] An example of enhanced information exchange via stress tests during a crisis is the US authorities' exercise of May 2009 (Board of Governors of the Federal Reserve System, 2009).

REFERENCES

Allen, F. and E. Carletti (2008), 'Financial System: Shock Absorber or Amplifier?', *BIS Working Paper*, 257.

Allen, F. and D. Gale (2000), 'Financial Contagion', *Journal of Political Economy*, 108 (1), 1–33.

Andersson, M. (2008), 'Ten Years with the Financial Stability Report', *Sveriges Riksbank Economic Review*, 1 February.

Banco Central do Brasil (2008), *Financial Stability Report*.

Banco de Espana (2008), *Financial Stability Report*.

Bank of Canada (2008), *Financial System Review*.

Bank of England (2008), *Financial Stability Report*.

Bank of Japan (2008), *Financial System Report*.

Basel Committee on Banking Supervision (2006), *Basel II: International Convergence of Capital Measurement and Capital Standards: a Revised Framework – Comprehensive Version*, Basel.
  (2008), *Principles for Sound Liquidity Risk Management and Supervision*, Basel.
  (2009), *Proposed Enhancements to the Basel II Framework*, Basel.

Board of Governors of the Federal Reserve System (2009), *The Supervisory Capital Assessment Program: Overview of Results*, Washington.

Borio, C. (2007), 'Change and Constancy in the Financial System: Implications for Financial Distress and Policy', *BIS Working Paper*, 237.

Cifuentes, R., G. Ferrucci and H. S. Shin (2005), 'Liquidity Risk and Contagion', *Bank of England Working Paper*, 264.

Committee of European Banking Supervisors (2005), *Annual Report*, London.

Committee on the Global Financial System (2005), *Stress Testing at Major Financial Institutions: Survey Results and Practice*, Basel.

Danmarks Nationalbank (2007), 'Macro Stress Testing of Danish Households', *Financial Stability*, May.
  (2008), *Financial Stability*.

De Bandt, O., C. Gauthier and P. St-Amant (2008), 'Developing a Framework to Assess Financial Stability: Conference Highlights and Lessons', *Bank of Canada Review*, Spring.

European Central Bank (2005), 'Assessing Financial Stability: Conceptual Boundaries and Challenges', *Financial Stability Review*, June.
  (2007), 'Global Macro-financial Developments and Expected Corporate Sector Default Frequencies in the Euro Area', *Financial Stability Review*, June.

European Commission (2008), *Memorandum of Understanding on Cooperation between the Financial Supervisory Authorities, Central Banks and Finance Ministries of the European Union on Cross-border Financial Stability*, Brussels.

Financial Stability Forum (2007), *Update of the FSF Report on Highly Leveraged Institutions*, May.
  (2008), *Report on Enhancing Market and Institutional Resilience*, April.

Goodhart, C. (2006), 'A Framework for Assessing Financial Stability?', *Journal of Banking and Finance*, 30, 3415–22.

Goodhart, C., P. Sunirand and D. Tsomocos (2006), 'A Model to Analyse Financial Fragility' *Economic Theory*, 27 (1), 107–42.

Haldane, A., S. Hall and S. Pezzini (2007), 'A New Approach to Assessing Risks to Financial Stability', *Bank of England Financial Stability Paper*, 2, April.

International Monetary Fund and World Bank (2005), *Financial Sector Assessment: A Handbook*, Washington DC.

Jenkinson, N. (2007), 'Developing a Framework for Stress Testing on Financial Stability Risks', *Speech given at the European Central Bank High Level Conference on Simulating Financial Instability*, 12–13 July.

Kohn, D. (2008), 'Condition of the Banking System', *Testimony Before the Committee on Banking, Housing, and Urban Affairs*, US Senate, June.

Misina, M., D. Tessier and S. Dey (2007), 'Stress Testing the Corporate Loans Portfolio of the Canadian Banking Sector', *Bank of Canada Financial System Review*, June.

Schinasi, G. (2006), *Safeguarding Financial Stability – Theory and Practice*, IMF.

Senior Supervisors Group (2008), *Observations on Risk Management Practices during the Recent Market Turbulence*, March.

Sveriges Riksbank (2008), *Financial Stability Report*.

Swiss National Bank (2008), *Financial Stability Report*.

Part II

Applications

8 Stress-testing credit risk: the Italian experience

Sebastiano Laviola, Juri Marcucci and Mario Quagliariello[*]

8.1 Introduction

In Italy a wide variety of approaches is used to measure the exposure of the banking system to different risks and its resilience to several kinds of shocks. Most stress-testing methodologies have been designed in 2004 within the International Monetary Fund (IMF) Financial Sector Assessment Program (FSAP) and subsequently improved.[1] In line with other countries' experience, the FSAP stress tests examined the impact of different shocks on the major Italian banking groups. The tests included both sensitivity and scenario analyses and they were performed using both top-down and bottom-up approaches, which provided sufficiently comparable results.

In this chapter we focus on credit risk for two reasons. First, it represents the most relevant risk Italian banks deal with. Second, while stress test procedures and sensitivity analyses for market risk are relatively better developed, there are no standardised methodologies for measuring the evolution of credit risk under different stress scenarios.

During the FSAP, the sensitivity exercise has been realised considering a 60 percent increase in the probability of default (PD) for all domestic exposures of Italian banks. This figure is slightly greater than the largest change historically observed in Italy (i.e., a 54 per cent increase in PD in 1993, after the European Monetary System (EMS) crisis). Sensitivity exercises are clearly very simple frameworks, in which PDs increase under a *ceteris paribus* assumption. To remove such an assumption scenario analyses have also been carried out along with single factor stress tests.

---

[*] Bank of Italy. The opinions expressed herein are those of the authors and do not necessarily reflect those of the Bank of Italy. Part of this chapter is based on the article 'Stress-testing credit risk: experience from the Italian FSAP', published in the *BNL Quarterly Review*, 59, 238. We are grateful to the editor, Alessandro Roncaglia, for granting us the permission to partially reproduce it here.
[1] For details, see IMF (2006).

The chapter is organised as follows. While section 8.2 briefly summarises the features of the Italian banking system, section 8.3 describes credit risk stress tests performed in the FSAP, illustrating both the approaches utilised and the hypotheses tested. Section 8.4 reports the results obtained with both top-down and bottom-up approaches. Section 8.5 draws some conclusions.

8.2 The Italian banking system: some stylised facts

In the last two decades, the Italian banking system has gone through an intense structural transformation. Institutional and regulatory reforms, large-scale consolidation and enhanced levels of competition in the market have substantially changed the banking environment.

In the 1990s the market was highly fragmented, with more than 1,000 credit institutions and a remarkable presence of state-owned banks. As a matter of fact, the average size of Italian banks was relatively small. In addition, business activities were strictly regulated and there were no universal banks. The structure of the banking industry evolved radically during the 1990s, with the massive privatisation of public institutions along with a relevant process of mergers and acquisitions.[2] Between 1990 and 2004, 620 mergers were recorded, involving target banks that accounted for 51 per cent of the assets of the entire banking system at the end of 1989. Since then, the average size of banks has increased substantially, and more than doubled between 1994 and 2004.

Consolidation and privatisation have permitted economies of scale in the production and distribution of financial services and increased risk diversification. Italian banks' profitability has improved, converging towards European standards. Furthermore, the proportion of income sources changed substantially. At the beginning of the 1990s profitability was essentially driven by the traditional intermediation business, also in connection with an overall economic environment characterised by high inflation and high nominal interest rates. The decrease of revenues from standard intermediation – as a

---

[2] In the 1930s state-owned banks became the dominant institutions in Italy. Even though they contributed to Italy's economic development after World War II, the deterioration of their performance has raised problems of efficiency and triggered discussions on possible reforms since the 1980s. The first step was the transformation of public banks into limited companies that started in 1990 with the Amato–Carli Law (law n. 218/1990). Privatisation was made easier by the general adoption of the limited company status by banks. Since 1990, all of the major Italian institutions have gradually been privatised.

consequence of fierce competition and more stable monetary policies – stimulated banks to enlarge the range of products and services supplied to clients thus allowing for diversification in revenue sources.

Notwithstanding these developments, the Italian banking sector still relies to a considerable extent on traditional intermediation products, therefore credit risk continues to represent the most relevant source of concern for credit institutions.

8.3 An analytical framework for stress-testing credit risk

As mentioned in Part I, stress-testing techniques have some inherent limitations: (1) the inability of macro stress tests to take into account potential second-round (or feedback) effects; (2) the difficulty to associate confidence intervals to the losses related to certain specified scenarios; and (3) the almost complete absence of non-linearities in most credit risk models.[3] As a consequence, the most pragmatic way to achieve a sound financial stability assessment is to adopt a variety of approaches, drawing conclusions upon inputs coming from a wide range of data, indicators and models.

Therefore, the stress-testing exercise has been performed using both bottom-up and top-down methodologies. The six largest limited company banks in Italy and three large cooperative banks have carried out the stress tests using their internal methodologies to generate results in the bottom-up approach. For the top-down approach, stress tests have been conducted at the aggregate level and also on a solo basis for the intermediaries belonging to the nine banking groups, which represent 62 per cent of the Italian banking system's assets. However, in the top-down exercise, individual bank data have also been used when this information was more detailed than that from the consolidated reports.

Banks have performed their simulations using a baseline macro scenario available at the beginning of 2005 as the benchmark for the assessment of the before-stress losses. The same baseline scenario has been used for the top-down exercises.

Given a fixed exogenous shock (or a combination of shocks), its impact on domestic macroeconomic variables has been estimated through the Bank of Italy Quarterly Model (BIQM). The output of the macroeconometric model has then been employed as an input for a reduced form econometric model

---

[3] See Chapters 2 and 3.

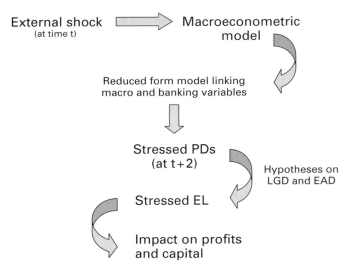

Figure 8.1   Stress-testing credit risk

linking macro and bank-specific variables. In this latter model the probability of default is the bank-specific dependent variable, while the macroeconomic indicators are the regressors. The substitution of the stressed figures for the macroeconomic variables allows estimating the stressed PDs in a given time horizon. Starting from the stressed PDs, it is possible to quantify the increase in expected losses (EL) using the formula

$$\Delta EL = (stressed\,PD - unstressed\,PD) * LGD * EAD$$

where LGD is the loss given default and EAD is the exposure at default.

The logical steps of the stress test simulations can be summarised as in Figure 8.1.

Given the lack of more specific data for the top-down methodologies, it has not been possible to use a complete Basel 2 framework in the simulations.[4] In other words, consistent with macro stress tests performed in the FSAPs of other industrialised countries, we could estimate a stressed expected loss, while it was not possible to estimate a stressed unexpected loss. Nevertheless, given the severity of the shocks on the expected loss the results we produced were quite conservative.

The losses or gains resulting from the stress test exercises have been measured in terms of (1) percentage of after tax profits, (2) percentage of

---

[4] On this issue, see Chapter 6.

capital buffer (i.e., bank capital in excess of the mandatory regulatory capital), and (3) new solvency ratio calculated according to Basel 1 prudential regulations but allowing for losses to be initially covered by pre-tax profits.

It is worth noting that the impact of the macroeconomic scenario on the banking system is propagated through two different, though not independent, mechanisms: (1) an increase in portfolios' riskiness, and (2) a contraction of profits. In the scenario analyses, the simulations have explicitly taken into account the second mechanism by assessing the impact of the stressed expected losses on estimated stressed profits (as in Casolaro and Gambacorta, 2004). This allowed us to incorporate the impact of market risks – as a result of changes in interest rates, equity and foreign exchange prices due to the macroeconomic shocks – in the scenario results.

Stress tests have been performed applying the shock to bank exposures as of December 2004 and considering a time horizon of two years. This time period is the minimum needed if one wants to fully capture the impact of the business cycle on the credit cycle, which in general can be even longer. Since the use of infra-annual data may require approximations, we prefer to focus on end of year results.

8.3.1 Scenarios

The scenarios selected were the following:
(1) A 70 per cent oil price increase from the level observed in the autumn of 2004 combined with a sudden global equity price decline of 30 per cent.
(2) A confidence shock in the US that triggers a 20 per cent appreciation of the euro with respect to the US dollar.
(3) A confidence crisis triggered by a large corporate failure in Italy, that implies a 35 per cent decline in stock prices combined with a 200 basis point increase in corporate spreads.

As mentioned above, the effects of these shocks on the Italian economy have been computed using the BIQM. The BIQM is a large-scale structural model which contains 96 behavioural equations, 885 endogenous and 663 exogenous variables, and a few non-linearities.[5]

The model is Keynesian in the short-run and neoclassical in the long-run. In the short-run the level of economic activity is determined by aggregate demand, while in the long-run it follows Solow's model of exogenous growth.

---

[5] A complete description of the model, including all the estimated equations, is given in Bank of Italy (1986).

In the short-run, the dynamics of the model are characterised by stickiness of prices and wages, inflation surprises and a putty-clay nature of the production process. In contrast, in the long-run, along the steady-state growth path, the dynamics are driven by capital accumulation, productivity growth, foreign inflation and demographics. In equilibrium, the model describes a full employment economy where output, employment and capital stock are consistent with an aggregate production function, relative prices are constant and inflation equals the exogenous growth rate of foreign prices.

The simulations of the macroeconomic shocks, arising from changes in some exogenous variables, have generated deviations with respect to a baseline projection over a two-year horizon.

Under scenario (1), oil prices per barrel jump by 70 per cent with respect to the baseline in the first quarter. At the same time, stock prices fall by 30 per cent and their impact on the economy goes through two channels: (i) the private sector wealth is proportionally eroded thus implying a downward revision of households' consumption plans, and (ii) firms face a higher cost for external financing. The effects for the Italian economy under this scenario are sizeable in terms of both a reduction in gross domestic product (GDP) growth and a decrease in households' consumption and gross fixed investments. The increase in consumer prices causes an aggressive reaction of monetary policy to the inflation mainly induced by the oil price shock.

Under scenario (2), the US dollar depreciation implies that the euro effective exchange rate appreciates. The competitiveness of Italian commodities reduces markedly. Two years after the depreciation of the US dollar, Italian GDP growth is slightly lower than the baseline, while the cumulated decrease in consumer prices is not relevant. For all the other variables, the impact of the depreciation is likewise quite modest.

Scenario (3) is built under the assumption that the cost of financing for Italian firms increases by 200 basis points in the first quarter, remaining at this new level for up to eight quarters. In addition, a further stock market price shock is assumed, with prices falling by 35 per cent, implying a sizeable drop in households' wealth. This is a typical scenario identifying a combination of idiosyncratic shocks that hit only the Italian economy. Thus, there are no implications for euro area monetary policy or exchange rates. The increase in corporate spreads heavily affects firms' investment behaviour, so that two years after the beginning of the shock total investment growth drops. At the same time, the cumulated drop in GDP growth is substantial. Total employment decreases, while domestic prices experience only a moderate decline.

8.3.2 Top-down methodologies

The tools that have been developed in order to carry out credit risk stress tests are reduced form econometric models, which are designed to estimate the impact of external macroeconomic shocks on banks' riskiness. In some cases, different statistical procedures may have similar or even overlapping goals (e.g., the estimation of future loan losses): this is a further explicit acknowledgement that cross-checks are an essential part of stress-testing and a necessary prerequisite for policy implementation.

The first way to estimate the relevant econometric relationships is the use of panel data techniques. As an example, Quagliariello (2007) estimates the reduced form relationships between the loan loss provision ratio and the default rate on one hand, and the business cycle indicators on the other.[6] The sample employed for the estimation includes over 200 Italian banks and covers the period 1985–2002. The sample is huge and represents around 90 per cent of the Italian banking system's consolidated total assets.

The main goal is to verify whether banks' performance is linked to the general economic climate and to understand the timing of banks' reactions to economic changes. The starting set of regressors is selected according to the insights provided by economic theory. In particular, the macroeconomic regressors include real GDP growth, the long-term real interest rate, the loan-deposit spread and stock exchange index changes. The lag structure of the explanatory variables is selected trading off parsimony with the need to account for the plausible delay with which macroeconomic shocks affect banks. The results of such a model can then be employed to carry out stress tests, mainly single factor stress tests. As an example, it is possible to set GDP growth at its lowest historical value, *ceteris paribus*. The main shortcoming of this approach is that any potential second round effect or policy response is neglected. Moreover, if the set of regressors includes many bank-specific variables, it is not very realistic to keep them constant.

Binary choice models may also be used in order to estimate borrowers' probability of default. Chionsini *et al.* (2005) estimate the PDs for all the corporate borrowers of Italian banks on the basis of a scoring model that employs several logit specifications. Exploiting the databases available at the Bank of Italy, balance sheet data and Credit Register information are jointly

---

[6] The default rate is built up as the ratio of the amount of loans classified as bad debts in the reference period to the performing loans outstanding at the end of the previous one. In order to improve the reliability and timeliness of such an indicator, the 'adjusted' bad debts as signalled by the Central Credit Register are used.

used to assess the probability of each firm being recorded as defaulted. Two separate multi-variate logistic models are estimated, respectively for the firms recorded in the balance sheet register and for those recorded in the Credit Register; the results generated by each model are then combined together in order to obtain the final estimation. With respect to previous releases, this methodology has the advantage that it is possible to exploit fully the higher frequency and the detailed information content of the Credit Register data, in principle available monthly (quarterly data are used in the estimation), with respect to the balance sheet data, available only once a year.[7] The model based on Credit Register information uses five variables out of about twenty ratios examined. The financial model employs separate functions for the main sectors of economic activity (manufacturing, trade, construction and services), in order to capture the specificities of the different segments. Six variables out of the fifteen examined have been selected, which refer to the main economic and financial profiles of all firms.

The authors have used the estimated PDs in order to carry out a stress test aimed at evaluating the impact of an adverse macroeconomic environment on the credit quality of the aggregate loan portfolio of Italian banks and on the overall capital buffer (that is, the amount of capital above the minimum solvency requirement) of the banking system. The exercise has tried to replicate the adverse circumstances of the economic recession experienced in Italy at the beginning of the 1990s. To this purpose, default probabilities have been computed using information on credit relations and balance sheet indicators related to 1993–4. The 'historical stress scenario' has been used to compute the average credit quality of the aggregate loan portfolio under the above-mentioned adverse scenario and the consequent increase in the capital requirement.

Finally, the impact of the business cycle on bank borrowers can be estimated using a vector autoregression (VAR) approach. With respect to cross-sectional or panel data techniques, VAR allows us to fully capture the interactions among micro and macroeconomic variables, providing a better framework for capturing possible feedback effects. This enables us to perform a more comprehensive assessment for financial stability purposes. Again, the estimated relations may be easily employed for carrying out stress-testing exercises in order to assess the resilience of the banking system in the presence of sudden unfavourable macroeconomic shocks.

---

[7] An earlier and partially different version of the model, with some applications, is contained in Fabi *et al.* (2004).

In the Italian FSAP, the VAR methodology has been used for the stress tests following Marcucci and Quagliariello (2008). They build a VAR from a small-scale macroeconomic model enriched with a micro equation that describes the behaviour of Italian banks' default rates. The macroeconomic model comprises an IS curve, a Phillips curve that corresponds to a backward-looking AS curve, an uncovered interest rate parity and a modified Taylor rule. Therefore, their VAR includes the following variables: (1) bank borrowers' default rate, (2) output gap, (3) inflation, (4) three-month interest rate, and (5) real exchange rate. The authors use a standard recursive identification scheme where the default rate and the output gap are assumed to react quite slowly to financial and monetary shocks. The default rate is assumed to be contemporaneously exogenous to the output gap and all the other variables. The contemporaneously exogenous variables are ordered first, so that variables at the front are assumed to affect the following variables contemporaneously, but to be affected by shocks to the following variables only after a lag. On the other hand, variables at the end are assumed to affect the preceding variables only after a lag, but are very reactive to shocks that hit the preceding variables. In the VAR, the financial variables are ordered at the end, since they respond immediately to shocks to the real side of the economy, whereas the default rate and the output gap are placed at the beginning, because of their sluggish reaction to financial and monetary shocks. Furthermore, the output gap is ordered after the default rate reflecting the prior belief that business cycles affect bank losses only after a substantial lag, as shown by Pain (2003) and Quagliariello (2007).

The results show that the Italian default rates follow a cyclical pattern, falling in macroeconomic upturns and increasing during downturns. They also document the presence of feedback effects.

8.3.3 Bottom-up practices

The Committee on the Global Financial System (2005) conducted two different surveys on the practices on stress tests developed by banks and found that G-10 intermediaries increasingly use these techniques for internal purposes ranging from risk management and capital allocation to strategic planning. The last survey, published in 2005, analysed sixty-four banks and investment firms. The results suggest that, while most large and complex institutions already have stress-testing arrangements in place, overall the use of a broad range of stress tests as a complement to existing risk management tools is not very widespread yet.

As far as Italy is concerned, according to a survey carried out jointly by the IMF and the Bank of Italy before the FSAP, there existed different methodologies across Italian banks. In particular, this survey has shown that stress tests for market risks are well developed. Regarding credit risk, internal ratings models have been developed in most cases while, in some cases, stress tests are used in the context of the broader activity of risk management. While sensitivity analyses are quite straightforward to implement once an adequate internal rating system has been put in place, in the scenario analysis the main technical challenge to be solved concerns the so-called macro link, that is, the possibility to estimate PDs (and LGDs) conditional to macroeconomic conditions.

For the FSAP, consistently with the goals and the spirit of the exercise, banks have assessed the impact of the macroeconomic scenarios using internal estimations. While some banks used their internal portfolio models in order to measure potential expected losses under unfavourable macroeconomic scenarios, most of them based their estimations on simpler frameworks.

Regardless of the complexity of the methodology employed, banks had to determine losses using before and after stress PDs, LGDs and EADs as inputs for their simulations. Banks using portfolio models also had to select adequate assumptions on the correlation across assets.

For the unstressed PDs, banks that at that time had already developed internal rating systems used their outcomes as the basis for the simulations. The other intermediaries based their simulations on either Merton's inspired default models or more simplified proxies for credit risk (default rates, scores, ratings), sometimes supplied by external providers. For the other risk parameters, regulatory figures have been typically used, but some banks also tried to employ preliminary internal evidence on LGDs. Regarding asset correlation, banks have either defined fixed conservative correlations or used the correlation of equity returns as a proxy for the correlation of asset returns, clustering obligors according to geographic and industry criteria.

For the purpose of stress-testing model parameters, few banks' portfolio models already included macroeconomic variables, which could be easily shocked in order to quantify the losses under stress conditions. Other banks have either developed econometric models in order to link their internal PDs to relevant macroeconomic indicators, or simply applied the changes of the aggregate default rates estimated by the Bank of Italy to their portfolios. The latter approach has been a pragmatic way out when time series for internal PDs were not sufficient for a proper statistical analysis of their dynamic properties.

8.4 Stress test results

8.4.1 Top-down simulations

As mentioned above, the credit risk shock consists of a 60 per cent increase in the PD of all banks' borrowers.

In the top down-approach, the PD is measured as the flow of new bad debts over the stock of performing loans in the previous period. With respect to Basel 2 rules, this is a narrower definition of PD since it does not include past-due exposures, but it is the only one for which long time series are available so far. For this reason, the increase in the PD translates in provisioning increases assuming a quite conservative LGD, equal to 60 per cent for the whole portfolio, independently of any collateral and guarantees held. Also, consistent with Basel 2, the EAD is assumed equal to the drawn amount of the performing exposures plus 75 per cent of the undrawn credit lines.

The LGD is the average loan loss provisioning rate on bad loans reported by the largest banking groups, which is considerably higher than the average 40–45 per cent LGD reported by G-10 countries in the third Quantitative Impact Study of the Basel Committee.

The effects of the macroeconomic scenarios on the PDs are reported in Table 8.1. As mentioned above, in the top-down simulations the profits themselves are affected by the shock and reduced or increased accordingly. The results refer to the simulations carried out using the updated baseline.

According to the simulations carried out using the VAR model described in section 8.3, in the worst scenario (scenario 1) the PDs of banks' borrowers increase by 98 per cent with respect to December 2004. In this scenario, the

Table 8.1 Macroeconomic stress-testing scenarios

	Scenario 1 Oil price increase and global equity prices decline by 30 per cent	Scenario 2 US dollar depreciation	Scenario 3 Increase in credit spreads and decline in Italian equity prices
Effect of changes in macroeconomic variables on banks' operating profits and borrowers' PDs (percent change after two years, December 2004)			
Banks' operating profits	−14.0	7.4	−17.9
Probability of default	98	42	58

Table 8.2 Stress test results

	Loss as percentage of after-tax profits December 2004		Loss as percentage of capital buffer at December 2004[a]		New CAR[b]	
	Weighted average	Largest loss	Weighted average	Largest loss	Weighted average	Min
Sensitivity to credit risk[c]						
Top-down	35.5	79.6	10.6	24.1	11.1	9.2
Bottom-up	36.4	94.9	10.9	36.4	11.1	9.2
Macroeconomic scenario tests						
Top-down						
Scenario 1[d]	73.8	171.5	17.3	39.4	11.0	9.2
Scenario 2[e]	22.2	49.6	7.4	16.9	11.1	9.2
Scenario 3[f]	47.5	111.6	10.3	23.3	11.1	9.2
Bottom-up						
Scenario 1[d]	33.3	104.3	10.0	40.0	11.1	9.2
Scenario 3[f]	16.6	45.9	5.0	17.9	11.1	9.2

Top-down results refer to the updated baseline scenario.
[a] Gains or losses as percentage of the capital in excess of the regulatory capital as of December 2004.
[b] Risk-weighted capital adequacy ratio, allowing for losses to be covered first by pre-tax profits.
[c] A 60 per cent increase in the probability of default of all credit exposures, except interbank exposures.
[d] The price of oil increases to US$85 per barrel and global equity prices decline by 30 per cent.
[e] Sustained 20 per cent depreciation of the US dollar with respect to the major currencies.
[f] Italian corporate spreads increase by 200 basis points and Italian equities decline by 35 per cent.

banks' operating profits decrease by 14 per cent (compared with 18 per cent in scenario 3).

Table 8.2 shows the impact of the extra provisions that banks need to make under stress in terms of after-tax profits and capital buffers.

With reference to the first scenario, on average, for the nine banking groups, the losses under stress represent 74 per cent of stressed after-tax profits and 17 per cent of capital buffers. The solvency ratio, calculated allowing for losses to be covered by pre-tax profits, remains virtually unchanged.

8.4.2 Bottom-up simulations

Banks have performed sensitivity analyses and two out of three scenario analyses. In the bottom-up approach, the PD is generally defined as the sum of bad and substandard loans. With respect to the top-down simulations, this is a broader definition, although it is not completely compliant with the new

Table 8.3 Top-down vs. bottom-up definitions

	PD	LGD	EAD
Top-down	Narrower	Higher	Higher
Bottom-up	Broader	Lower	Lower

Capital Accord definition. For the LGD, most banks have employed values equal or close to regulatory LGDs; some of them have used LGDs obtained from internal calculations. The exposure at default is typically equal to the credit exposures used plus a certain percentage of the difference between exposures committed and granted, guarantees, etc.

Table 8.3 provides a summary of the different definitions of PD, LGD and EAD used in the top-down and bottom-up approaches.

Results for the bottom-up simulations are also reported in Table 8.2. Consistent with the top-down results, the first scenario has the greatest impact on banks' profits and capital buffers. For the nine banking groups, the extra provisions arising from the worst stress scenario represent on average 33 per cent of the after-tax profits and 10 per cent of the capital buffers. The after-stress solvency ratio is calculated allowing for losses to be covered by pre-tax profits and is substantially unchanged.

8.4.3 A comparison between top-down and bottom-up impacts

The final goal of stress tests is to obtain a reliable estimate of the impact of shocks on the banking system. The interpretation of the results is therefore an important step of the process to understand to what extent the different techniques employed provide comparable outcomes. However, given the different assumptions and modelling strategies underlying the various approaches, top-down and bottom-up scenario simulations are hardly comparable. Therefore, a direct comparison of different results can be made using the sensitivity analyses (Table 8.4).

The results are definitely encouraging. The choice of PD, LGD and EAD definitions has ensured consistency of the results across different approaches. Regardless of the metrics, the impacts are on average similar although there are differences when one looks at the range between minimum and maximum values.

A further check of the consistency between the results emerging from different approaches is provided in Table 8.5, which reports the ranking of

Table 8.4 Sensitivity analysis: comparison of top-down and bottom-up results[a]

	Average		Minimum		Maximum	
	TD	BU	TD	BU	TD	BU
After-tax profits	35.5	36.4	19.4	15.8	79.6	94.9
Capital Buffers	10.6	10.9	5.3	6.2	24.1	36.4
New CAR	11.1	11.1	12.0	12.0	9.2	9.2

[a] TD = Top-down approach; BU = Bottom-up approach.

Table 8.5 Sensitivity analysis: comparison of top-down and bottom-up banks' ranking (impact on capital buffers)

Ranking[a] TD	1	2	3	4	5	6	7	8	9
BU									
1			B3						
2					B4				
3	B7								
4				B6					
5		B5							
6							B9		
7								B1	
8						B2			
9									B8

[a] TD = Top-down approach; BU = Bottom-up approach.

the banks involved in the exercise according to the impact on their capital buffers.

Banks in (or close to) the main diagonal are ranked in a similar way by the top-down and bottom-up methodologies. As an example, the impact on bank 3 (B3) is ranked as the third most relevant impact according to the top-down approach and the first according to the bottom-up one. Overall, top-down and bottom-up approaches demonstrate an acceptable degree of convergence in classifying banks on the basis of their vulnerability to credit risk under different stress hypotheses.

All in all, the comparison reveals that, in the event of very unfavourable macroeconomic shocks, top-down exercises can provide on average reliable signals on the resilience of the banking system on one hand and the single intermediaries on the other. Since bottom-up simulations are resource-intensive and quite expensive for banks, this suggests that top-down stress tests can be a relatively cost-effective approximation for periodical assessments of financial stability.

8.5 Conclusions

Setting the stage for adequate stress-testing procedures is not an easy task. In fact, the level of complexity tends to increase very rapidly when many variables and risk factors are involved. A certain degree of simplification and some discretionary assumptions are therefore needed in order to keep the simulations at a manageable level. Furthermore, most of the statistical techniques that are commonly used have some inherent limitations, such as the inability to take into account potential feedback effects, the difficulty in assigning confidence intervals to the losses associated with certain specified scenarios or to consider asymmetries and other non-linearities. As a consequence, the most pragmatic way to achieve a sound financial stability assessment is to use a variety of approaches, drawing upon input from a wide range of data, indicators and models. In that respect, expert judgments may somehow help when data availability and statistical methods are not sufficient.

Within the FSAP for Italy, stress tests examined the impact of a variety of shocks on the nine major Italian banking groups. The tests were performed using both top-down and bottom-up approaches, which provided sufficiently comparable results. For the sensitivity analysis, the size of the shocks to assess market risk, sovereign risk, interest rate risk and liquidity risk in the banking book was in line with those applied in other FSAPs for euro area countries, while the credit risk shock exceeded the largest historical shock. In addition, the impact of various adverse macroeconomic scenarios was assessed. Specifically, an adverse macro scenario in which oil prices increase by 70 per cent causing a global slowdown, and global equity prices decrease by 30 per cent, had the largest impact. Overall, stress test results suggested that the Italian banking sector was resilient to many kinds of shock. Profits appeared in most cases sufficient to cover losses arising from the calibrated shocks. Furthermore, existing capital buffers remained comfortably above the minimum regulatory solvency ratios.

The implementation of macroeconomic stress-testing programs such as those underlying the FSAPs has advanced the development of internally consistent stress-testing procedures. However, the state of the art is still evolving; further work in this field will allow the relaxing of less realistic assumptions, improving the methodologies and making results more reliable. As the 2007–8 financial crisis revealed, a priority for credit risk is the analysis of its links with other risk types. Indeed, credit risk tends to interact with other risks – such as market and liquidity risks – particularly in extreme market conditions. Stress tests should consider these interlinkages in order to depict a more accurate picture of the impact of financial instability on banks.

REFERENCES

Banca d'Italia (1986), 'Modello Trimestrale dell'economia Italiana', *Banca d'Italia Temi di discussione*, 80.

Busetti, F., A. Locarno and L. Monteforte (2005), The Bank of Italy Quarterly Model, in G. Fagan and J. Morgan (eds.), *Econometric Models of the Euro Area Central Banks*, Cheltenham: Edward Elgar.

Casolaro, L. and L. Gambacorta (2004), 'Un Modello dei Conti Economici per il Sistema Bancario Italiano', *Banca d'Italia Working Papers*, 519.

Chionsini, G., F. Fabi and S. Laviola (2005), *Analisi del Rischio di Credito: un Modello per la Stima della Probabilita' di Insolvenza delle Imprese*, Banca d'Italia, mimeo.

Committee on the Global Financial System (2000), *Stress Testing by Large Financial Institutions: Current Practice and Aggregation Issues*, Basel.

  (2005), *Stress Testing at Major Financial Institutions: Survey Results and Practice*, Basel.

Fabi, F., S. Laviola and P. Marullo Reedtz (2004), 'The Treatment of SMEs Loans in the new Basel Capital Accord: Some Evaluations', *BNL Quarterly Review*, 228, March.

International Monetary Fund (2006), *Financial Sector Stability Assessment – Italy*. Washington DC.

Marcucci, J. and M. Quagliariello (2008), 'Is Bank Portfolio Riskiness Procyclical? Evidence from Italy using a Vector Autoregression', *Journal of International Financial Markets, Institutions and Money*, 18, 1.

Pain, D. (2003), 'The Provisioning Experience of the Major UK Banks: a Small Panel Investigation', *Bank of England Working Paper*, 177.

Quagliariello, M. (2005), 'Assessing Financial Stability at the Bank of Italy: Data Sources and Methodologies', *Irving Fisher Committee Bulletin*, 23.

  (2007), 'Banks' Riskiness over the Business Cycle: a Panel Analysis on Italian Intermediaries', *Applied Financial Economics*, 17, 2.

Terlizzese, D. (1994), 'Il Modello Econometrico della Banca d'Italia: una Versione in Scala 1:15', *Ricerche Quantitative per la Politica Economica*.

9 Stress-testing US banks using economic-value-of-equity (EVE) models

Mike Carhill[*]

9.1 Introduction

Since the early 1980s, American banks have been using 'economic-value-of-equity' (EVE) models to help measure and manage their banking-book interest rate risk (IRR). These models estimate the fair value of the institutions' financial instruments as a function of the current interest rate environment (the 'base-case' EVE). The modeller then specifies alternative stress scenarios, and estimates the resulting change from base-case EVE. This change is usually expressed as a percentage of the base-case estimate.

Banks develop and use internal EVE models to quantify and control their interest rate risk. For executive management and bank supervisors, a common benchmark interest rate scenario is an instantaneous plus/minus 200-basis-point shock to the current yield curve. That benchmark is typically used to set a risk limit, e.g., the banking-book IRR manager will tolerate an exposure of no more than 20 per cent of base-case EVE for the 200-basis-point shock.

Banking supervisors also have their own EVE models. The OCC uses these to estimate banks' exposure under a common set of assumptions, allowing peer comparisons. This provides a basis for supervisory actions against banks that have excessive exposures relative to industry norms.

For the middle management responsible for interest rate risk, EVE models are used for day-to-day management. For that purpose, the shocks are estimated in a comprehensive range, e.g., 10-basis-point increments up to the 100-basis-point shock, or whatever is deemed the maximum shock likely before the manager can react. The result is a 'valuation profile' showing the value of the instrument as a function of the level of interest rates. The interest

* Office of the Comptroller of the Currency (OCC). The views herein are those of the author and not necessarily those of the OCC.

rate changes can have multiple dimensions, but for expository purposes a single-factor interest rate model suffices, so the valuation profile has two dimensions, value and interest rates. The use of valuation profiles is pervasive in the industry at the instrument or sub-portfolio level, but some – arguably, most – asset–liability (A/L) managers are dubious about the usefulness of enterprise-wide EVE. There are two themes that underlie this dubiousness.

First, many argue that the model uncertainty is very large relative to the estimated level of risk. Below, we analyse the model uncertainty. Fortunately, EVE has the important mathematical characteristic that it is linear in the balance sheet components. Because of this linearity, estimation uncertainty at the enterprise level is entirely determined by estimation uncertainties at the instrument or sub-portfolio level. If modellers can characterise those uncertainties, they can also determine the reliability of the estimates at the enterprise level.

We confirm the argument that the EVE model uncertainty is too large to precisely quantify the level of risk or to precisely estimate the base-case value of the firm. However, when considering changes in interest rates, the uncertainties are manageable. Banks can use the models to evaluate risk-management options and trends in their risk, and can identify the sources of their risk and the consequences of alternative portfolio changes. Supervisors can use the models for peer comparisons. While EVE uncertainty is high relative to a low- or moderate-risk bank, it is much smaller relative to the risk of a high-risk bank, and bank executives and supervisors can be confident when the EVE models identify a high-risk portfolio.

The second theme is that the EVE models invite mismanagement of interest rate risk by creating too much transparency. While this may seem a perverse position, and asset–liability managers explicitly raise this concern only rarely, the argument is valid. Asset–liability management is one of the most quantitatively complex areas of banking, and generally is little understood by non-specialists. Particularly at banks that prefer to profit from credit risk rather than financial types of risk, executive management is often surprised by the amount of risk that EVE models reveal, and have unrealistic expectations about the practical ability to eliminate the risk.

Whatever the merits of this concern about transparency, US banking supervisors have firmly decided that executive management is responsible for establishing their bank's risk strategy, and for middle management's compliance with that strategy. It is not the asset–liability manager's responsibility to determine the bank's strategy; rather, the responsibility is to provide executive management with the information necessary to choose and monitor the strategy. From the perspective of banking supervisors and shareholders, transparency has its merits.

Given an understanding of their limitations, the major attraction of EVE models is the expression of risk in very concrete economic terms as the percentage or dollar value of equity at risk to plausible changes in the interest rate environment. As a validation exercise, publicly traded firms can compare the estimated interest rate sensitivity of EVE to the interest rate sensitivity of their stock valuations. A divergence shows a difference between the model's and the market's view of the bank's interest rate exposure, which may be due to the modeller's superior information or his excessive pessimism or optimism.

Hitherto, OCC is not aware of any bank that has incorporated credit risk into their EVE stress-testing. However, in the past decade banks and bank regulators have made major investments and commitments to enterprise-wide credit risk measurement and stress-testing, particularly with Pillar I and Pillar II of the Basel 2 capital regulations (OCC, 2007). EVE models, which already provide a very useful tool for estimating the gains and losses from changes in the interest rate environment, can be rigorously extended to incorporate credit risk and evaluate the bank's exposure to stressful economic environments. Because of the investments required for large banks to conform to Basel 2, the additional expenditures needed to develop sound stress tests for credit risk are relatively small. It seems promising that at least some banks will develop enterprise-wide stress-testing by adapting the Basel 2 – Pillar I data investments to incorporate credit risk in their EVE models.

9.2 The EVE concept

In principle, EVE models measure a bank's gains and losses as a function of the economic environment. In practice, measurement of distant-horizon gains and losses can be problematic, and the majority of bank managers place a greater reliance on shorter-term risk modelling, such as accounting income at risk the next quarter to (at most) the next eight quarters. Such models can be very reliable and informative. However, a bank's solvency is a function of economic values, not accounting income. EVE assesses solvency.

Most EVE models use a 'liquidation' approach, estimating the fair value of the firm as if it were to be liquidated in an orderly fashion. This approach captures the economic value of any lucrative transactions to which the bank is currently a party, possibly including ongoing business with existing customers, but ignores the 'going concern' franchise value associated with the opportunities to enter into lucrative transactions in the future.

In practice, most EVE models treat non-financial assets at historical cost, usually for both current interest rates and for alternative scenarios. Most models also ignore new business with existing customers; the liquidation model could in principle capture new business with both existing and new customers, but, particularly for new customers, the estimates would generally be too unreliable for business purposes. Indeed, banks with good validation processes generally conclude that the accounting-income-at-risk models do not provide useful income predictions at horizons of more than a few months, illustrating the difficulties of forecasting new business.

While the model can accommodate any number of different asset and liability categories, the basic methodology can be illustrated with only one liability and one asset category. For a typical bank, the model first converts book values to market values at current interest rates (see Table 9.1).

Book value equity is $10, or 10 per cent of assets. Because the economic environment is favourable, the loans generate a premium, while the deposits generate a discount (by convention, the deposit discount is referred to as the 'core-deposit premium' which will follow hereafter). Hence, supposing that the loans have a 5 per cent premium, and the deposits a 5.55 per cent premium, the EVE in the current environment (base-case EVE) is $20, or two times book value. However, if the yield curves shifts upwards by 200 basis points in a short period of time, most banks will suffer a modest decline in their estimated EVE as the decline in asset values outpaces the increase in deposit premiums.

Conceptually, leverage has the same implications for economic equity-at-risk as for book equity-at-risk. For a given portfolio composition of assets and liabilities, a lower EVE-to-assets ratio will produce a higher interest rate sensitivity of EVE, and make the sensitivity estimates more sensitive to the model assumptions.

Table 9.1 An application of EVE models

Book value	
Assets	Liabilities
$100 Loans	$90 Deposits
Economic value	
Assets	Liabilities
$105 Loans	$85 Deposits

For enterprise-wide stress-testing, the most attractive mathematical feature of EVE arises from the structural relation between interest rates and the value of the assets and liabilities. Since a common factor drives all of the balance sheet items, there is no role for estimating correlations between items. Hence, EVE is linear in the bank's positions. While EVE estimates can require very complex models for each financial position, the absence of dependency structures greatly enhances the reliability and simplicity of the model's risk-aggregation process.

If the modeller attaches a probability to the stress scenarios, the EVE model becomes a value-at-risk (VaR) model. Indeed, a reasonably professional modeller should be able to provide executive management with a clear and extensive discussion of the likelihood of any given stress scenario and hence the likelihood of that profit or loss associated with that scenario. However, the attachment of a precise probability to any given stress scenario is arbitrary, particularly for those unusual scenarios that could threaten the bank's solvency, so we do not advocate the VaR extension of EVE.[1]

9.3 Future business

New business can occur with future customers and with current customers. Future customers, while arguably a significant component of the value of a bank charter, are probably too hypothetical to be reliably modelled, and we have not observed banks make an effort to do so. However, many modellers attempt to capture new business with existing customers, certainly an important component of a bank's economic value-of-equity.

If all new business is incorporated, base-case equity estimates from the EVE model are also estimates of stock market valuations. The stock market then provides an interesting avenue for model validation. However, in the typical case where no new business is included in the model, the stock market is usually considerably higher than the EVE estimates.

9.3.1 Non-maturity deposits

The most prominent example of new business with existing customers is deposits with indefinite maturity. In the US, this category comprises

---

[1] See Chapter 4.

transactions deposits (which can be non-interest-bearing or interest-bearing), savings accounts and money market deposit accounts.

Although an EVE model is essentially a fair-value model of the balance sheet, fair-value accounting standards require institutions to carry these deposits at par (Financial Accounting Standards Board (FASB), 2007; particularly standards 107, 157 and 159). The FASB's reasoning is that these instruments are instantaneously demandable at par, hence must be carried at par. However, in a statistical sense, any given deposit account will persist for several years and will carry below-market all-in costs, and will have an economic value well below the par value.

The literature is clear both that the economic value of most banks' indefinite-maturity deposit liabilities is significantly below par, and that the rents tend to increase when interest rates rise. Carhill (1997) reconciled earlier research and established that the value of the liabilities had averaged about 6 per cent below par over the 1981–94 period. Flannery and James (1984) established that the stock market regarded the effective maturity of these (demandable) deposits as at least greater than one year. Hannan (1994) established that the interest rates paid on the deposits were sticky upwards but flexible downwards, a rather nice characteristic for a liability.

Defined-maturity retail certificates of deposit are a major source of funds for banks, typically 20–40 per cent of assets. As with non-maturity deposits, these often provide a below-market source of funds. These deposits have optionality in the form of rollover and an implicit put option, but most banks model them as optionless instruments, so that their valuation and interest rate sensitivity is straightforward.

9.3.2 On-going lending relations

On the asset side, on-going lending relations are analogous to non-maturity deposits. This is particularly the case for home-equity lines of credit and credit card receivables, which have indefinite maturities. The draw and pay-down patterns for these lines of credit can be estimated statistically, as is currently required by the gain-on-sale accounting that applies to asset securitisations. Although current accounting standards do not permit the recognition of future increases in balances drawn, some firms estimate future increases in order to better understand the economic values of the loans.

Another major item is unsecured commercial and industrial loans, which frequently have a short maturity, e.g., one year, with the expectation that the lender will renew the loan at maturity for those businesses whose credit worthiness does not deteriorate. These loans carry coupon rates substantially above risk-free market rates. While most of the extra coupon compensates for defaults, the loans may well earn positive premiums, at least in good economic times. We have not seen a bank that has researched this rollover. It would be a major step forward in EVE modelling if banks would research the value of these loans in more detail.

9.4 Model uncertainty

In the context of static liquidation EVE models, model uncertainty is dominated by two components of the balance sheet: non-maturity deposits and non-earning assets and liabilities. The interest rate sensitivity of any instrument can never be estimated or forecasted with absolute precision, but the uncertainty about these two components so greatly swamps the uncertainty about other components to the extent that, comparatively, uncertainties arising from other items are negligible, at least for diversified banks.

9.4.1 Non-maturity deposits

Many banks have conducted attrition studies of their non-maturity deposits. These studies typically show that about 30 per cent of accounts close in the first year, but those that survive the first year attrite very slowly and steadily over the next twenty years or so. For modelling purposes, this history suggests a twenty-year amortisation (in practice most banks arbitrarily truncate the amortisation at ten years, for conservatism).

Against this long life, the deposits have well below-market interest rates. As of June 2008, US banks paid an average interest rate of about 0.75 per cent for money market accounts and an average rate for interest-bearing transaction accounts of about 0.25 per cent (Bank Rate Monitor, 2008). This compares to one-year (five-year) swap rates of about 3.4 per cent (4.5 per cent) at the same point in time. Banks incur higher expenses in managing these accounts than for most other assets and liabilities, but all-in costs certainly remain below market.

The academic studies noted in section 9.3.1 agreed on an average or base-case premium of about 6 per cent of par, but studies have not produced a consensus on the interest-rate sensitivity of the premiums (Ellis and Jordan (2001) provide a survey of the literature). Econometrically, the problem is that deposit balances and interest rates respond to changes in market rates with a long and variable lag, and long and variable lags have severe consequences for the reliability of econometric estimates.

However difficult the task, banks must estimate the sensitivity for their internal asset–liability modelling. No consensus approach has emerged. A plurality, but probably not a majority, use attrition studies to determine the expected deposit lives, assume that current deposit rates will remain constant unless interest rates change and rely on expert judgment to estimate how deposit interest rates ('offer rates') will respond to changes in market rates. Conventional static discounted cash flow calculations then deliver value estimates for the base-case and stress scenarios.

Because there is no industry consensus as to methodology, and due to the importance of expert opinion in banks' modelling efforts, we developed an informal 'OCC consensus range', designed to reflect the views of the middle 80 per cent of A/L managers. These are the assumptions used for the supervisory model that the OCC uses on exams. (The National Credit Union Administration adopted a similar approach to non-maturity deposits, based on the survey in Ellis and Jordan (2001)). While participating in bank exams, we have collected the value-sensitivity estimates of twenty-five banks for the plus-200-basis-point parallel interest-rate shock. Almost all banks suffer EVE declines for rising rate scenarios; so the larger the estimated increase in premiums for the plus-200 shock, the more 'optimistic' are the assumptions.

The results from the twenty-five banks are listed in the Appendix. Excluding the highest and lowest estimates, the estimated increase in premiums for the plus-200 shock ranged from 1.7 per cent to 6.1 per cent. This somewhat overstates the differences, because banks differ in the proportion of transaction versus money market deposits, and there is consensus that the premiums for transaction deposits are much more responsive to rising rates. Moreover, these estimates were collected over the course of an interest rate cycle, with premiums more sensitive to the 200-basis-point shock when rates are low than when rates are high.

The results demonstrate that the range of reasonable expert opinion is at least as wide as the OCC consensus range. Sixteen banks fell within the consensus range or very close to one end or the other, but nine fell significantly outside the range. It appears that, loosely speaking, most experts believe that the deposit premiums would increase by about 2 to 5 per cent for the plus-200 shock, a range of three percentage points.

This would not be such a major problem if non-maturity deposits were not such a large proportion of liabilities. Suppose that in the base case a bank has $90 in liabilities, of which $45 are non-maturity deposits, and $100 in assets, for a base-case EVE of $10. For the plus-200 shock, the range of 2 to 5 per cent implies a dollar gain on the deposits ranging from $0.90 (9 per cent of base-case EVE) to $2.25 (22.5 per cent). If the bank's net loss on the other assets and liabilities happened to come to $0.90, the percentage of EVE at risk for the plus-200 shock would fall anywhere between 0 and 13.5 per cent, given the reasonable range of deposit assumptions.

For most banks, a range of more than 10 per cent of base-case means that EVE is nearly useless for determining the absolute level of risk. Banks' internal models generally estimate a level EVE at risk to the plus-200 shock between 0 and 20 per cent. Using the optimistic end of the deposit assumptions and the OCC EVE model, we also find that most banks fall below 20 per cent. (As a rule of thumb, examiners classify the banks above 20 per cent as 'high' under our risk-assessment system.) So the arbitrary difference between the two ends of the deposit-assumption range is about equal to the total risk of a typical bank.

9.4.2 Non-earning assets

The difficulties in estimating the interest rate sensitivity of deposits receives much attention in the US, but the issue of non-earning assets and liabilities receives almost no attention. These items constitute the balance sheet representation of the infrastructure of a bank. Non-earning assets usually fall between 5 to 10 per cent of assets and include physical plant, cash and reserves to support deposits, and miscellaneous non-financial investments such as payment processing. Non-earning liabilities include such items as accounts payable and typically range from 1 to 5 per cent of liabilities. The difference in non-earning assets and liabilities ranges by up to as much as 5 per cent of total assets and thus these items make a large net contribution to total base-case or accounting equity.

The assignment of maturities to non-earning items is largely arbitrary. Consider cash reserves to support deposits. Viewed from a cash liquidation perspective, the value of cash is invariant, hence it should be carried as overnight. Viewed as part of the business of banking, idle cash provides a necessary stream of services with a value that is independent of interest rates, and should be classified as a perpetuity.

The choice between the two arguments is arguably an arbitrary one. Most banks classify non-earning items as overnight, but some treat the items as perpetuities, and some split the difference and assign intermediate maturities. If the difference between non-earning assets and liabilities comes to 5 per cent of total assets, with long-term rates at 6 per cent, moving the items from overnight to perpetuity increases EVE at risk by 12.5 of base-case EVE, similar to the valuation uncertainty raised by non-maturity deposits.

It would be most convenient to ignore non-earning items and leave them out of the model altogether, but the model would then substantially overstate the bank's leverage. This would greatly increase the estimated percentage sensitivity of EVE. Arguably, by treating the items as overnight, the model remains silent on the sensitivity but without greatly misstating the base-case equity ratio.

9.4.3 Other activities

On several occasions, we have compared the EVE valuation profile produced by the OCC model to those produced by a bank's EVE model, with the OCC model adopting the bank's assumptions for deposits and non-earning items. On a couple of occasions, we uncovered material programming errors in the bank's models. Aside from those errors, on no occasion did our model differ materially from the bank's. However, it is useful to discuss the modelling issues for other instruments that banks typically hold.

To conserve computational resources, banks use static discounted cash flow modelling for instruments with no optionality, such as Treasury bonds. The valuation profile for optionless instruments is very nearly linear, with the slight 'positive convexity' universally ignored for the purposes of asset–liability management. ('Positively (negatively) convex' instruments have values that are increasing (decreasing) in interest rate volatility.)

When instruments have significant optionality, the valuation profile becomes non-linear and requires stochastic path valuation techniques. This requires the modeller to supply implied forward short-term interest rates, which are typically taken from the swap market; the forwards can be calculated by the modeller but are readily available from market data vendors.

The modeller must also provide a probabilistic volatility structure for interest rates. The most common convention is to use the implied volatilities from the fixed-income derivative markets, also readily available from vendors.

Among Wall Street modellers, the convention is to develop assumptions for the dependency structure between short-term and longer-term rates, resulting in multiple interest rate factors. However, our own internal validation efforts show that, for the levels of precision involved in EVE modelling, one-factor models are preferred, as they are easier to implement and thus less prone to model error. However, even in the one-factor models, the modeller should provide the one- to ten-year term structure of implied volatility, as base-case valuations and risk estimates can vary significantly if the slope of the implied-volatility term structure is not captured.

Relative to discounted cash flow modelling, stochastic path option valuation requires a much greater investment in computational resources, staff training and option research, so banks prefer to ignore options for most of their financial instruments. For example, non-maturity deposits have the very attractive feature that offer rates are 'sticky upwards, flexible downwards' so the premium values are probably increasing in interest rate volatility (Hannan 1994). Nevertheless, most banks ignore this feature, probably because the large uncertainties associated with the deposits make the positive convexity too putative to be worth capturing.

It is standard practice to use stochastic path techniques for the residential mortgage loans and mortgage-backed securities, which have strong negative convexity. The cause of the negative convexity is the costless call option that banks typically include in the loans. Because retail consumers lack the information needed for optimal exercise of their option, banks need to develop or acquire a statistical model of that exercise, and the models forecast only imprecisely. This creates model uncertainty that bank modellers track fairly carefully, but not so much uncertainty as to significantly affect the bottom-line EVE-at-risk estimates.

Prior to 2000, banks generally did not capture options residing outside the residential mortgage portfolio, but some banks have been improving their modelling. This is particularly the case in long-term fixed-rate commercial lending and commercial real-estate lending. While these loans typically have 'make-whole' prepayment penalties that would remove the interest rate incentive to prepay, lending officers tend to waive the penalties in order to maintain business relations. This problem became particularly acute during the period of very low interest rates that the US experienced in 2001–3.

Fixed-maturity certificates of deposit have an implicit put option that creates an incentive for depositors to withdraw funds when rates rise. Similar to commercial lending, deposits generally have an interest penalty to discourage exercise of the put, but banks tend to waive this in the interests of customer relations. Both an internal bank study we reviewed and Gilkeson *et al.* (1999) provide evidence that the value of this option is economically significant and should be captured by the A/L models.

Most large banks raise a significant proportion of their funding by issuing long-term non-deposit debt. These debts can have complex options structures; many banks issue puttable debt where the option value lowers the coupon significantly. Obviously, these options should be captured in the models.

One of the major benefits that banks earn from credit card lending is the interchange fee of about 1 to 2 per cent of balances. This fee is not rate-sensitive, creating an exposure to rising rates. However, most banks treat the card loans as overnight, though some have a more thoughtful approach. While not a major balance sheet item for most banks, these assets potentially have quite complex optionality that has received little study of which we are aware. Keller (1997) provides an expert discussion of the issues.

The last major potential source of interest rate optionality is the non-residential retail portfolio, particularly auto lending. Auto loans generally carry fixed rates for a four or five years' maturity, with no prepayment penalty. However, the relatively low balances, against the costs the borrowers incur to refinance, helps mute the prepayment incentive. Banks' internal studies that we have reviewed have been mixed as to the rate sensitivity of auto prepayments, but none found sensitivity approaching that of mortgage loans.

9.5 Credit risk

The only major departure from current standard practice that is needed in order to use EVE for enterprise-wide stress-testing is the incorporation of credit risk. This would allow a bank to perform 'what if' experiments for plausible changes in the economic environment, to determine what damage adverse developments might do to the bank. For example, for several years we have advocated that banks assess the EVE losses that would result from a 'stagflation' scenario. While we know of several banks that are moving towards that capability, at present we have not observed any bank that can persuasively model such stress scenarios.

Conceptually, acquiring this capability would not require any new thinking, as finance theory treats the default option similarly to other options that can be reliably included in EVE models. However, in practice, meaningful incorporation of credit risk requires the development of persuasive factor-driven credit-risk modelling for the banking book, which in turn requires banks to innovate in the way they have traditionally approached credit risk.

Until now, banks have generally worked with credit-scoring models which were based on the characteristics of borrowers. For business purposes, this has evidently been adequate to the task. Business needs have not required an understanding of the relation between environmental risk factors and portfolio credit losses; by rank ordering using borrower characteristics, banks are able to avoid lending to the worst credits and remain profitable in normal economic environments.

One area of lending where the environment has already been incorporated is residential mortgage lending, where there is a good understanding of the relation between home prices and defaults.

Similar relations exist between other macroeconomic variables and defaults, and it is in principle straightforward to quantify the relations via a research agenda. For retail lending other than residential mortgages, a discussion of one practical implementation is presented in Breeden (2003), though in discussions some bankers have taken issue with Breeden's evidence of a correlation between macroeconomic factors and defaults.

For corporate defaults, the evidence of correlation is particularly clear. The 1991 and especially the 2001 US recessions saw sharp spikes in corporate defaults (Das *et al.*, 2007). Prospects in this area appear particularly promising for persuasively establishing the relation between macroeconomic risk factors and credit losses.

The utility for stress-testing portfolio credits will depend on the persuasiveness of the research into the relation between risk factors and credit losses. This will require some investment by banks, but those banks that have implemented the Internal Ratings Based (IRB) approach of Basel 2 have already made extensive investments in data and research, and the remaining investment necessary to conduct this research is trivial relative to the large amount of shareholder wealth at stake.

While the success of this research cannot be guaranteed in advance, it could potentially answer probably the most fundamental question confronting a bank's top management team: how will my bank fare through the various plausible changes in the economic environment? This benefit probably exceeds the combined total of all the other benefits from the IRB implementation. If this proves true, it seems a compelling investment.

9.6 Conclusions

EVE modelling uses the percentage sensitivity of equity, the most economically meaningful expression of risk available to investors and creditors, and therefore to bankers and banking supervisors. Against this attraction is the problem of irreducible uncertainty in the modelling estimates. This uncertainty will naturally increase if the models are extended to include credit risk.

It is not surprising that EVE has such uncertainty. EVE models are among the most ambitious used in banking. Not only must the model estimate the value of the firm, it does so for (in principle) every economic environment. Fortunately, the uncertainties can be identified and quantified, if not reduced.

Possibly, banks that adopt EVE for enterprise-wide stress-testing will, after a few years, come to see the model as an indispensable and routine component of their executive risk-management information systems. Supervisors would regard it as the single most interesting risk report that the bank produces.

Appendix Variation of deposit sensitivity estimates across banks

The Risk Analysis Division is often asked to run the OCC EVE Model at IRR exams. One of the most contentious aspects of EVE measurement is the effective duration of core deposits. We currently pay particular attention to the impact of a 200-basis-point increase in rates on the hedge value provided by core deposits. We refer to the decline in value of the core deposits (liabilities) as a hedge because they offset the decline in assets as rates instantaneously increase. The decline in liabilities offsets the decline in assets, thus hedging the impact to equity.

We have conducted our own research, reviewed the literature on non-maturity deposits and interviewed numerous bankers in exam settings. We have concluded that the problem of a long and variable lag between changes in market conditions and changes in banks' deposit bases causes statistical analysis, by itself, to be unreliable. Statistics are useful, but most banks overlay the statistics with their expert judgment on the rate sensitivity of their deposit bases.

We have estimates from twenty-five banks' EVE models to compare to the OCC pessimistic and optimistic assumption sets. Several banks, mostly community banks in relatively uncompetitive markets, are moderately more optimistic than the OCC's optimistic range. A few are more pessimistic than the OCC's pessimistic range.

Bank	Bank +200	Rank	OCC Pess. + 200	OCC Opt. + 200
15	6.9	1	3.0	4.5
17	6.1	2	2.2	3.1
20	5.3	3	2.9	5.0
25	5.1	4	3.2	5.2
21	4.8	5		3.8
8	4.7	6	3.6	4.1
22	4.5	7	3.2	4.9
6	4.4	8	2.4	4.1
23	4.4	9	2.8	4.2
4	4.1	10	2.8	4.1
24 (using OTS model)	4.0	11	1.9	4.8
9	3.9	12	2.4	4.2
16	3.8	13	3.6	4.6
13	3.8	14	2.7	4.5
18	3.4	15	3.2	4.4
2	3.2	16	2.5	4.6
7	3.0	17	2.9	3.9
5	2.8	18	2.7	4.3
19	2.8	19	2.9	4.2
10	2.6	20	3.0	4.5
11	2.6	21	2.2	3.5
14	2.3	22	2.7	3.9
3	2.1	23	2.8	4.1
1	1.7	24	2.3	4.3
12	0	25	3.8	5.3
Olson Research Associates-Mean		3.6	0	
Olson Research Associates-Max		10.4	0	
Olson Research Associates-Min		1.4	0	

Figure 9.1   An application of EVE models
Note: Bank 24 used the assumption developed by the Office of Thrift Supervision, which uses a point estimate rather than a range for the deposit assumptions.

REFERENCES

Bank Rate Monitor (2008), 27 (24), June.

Berkovec, J. A. and J. N. Liang (1991), *Deposit Premiums of Failed Banks: Implications for the Values of Deposits and Bank Franchises*, Board of Governors of the Federal Reserve System, May.

Breeden, J. (2003), 'Portfolio Forecasting Tools: What you Need to Know', *RMA Journal*, 86 (2), October, 78–87.

Carhill, M. (1997), 'Accounting Income and Market Prices: Explaining Core-Deposit Premiums', *Managerial Finance*, 23 (2), 42–64.

Das, S., D. Duffie, N. Kapadia and L. Saita (2007), 'Common Failings: How Corporate Defaults are Correlated', *Journal of Finance*, 62 (1), 93–118.

Ellis, D. M. and J. V. Jordan (2001), *The Evaluation of Credit Union Non-Maturity Deposits*, National Economic Research Associates (NERA), 10 September.

Financial Accounting Standards Board (2007), *Statement of Financial Accounting Standards*, 159.

Flannery, M. J. and C. M. James (1984), 'Market Evidence on the Effective Maturity of Bank Assets and Liabilities', *Journal of Money, Credit, and Banking*, 16 (4), 435–45.

Gilkeson, J. H., J. A. List and C. K. Ruff (1999), 'Evidence of Early Withdrawal in Time Deposit Portfolios', *Journal of Financial Services Research*, 15 (2), 103–22.

Hannan, T. H. (1994), 'Asymmetric Price Rigidity and the Responsiveness of Customers to Price Changes: the Case of Deposit Interest Rates', *Journal of Financial Services Research*, 8 (4), 257–67.

James, C. (1991), 'The Losses Realized in Bank Failures', *Journal of Finance*, 46 (4), 1223–42.

Keller, J. W. (1997), 'Managing the Interest-Rate Risk of a Card Portfolio', in A. G. Cornyn, R. A. Klein and J. Lederman (eds.), *Controlling and Managing Interest-Rate Risk*, New York Institute of Finance, 408–22.

Office of the Comptroller of the Currency (2007), Risk Based Capital Standards: Advanced Capital Adequacy Framework–Basel II – Final Rule, *Federal Register*, December, 69287–445.

10 A framework for integrating different risks: the interaction between credit and interest rate risk

Steffen Sorensen and Marco Stringa[*]

10.1 Introduction

As described in the previous chapters, credit and interest rate risk are two of the most important sources of risk for commercial banks. According to commercial banks, interest rate risk is a significant source of market risk, and, after credit risk, is the second most important source of risk.[1] The Standard and Loans (S&L) crisis in the US is an example of the significance of interest rate risk.[2] While banks and regulators are aware of the importance of both risks, they tend to manage them separately. However, credit risk and interest rate risk are intrinsically related to each other and not separable. Ignoring this interdependence may potentially have implications for banks' stability during severe downturns.

The separate treatment has been reflected in most stress tests, which have focused on either credit risk or interest rate risk. For example, traditional macroeconomic stress tests aimed to assess the deterioration in banks' asset quality following an adverse macroeconomic shock (see Sorge, 2004 for a survey). Although these have established that credit risk may significantly reduce the profitability of banks and threaten their solvency, they often fail to recognise the interdependence between credit and interest rate risk. To capture this interdependence it is fundamental to take into account the whole balance sheet. For example, following a sharp deterioration in asset quality, a bank subjected to a downgrade may face higher funding costs, which could amplify the losses to the bank. It is therefore necessary to consider the

---

[*] Barrie and Hibbert and Bank of England respectively. This chapter is largely based on the article: 'The Integrated Impact of Interest Rate and Credit Risk on Banks: an Economic Value and Capital Adequacy Perspective', Bank of England, Working Paper 339, January 2008. The views expressed in this chapter are those of the authors, and not necessarily those of Barrie and Hibbert and the Bank of England.
[1] See IFRI–CRO (2007).   [2] See Curry and Shibut (2000) for an overview of the S&L crisis.

whole portfolio of the bank – assets, liabilities and off-balance sheet items – to obtain the full impact of the unexpected macro shock on a bank's stability.

Stress tests that fail to model the whole portfolio of the bank also fail to account for the asset-liability re-pricing mismatch.[3] This mismatch arises as a result of one of the defining functions of the banking system: borrowing money at short maturities to lend to households and companies at longer maturities. This mismatch is the key source of interest rate risk for commercial banks as changes in the default-free interest rates tend to feed through more quickly on interest paid on liabilities than interest earned on assets. As a result, net interest income may decrease following an interest rates rise unless a bank has fully hedged this risk through, for example, off-balance sheet items.

But the re-pricing mismatch may also affect banks' exposure to credit risk. Indeed, net interest rate income is not only affected by changes in default-free interest rates, but also by credit risk. This is because credit spreads can be adjusted to reflect changes in the banks' own or borrowers' credit risk. And the timing of such an adjustment will depend on the above-mentioned re-pricing mismatch.

Therefore, stress tests need to capture not only the direct impact of changes in macroeconomic variables, such as unemployment, on banks' expected write-offs, but also their indirect impact via potential changes in default-free interest rates. And besides the re-pricing mismatch, changes in default-free interest rates will affect banks' write-offs.

Although we claim that interest rate risk is an important source of risk which has to be considered alongside credit risk, its importance has found mixed support in the literature. Starting with Flannery and James (1984) several papers find a strong negative impact of interest rates on bank stock returns (see Fraser *et al.*, 2002 for a more recent study). Chen and Chan (1989), however, argue that this is highly dependent on the sample period. Using econometric analysis of annual aggregate net interest income in different countries, English (2002) concludes that it seems unlikely that interest rate changes are an important factor for the stability of a banking system. Similarly, Maes (2004) finds weak empirical evidence when looking at aggregate net interest income in the Belgian banking sector. But annual net-interest income may be too aggregated to disentangle the complex effects of interest rates on banks' riskiness: initially a rise in interest rates will compress margins between short-term borrowing and long-term lending, depressing net-interest

---

[3] The re-pricing characteristic of an asset or liability need not be the same as its maturity. For example, a flexible loan can have a maturity of twenty years even if it can be re-priced every three months.

income. After a few quarters, once higher rates are passed on to borrowers, net-interest income will increase. Hence it is perhaps not surprising that an econometric analysis of annual net-interest income finds it hard to support the importance of interest rate risk.

One of the simplest sensitivity tests is gap analysis, where banks or regulators assess interest rate risk by purely looking at the net re-pricing mismatch between assets, liabilities and off-balance sheet items.[4] Using this approach as well as a model by the Office of Thrift Supervision, Voupt and Wright (1996) conclude that interest rate risk is not a major source of risk for most banks in the risk environment of the mid-1990s. But standard and more sophisticated gap analysis have a number of problems (e.g., see Staikouras, 2006). Most importantly these tests implicitly assume that shocks to the default-free yield curve have no impact on the credit quality of assets. And this is a strong assumption as higher probability of default and lower recovery rates are more likely in periods of increasing interest rates.

The above discussion suggests that it is important to use a consistent framework to conduct a macro stress test that simultaneously captures the impact of credit and interest rate risk. Jarrow and Turnbull (2000) are among the first to show theoretically how to integrate interest rate and credit risk. Jarrow and van Deventer (1998) show that in terms of hedging a bond portfolio, both credit and interest rate risk have to be taken into account. But these papers look at the integrated impact of credit and interest rate risk on assets only, they do not aim to assess the impact of interest and credit risk on banks' whole balance sheets. Barnhill and Maxwell (2002) and Barnhill et al. (2001) attempt to measure credit and market risk for the entire portfolio of a bank. They use a simulation framework to re-value assets and liabilities depending on the state of several systematic risk factors. To assess the stability of a bank, they focus on the distribution of the economic value. But they ignore one of the most important sources of interest rate risk – the above-mentioned re-pricing mismatch between assets and liabilities. Further they do not take off-balance sheet items into account.[5]

We propose a general framework that can be used as a stress test to measure the stability of a bank subject to correlated credit and interest rates. Our framework captures (1) impact of credit risk on the whole portfolio,

---

[4] Generally, gap analysis allocates assets, liabilities and off-balance sheet items to time buckets according to their re-pricing characteristics and calculates their net difference for each bucket. Gap analysis may therefore not capture non-linearities and will underestimate the impact of interest rate risk.

[5] The papers also look at a maturity mismatch of +/− one year and conclude that this is important. But +/− one year is clearly too simplistic to capture the full impact of the maturity mismatch on the riskiness of banks.

(2) interest rate risk stemming from the re-pricing mismatch between assets, liabilities and off-balance sheet net positions as well as basis and yield curve risk, and (3) interdependence between credit and interest rate risk.

We consider non-tradable exposures in the banking book of a hypothetical bank and model corporate and household credit risk directly. And more importantly, we model the complex cash flows from liabilities with different re-pricing characteristics rather than assuming a simple cash account. The approach also takes account of interest rate-sensitive off-balance sheet items. And in contrast to the existing literature, we are also able to assess the impact of a severe stress scenario on risk-adjusted discount rates, write-offs, net interest income, capital ratios and net profits. This framework could thus be used to extend standard credit risk stress tests to account for complex integration of different sources of risk.

An economic value, as well as a capital adequacy condition, needs to be checked to assess the impact of the adverse macroeconomic scenario. The economic value condition provides a long-term view of banks' health based on economic fundamentals and is simply based on risk-adjusted discounting of future cash flows. But this is not a sufficient metric to assess banks' stability. For example, it may be the case that a particular path of profits leads a bank to be undercapitalised in the short run because of severe losses which are outweighed by future profits. And because of market or regulatory constraints the bank may find it difficult to continue to operate as it may be subject to liquidity runs. Assessing the risks to the bank in the short- to medium-term requires projecting the banks' write-offs, net-interest income and capital requirements in a consistent fashion.

The rest of the chapter is organised as follows. Section 10.2 briefly describes the general framework and section 10.3 discusses the various risks on the balance sheet of a hypothetical bank and assumptions made on this bank's behaviour. This section also discusses models to link credit and interest rate risk to macro variables and the economic stress the bank is facing. Using these building blocks, section 10.4 illustrates why measuring interest rate risk and credit risk separately may over/underestimate losses to the bank. Section 10.5 considers future challenges and section 10.6 concludes.

10.2 A framework for integrating interest rate and credit risk

While this section does not provide a full account of the framework proposed by Drehmann *et al.* (2008), it aims to explain the main intuition for the framework with particular focus on the integration of credit and interest rate risk.

10.2.1 Integration of risks

The economic value EVA^i of a generic asset i with maturity T is simply the risk-adjusted discounted value of future coupon payments C and the principal A:

$$EVA^i_t = \sum_{k=1}^{T} D^i_{t+k} C^i_0 A^i + D^i_{t+T} A^i \tag{1}$$

We assume that all assets are equivalent to bullet bonds – i.e., repay the principal only at maturity and pay a constant coupon C^i_0 priced at time $t=0$. Such an asset could, for example, be a fixed-interest rate bond with no embedded options or a simple bank loan. The discount function is given by:

$$D^i_{t+k} = \prod_{l=1}^{k} d^i_{t+l-1;t+l}, \tag{2}$$

where d is the period by period risk-adjusted discount factor which is equal to the inverse of $1+R$, the risk-adjusted interest rate. In continuous time, R equals the risk-free rate plus a credit risk premium. In discrete time the following relation holds:[6]

$$R^i_{t+l-1,t-l} = E_t \left(\frac{r_{t+l-1,t+l} + PD^i_{t+l-1,t+l} \times LGD^i_{t+l-1,t+l}}{1 - PD^i_{t+l-1,t+l} \times LGD^i_{t+l-1,t+l}} | \Omega_t \right), \tag{3}$$

where $r_{t+l-1,t+l}$ is the forward risk-free interest rate between $t+l-1$ and $t+l$ known at time t. LGD^i is the expected loss given default for borrower i which, for simplicity, is assumed to be constant. $PD^i_{t+l-1;t+l}$ is the risk-neutral probability of default of borrower i between $t+l-1$ and $t+l$ conditional on surviving until $t+l-1$. Expectations are taken conditional on the time t available information set, Ω_t.

Assets and liabilities need to be re-priced according to their contractual characteristics as empirical coupon rates are not observable. To do so, it is assumed that at the time of issuance the economic value of a security (an asset

---

[6] The formula assumes that the same loss given default (LGD) applies to both coupons and principal and that the liquidity premium is zero. See Duffie and Singleton (2003, 134) for a derivation.

or a liability) is equal to its face value. This implies that $EVA_{t=0}^i|\Omega_0 = A^i$ in equation (1). Solving for $C_{t=0}^i$ we obtain:

$$C_0^i = \frac{1 - D_T^i}{\sum_{k=1}^{T} D_k^i} \tag{4}$$

Equations (3) and (4) are crucial for understanding the channels through which credit and interest rate risk impact on a security. First, both the expected risk premium and the expected default-free yield curve depend on a common set of macroeconomic risk factors. And unexpected changes in the macro factors therefore impact both credit and interest rate risk. Second, unexpected movements in the default-free yield curve do change borrowers' and the bank's own credit risk.[7]

It follows that when economic conditions change, the discount factors (D_{t+k}) of a security will adjust instantaneously to reflect changes in the yield curve, and in the security's LGD and PD. But as coupon rates remain fixed until the security is re-priced, the economic value of the security will diverge from face value. Economic and face value will be equal again only when the security can be re-priced, as coupon payments will then reflect the new economic environment.

These insights also apply to the whole portfolio of the bank. But while the economic value will reflect all changes in economic conditions instantaneously, income will adjust sluggishly depending on the re-pricing characteristics of the bank's assets, liabilities and off-balance sheet items.

The economic value of the bank, EVB, is the economic value of its assets (EVA) minus the economic value of its liabilities (EVL):

$$EVB_t = EVA_t - EVL_t \quad \text{with} \quad EVA_t = \sum_{i=1}^{N} EVA_t^i \text{ and } EVL_t = \sum_{j=1}^{M} EVL_t^j \tag{5}$$

N refers to the number of different assets on the bank's balance sheet and M to the number of different liabilities.

From a regulatory perspective it is not the economic value of liabilities but the banks' ability to repay liabilities at par when due which matters most. Therefore, our first condition to judge the riskiness of a bank is to calculate

---

[7] There may also be a feedback from credit risk to interest rates. Such an effect should, however, partially be embedded in the macro model used to simulate the systematic risk factors in the following.

whether the economic value of assets falls below the face value of liabilities, with $FVL_t = \sum_{j=1}^{M} L_t^i$.

10.2.2 Short- medium-term stability criteria

An economic value condition is not a sufficient metric to assess banks' stability. Whereas the economic value may suggest that the long-term health of the bank is not threatened by an unexpected macro shock, the bank may still be undercapitalised in the short- to medium-term. This provides an important dimension to risk assessment as an undercapitalised bank may be subject to regulatory interventions or liquidity runs. We look at whether the bank's capital relative to its risk-weighted assets (RWA) remains above the regulatory minimum, k, in all periods in the medium term W:

$$\frac{SF_t}{RWA_t} > k \qquad \text{for all } t < W, \tag{6}$$

where SF is expected shareholder funds.[8] Under the Internal Ratings Based (IRB) approach the ratings change with the stress to reflect the changing PD and LGD for each of the asset classes (see Bank for International Settlements, 2004).

10.2.3 Projection of shareholder funds

As mentioned above, future coupons cannot be observed. We assume that at time zero the economic value of each asset is equal to its face value. This allows us to derive initial coupon payments. This assumption is applied every time an asset or a liability is re-priced. Four additional assumptions are needed in order to forecast SFs. First, exposures within an asset class are infinitely fine-grained, i.e., individual exposures within an asset class are small. This assumption is in line with the basic Basel 2 formula. Second, once deposits mature, depositors are willing to roll over their deposits with the same re-pricing characteristics unless the bank defaults on its obligations. Third, the bank does not actively manage its portfolio composition: once assets mature, the bank continues to invest in new projects with the same re-pricing and risk characteristics as matured assets. But the bank changes coupon rates to the extent that credit risk and default-free interest rates have changed to

---

[8] For simplicity we assume this is the only capital of the bank.

reflect the new economic environment. Fourth, the bank uses its free cash flows to pay back the most costly liabilities maturing, rather than invest in new assets or expand its balance sheet. If *SFs* decrease by more than write-offs, the bank is able to attract new interbank deposits. The behavioural assumptions are to a certain degree arbitrary but they are the simplest possible rules.

Deriving expected *SF* in each future period requires tracking expected net profits which either grow by retained earnings (i.e., profits after taxes and dividend payouts) or decrease by losses, in which case no taxes and dividends are paid.[9] *SFs* are therefore computed as:

$$SF_t = \theta \max(0; NP_t) + \min(0; NP_t) + SF_{t-1}, \tag{7}$$

with $\theta < 1$ given that the bank pays taxes as well as dividends.

Expected net profits (NP_t) between period $t-1$ and t are the sum of expected net-interest income plus other expected income (OI_t) minus expected write-offs (WR_t) and expected costs (C). Expected net-interest income in turn is the sum of the expected total cash flows the bank receives from all its assets (CFA_t), minus expected total cash flows it pays on its liabilities (CFL_t).

$$NP_t = (CFA_t - CFL_t) - WR_t + OI_t - Cost_t \tag{8}$$

Other income and costs are assumed constant.

10.3 Building blocks of the stress test

This section discusses the main building blocks of the macro stress test using the framework presented so far.

10.3.1 The hypothetical bank

We have constructed a hypothetical but realistic bank with five asset classes, three liability classes, shareholder funds and interest rate swaps as off-balance sheet items (Table 10.1).

We allocate assets, liabilities and off-balance sheet items into five re-pricing buckets. The balance sheet is constructed such that shareholder funds, profitability (in terms of return on equity and on assets), the cost–income ratio and

---

[9] I.e., an implicit assumption that the bank pays dividends proportionally to its income as long as it is able to do so. Furthermore, it is assumed that losses cannot be carried forward to offset future taxes.

Table 10.1: A hypothetical balance sheet

	Time buckets						
	0–3 months	3–6 months	6–12 months	1–5 years	> 5 years	Non-interest bearing funds	Total
Assets							
Total loans and advances to banks	5,500	1,900	500	100	100	0	8,100
Total loans and advances to customers	86,900	12,200	5,000	17,800	12,300	0	134,200
Total households	44,700	10,600	2,400	10,600	5,600	0	73,900
Mortgage	24,600	9,800	1,200	7,200	2,400	0	45,200
Fixed-rate mortgages	0	0	1,200	7,200	2,400	0	10,800
Variable-rate mortgages	24,600	9,800	0	0	0	0	34,400
Credit cards	20,600	800	1,200	3,400	3,200	0	28,700
Total PNFC/NPISH[a]	42,200	1,600	2,600	7,200	6,700	0	60,300
Treasury bills and other debt securities	6,700	2,300	2,100	3,400	3,200	0	17,700
Total assets	99,100	16,400	7,600	21,300	15,600	0	160,000
Liabilities							
Total deposits by banks	17,900	1,290	250	100	150	0	19,691
Total deposits to customer accounts	88,000	2,610	3,000	2,700	200	6,000	102,509
Total households	44,000	1,305	1,500	1,350	100	3,000	
Total PNFC/NPISH[a]	44,000	1,305	1,500	1,350	100	3,000	
Debt-like instruments	18,850	2,850	2,850	3,190	1,260	0	29,000
Shareholders funds – equity						8,800	8,800
Total liabilities (excl shareholder funds)	124,750	6,750	6,100	5,990	1,610	6,000	151,200
Total liabilities	124,750	6,750	6,100	5,990	1,610	14,800	160,000
Off-balance sheet items	8,050	–8,050	100	–910	3,610		2,800
Interest rate sensitivity gap	–17,600	1,600	1,600	14,400	17,600		

[a] Private non-financial corporations (PNFC) and non-profit institutions serving households (NPISH).

the interest rate sensitivity gap match very closely an average commercial bank.

The shaded area in Table 10.1 is the part of the balance sheet typically taken into account in macroeconomic stress tests. The table highlights why simple macro stress tests may mis-estimate the risks to the bank as liabilities and off-balance sheet items are not taken into account. Furthermore, stress tests often do not account for the full re-pricing matrix for assets and liabilities.

10.3.2 Stress scenario and macro model

We consider a combination of three shocks originally used for the UK Financial Sector Assessment Program (FSAP) in 2002: a 12 per cent decline in UK residential and commercial property prices, a 1.5 per cent unanticipated increase in UK average earnings growth and a 15 per cent unanticipated depreciation in the trade-weighted sterling exchange rate. All the scenarios are run from 2005 Q1 and forecasted over a three-year horizon.

As with any other macro stress test a macroeconometric model is needed to capture the correlations between the macro data. We use the Bank of England Quarterly Model. As a baseline scenario we use the projections from the Bank of England Inflation Report in February 2005 with interest rates assumed to follow market expectations. The stress test scenario is fed through the Bank of England Quarterly Model. One of the key characteristics of this stress is that default-free interest rates, across all maturities, change quite significantly. It is also important to model the monetary policy reaction to the initial shock. In line with general macro stress-testing practices we assume a mechanical Taylor rule.

By using models linking the probability of default of different asset classes and the default-free term structure of interest rates to macro variables, allows us to undertake a scenario analysis and simulate the economic value as well as capital adequacy for normal and highly adverse economic conditions.

10.3.3 Credit risk models

We use a number of models to link PDs to macroeconomic variables. The models are described in Bunn *et al.* (2005). An example of such a mortgage PD equation is given by:

$$a_t = 1.23 + 0.30m_{t-1} + 0.086u_{t-1} - 1.06UD_{t-1} + 1.41a_{t-1}$$
$$- 0.51a_{t-2} - 0.52LF_t, \tag{9}$$

where a is the logarithm of mortgages in arrears of more than six months, m is mortgage income gearing, u is unemployment, UD is undrawn equity and

LF is the loan-to-value ratio of first-time borrowers. The *PD* of other asset classes is modelled by similar equations. The corporate *PD* model links the corporate liquidation rate to macro variables and the credit card *PD* model links credit card arrears of more than three months to macro variables. A key characteristic of these models is that interest-rate-sensitive variables, such as income gearing, are significant determinants of *PDs*.

In the base simulation, we assume that the *LGD* is fixed and not changing in the stress scenario. Slightly worse-than-average industry numbers suggest, we assume, that the *LGD* on interbank loans is 40 per cent, the *LGD* on mortgage loans is 30 per cent, the *LGD* on credit cards is 80 per cent and the *LGD* on corporate loans is 60 per cent. Below we analyse the impact of an increase in *LGD* in the stress scenario.

In the base simulation, the bank's own *PD* is not modelled. We assume that the risky interbank curve is forecasted simply by adding a constant spread to the default-free term structure of thirty basis points.

10.3.4 Model of the nominal default-free term structure

A model is needed to link the government, default-free, yield curve to macro variables. There are a number of different yield curve models that could be used. We use a term-structure model for the UK similar to the model proposed by Diebold *et al.* (2006) with three latent factors and three observable macroeconomic variables – GDP, inflation and policy interest rates. Estimating the term structure model on UK data and linking it to macro variables allow us to forecast the default-free yield curve across maturities up to ten years conditional on a given macro scenario. As we can see in Panel B in Figure 10.1, the stress scenario implies a very strong increase in the default-free term structure of interest rates across all maturities. As interest rates increase substantially the scenario also implies a strong increase in *PDs* on the bank's asset side. The increase is particularly strong for mortgage arrears.

10.4 Illustrative simulations

Based on the FSAP stress discussed above, this section illustrates how the bank's stability is affected by the shock given the set of assumptions described above. We also investigate the consequences of relaxing some of these assumptions.

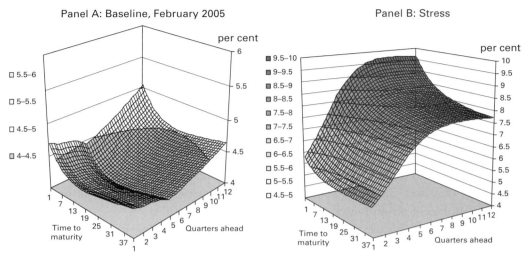

Figure 10.1   Evolution of the default-free term structure over the next twelve quarters in the base and stress scenario respectively

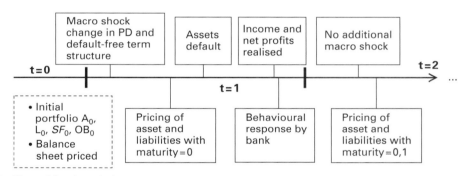

Figure 10.2   Steps of the stress test

10.4.1 Summary of the stress test and bank behaviour

Figure 10.2 summarises how the stress test works. In the initial period the bank is assumed to start operations. It has an initial portfolio of assets, liabilities and off-balance sheet items (Table 10.1). These are all priced to reflect the default-free term structure and the *PD*s conditional on the baseline macro scenario. The FSAP shock is assumed to take place immediately after. At the end of the first period the bank re-prices assets and liabilities that need to be re-priced. Due to the macro shock, some assets may default and net interest income is realised. We do not assume that there are any further macro shocks after the first period. In the following quarters more and more assets and liabilities gradually need re-pricing to reflect the changing macro environment.

10.4.2 Impact on capital adequacy

Judged from an economic value perspective, the macro stress does not appear large enough to threaten the stability of the hypothetical bank. The combined impact of credit and interest rate risk reduces the economic value of the bank by 21 per cent in the stress scenario. Although this represents a material fall, the net economic value of the bank remains positive.

Even though the economic value condition is not violated, it may still be the case that in the short or medium term the bank makes losses which could threaten its capital. For this reason we track the bank's expected capital adequacy over the next three years following the stress. While the capital ratios fall substantially, the macro stress does not appear to threaten the stability of the bank as the capital ratio always remains well above the regulatory minimum (Figure 10.3).

It is useful to decompose the change in the bank's profits following the stress scenario into expected write-offs and expected net-interest income.

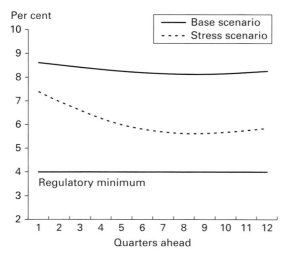

Figure 10.3   Shareholder funds as a proportion of risk-weighted assets

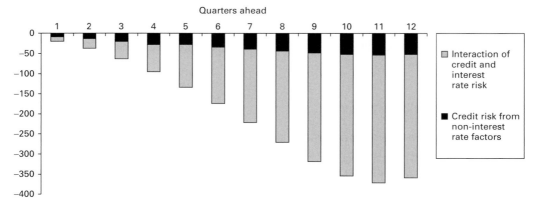

Figure 10.4   Impact on write-offs

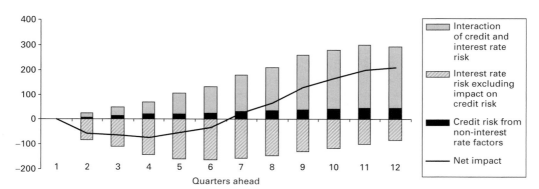

Figure 10.5   Impact on net-interest income

10.4.3 Impact on write-offs

Following the macro stress, expected write-offs increase (Figure 10.4), contributing negatively to the bank's profits. The largest impact occurs eleven quarters ahead. The figure also shows that most of the increase in expected write-offs arises as a direct effect of the sharp increase in default-free interest rates.

10.4.4 Impact on net-interest income

Next we consider the change in net-interest income caused by the macro shock. Figure 10.5 disentangles the complex effects of interest rate and credit risk on net-interest income. As gap analysis suggests, pure interest rate risk decreases net-interest income as margins are compressed. Pure interest rate risk, however, does not take account of the impact of interest rates on credit quality nor the interaction between interest rates and other credit risk determinants. The increase in credit risk has two opposing effects on net-interest income. On the one hand, net-interest income is negatively affected as borrowers default on coupon payments. On the other hand, there is a positive impact of credit risk on net-interest income because, over time, the bank increases the credit spread on loans that are re-priced. As we notice in Figure 10.5, this effect becomes particularly strong in the second year. However, it is fundamental to recognise that Figure 10.4 may provide an underestimation of the impact of the stress on net-interest income. This is because, as we will show in section 10.4.6, the positive impact of credit risk is inflated by assuming that the banks' own credit spreads remain constant.

10.4.5 Total impact

By combining the impact of changes in write-offs and net interest rates income with the FSAP stress we can obtain the combined impact on net profits in Figure 10.6. From Figure 10.6 it is evident that following the FSAP shock, the rise in interest rates is the main cause of the fall in net profits as it drives both the squeeze in net margins and the rise in write-offs.

Figures 10.4 and 10.5 clearly illustrate why credit and interest rate risk have to be assessed jointly and simultaneously for the whole portfolio. If the stress test only focused on the impact of credit risk on write-offs and ignored net interest income, it would underestimate the negative impact on net profits by

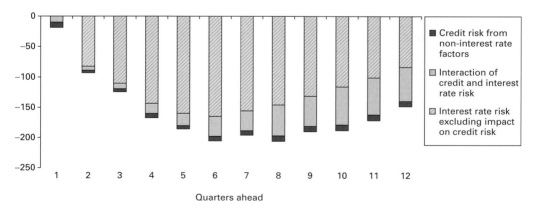

Figure 10.6   Impact on net profits

over 50 per cent. By contrast, in the third year the bank has re-priced a large proportion of its assets, leading to an off-setting increase in net interest income. Had the stress test only focused on the impact of the increasing write-offs, the negative impact on net profits would have been overestimated by nearly 100 per cent in the third year.

From Figure 10.6 we can also see that were the bank to assess the impact of higher interest rates on its book by purely undertaking a sensitivity analysis based on its re-pricing mismatch, it would underestimate the negative impact of the shock by around 30 per cent over the three-year period.

10.4.6 Sensitivity tests

We conduct a number of sensitivity tests to our assumptions. Compared to the above simulation we change three assumptions. First, we consider a scenario where while the increase in the default-free interest rates is passed on to the borrower as soon as for variable-rate mortgages, the credit spread on these assets cannot be changed until maturity.

Second, we allow the LGD to increase with the adverse macro conditions. While we have no model to link the LGD to macro variables, we simply increase the LGD for all asset classes by 33 per cent and assume it declines linearly to the long-run levels over the final 10 years.[10]

Finally, we allow the bank's own credit spreads to change with the stress. By using an ordered probit model (see Pagratis and Stringa, 2009), we link rating changes to macro factors and balance sheet variables. The implied rating is then mapped to spreads by using the average credit spread term structure of sterling corporate bonds between 2003 and 2006. If the bank's rating falls below a given threshold, we also assume that the bank no longer has access to the interbank market. In this case the bank will have to raise more funds through the debt market at a higher spread given the lower rating.

By changing these assumptions, we find that profits are significantly lower in the stress scenario. The bank is downgraded twice after the second year, which in turn implies that it has to pay a higher spread in the debt market. Following an increase in the cost of debt the bank incurs losses in the third year. But, the bank capital adequacy continues to remain above the 4 per cent threshold (Figure 10.7).

---

[10] An increase of around 33 per cent is a reasonable assumption consistent with the findings of Frye (2003).

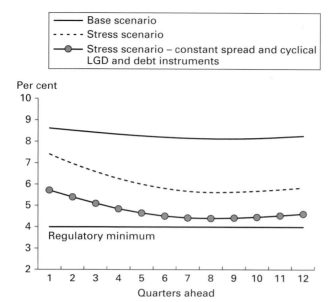

Figure 10.7   Capital adequacy with debt, constant spreads and cyclical loss given default (LGD)

10.5 Future challenges to capture integration in macro stress tests

We have discussed a stress test to assess the complex interactions between credit and interest rate risk and their impact on the stability of a bank in the short, medium and long term. A number of challenges remain for macro-economic stress-testing.

First, in our framework we do not consider liquidity risk. For example, in a severe macroeconomic stress, depositors could withdraw their deposits even if the bank's capital remains above the regulatory minimum. Incorporating the likelihood of a bank run conditional to the macro stress could be very useful given the long history of bank runs from the Dutch Tulip manias (1634–7) and the British South Sea Bubble (1717–19), to the US savings and loan crisis of the 1980s and 1990s and to the more recent examples following the credit shock begun in the second half of 2007.

Second, a bank's liquidity position also depends on the availability of credit in the interbank market. Hence it would be important to get a better understanding of how interbank lending changes over the economic cycle and how access to the interbank market depends on a bank's own *PD* and rating. The developments in the credit markets since August 2007 emphasise the importance of this point.

Third, it would be interesting to allow the bank to actively manage its portfolio to maximise its profits. This, however, will not be a straightforward exercise. Finally, it would be useful to get a better understanding of how demand for loans changes with the economic cycle. Rather than assuming that loans rollover once re-priced, it would be important to have a model where the demand for loans changes with the adverse macro environment. While there may be a large literature on each of the above topics, it would be useful if it could be drawn together to get a better understanding of risks to banks.

10.6 Conclusions

Credit and interest rate risk are the two most important risks faced by commercial banks. Given that they are intrinsically related, they cannot be measured separately. Many studies focus only on the combined impact of interest rate risk and default risk on assets. But a bank's profitability and net worth depend not only on default risk of assets but also on the overall credit quality, liabilities and off-balance sheet items as well as the re-pricing characteristics of its banking book.

Understanding these interactions is an important challenge for macro stress-testing. Measuring the combined impact of credit and interest rate risk on banks' profitability requires a consistent framework that allows us to detect the complex relation between the profitability of a bank and various risks. This chapter illustrated a framework that can be used to compute a bank's economic value as well as its short to medium term profitability and capital adequacy. An application illustrated why it is fundamental to assess the impact of interest rate and credit risk jointly on assets, liabilities and off-balance sheet items.

While the framework is relatively simple, it provides a tool to understand the combined impact on banks of different risks. The chapter also discusses a number of extensions that could be explored to get an even better understanding of the risks to banks.

REFERENCES

Bank for International Settlements (2004), *International Convergence of Capital Measurement and Capital Standards*, Basel.

Barnhill, T. M Jr and W. F. Maxwell (2002), 'Modelling Correlated Market and Credit Risk in Fixed Income Portfolios', *Journal of Banking and Finance*, 26, 347–74.

Barnhill, T. M. Jr, P. Papapanagiotou and L. Schumacher (2001), 'Measuring Integrated Market and Credit Risk in Bank Portfolios: an Application to a Set of Hypothetical Banks Operating in South Africa', *Milken Institute*.

Bunn, P., A. Cunningham and M. Drehmann (2005), 'Stress Testing as a Tool for Assessing Systemic Risk', *Bank of England Financial Stability Review*, June, 116–26.

Chen, C. and A. Chan (1989), 'Interest Rate Sensitivity, Asymmetry and Stock Returns of Financial Institutions', *Financial Review*, 24 (3), 457–73.

Curry, T. and L. Shibut (2000), 'The Cost of the Saving and Loan Crisis: Truth and Consequences', *FDIC Banking Review*, 13, 26–35.

Diebold, F. X. and C. Li (2006), 'Forecasting the Term Structure of Government Bond Yields', *Journal of Econometrics*, 130, 337–64.

Drehmann, M., S. Sorensen and M. Stringa (2008), 'The Integrated Impact of Credit and Interest Rate Risk on Banks: an Economic Value and Capital Adequacy Perspective', *Bank of England Working Paper*, 339.

Duffie, D. and K. J. Singleton (2003), *Credit Risk*, Princeton University Press.

English, W. B. (2002), 'Interest Rate Risk and Bank Net Interest Rate Margin', *BIS Quarterly Review*, December, 67–82.

Flannery, M. J. and C. M. James (1984), 'The Effect of Interest Rate Changes on the Common Stock Return of Financial Institutions', *Journal of Finance*, 39 (4), 1141–53.

Fraser, D. R., J. Madura and R. A. Wigand (2002), 'Sources of Bank Interest Rate Risk', *The Financial Review*, 37 (3), 351–67.

Frye, J. (2003), *LGD in High Default Years*, Federal Reserve Bank of Chicago, mimeo.

IFRI–CRO Forum (2007), *Survey on Economic Capital Practice and Applications*, International Financial Risk Institute (IFRI) and Institute of the Chief Risk Officers (CRO).

Jarrow, R. M. and S. M. Turnbull (2000), 'The Intersection of Market and Credit Risk', *Journal of Banking and Finance*, 24, 271–99.

Jarrow, R. M. and D. R. van Deventer (1998), 'Integrating Interest Rate Risk and Credit Risk in Asset and Liability Management', in *Asset and Liability Management: the Synthesis of New Methodologies*, Risk Books.

Maes, K. (2004), 'Interest Rate Risk in the Belgian Banking Sector', *National Bank of Belgium Financial Stability Review*, June, 157–79.

Pagratis, P. and M. Stringa (2009), 'Modelling Bank Credit Ratings: a Structural Approach to Moody's Credit Risk Assessment', *International Journal of Central Banking*, forthcoming.

Sorge, M. (2004), 'Stress-testing Financial Systems: an Overview of Current Methodologies', *BIS Working Paper*, 165.

Staikouras, S. K. (2006), 'Financial Intermediaries and Interest Rate Risk: II', *Financial Markets, Institutions and Instruments*, 15 (5), 225–72.

Voupt, J. V. and D. M. Wright (1996), 'An Analysis of Commercial Bank Exposures to Interest Rate Risk', *Federal Reserve Bulletin*, 77, 625–37.

11 Stress-testing linkages between banks in the Netherlands

Iman van Lelyveld, Franka Liedorp and Marc Pröpper[*]

11.1 Introduction

Assessment of the stability of the financial sector is well established in the Netherlands. Spurred by the International Monetary Fund's (IMF) Financial Sector Assessment Program (FSAP) in 2004 and by increased attention for financial stability, as witnessed by the creation of a separate financial stability division at the central bank (De Nederlandsche Bank, DNB), many issues have been studied.

An example is the analysis conducted and reported in the bi-annual *Overview of Financial Stability* in the Netherlands, highlighting *inter alia* operational problems in payment systems and the effect of (failing) credit risk transfer on the soundness of financial firms. Sometimes such analyses come eerily close to reality, as was the case with the securitisation scenario computed in mid-2007 (DNB, 2008). In this scenario banks were asked to compute the cost of taking their most recent securitisation back on the book. Liquidity effects found in this scenario were limited because of the short time horizon considered. In reality, in the late summer of 2007, the vulnerability of banks with the so-called originate-to-distribute model, in which banks securitise issued loans and sell them to interested investors via special legal entities, emerged prominently. Rising sub-prime mortgage default rates and growing doubts about the nature and value of the assets of special legal entities led to widespread downgrading of structured credit products containing such loans. This in turn caused the market financing of these entities to evaporate, generating uncertainty about possible draw downs of credit lines at sponsor banks. Indeed, some banks had to take the securitised loans back on their balance sheets. Also markets for other structured credit products dried up,

---

[*] De Nederlandsche Bank. The contents of this chapter reflect the opinions of the authors and do not necessarily reflect the views of De Nederlandsche Bank.

contributing to the uncertainty about valuations. Internationally, many banks were confronted with the impact of the turmoil, putting their liquidity and solvency positions under pressure.

Another example is the ongoing analysis of Dutch banks as operating in a network; this will be the focus of the current chapter. In this type of analysis we study interrelationships between participating banks. Naturally, understanding the risks in individual institutions is important as well, but this is not the focal point here. We will discuss two related examples of such network analyses: the interbank loan market and the interbank large value payment system.

The first analysis considers the contagion effects of bank defaults in the interbank market. In this market banks buy and sell liquid funds which are largely unsecured and of a short-term nature. Given the large notional values even small probabilities of default would introduce considerable risk into the system. Using various methods the linkages between banks are estimated. Given a matrix of the linkages, each of the banks is toppled in turn. The impact on other banks and the banking system as a whole upon this failure is analysed. For instance, the number and type of banks that fail following the first bankruptcy is measured, as well as the losses in terms of total assets.

In the second type of analysis the network topology of large value payments between Dutch banks in the TARGET system is considered.[1] We will briefly discuss the various network measures available and then turn to a sensitivity analysis. We will, for example, remove some of the banks (nodes) from the network and see how this affects the structure of the remaining network.

The setup of this chapter is straightforward. We first provide a brief overview of the Dutch banking sector as a background to the next two sections. These sections will, in turn, discuss the interbank loan market and the interbank payments network. Finally, we conclude and discuss the results of these two interrelated analyses.

11.2 The Dutch financial landscape

The final decades of the twentieth century saw a distinct change in the Dutch financial landscape. Globalisation, conglomeration, the blurring of boundaries between banking, insurance and securities activities, the single market for financial services in the European Union and the birth of the euro, all changed the arena. The liberalisation of capital markets in the Netherlands in

---

[1] Trans-European Automated Real-time Gross Settlement Express Transfer system.

the 1980s had eliminated restrictions on the cross-border activities of financial institutions. Subsequent developments in information and communication technology made these activities economically profitable. However, in order to be successful players in a global financial market, the banks in the Netherlands had to realise economies of scope and scale, first nationally and then internationally. Growth was stimulated by the abolishment in 1990 of the ban on banking–insurance mergers, paving the way for the creation of large financial conglomerates. Immediately after the prohibition was lifted, a process of mergers and acquisitions ensued (Van der Zwet, 2003). In fact, the Netherlands was one of the pioneers in the area of 'bancassurance'.[2] Growth was not only realised cross-sector but also cross-border by expanding international activities.

The banking sector is important for the Netherlands. Total banking sector assets are almost six times gross domestic product (GDP), a ratio which is among the highest in Europe. In terms of Tier-1 equity, the largest Dutch banks also feature in the top twenty-five of the world. In addition, the banking sector in the Netherlands is very concentrated. The largest three banks hold three quarters of total savings and deposits. Other measures of bank activity, like total assets or income, show similar results. Nevertheless competition, especially in the residential mortgage market, is intense.

Dutch banks are relatively internationally oriented. About two-fifths of total assets are held in foreign countries, while more than half of the consolidated income is earned outside the Netherlands.

The fact that the market is concentrated and firms are large, implies first of all that prudential concerns very quickly turn into financial stability concerns. This has a number of consequences. First of all, given the blurring of boundaries between financial sectors and products in the Netherlands since 1990, it was obvious that more cooperation was needed between the Dutch supervisors, both in the area of prudential supervision and in that of conduct-of-business supervision. An important reason for cooperation is that sectoral regulation might fail to capture the risk characteristics of a financial conglomerate as a whole. Financial conglomerates call for a consolidation of prudential supervision. Moreover, the increase in the number of financial conglomerates in the Netherlands has been accompanied by a blurring of the boundaries between traditionally distinct products. A specific

---

[2] The 'bancassurance' model has received mixed support. In earlier years firms like Citigroup expanded across sectors, while recently there seems to be a trend to roll back such diversifying acquisitions. See Van Lelyveld and Knot (2008) for an analysis of the value effect of cross-sectoral M&As.

example for the Netherlands is a mortgage combined with a unit-linked life insurance policy; this hybrid financial product embodies banking, securities and insurance components. A harmonised supervisory approach towards complex products with mixed features safeguards the level playing field. Similarly, adequate conduct-of-business supervision requires that for similar products and markets a similar regime is applicable, regardless of the sector of the supplier.

Second, especially in a highly concentrated banking system as that of the Netherlands, it is in practice difficult to draw a line between the responsibility for systemic stability, including the function of lender of last resort, and that for prudential supervision. Recent experiences have shown that this is an issue in other countries as well. Moreover, it is no coincidence that with the development of new, complicated products and the intensification of cross-sector and cross-border linkages, the attention for financial stability issues and the interplay between macro- and micro-prudential risks has increased. In view of the high degree of concentration in the banking sector, systemic and prudential supervision are appropriately placed within the central bank.

11.3 Interbank loan market

11.3.1 Review of the literature

There is a small but growing body of literature modelling the interbank loan market. Basically the approach consists of taking the matrix of all bilateral exposures between banks and then letting one (or more) banks default, either randomly or dependent on a model which assesses banks' sensitivity to some risk. Authors have, mainly driven by data availability, taken various approaches to determining the matrix. A good review is for instance provided by Upper (2007); this section will therefore only provide a concise summary.[3]

The analysis of the structure of the interbank loan market as a source of financial sector contagion is relatively recent. Theory discerns both direct and indirect contagion (De Bandt and Hartmann, 2001), based on the type of linkages between institutions. Direct contagion results from direct (financial) linkages between banks, such as credit exposures. Indirect contagion is the result of expectations about a bank's health and about the resilience of the sector, given developments at another bank. The exposure of banks to similar

---

[3] This section builds on Van Lelyveld and Liedorp (2006).

events, such as asset price fluctuations, does not create a direct link between banks and hence cannot result in direct contagion. Although these two contagion channels can work separately, direct contagion and indirect contagion are obviously not mutually exclusive and may even reinforce each other. For instance, one bank failure may lead to further bank failures through direct linkages and may induce further bankruptcies if depositors *assume* the existence of linkages between banks (regardless of whether these assumptions are true or not). In this section, we focus on direct linkages – or direct contagion – between banks.

In the literature it has become clear that the structure of the interbank loan market is of crucial importance for contagion. It determines the impact of a shock to an individual bank on the entire system of banks. Allen and Gale (2000) distinguish three types of interbank market structures. First, they define a complete structure as one where banks are symmetrically linked to all other banks in the system. Second, an incomplete market structure exists when banks are only linked to neighbouring banks. A special case of this structure is introduced by Freixas *et al.* (2000): the money centre structure. In this structure, the money centre bank is linked symmetrically to the other banks, while the latter have no links among themselves. Third, an incomplete market structure is defined as one where two or more separate (but internally connected) markets exist simultaneously. Because of diversification effects a complete market structure may give the highest level of insurance against an unexpected liquidity shock hitting an individual bank. However, such a structure might also propagate shocks more easily through the system of banks, as shocks will not remain isolated at one bank or at a cluster of banks.

Empirical studies that try to model the structure of the interbank market and (the impact of) contagion risks have been carried out for several countries. These studies include Elsinger, *et al.* (2006), Degryse and Nguyen (2007), Upper and Worms (2004), Van Lelyveld and Liedorp (2006), Mistrulli (2007), Blåvarg and Nimander (2002) and Wells (2002) to mention just a few. Most of these studies use balance sheet data or large exposures data as proxies to determine the interbank market structure. Blåvarg and Nimander (2002) and Mistrulli (2007) use reported bilateral data to model contagion risk. Mistrulli (2007) concludes for the Italian case that estimates based on aggregate data may underestimate contagion risk.[4] Mueller (2006) explores the Swiss

---

[4] However, this conclusion is based on a comparison of the results using on the one hand maximum entropy (banks' exposures are evenly spread over all other banks in the system) and on the other hand the reported bilateral exposure data. Given the presence of a money centre bank structure in the Italian

interbank market using data from the Swiss national bank. Applying network analysis, she discerns systemically important banks and possible contagion paths.[5] Furfine (1999) estimates contagion risk in the US interbank market, but uses bilateral data from the payments system Fedwire to build the interbank market structure. The majority of these studies finds that contagion effects are small, especially since high loss rates are rare.

The work described below relates to these studies in several ways. For one, we based our analysis on balance sheet data and large exposures data as well. Furthermore, we used different loss rates to test the strength of the system under different shocks. However, we describe a second variant in which we incorporated the input of banks themselves with respect to their bilateral exposures. This provides the opportunity to test the usefulness of the large exposures data for estimating the interbank market structure.

11.3.2 Data description

As is common in this type of approach (Upper, 2007), we first constructed a matrix of interbank exposures. The structure of interbank linkages between N banks would then be fully represented by this NxN matrix of exposures (see Figure 11.1). The columns represent banks' lending while the rows represent banks' borrowing. Hence, the matrix elements x_{ij} in Figure 11.1 represent the liabilities of bank i towards bank j. The row and column totals (i.e., each bank's total interbank lending and borrowing, a_j and l_i) are known. Clearly, a bank does not lend to itself: the cells on the main diagonal from upper left to bottom right are all zeros.[6]

In the Netherlands it is difficult to estimate the cells of the matrix, as there is no credit register providing bilateral exposures. An often-used alternative source of information is the large exposures reporting. Based on such reports and using the assumption that the distribution of large exposures over interbank counterparties is the same as in the interbank market itself, we can estimate a lending matrix using the RAS algorithm.[7] A specific contribution of our study was to compare the outcomes based on the large exposures data to

---

interbank market, it is clear that the assumption of maximum entropy, or maximum spread, becomes less appropriate.

[5] Measuring, for example, the number and size of interbank linkages, the distance from other banks, the importance of counterparts and the position in the network. See also the second part of this chapter which discusses a similar approach applied to the Netherlands.

[6] Moreover, not all banks need to be both a lender and a borrower at the same time. In fact, a bank need not be active in the interbank market at all.

[7] Blien and Graef (1997).

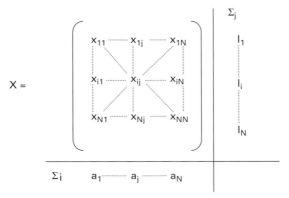

Figure 11.1   The interbank lending matrix
Source: Upper and Worms (2002).

the outcomes based on data requested specifically from the ten largest institutions. The concentrated nature of the Dutch banking sector, as described earlier, assures coverage of over 90 per cent of total assets.[8] Given these two data sources, we constructed two matrices and used these for our scenario analysis as described in section 11.3.3.

11.3.3 Scenario analysis

Our basic approach is to assume that one of the participating banks suddenly defaults and that consequently (part of) the exposure on this particular bank become worthless. If the exposure of another bank to this failed bank is larger than its Tier-1 capital, this second bank defaults as well (we call this the first round). Then, if the combined exposure of another bank to these two or more failed banks is again larger than its Tier-1 capital, this bank also defaults (we call this the second round). This process continues until no additional banks default. In this way the default at one bank could lead to a contagious series of defaults at other banks. As there are no reliable data on the loss rate in case of default, we vary over several loss rates (25 per cent, 50 per cent, 75 per cent and 100 per cent). For each individual bank there is a scenario in which it suddenly defaults. Alternatively, there are scenarios in which (geographical) groups of banks initially default.

---

[8] For the banks not included in the sample (i.e., the smaller banks) we assumed that bilateral exposures would be distributed according to maximum entropy. We also estimated a maximum entropy matrix without any prior information as discussed in Van Lelyveld and Liedorp (2006).

Completely idiosyncratic shocks are rare and thus our assumption of a single bank failure due to some exogenous shock might be a relatively strong one. It seems more likely that several banks will be simultaneously affected in case of a shock. Moreover, bankruptcy is often preceded by a period of distress and thus other banks are able to take measures in time. In contrast, the nature of operational risk events is different as exemplified by the Barings case. There, activities of a single trader led to the demise of the entire bank. In this case, the factor that triggered the failure was idiosyncratic to Barings bank, and other banks were not directly influenced by this shock. Further, such a severe scenario analysis may be useful in determining the sequence and path of possible contagion. Modelling the probability of default conditional on the state of the economy and/or crisis would be a possible future improvement (Elsinger *et al.* 2006).

We will not present the full analysis here but provide a flavour of the type of analysis conducted and then turn to the conclusions in section 11.3.4. As described earlier, we use large exposure data and survey data. The scenario analysis gives us a distribution of possible outcomes. The left panel of Figure 11.2 shows the mean of the distribution of the cumulative number of failed banks per round and per loss rate (based on the large exposures data), while the right panel shows the mean of the cumulative assets of these failed banks per round and per loss rate.[9] Note that 'assets affected' is defined as the total assets of the failed banks. A bank may suffer losses following a bankruptcy, but these losses are not included in the measure of assets affected if it does not fail consequently. However, every loss does make the respective bank more vulnerable to subsequent losses in future rounds. For both panels the cumulative effects obviously increase when the loss rate is increased. When we use a 75 per cent loss rate the contagion path lasts longer, as there are more rounds compared to the use of lower loss rates. With a higher loss rate (100 per cent), the failure of all banks that can be affected has already been triggered earlier in the process, such that all banks that can be affected have already been affected in previous rounds. Hence, no banks are left to be affected in the higher rounds.

We then compared the results based on the large exposures data with the results using the survey data, and found that the large exposures data provided a good approximation to the survey – or real – data. Other measures of interest (not shown here) include the relationship between the size (total assets) of the

---

[9] The initially defaulting bank is excluded in these measures.

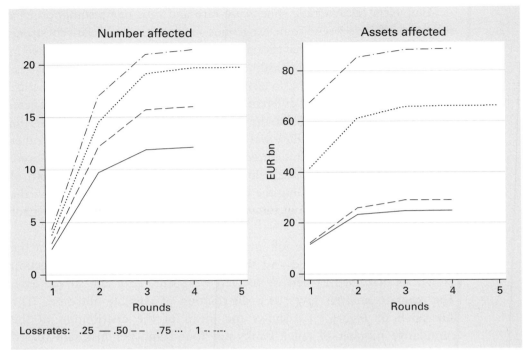

Figure 11.2 Cumulative effects of simulated failures
Source: Van Lelyveld and Liedorp (2006).

failing bank and the size of the contagion effects: do bigger banks cause higher distress? Further, we looked at the sensitivity of our outcomes to the use of different loss rates in more detail. Finally, we analysed which geographical region posed the biggest risk to the stability of the Dutch interbank market. This risk measure turns out to be the most relevant for our analysis, as exposures on foreign counterparties in certain geographical regions (specifically Europe or the US) have the largest impact on the Dutch banking sector. If these scenarios trigger the failure of even one of the large banks in the system, then the highest number of banks and the most assets are affected.

11.3.4 Results

Our analysis showed that the most important risks in the Dutch interbank loan market stem from exposures on foreign counterparties, in particular European and North American counterparties. This result holds regardless of the information source used. The national interbank market only seems to carry systemic risks if a large bank fails, although even in this extreme and unlikely event not all the remaining banks are affected. In fact, none of the large bank failures trigger the failure of another large bank. The Dutch banking system hence cannot be pictured by one single line of dominos and the amounts outstanding per counterparty are relatively small (i.e., losses are limited).

The analysis also showed that the distribution of the exposures in accordance with maximum entropy (maximum dispersion) is not appropriate for estimating bilateral exposures in a concentrated market, such as the Dutch market. In addition, for an accurate assessment of the risks in the interbank market, there is no clear advantage in using either the large exposures data report or survey data. Both data sources give an adequate and similar overview of the systemic risks in the interbank market. At the individual bank level, however, there are material differences. Working from the premise that the survey data are a more reliable source of information since they have been specially requested, this implies that the large exposures data reports are not well suited for monitoring the individual interbank exposures of a particular bank. However, for estimates of contagion effects at the macro level, the large exposures data form an appropriate (and easier) data source.

The most important conclusion, based on the research presented, is that in order to make the analyses more informative, information about foreign exposures is necessary. As the largest contagion effect flows outside the domestic market, we do not know how this affects the foreign counterparties and what reciprocal effect this may have on Dutch banks. Other studies in this area suffer from the same issue. In an increasingly integrated market, like the interbank loan market, it might therefore be fruitful to merge the various analyses.

On the whole, our simulations suggest that contagious defaults are unlikely, although we cannot rule them out completely. An important caveat is that we do not model behavioural reactions. Especially in a crisis that is developing over time, it is important to model the reaction of participating banks to market events. Similarly, we did not attach any probabilities to the default of banks.

11.4 Payment networks[10]

A different perspective on the linkage between banks in the Netherlands is provided by analysing the patterns in payment systems. Here, we focus on the

---

[10] This section draws on Pröpper *et al.* (2008).

Dutch large value payment system which is operated by the central bank and forms part of the European system for euro-denominated payments. In this payments system the participants, mainly banks, transfer large value funds to each other. These payments reflect economic transactions by bank clients (e.g., an employer who transfers wages to employees) or from the banks' own accounts (e.g., interbank loans). An important difference with the approach discussed in section 11.3 is that the information provided by the payments stream is much more ethereal. In the interbank loan market banks are linked as long as a bank has an exposure on another bank. In payment streams the link between banks ceases to exist as soon as the payment is settled. Presently this generally occurs quite rapidly and without recourse.

This section highlights the main aspect of a study into the Dutch payment system. It will first provide a description using conventional measures and then turn to network analysis measures. We will then show how these measures can be used to, for instance, analyse the failure of important banks or to analyse the 2007 sub-prime turmoil.

11.4.1 Traditional descriptions of payment networks

Traditionally, networks have been described in terms of, for instance, the volume of transactions, the value transferred or the number of participants, and for many purposes this is adequate. In terms of these metrics, the Dutch system is an active, medium-sized network and thus exemplary for many smaller countries. The figures in Table 11.1 show that the European TARGET and US Fedwire systems are both large payment systems of the same order of magnitude. The Dutch large value payment system (Top) is clearly smaller, although the average transaction value is relatively high.

11.4.2 Network measures

Network analysis, which is of a more recent date, considers not so much the individual banks or nodes, the technical term used for network participants, but the relation between these nodes. In terms of friendships, for instance, the focus would not be so much on individuals but on their relationships with others. How many people do they know and how many people do they, in turn, know? How often do they interact with them? Using what medium? Are friends of those friends, friends as well? Measures have been developed

Table 11.1 Key daily payment characteristics for Top (NL), TARGET (EU), CHAPS (UK) and Fedwire (US)

	Top	TARGET	CHAPS	Fedwire
Participants	155	10,197	N/A	6,819
Transactions (x1,000)	151 (18.1)	312	116	519
Value (€bn)	151 (173)	1,987	297	1,634
Trans. value (€m)	9.9 (9.5)	6.4	2.6	3.1

Source: Top (DNB), Target (ECB bluebook), CHAPS and Fedwire (BIS). The period is 2005 except for TOP where the data are for June 2005–May 2006. The TOP system is with evening settlement in brackets.

for friendship networks and other types of networks and we will discuss a selected number below (see Box 11.1).[11]

As mentioned above, the time dimension is important in the analysis of payment networks. In a short time span, not many transactions will take place. The number of connections (the degree), or any other measure of being connected, will thus be low as well. As the observation period increases the number of transactions recorded will increase. Typically, network measures are being computed using a one-day snapshot of the data. It is not clear, however, that this is the optimal period. In Figure 11.3, we show the development over time (x-axis in minutes of observations) of several important network measures. Note that the x-axis, and in some cases the y-axis as well, is on a logarithmic scale.

Figure 11.3 shows that major developments take place mostly in the first hour of network formation, consequent growth (up to one day) is more gradual. The *size* of the network (top left) measured 88 ± 6 nodes on an hourly basis and 129 ± 5 nodes on a daily basis. *Connectivity* (top right), the fraction of actual to possible links, provides a better view on the relative growth of nodes and links. This measure shows that the network remains very sparse over all time periods. Connectivity rapidly declines from 0.16 ± 0.12 after 1 minute to a minimum of 0.04 ± 0.01 after approximately 30 to 60 minutes, to increase thereafter at a lower pace to 0.07 ± 0.00 after 1 day and 0.12 after 257 days. The explosion of nodes in the first hour suppresses connectivity, because the growth of links does not keep up with the growth of nodes. After one hour, however, the situation reverses. At all times the network keeps its low connectivity and remains far from connected. Even after 257 days 88 per cent of all theoretically

[11] See Dorogovtsev and Mendes (2003) for an overview of the methods used.

Box 11.1 Network properties

The most basic network properties are the number of *nodes (n)* and *links (l)*.[12] The former is often referred to as the *size* of the system. The relative number of links *l* to the possible number of links determines the network *connectivity (c)*. Alternatively, it is the probability of two nodes sharing a link. *Reciprocity*, finally, is the fraction of links with a link in the opposite direction. A *path* is an alternating sequence of connected nodes and links that starts and terminates at a node. If all links represent unit length, *path length* l_{ij} between nodes *i* and *j* is the length of the shortest path between the nodes. Network *eccentricity (e)* is defined as the largest of the observed path lengths.

The number of links between one node *i* and other nodes determines the *node degree (k_i)*. In a directed network these connections consist of incoming and outgoing links, which respectively determine the *in-degree ($k_{in,i}$)*, the *out-degree ($k_{out,i}$)*, and *node degree (k_i)* by $k_i = k_{in,i} + k_{out,i}$. Every link contributes exactly one unit to both the out-degree of the node at which it originates and to the in-degree of the node at which it terminates. The *average degree (k_{avg})* of a network is the relative number of all links to all nodes. The *maximum in-degree* and the *maximum out-degree* are determined by the maximum degree values and the maximum deviations (to the upside) from the respective average degree values.

Degree correlations between neighbouring nodes provide additional information on the network structure. In an uncorrelated network the degree of one node is independent of its neighbouring nodes: being popular does not mean your friends are popular as well. Degree correlations therefore provide information on whether nodes are generally connected to nodes with comparable degree, to nodes of different degree, or if there is no relation at all.

Another concept to describe the correlation between nodes is the *clustering coefficient (C_i)*, which gives the probability that two neighbours of a node share an undirected link among themselves. It marks the density of connections in the direct neighbourhood of a node (cliquishness). The meaning of the coefficient becomes particularly clear in a social context where it is the extent of the mutual acquaintance of friends. The clustering coefficient ranges from 0 for a tree network to 1 for a completely connected network.

possible links have not been used for a single transaction. *Reciprocity*, the fraction of links with a link in the opposite direction, displays a rapid increase in the first hour to on average 0.44 and increases at a lower rate to on average 0.63 after one day. It means if there is a link in one direction a link in the opposite direction is very likely.

11.4.3 Sensitivity to shocks

Given the description of the network measures, we will now discuss how the network is affected if one (or more) participants are taken out of the system.

---

[12] See Dorogovtsev and Mendes (2003) and Soramäki, *et al.* (2007).

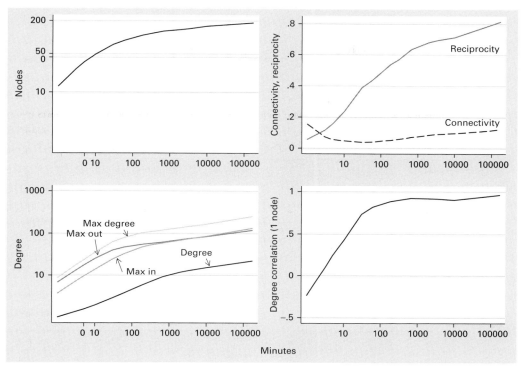

Figure 11.3   Selected network measures
Source: Pröpper *et al.* 2008.

As we cannot model adaptive behaviour, this is a static exercise. Removing a certain number of nodes will always, regardless of the order of taking them out, lead to the same result in the end. The ordering (or path dependence) of taking them out can reveal that certain nodes are particularly important to the system.

In Figure 11.4, we show the change in a number of measures (y-axis) after the removal of nodes, ordered from the most highly connected node ('−1') to lowly connected nodes. The network becomes smaller and even sparser as, for instance, shown by the *degree* values (top left panel). Further, it increases the path lengths between the remaining nodes. In the removal of the seventh node this phenomenon is outweighed by the accompanying loss of the single link nodes and the shortest paths between them and all other nodes. Specifically, the top right panel shows that *path length* and maximum path length, or *eccentricity*, increase from 2.2 to 2.5 and from 3.3 to 4.2, respectively. The bottom left corner shows that the local structure starts to break down.

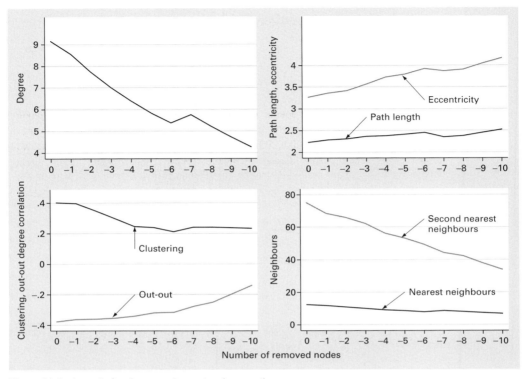

Figure 11.4 Impact of node removal on network properties
Source: Pröpper *et al.* (2008). The panels show (1) degree, (2) path length and eccentricity, (3) clustering and out-out degree correlation, and (4) nearest and second nearest neighbours (z1 and z2).

Clustering, or the local density of connections, decreases from 0.40 to 0.23. The removal of nodes two to four has a disproportionately negative impact on clustering in comparison to the other nodes. The *out-out degree correlation* increases more steadily from −0.38 to −0.14 (= loss of correlation).[13] The outcomes for *nearest neighbours* and *second nearest neighbours* confirm this breakdown in structure (bottom right panel).

The analysis shows that although the Dutch financial sector is quite concentrated, removing important banks does not produce the same cliff effects as would be the case in a typical centre–periphery structure. In such a structure, the removal of a bank in the periphery hardly affects the network, while the removal of the bank in the centre leads to an immediate breakdown of the structure.

[13] In-in degree correlation increases from −0.38 to −0.10. In-out degree correlation decreases from 0.93 to 0.59.

Box 11.2 The market turmoil in 2007

Network measures can also be useful to look at the effects of the turmoil which started in 2007 on the structure of bank relationships. Some previously liquid credit markets abroad have quickly dried up due to a loss of confidence between counterparties and we might see this reflected in payment patterns in the large value payment system. Payments are, after all, a mere reflection of economic agents' decisions and actions. To analyse whether market turbulence has affected the payments patterns we show selected measures in Figure 11.5. The dotted (solid) line shows 2006 (2007) data.[14] The vertical lines denote events which we considered negative or positive. We conclude that it has not *materially* affected the network structure of the payment system during the investigated period. Severe disruptions in the payment system would inevitably have shown up in the discussed measures. There does seem to be an effect on the level of the measures as the payment activity (not shown here) proved higher during the investigated turmoil period in 2007 than in the corresponding period in 2006. In addition, there does not seem to be an effect related to the positive and negative events.

These network measures are also useful to analyse real events in the financial sector, such as the 2007–8 sub prime crisis (see Box 11.2).

11.5 Conclusions

This chapter discussed two different approaches to gauge the risks in the Dutch financial markets. First, we analysed the interbank market, where banks extend short-term loans to each other. Then we turned our attention to the large value payment system. In the analyses we tried to uncover hidden risks by first unravelling the structure of the market and in particular the way the participants are linked to each other. We then conducted a number of tests to stress the structure. In the case of the interbank market we analysed what would be the result of the default of (groups of) banks. We included second round effects but did not model reactions of market participants. As reliable information on loss rates (given default) is not available, we computed our results subject to a range of loss rates. In the case of Dutch payment system analysis we conducted an experiment by removing one by one the most

---

[14] We have not yet extended this data period due to the computational burden.

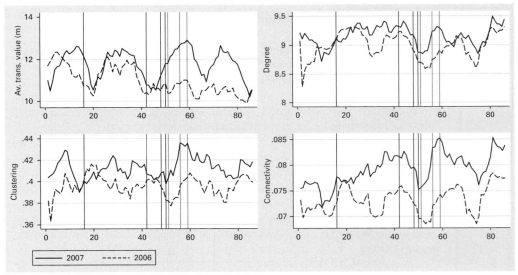

Figure 11.5 Development of a selection of traditional system measures and network properties over time
Source: Pröpper *et al.* (2008). The panels are (1) transaction value, (2) degree, (3) clustering and
(4) connectivity. To make the two sets of data comparable we started both series on the same day of the
week. Further, we dropped all days corresponding to Dutch public holidays. The series are five-day moving
averages.

important players. We also looked at the 'natural experiment' that the 2007–8
financial crisis has provided us.

While such analyses are extremely useful for assessing the stability of the
financial sector, there are important challenges in this area of research. As
noted above, we did not model participant reactions. It is, for instance, likely
that if banks observe another bank to be in trouble, they will try to reduce net
exposures on the bank in question, either by calling in loans or by borrowing
more from the bank. Modelling reaction functions, especially in times of
stress, is particularly difficult.[15] A second problem is that data collection is
generally organised within countries or regions. Information about exposures
generally stays within national jurisdictions. Payment systems may operate
across borders but information on individual payments is generally kept
within national boundaries. Thus, while financial markets become increasingly intertwined, data collection, and thus our ability to do wide-ranging
analyses, is lagging.

---

[15] A possible avenue could be the use of experimental economics as in Heijmans *et al.* (2008).

REFERENCES

Allen, F. and D. Gale (2000), 'Financial Contagion', *Journal of Political Economy*, 108, 1–33.

Blåvarg, M. and P. Nimander (2002), 'Interbank Exposures and Systemic Risk', *Sveriges Riksbank Economic Review*, 2, 19–45.

Blien, U. and F. Graef (1997), 'Entropy Optimizing Methods for the Estimation of Tables', in I. Balderjahn, R. Mathar and M. Schader, *Classification, Data Analysis and Data Highways*, (eds.), Springer Verlag.

De Bandt, O. and P. Hartmann (2001), 'Systemic Risk, A Survey,' *CEPR Discussion Paper Series*, 2634.

Degryse, H. and G. Nguyen (2007), 'Interbank Exposures, An Empirical Examination of Contagion Risk in the Belgian Banking System', *International Journal of Central Banking*, 3, 123–71.

DNB (2008), *Overview of Financial Stability in the Netherlands*.

Dorogovtsev, S. N. and J. F. F. Mendes (2003), *Evolution of Networks*. Oxford University Press.

Elsinger, H., A. Lehar and M. Summer (2006), 'Risk Assessment for Banking Systems', *Management Science*, 52, 1301–14.

Freixas, X., B. Parigi and J. C. Rochet (2000), 'Systemic Risk, Interbank Relations and Liquidity Provision by the Central Bank', *Journal of Money, Credit & Banking*, 3, 611–38.

Furfine, C. H. (1999), 'Interbank Exposures, Quantifying the Risk of Contagion', *BIS Working Paper*, 70.

Heijmans, R., R. Bosman, F. v. Winden and K. Abbink (2008), 'Stress Situations in Large Value Payment Systems, An Experimental Approach', mimeo.

Mistrulli, P. E. (2007), 'Assessing Financial Contagion in the Interbank Market, Maximum Entropy Versus Observed Interbank Lending Patterns', *Bank of Italy Working paper*, 641.

Mueller, J. (2006), 'Interbank Credit Lines as a Channel of Contagion', *Journal of Financial Services Research*, 29, 37–60.

Pröpper, M. H., I. P. P. Van Lelyveld, and R. H. Heijmans (2008), 'Towards a Network Description of Interbank Payment Flows', *DNB Working Paper Series*, 177.

Soramäki, K., M. L. Bech, J. Arnold, R. J. Glass and W. E. Beyeler (2007), 'The Topology of Interbank Payment Flows', *Physica A*, 379, 317–33.

Upper, C. (2007), 'Using Counterfactual Simulations to Assess the Danger of Contagion in Interbank Markets', *BIS Working Paper*, 234.

Upper, C. and A. Worms (2004), 'Estimating Bilateral Exposures in the German Interbank Market, Is There a Danger of Contagion?', *European Economic Review*, 48, 827–49.

Van der Zwet, A. (2003), 'The Blurring of Distinctions between Different Financial Sectors, Fact or Fiction?', *DNB Occasional Studies*, 2.

Van Lelyveld, I. P. P. and K. Knot (2008), 'Do Financial Conglomerates Destroy Value?', *Journal of Banking and Finance*, forthcoming.

Van Lelyveld, I. P. P. and F. R. Liedorp (2006), 'Interbank Contagion in the Dutch Banking Sector', *International Journal of Central Banking*, 2, 99–134.

Wells, S. (2002), 'UK Interbank Exposure, Systemic Risk Implications', *Financial Stability Review, Bank of England*, December, 175–82.

12 An integrated approach to stress-testing: the Austrian Systemic Risk Monitor (SRM)

Michael Boss, Gerald Krenn, Claus Puhr and Martin Summer[*]

12.1 Introduction

The Systemic Risk Monitor (SRM) is a quantitative risk assessment model that aims at a new approach to financial stability analysis for banking systems. The central idea is the combination of tools from modern risk management with a network model of interbank loans in a framework that can be applied to bank data usually available to central banks. The key innovations of the model include conceptual as well as applied aspects. The network perspective of the banking system constitutes the conceptual side, whereas the construction of an integrated framework that is also applicable in the daily work of an institution with the mandate to safeguard financial stability addresses the applied side. Combining together new and established concepts from risk management with real world applicability was the guiding principle behind the development of the SRM.

Why is there an interest in risk analysis for banks at a system level? And what additional insights can be gained from such an approach in contrast to traditional risk analysis with its focus on individual institutions? As seen in Chapter 11, looking at banks individually conceals two important sources of risk that can potentially result in the joint failure of banks and in extreme situations even a large-scale breakdown of financial intermediation: first, banks might have correlated exposures and an adverse economic shock may directly result in simultaneous multiple bank defaults; second, troubled banks may default on their interbank liabilities and hence cause other banks to default, triggering a domino effect. Large-scale breakdowns of a financial system – often described by the term systemic risk – are the cause of enormous economic and social

---

[*] Oesterreichische Nationalbank (OeNB). The views presented in the chapter are those of the authors and do not necessarily reflect those of the OeNB.

costs. The awareness that the major drivers of this risk are hidden at a single institution level spurred the initial interest in models like the SRM that permit a novel interpretation of readily available data in a way that indicates potential build up of systemic risk before a crisis materialises.

In order to integrate both causes of systemic risk, the SRM has to analyse market and credit risks of all banks simultaneously. At the same time financial linkages and their role in the propagation of shocks in the banking system have to be studied. The main challenge lies in finding a tractable way to model the integration of the two major sources of systemic risk. In the SRM framework this task is performed by the network model. Since the risk of bank defaults – in particular of joint defaults – is at the core of financial stability, the network model with its ability to distinguish default events that directly result from changes in risk factors from defaults that result indirectly from contagion through interbank relations is of central interest. Apart from analysing bank defaults, the SRM provides loss distributions for market risk, credit risk and contagion risk as well as for the combination of these risk categories.[1]

A model has of course another main advantage: it allows the assessment of situations that have not yet occurred. This includes severe experiments about situations of financial distress and crises. Having a clear idea about the implications of certain stress scenarios for the financial system adds significant value for an institution in charge of safeguarding financial stability.[2] Hence implementing an advanced tool for stress-testing the banking system was another reason for the development of the SRM by Austrian authorities.

This chapter gives an overview both of the theoretical as well as of the practical aspects of the SRM. Section 12.2 gives a descriptive account of the Austrian banking system and the supervisory framework. Section 12.3 discusses the theoretical framework of the SRM. Section 12.4 provides a detailed description of the data input and section 12.5 discusses the current applications of the model. Section 12.6 describes how the model output is used in the daily practice of the Oesterreichische Nationalbank (OeNB). Section 12.7 shows three stress-testing examples and the final section 12.8 draws conclusions.

---

[1] For a survey of related research, see Chapter 3.   [2] See also Chapter 7.

12.2 The Austrian banking system

12.2.1 Structure of the banking system

Austria, compared to other European countries, has one of the most densely populated banking systems. At end-2007 a total of 870 banks operated in Austria and held a consolidated balance sheet total of €1,073 bn. A still on-going concentration process has been observed in the past, which saw the total number of Austrian credit institutions decline from 995 at end-1997 to the current level, while total assets on an unconsolidated basis increased from €436 bn to €900 bn over the last ten years. This development was driven in particular by concentration in the tiered sectors of the Austrian banking system, which still account for the vast majority of Austrian banks in terms of licenses granted by the Austrian Financial Market Authority (FMA).[3] Table 12.1 gives an overview of the structure of the Austrian banking system in terms of sectors and size.

Within the SRM all Austrian banks are considered, with the exception of EU member state branch offices and banks reporting zero total assets due to the fact that they do not have any operational business though they are legally existing, which results in a total of 824 banks.

Another significant development during the last decade was the formation of clusters of smaller banks within the tiered sectors of the Austrian banking system that became increasingly tied to central institutions through cross-guarantee schemes. This development produced a few relatively large banking groups. Furthermore, the traditional multi-sector structure of the Austrian banking system – stemming from historical differences in lines of business and ownership – has changed significantly in recent years, and the vast majority of banks now effectively operate as universal banks. Finally, the most important development followed the economic stabilisation in Central, Eastern and South Eastern Europe (CESEE) at the turn of the millennium. Banking activities entered a path of sustained expansion, boosted by the resumption of robust economic growth and the anchor of European Union (EU) integration or proximity. EU-15 banks began to enter the markets in significant numbers, taking advantage of further large-scale privatisations. Austrian banks seized the opportunity of their early expansion and became some of the largest foreign investors in terms of control of total banking assets

---

[3] The tiered sectors are savings banks, as well as Raiffeisen and Volksbank credit cooperatives.

Table 12.1 The Austrian banking system at end-2007

Breakdown by sectors

	Joint stock banks and private banks	Savings banks	State mortgage banks	Raiffeisen credit cooperatives	Volksbank credit cooperatives	Building and loan associations	Special purpose banks	EU member state branch offices
Number of banks	51	56	11	558	69	4	93	28
Total assets (€bn)[a]	251	150	88	222	69	21	87	11

Breakdown by size

	Big banks	Large banks	Medium-sized banks	Small banks
Definition in terms of total assets	The 6 largest banks[b]	Above €2 bn	Below €2 bn but above €500 m	Below €500 m
Number of banks	6	47	74	743
Total assets (€bn)[a]	411	326	68	94

Notes:
[a] Total assets on an unconsolidated basis;
[b] Excluding special purpose banks; for banking groups only the mother institution is included
Source: OeNB

in the region. The successful cross-border diversification strategy of several Austrian banking groups contributed substantially to the system's overall positive profit development, since margins in CESEE still remain relatively high. This positive impact on profitability is expected to continue, although on a less pronounced basis as margins adapt to EU levels and are therefore expected to decline.

12.2.2 The Austrian supervisory framework

In light of the continuously increasing complexity of global financial markets an integrated supervisory agency, the Austrian Financial Market Authority (FMA), was established in April 2002. Although the FMA took charge of bank licensing, authorisation and notification procedures, as well as banking supervision, the OeNB remained in charge (of parts) of the supervisory process, a mandate which has been extended by an amendment to the Austrian national bank act in January 2008.[4]

As on-site supervision of the Austrian banking system with more than 800 legally independent banks is demanding in terms of time and human resources, some concessions in terms of inspection frequency have to be made. Thus, off-site analysis plays a major role in the Austrian supervisory process, the reason the OeNB and the FMA place great emphasis on developing sophisticated off-site analysis models to make full use of the resources of both authorities. Beginning in 2002 the OeNB launched several projects aimed at developing new tools for quantitative financial stability analysis and off-site banking supervision.[5] The Systemic Risk Monitor formed a part of this effort.[6]

12.3 Theoretical foundations of the SRM

The main purpose of the SRM is its application in the stability analysis of the Austrian banking system. In order to truly deserve its name – suggesting a risk analysis tool at the systemic level – the SRM has to consist of a collection of

---

[4] The OeNB's bank analysis and inspection activities primarily focus on two areas: on-site bank inspections and individual bank analyses. On the basis of supervisory reporting data, the OeNB regularly assesses the risk levels of individual banks and reviews their compliance with legal regulations. The on-site bank inspections conducted by the OeNB are commissioned by the FMA.
[5] In these projects, OeNB expertise from financial analysis and research was combined with expertise from the FMA, the University of Vienna, the University of Applied Sciences, Vorarlberg and the University of Technology, Vienna.
[6] See OeNB/FMA (2005).

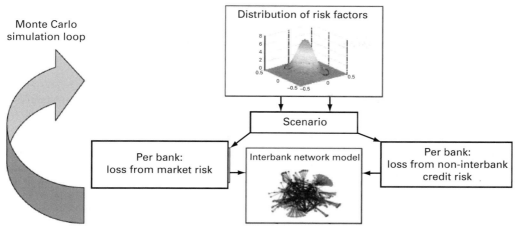

Figure 12.1   Basic structure of the SRM
Source: OeNB.

risk assessment models applied to the Austrian banks at the individual firm level. The SRM meets this requirement primarily by the following two features: first, the impact of market and credit risk is calculated simultaneously for all banks in the system, thus facilitating an assessment of how different banks depend on the same risk factors; and second, the risk of interbank contagion within the Austrian banking system is explicitly accounted for by means of a network model. Figure 12.1 displays the basic structure of the model underlying the SRM.

From Figure 12.1 it can be seen that the SRM makes use of a Monte Carlo simulation. In every loop of the simulation, a scenario is drawn from a multi-variate distribution of risk factors (top). Risk factors are defined as logarithmic differences within one quarter in the levels of market prices and market interest rates (market risk factors) and of macroeconomic variables that have an impact on default probabilities (macroeconomic risk factors).[7] The risk factor distribution is estimated based on historical data. Once a scenario is drawn, the SRM associates with it a certain loss figure for every bank in the Austrian banking system.[8] These figures reflect potential losses that the banks incur within the quarter that follows the reference date under the assumption that their balance sheets remain constant from the reference

---

[7] In the case of interest rates, simple differences instead of logarithmic differences are used. See Section 12.4. For macroeconomic variables that represent a rate (as e.g., the unemployment rate), simple differences instead of logarithmic differences are used.

[8] As market risk positions could benefit from the scenario, a bank can also incur a negative loss, i.e., a gain.

date onwards.[9] This is done separately for banks' positions exposed to market risk (left hand side of Figure 12.1) and for non-interbank loan portfolios exposed to credit risk (right hand side). Banks' capital positions at the reference date – adjusted for interbank claims and liabilities – are then reduced by market and credit risk losses, yielding their capital positions at the end of the quarter before clearing the interbank market. This serves as an input to the network model (bottom of Figure 12.1) which determines banks' abilities to serve their interbank liabilities given the actual payments from other banks. If a bank is not able to pay back its debt in the interbank market, it is technically insolvent. The network clearing algorithm not only determines immediate insolvencies that occur in the first round through market and credit risk losses (fundamental defaults), but also contagious insolvencies triggered by the insolvency of another bank (contagious defaults). By calculating the consequences of many scenarios in the Monte Carlo simulation, a set of risk parameters at the level of each individual bank in the system is produced. This includes the relative frequency of a bank's insolvencies in the total number of Monte Carlo simulations, which is interpreted as its probability of default within three months, or the loss distribution for credit risk, market risk and interbank contagion risk.

Besides the analysis of the current situation of the banking system, the SRM can be used for stress-testing in various ways. For instance stress tests can be performed by setting one or more risk factors to predefined stressed values, reflecting for example a hike in interest rates. The other risk factors are then sampled from their multi-variate distribution conditional on the constraint that certain risk factors are at their stressed values. However, other types of stress tests can be conducted within the SRM framework as well (see section 12.5.2).

The boxes shown in Figure 12.1 form the main building blocks of the SRM framework. The following sections briefly describe how these building blocks were actually modelled.[10] It should be noted, however, that alternative approaches for the modelling of each building block are possible as well.

---

[9] The constant balance sheet assumption demanded for a reasonable and commensurate time horizon for both credit and market risk. However, while one quarter is relatively short for the first risk category, it is rather long for the latter.

[10] For a detailed description of the underlying model of the SRM see Boss *et al.* (2006). The scientific foundation is given in Elsinger *et al.* (2006).

12.3.1 Risk factor model

In the SRM uncertainty is described by a combination of exogenous and endogenous risks. The exogenous risk drivers are captured by a multi-variate distribution of risk factors that affect the value of the non-interbank positions whereas the value of interbank exposures is determined endogenously by the network model. Utilising the hypothesis of constant balance sheets, uncertainty in the SRM evolves over three months, which therefore also represents the reference period for risk factors, i.e., risk factors refer to differences within one quarter. As the risk factor distribution is used in a Monte Carlo simulation, it should allow for an efficient algorithm for randomly drawing from it and – in the case of stress-testing when certain risk factors are set to pre-defined values – also from the conditional distribution.

The choice of risk factors is determined by the data that are available to describe bank portfolios. On the one hand are aggregate positions that depend on market risk factors, namely interest rates, stock indices and exchange rates. On the other are individual loans that are sensitive to credit risk, which in turn is driven by macroeconomic fundamentals that have an influence on the default rates of the corporate and household sectors. While market risk factors if at all show rather limited autocorrelation, for macroeconomic risk factors there is usually a significant impact of lagged values. Therefore, macroeconomic risk factors are preprocessed in a vector auto regression (VAR) and the residuals of the VAR model finally enter the multi-variate distribution of risk factors.

For deriving the multi-variate risk factor distribution, a copula approach is used, consisting of two steps: first a model for the uni-variate marginal distributions is chosen and the dependence between risk factors is then accounted for separately.[11]

The choice of a model for the marginal distributions relies on statistical out-of-sample tests of the three-month density forecasts produced by a group of reasonable models for the time series relevant to the SRM. This way, a single marginal model is selected to cover all risk factors, rather than picking for each factor the optimal model. The motivation for this strategy is parsimony and robustness under the inclusion of new risk factors. The candidate marginal models are intended to be simple but suited to accommodate for the most prominent stylised facts that have been observed for most of the time series of interest: volatility clustering

---

[11] See Chapter 5.

and fat tails.[12] This led to considering the normal distribution, the *t* distribution and a model that combines a kernel estimator for the distributional centre and – according to extreme value theory – a generalised Pareto distribution for the lower and upper 10 per cent tails.[13] To allow for volatility clustering, also uni-variate GARCH (1,1) models were considered, i.e., the GARCH residuals were fitted to the marginal models. Using a test procedure that combines a Kolmogorov–Smirnov test and a test proposed in DeRaaij and Raunig (2002), the extreme value theory model combined with GARCH (1,1) gave overall the best out of sample distribution forecasts.

Once the model for the marginal distributions is chosen, dependence between risk factors is modelled separately by a copula. The marginal distributions and the copula uniquely determine the multi-variate distribution, a fact that is known as Sklar's theorem (see Nelsen, 2006). The SRM uses a grouped *t* copula for dependence modelling since it accommodates for a stylised fact about the dependence between financial market data, namely that extreme comovements of two risk factors have a higher probability than implied by the dependence structure of a multi-variate normal distribution (tail-dependence).[14] In the grouped *t* copula, different groups of risk factors can have different levels of tail dependence. The SRM uses the following four groups of risk factors: macroeconomic risk factors, interest rates, foreign exchange rates and equity price indices.

12.3.2 Market risk model

For evaluating market risk, the change in the portfolio value of a specific bank in response to the market risk factors has to be determined. In that respect, supervisory reporting gives a somewhat coarse picture of banks' portfolios and hence of their dependence on these risk factors.[15] Based on the available data, these risk factors include in the SRM (1) interest rates for four different maturities and major currencies, (2) a domestic and a world stock market equity index, and (3) exchange rates of major currencies *vis à vis* the euro.

---

[12] Stylised facts apply especially to market risk factors at higher frequencies but could not be ruled out *a priori* for the quarterly frequency used in SRM.

[13] For the latter distribution see e.g., McNeil and Frey (2000).

[14] For an application of the grouped *t* copula in credit risk, see Daul *et al.* (2003).

[15] See Section 12.4.1 for available reporting data on market risk positions.

The various data sources specify banks' aggregated exposures to the individual risk factors. Thereby, options are accounted for by their delta-weighted underlying. For example, symmetric interest rate derivatives are broken down to plain vanilla bonds according to the standardised method of the Basel regulatory capital regulations for market risk. For each bank, the change in portfolio value induced by the market risk factors is then determined by multiplying risk factor exposures by the risk factors in a first step and then summing up these products over all individual risk factors. This yields a first order approximation of the change in portfolio value, neglecting any non-linear effects due to exposures in complex derivative instruments as well as those through potential simultaneous dependencies on risk factors.[16,17]

12.3.3 Credit risk model

In the market risk model, a certain combination of market risk factors identifies the portfolio loss in a deterministic way. Opposed to that, a certain combination of macroeconomic risk factors does not specify one single credit loss figure, but rather a whole distribution of possible credit portfolio losses. The SRM therefore calculates the credit loss distribution for each bank in the system by means of a credit risk model and then randomly draws from these distributions in order to arrive at credit losses.

The credit risk model used by the SRM is based on CreditRisk+ (see Credit Suisse, 1997), which is adapted to take explicitly into account the dependence of probabilities of default (PDs) on the state of the economy. However, the approach could also be based on other credit risk approaches like the straightforward Monte Carlo simulation.[18] The average PD of a loan in a particular industry sector is assumed to be a function of the

---

[16] In some cases, this approximation error might be substantial. A comparison of results between stress tests performed by the OeNB and by Austrian commercial banks (see Boss et al., 2008) even showed different signs of the scenario impact in the case of foreign exchange risk, which in all likelihood is due to the fact that options play a relatively important role in banks' foreign currency business but cannot be adequately re-priced by a linear approximation given the relatively large movements in exchange rates assumed as stress scenarios.

[17] Consider for example a 10 per cent decrease in foreign equity prices combined with a 10 per cent depreciation of the respective foreign currency, which results in an exact loss of 19 per cent in the underlying exposure, while the first order approximation yields a loss of 20 per cent.

[18] This approach was used for instance in Boss (2002), which also provides some technical details regarding estimation and model selection with respect to an antecessor of the model that links credit risk to the economic environment presented in the following. In the current implementation of the SRM, however, the estimation is based on the method proposed by Papke and Wooldridge (1996).

macroeconomic risk factors whose parameters are estimated from historical data. The functional form is assumed to be the logistic function of a linear combination of a set of macroeconomic risk factors plus a noise term. This specification assures that a PD – according to its definition – can only take values between zero and one. Quarterly data on historical default rates – interpreted as realisations of average PDs – are available for thirteen industry sectors and for several business cycles.[19] From a predefined pool of macroeconomic risk factors a maximum of four variables is chosen for each of the sectoral models in a selection procedure that is intended to identify parsimonious models. For determining sectoral average PDs for given values of macroeconomic risk factors, residuals drawn from the multi-variate risk factor distribution are combined with the macroeconomic VAR model and are plugged into the respective estimated models.

The average industry sector PDs are not used directly in the credit risk model, as ratings of individual obligors are available in the central credit register. From these ratings, PDs of individual obligors are derived and adjusted by the relative change of the average sector default probabilities within the next quarter implied by models linking industry-specific sectoral PDs to macroeconomic variables. The PD of an obligor that is used in the credit risk model is thus given by the PD according to the central credit register times the ratio of the sectoral PD predicted by the model for the next quarter to the actual sectoral PD.

Once obligor's PDs are determined, the credit risk model closely follows the CreditRisk+ framework. Given a realisation of the macroeconomic risk factors, loan defaults are assumed to be conditionally independent. In order to facilitate the efficient computation of the portfolio loss distribution, CreditRisk+ pools similar exposure volumes into exposure buckets and exploits the fact that if PDs are small, the number of defaults within a sample of obligors who default independently of each other is well approximated by a Poisson distribution.[20] The parameter of this distribution is given by the expected number of defaults, i.e., by the sum of the PDs of the individual obligors in the sample.

As the SRM repeatedly draws macroeconomic risk factors from the multivariate risk factor distribution, PDs are themselves stochastic. Consequently,

---

[19] For a more detailed description of the data input to the credit risk model see Section 12.4.2.
[20] An exposure bucket is defined by a predetermined exposure unit. For instance, if exposures are expressed in units of €100,000, all exposures smaller or equal to 100,000 are pooled into exposure bucket no. 1.

the resulting credit loss distribution assigns a higher probability to extreme losses than a model with fixed PDs.

12.3.4 Network model

Once loss figures for positions exposed to market risk and for non-interbank loans have been calculated for every bank in the system, the network model comes into play. It answers the question of whether banks *potentially* could pay back their interbank liabilities at the end of the three-month time horizon given that the losses have reduced their initial capital. If a bank is not left with enough capital to do so, it is insolvent.[21] The value of shares that other banks hold in insolvent banks is zero and the value of debt is whatever creditors can realise from the remaining asset value under a proportional sharing rule. This potentially reduced value of claims may induce further insolvencies of banks that initially had stayed solvent. The network clearing algorithm works out this value adjustment process which – given the complexity of the system of interbank debt and equity holdings – is a non-trivial task. Besides the losses due to market and credit risk that banks incur during the three-month time horizon and banks' initial capital positions (see Box 12.1), the matrices of bilateral interbank debt and equity holdings represent a crucial input to the network model (see section 12.4.3).

The SRM network model is an extended version of Eisenberg and Noe (2001) presented in Elsinger (2007) with the inclusion of interbank share holdings representing an innovation. In case of a bank's insolvency, the virtual clearing algorithm has to respect three criteria: (1) limited liability, which requires that the total payments made by a bank must never exceed the cash flow available to the bank, (2) the priority of debt claims, which requires that stockholders in the bank receive no value unless the bank is able to pay off all of its outstanding debt completely, and (3) a proportional sharing rule, which requires that in case of insolvency all creditors are paid off in proportion to the size of their claims. Another innovation of the SRM network model is the possibility to include a seniority structure within interbank liabilities. This feature, however, is not used in the current implementation of the SRM as no data on the seniority of interbank liability is available.

---

[21] As banks tend to become insolvent in practice before all of their capital is exhausted, in a future version it is planned to use an even more stringent rule for banks' insolvencies, namely a capital adequacy ratio falling below 4 per cent. This has been applied in the example presented in section 12.7.3.

From the network model it is not only possible to gain information about insolvencies of individual banks but also insights regarding systemic stability. The default of a bank is called fundamental if that bank is not able to pay back its liabilities under the assumption that all other banks can do so. A contagious default occurs when a bank becomes insolvent only because other banks are not able to pay back their interbank debt. This distinction allows for analysing insolvencies that result directly from risk factor movements as well as insolvencies that indirectly result from second round effects of insolvency contagion through interbank relations.

12.4 Input data of the SRM

Two different categories of input data are used by the SRM: (1) individual banks' data reported to the OeNB that reflect their on- and off-balance sheet positions and supervisory information like regulatory capital, and (2) time-series data from external sources reflecting historical movements of market and macroeconomic risk factors. The latter time series are taken from the OeNB's macroeconomic database, all other input data is described in the subsequent sections of this chapter.[22]

12.4.1 Data for the market risk model

To assess market risk, net positions of all on- and off-balance sheet assets and liabilities in foreign currency, equity and interest rate-sensitive instruments according to supervisory reports are considered. For foreign exchange rate risk the net open positions in USD, JPY, GBP and CHF as reported by banks are used. Regarding equity risk domestic and non-domestic equity exposures are differentiated, where the net exposure in the Austrian Traded Index is used for the first and the sum over all reported foreign stock market indices is used for the latter. For interest rate risk, net open positions in EUR, USD, JPY, GBP and CHF with respect to four maturity buckets are derived from the interest-rate risk statistic. The maturity buckets refer to the re-pricing maturities of the underlying instruments and include: up to six months, six months to three years, three to seven years and more than seven years. For the valuation of net

---

[22] Currently the SRM uses eight macroeconomic risk factors: gross domestic product (GDP), the consumer price index (CPI), the unemployment rate, gross capital formation including and excluding equipment, the German Information and Forschung (Ifo) business climate index, global industrial production and a global equity price index.

positions in these maturity buckets, the three-month, one-year, five-year and ten-year interest rates in the respective currencies are used. Historical time series for interest rates, exchanges rates and stock market indices are taken from Bloomberg's financial database. In some cases time series are complemented by data from additional sources in order to extend quarterly time series beyond their availability in Bloomberg.[23] Consequently, the starting points of most of them date back to 1970, but at least to the early 1980s.

12.4.2 Data for the credit risk model

To analyse credit risk, in addition to supervisory reports the OeNB's central credit register is used which provides detailed information on banks' loan portfolios to non-banks, including the lender's assessment of the debtor's creditworthiness, i.e., rating. In the SRM, the riskiness of an individual loan to a domestic customer is assumed to be characterised by two components: the aforementioned rating and the default frequency of the industry sector the customer belongs to, which are taken from the Austrian debt collector Kreditschutzverband von 1870 (KSV).

The central credit register contains data on the outstanding volume of all credit risk-affected on- and off-balance sheet instruments, loan loss provisions and collateral as well as banks' internal debtor ratings for all loans exceeding a volume of €350,000 on a bank-by-bank and obligor-by-obligor basis.[24] The bank's internal rating is reported to the credit register and mapped by the OeNB onto a master scale which allows assigning a PD to each debtor. In cases where obligors have loans at more than one bank, the ratings assigned by banks to a specific customer can differ, whereby the SRM uses by default the highest, i.e., most risky, rating.

Regarding the classification of loans in the SRM, domestic loans to non-banks are assigned to thirteen industry sectors based on the NACE classification of the debtors.[25,26] Furthermore cross-border loans are classified according to nine regional sectors for both foreign banks and non-banks, leading to a total of eighteen non-domestic sectors.[27] For domestic loans

---

[23] Additional data sources include central banks (Bank of England, German Bundesbank, Swiss National Bank), as well as Thomson's Datastream database.

[24] This includes securitised and non-securitised loans, credit lines, guarantees and commitments.

[25] The thirteen sectors include: basic industries, production, energy, construction, trading, tourism, transport, financial services, public services, other services, health, households and a residual sector.

[26] Nomenclature of economic activities (NACE) is a European industry standard classification system.

[27] The nine regions are: Western Europe, Central-, Eastern- and South-eastern Europe, North America, Latin America and the Caribbean, Middle East, Asia and Far East, Pacific, Africa, and a residual sector.

below the threshold volume of the central credit register, information of the supervisory reports is used which provides the number of loans to domestic non-banks with respect to different volume buckets. No comparable statistics are available for non-domestic loans. However, one can assume that the largest part of cross-border lending exceeds the threshold of €350,000 and hence not much information on smaller cross-border exposures is lost.

The KSV database provides time series of insolvencies in most NACE branches at a quarterly frequency starting in 1969. This information is complemented by data on the total number of firms in each sector according to Statistics Austria. This allows for the calculation of time series of historically observed default frequencies in the thirteen domestic industry sectors by dividing the number of insolvencies by the number of total firms for each industry sector and quarter. The time series of default frequencies are then interpreted as sectoral average PDs. To construct insolvency statistics for the private and the residual sectors, where no reliable information on the number of insolvencies and sample sizes is available, respective default frequencies for the overall Austrian economy are used. PDs for the non-domestic sectors are calculated as averages of the default probabilities according to the ratings that are assigned by all banks to all customers within a given foreign sector.

12.4.3 Data for the network model

The network model of the SRM requires a matrix of bilateral financial relations among domestic banks in terms of debt and equity as data input. The matrix of interbank loans and liabilities of individual Austrian banks, however, can only be partially reconstructed from supervisory reports and the central credit register. Hence, the full bilateral structure of exposures has to be estimated. By entropy maximisation, which allows for estimation under the constraint of partial information, the interbank liability matrix is estimated in such a way that it fulfils all constraints derived from the available information.[28] Information from the central credit register and the supervisory reports was used to define constraints on the interbank liability matrix regarding (1) the lower bound of individual cells, (2) the exact value of the sum of each row (total interbank loans), (3) the lower and upper bound of the sum of each

---

[28] See Blien and Graef (1997) on how entropy maximisation can be used to estimate a consistent matrix of mutual relationships (in the present context loans and liabilities) between entities (banks) on the basis of partial information.

column (total interbank liabilities), and (4) the lower bound of the sum of rows and columns of sub-matrices of the interbank liability matrix corresponding to the seven sectors of the Austrian banking system.[29]

Because these constraints show some inconsistencies, the algorithm for entropy maximisation does not converge for the full set of constraints.[30] Hence, a first estimation with all constraints and the lower bound of individual cells as a prior is followed by a second run neglecting the constraints on sectoral sub-sets and the result from the first run as a prior. Now the algorithm converges, however in the case of the Austrian banking system it tends to assign small values to a relatively large number of entries corresponding in most cases to small banks, for which, as a rule, information is less easily available. As this would most likely not be justified by actual interbank relations, values below a threshold of €10,000 are set to zero after convergence and the resulting matrix is used as a prior in an iterative re-estimation until no further entries fall below the threshold after convergence.

In addition to interbank loans and liabilities the network of the Austrian banking system is defined through mutual equity holdings of Austrian banks in other domestic banks. The integration is straightforward, as equity holdings are directly reported within OeNB's supervisory reporting scheme.

12.5 Application of the SRM

12.5.1 Regular simulations

The SRM is used, first of all, for regular simulations of the impact on banks of ordinary (i.e., unstressed) future economic conditions. In every loop of the simulation, a scenario is drawn that consists of a set of macroeconomic and market risk factors. These are used to calculate the impact of the state of the economy on banking risks under the assumption that banks' balance sheets remain constant over the simulated horizon of one quarter. Following the steps illustrated above, estimated market and credit risk losses reduce a bank's capital position, which determines whether the bank is still able to serve its interbank liabilities.[31] Banks that are no longer able to do so default, which, in turn, may trigger contagion to other counterparties.

---

[29] By convention it is assumed that cell (i,j) of the interbank liability matrix represents the volume of loans granted by bank i to bank j, or vice versa the liability of bank j to bank i.

[30] These inconsistencies arise due to slightly differing reporting requirements and cut-off dates of the different data sources.

[31] For the role of capital in the SRM refer to Box 12.1.

Drawing many scenarios from the joint distribution of risk factors in a regular SRM simulation yields economically consistent risk parameters, i.e., probabilities and distributions, as SRM output, rather than point forecasts like many other stress testing tools. Each of the individual modules of the SRM can be turned off individually or, in principle, substituted by other modelling approaches.[32] All these features lead to a wide array of possible sensitivity analyses, simulations and robustness checks, particularly in light of the SRM's stress-testing capabilities.

12.5.2 Stress tests

The framework of the SRM can be used to perform stress tests in various ways. Typically, a stress test is defined by setting one or more risk factors to their stressed values. This can apply to market and/or macroeconomic risk factors, the latter implying stressed PDs through the model linking macro variables to domestic PDs as described in section 12.3.3. Alternatively, the PDs can be stressed directly. The impact of the stress test is then calculated for the single scenario defined through the stressed values of risk factors, or it is based on a full Monte Carlo simulation, where the stressed risk factors are fixed and the remaining ones are drawn from the joint risk factor distribution. Drawing from the joint distribution can either be done unconditionally or conditional on the fixed risk factors. Another way to define stress tests is to apply direct shocks to banks' capital before clearing the interbank market. The size of the shock can be defined in a rather general way, e.g., by just forcing a certain bank to default or by reducing the capital of every bank by a fixed share of its loan portfolio. In principle the various ways of defining and calculating stress tests can be arbitrarily combined. In the following, however, the most common ways to use the SRM for stress-testing will be discussed in the light of generally known stress-testing techniques.

Single scenario stress tests and sensitivity analyses

In these straightforward types of stress tests one or more risk factors are set to their stressed values and for this single scenario market- and

---

[32] It is for instance possible to calculate the expected loss conditional on the current economic environment by simple parameterisation, i.e., by running a single scenario in which macro risk factors are fixed at their current levels (or any other, for that matter), turning off the market risk module and changing the method in the credit risk module described in section 12.3.3 to a straightforward expected loss calculation, while at the same time still observing potential contagious effects in case of fundamental defaults with the network model or alternatively turning off the network component as well.

credit-risk portfolios are re-valued. Finally, the interbank market is cleared, to determine fundamental and contagious defaults. These stress tests can be based on a single risk factor (sensitivity analyses), including macroeconomic and market risk factors as well as sectoral or regional PDs, or any combination of these (scenario analyses).[33] The stress itself can be defined in terms of absolute or relative changes with respect to the reference date, or in terms of a designated stress level, e.g., a historic worst case of a sectoral PD. Other risk factors are set to zero or, in case of PDs, are fixed at their values at the reference date.[34] As already mentioned, in order to assess different risk categories on a stand-alone basis one or more modules of the SRM can be turned off. For example, for a typical market risk sensitivity analysis, the credit risk model is not run.

Simulation stress tests and macro stress-testing

Simulation stress tests are defined analogous to single scenario stress tests. In a simulation stress test, however, the SRM capitalises on its Monte Carlo simulation foundation. A large number of scenarios is generated, where one or more risk factors are set to their stressed values and the remaining risk factors are drawn from the joint risk factor distribution. This can be done unconditionally, i.e., by drawing all risk factors as it is done in a regular simulation, then overwriting the values of the risk factors to be stressed by their designated stress values. Similarly, domestic sectoral and non-domestic regional PDs can be stressed where in the first case PDs according to the drawn macro risk factors are simply overwritten by stressed values.

The most sophisticated way of stress-testing with the SRM, however, is to first fix the risk factors to be stressed at their designated stress values, and in a second step to draw the scenarios from the joint distribution conditional on the fixed risk factors.[35] This procedure takes advantage of one of the main features of the SRM, namely the fact that a grouped t copula is used to model the joint distribution of risk factors. This approach addresses a phenomenon which is usually referred to as correlation break down – i.e., stochastic dependencies between risk factors in

---

[33] See Chapter 2.
[34] Note that risk factors are defined in terms of changes of underlying variables (see section 12.3.1).
[35] Note that this is not possible in the case of stressing PDs.

periods of stress can potentially diverge from those in normal times – by the copula's ability to capture tail dependencies.

Hence, by drawing from the conditional risk factor distribution, consistent stress scenarios for all risk factors are generated, whereby this type of stress test can be viewed as a macro stress test, which usually refers to a stress test where several risk factors are stressed simultaneously and in a consistent way. Actually, this is even the case if only one risk factor is explicitly stressed as the other risk factors are implicitly set to values consistent with the stressed value through the conditional drawing from the joint distribution. Typically, in macro stress tests the consistent macro scenarios are generated through a structural or vector autoregressive macroeconomic model. These models are generally not capable of accounting for the fact that statistical dependencies between risk factors in crisis situations could diverge from those in normal times, while this is explicitly accounted for within the SRM through the copula approach. However, the time series on which the estimation of the joint risk factor distribution is based need to comprise periods of stress in order to actually capture potential tail dependencies in the estimated distribution. Examples of these simulation stress tests can be found in section 12.7.1.

Stressing banks' capital

Another type of stress test within the SRM framework refers to shocks to banks' capital before clearing the interbank market.[36] These shocks can either be idiosyncratic or systemic. Stress test of the former type is the modelling of the default of a single bank by setting its capital before clearing to a value below its overall interbank claims. Consequently the bank is unable to fulfil its interbank liabilities, which potentially affects the payment ability of other banks and hence allows assessment of contagion risk through the interbank market.

However, this concept can be generalised in two ways: with the SRM it is possible to (1) deduct any amount from a bank's capital, and (2) extend the shock from an idiosyncratic problem at one bank to a systemic crisis in which the capital of more than one bank is affected. In principle, the amount deducted can be determined by any function depending on either

---

[36] For the role of capital in the SRM refer to Box 12.1.

the stress scenario or any of a bank's balance sheet positions. For example, the SRM is used to analyse the impact of the default of a large Austrian corporate customer, to which many banks in the system have large exposures, by deducting 80 per cent of their respective outstanding volume from their capital before clearing the interbank market. Section 12.7.2 provides a detailed example based on the risk emanating from foreign-currency lending.

12.6 Output data of the SRM

12.6.1 Results produced by the SRM

The SRM, based on individual bank portfolios and a Monte Carlo simulation generating scenarios from a risk-factor distribution, provides its main results in the form of matrixes from which a wide range of different statistics can be calculated. Each of these matrixes is of the dimension number of banks times the number of scenarios. Simulation results for credit, market and contagion risk are stored in separate matrixes, which contain the losses for each risk category for each bank in each scenario, whereby the contagious risk losses refer to the sum of one bank's claims in the interbank market that could not be paid due to other banks' (fundamental or contagious) defaults after clearing the interbank market. Furthermore, the SRM stores a matrix of the same size with flags indicating fundamental, contagious or no default for each bank in each scenario.

   This data can be used to analyse simulation results in various ways. First, loss matrixes can be used to calculate statistics of the loss distribution, like expected loss, standard deviation and quantiles for credit, market and contagion risk as well as for total risk corresponding to the sum of the three individual risk categories. Second, losses can be related to capital and other risk buffers, like provisions, in order to assess the risk-bearing capacity (see Box 12.1). Third, the matrix indicating bank defaults can be used to derive PDs for fundamental, contagious and total defaults by dividing the number of respective defaults by the number of total simulations. Loss statistics as well as PDs can be calculated for a single bank, the overall system, and various aggregates below the total. Currently, the SRM provides aggregates according to size, the formal Austrian banking sectors,

---

Box 12.1 Using capital for assessing banks' resilience

The definition of banks' capital is crucial for the SRM as it defines the risk-bearing capacity of a bank, i.e., how much buffer is available to absorb losses due to market, credit and/or contagious risk losses, as a bank defaults in the SRM when losses exceed capital. Besides capital in its narrow definition (e.g., Tier-1 or Tier-2 capital) previously made loan loss provisions or even profits could be accounted for. Hence, the SRM provides several options for the definition of capital ranging from a very strict to a rather broad definition. These definitions include: (1) Tier-1 capital, (2) regulatory capital as defined by the Austrian Banking Act, and (3) regulatory capital as defined by the Austrian Banking Act plus existing general and specific loan loss provisions, where option (3) is the default setting of the SRM. Depending on the choice of capital definition results in a given simulation can vary substantially.

However, it is planned to change the standard criterion for bank defaults in a future version of SRM as follows: first, as an additional important risk buffer profits shall be taken into account. Second, because in practice banks would most likely become insolvent before all their capital is exhausted, they will be assumed to default, if their capital adequacy ratios (CARs) or Tier-1 ratios fall below the 4 per cent threshold.[37]

---

peer-groups defined according to statistical similarities for internal off-site banking analysis and the Austrian provinces.[38]

Moreover, the default matrix serves as a basis for further interbank contagion analysis. By defining a range of scenarios, whereby in each scenario exactly one bank defaults exogenously, it can be investigated which banks default contagiously triggered by the fundamental default of which bank and vice versa. In addition, probabilities of systemic events can be derived by dividing the number of scenarios in which the number of defaults – or alternatively the share of defaulting banks in total assets – exceeds some predefined threshold by the total number of scenarios. This is obviously also the case for the scenarios themselves, as macro as well as market risk factors are stored as output as well.

12.6.2 Dissemination of the results

Results of the SRM – regular simulations as well as the various possible stress tests – are published periodically to an internal as well as an external audience.

---

[37] This approach is also used by Alessandri *et al.* (2007) and has already been implemented for the SRM stress tests conducted for the Austrian FSAP update in 2007 (see section 12.7.3).

[38] See section 12.2.1.

In addition, *ad hoc* simulations are run on an event-by-event basis that range from international stability assessments like the International Monetary Fund's (IMF's) Financial Sector Assessment Program (FSAP) to incident-based internal risk assessments, e.g., in case of supervisory concerns regarding a particular bank and/or market developments.

Publication in the Austrian Financial Stability Report

The general public is addressed via the OeNB's biannual *Financial Stability Report (FSR)* which includes aggregated stress test results. Since the roll-out of the SRM in 2006, these stress test results have been based on three SRM simulation stress tests and a regular simulation without stress as the baseline scenario.[39] In addition, the methodological change that came about with the introduction of the SRM in issue 11 of the *FSR* was accompanied by the publication of a study offering a detailed description of the SRM in the special topics section of the same issue.[40]

Integration in the Austrian Banking Business Analysis

For the purpose of risk-based supervision, SRM results enter the Austrian Banking Business Analysis (ABBA), a supervisory framework cooperatively established by the FMA and the OeNB, driven by the importance of off-site supervision in Austria.[41] ABBA's main objective is the categorisation of banks based on a risk/relevance classification in order to ensure efficient resource allocation in the supervisory process. This risk orientation is achieved by a systematisation of the results of independent supervisory tools to yield a quarterly report, which provides a consistent risk assessment of individual Austrian banks.[42]

Although the SRM has initially been developed as a software tool to assess systemic risk, results on an individual bank level proved accurate and robust enough to include results in the ABBA framework. In addition, features like the quantification of contagion risk added aspects to the analytical depth of the ABBA suite of tools that had not been addressed prior to the inclusion of the SRM. Hence, SRM results for individual banks enter the quarterly ABBA aggregation process, closing the analytical gap between a macro prudential financial stability stance and a banking super-vision point of view.

---

[39] A detailed example with current data is provided in section 12.7.1.   [40] See Boss *et al.* (2006).
[41] On the link between macro surveillance and micro supervision, see also Chapter 13.
[42] See OeNB/FMA (2005).

Box 12.2 Performing *ad hoc* simulations

The use of the SRM is not confined to periodic assessment and reporting. In fact, it has been employed in a wide variety of ways, for which its capability to shock a bank's capital before clearing the interbank market proved most useful. Questions ranging from the risk associated with high levels of foreign-currency lending in the western part of Austria, to supervisory concerns regarding particular banks in times of turmoil have been addressed and – subject to certain model constraints – could be answered almost immediately.

The main reason these questions could be addressed without further ado is the fact that the SRM is a fully developed software tool. Authorised OeNB analysts are granted access via a graphical user interface from their desks that provides them with the possibility to run certain predefined simulations (including the regular stress tests described above) as well as to parameterise individual simulations themselves.

Next to these truly *ad hoc* simulations the SRM has been put to use for various one-off exercises that, nevertheless, had been planned well in advance. Section 12.7.3, for instance, describes the recently finished FSAP follow-up.

Supervisory information system

On top of the integration of SRM results into the ABBA framework, detailed results on a bank-by-bank basis are published quarterly in the Austrian supervisory information system, jointly operated by the FMA and the OeNB. These results are released to an authorised internal audience from both institutions and include absolute and relative market, credit and contagion risk losses, as well as their aggregate total in the mean and for selected percentiles. Again, these results are available for a regular simulation without stress and three standardised stress scenarios. In addition, results of a systematic stress test simulating the default of each bank, by wiping out its capital are on-hand. This provides supervisors with information on banks that either (1) cause contagious defaults or (2) are affected through interbank contagion. Moreover, for each individual bank relative results in terms of capital are put in relation to the aggregate of the entire banking system, and various sub-aggregates: (1) by sector, (2) by size, and (3) by a qualitatively defined peer-group (see Box 12.2).

12.7 Some examples of stress tests with the SRM

This section presents three examples that highlight how the SRM can be used to perform stress tests. The first example shows a standard simulation accompanied by two simulation stress tests, one sampling scenarios from the joint distribution of risk factors conditional on the fixed values of stressed risk factors and one shocking PDs directly. In the second example, banks' capital before clearing the interbank market is shocked. The last example shows how the SRM was used in 2007 for the update of the Austrian Financial Sector Assessment (hereafter FSAP-2007) to assess the impact of a multi-period macroeconomic stress scenario on the Austrian banking system.

12.7.1 Standard SRM simulations

Since 2006, results of standard SRM simulations are calculated regularly for internal purposes and for publication on an aggregated level in the Austrian Financial Stability Report (see section 12.6.2). This includes a simulation without stress corresponding to the baseline scenario and two simulation stress tests assuming an increase in euro interest rates by 120 basis points and a doubling of domestic PDs.

Figure 12.2 shows the density functions of the loss distributions for the aggregated Austrian banking system according to the baseline simulation for credit, market, contagion and total risk, where the latter refers to the sum of the three previous risk categories. The simulation is based on data as of end-2007 and hence shows loss distributions over the first quarter of 2008. The expected loss due to credit risk is around €8.6 bn for the first quarter of 2008, while market risk is expected to generate profits of around €0.1 bn over the same period. Expected losses due to contagion risk are negligible and hence in total the expected loss amounts to about €8.5 bn.

The figure also shows the quantiles of the loss distributions for some commonly used probability levels. For example, the 95 per cent quantile of a loss distribution corresponds to the amount of loss which is not exceeded in nineteen out of twenty cases, i.e., with a probability of 95 per cent. Accordingly total losses due to all risk categories in the first quarter 2008 will not exceed €10.5 bn, €11.2 bn and €13.6 bn with probabilities 95, 99 and 99.9 per cent. Again, credit risk is the most important component of total risk, however at the 99.9 per cent quantile market risk losses amount to about €2.4 bn and losses due to interbank contagion to roughly €1.8 bn. The loss distributions in absolute terms shown in Figure 12.2 do not account for loan loss provisions banks already have in their books. In addition, in order to assess the risk-bearing capacity of banks, one is interested in the relation between losses and capital, which serves as a final buffer against losses.

This is the aim of the presentation of results in Table 12.2, which shows expected losses and quantiles of the loss distributions for the entire Austrian

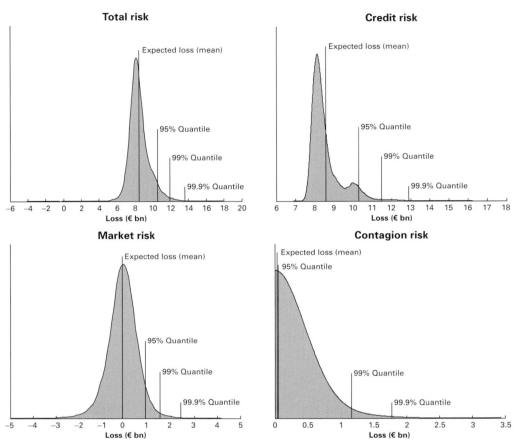

Figure 12.2   Density functions of loss distributions for the aggregated Austrian banking system according to the baseline simulation over the first quarter 2008
Source: OeNB.

banking sector over the first quarter of 2008 relative to capital, with risk provisions existing at end-2007 being deducted from respective losses.[43] In addition to the baseline simulation, results for the two stress tests mentioned above are shown. For credit risk, contagion risk in the interbank market and total risk, a negative value means that existing corresponding loan loss provisions exceed the expected value or the quantiles of the related loss distribution. In the case of market risk, no risk provisions were taken into account, so that a negative value indicates a profit.

[43] See notes to Table 12.2.

Table 12.2 Results of baseline and stress test simulations for the aggregated Austrian banking system for the first quarter 2008

%		Baseline simulation	Doubling of domestic probabilities of default	Increase of euro interest rates by 120 basis points
Total risk	Expected loss	−1.8	−0.1	−0.4
	95% quantile	0.9	2.7	2.1
	99% quantile	2.8	4.5	3.9
	99.9% quantile	4.5	7.7	6.7
Credit risk	Expected loss	−1.6	0.1	−1.6
	95% quantile	0.6	2.4	0.6
	99% quantile	2.5	4.1	2.4
	99.9% quantile	4.0	6.4	4.7
Market risk	Expected loss	−0.2	−0.2	1.2
	95% quantile	1.1	1.2	2.0
	99% quantile	1.9	1.9	2.4
	99.9% quantile	3.0	3.2	2.8
Contagion risk	Expected loss	0.0	0.0	0.0
	95% quantile	0.0	0.0	0.0
	99% quantile	1.4	1.4	1.4
	99.9% quantile	2.2	2.4	2.4

Note: Figures denote the expected value and the quantiles of the loss distribution in the relevant risk category in per cent of capital for the first quarter of 2008. Loss from credit risk was adjusted for provisions related to claims on domestic and foreign non-banks as well as on foreign banks; loss from contagion risk in the Austrian interbank market – which corresponds to the credit risk *vis à vis* domestic banks – was adjusted for provisions related to claims on domestic banks. Correspondingly, total risk was adjusted for total loss provisions.
Source: OeNB

     The simulation without a crisis scenario yields a mean value of −1.8 per cent for total risk. This means that existing risk provisions at end-2007 (€9.9 bn) surpassed the losses expected to arise in the first quarter 2008 from credit, market and contagion risk in the interbank market (€8.5 bn) by €1.4 bn, which corresponds to 1.8 per cent of total capital (which amounts to €78 bn). With regard to credit risk, existing provisions for loans to non-banks and foreign banks exceeded losses expected to arise from these claims by a value corresponding to 1.6 per cent of capital. Regarding contagion risk in the interbank market provisions for loans granted to domestic banks were deducted from the expected loss, the result in per cent of capital, however, is insignificant. In the case of market risk, no risk provisions were taken into consideration; thus, the value listed can be interpreted as an expected profit in the amount of 0.2 per cent of capital. In the quantiles, the losses arising from all individual risk categories surpass existing loss provisions up to 4.5 per cent of capital corresponding to the 99.9 per cent quantile of the total risk distribution.

The stress test that assumes a doubling of domestic customers' PDs shows a rather limited impact and existing loan loss provisions still surpass the expected total loss, though by a mere 0.1 per cent of capital. This is due to the fact that a doubling of domestic PDs increases expected credit risk loss only by 16 per cent from €8.6 bn to €9.9 bn, as the major part of the expected loss is due to loans that have already defaulted. However, at the quantiles a doubling of domestic PDs shows a rather significant impact. At the 99.9 per cent quantile the loss adjusted for existing credit risk provisions corresponds to 7.7 per cent of capital. However, it should be noted that for stress scenarios a quantile corresponds to an event that can be interpreted as a crisis in addition to the crisis scenario hypothesised in the stress test. Assuming that the stress scenario has a probability of 0.1 per cent, the probability for both events to happen simultaneously – the stress scenario occurs and the 99.9 per cent quantile of the loss distribution is exceeded – amounts to 0.0001 per cent – a composite event that can be expected to happen once in a million quarters, or 250,000 years, according to the SRM horizon.[44]

An increase of euro-area interest rates by 120 basis points would have somewhat less impact on the total expected loss, though expected market risk losses are substantial and amount to 1.2 per cent of capital. However, as expected credit risk losses do not change compared to the baseline scenario, in total existing credit risk provisions surpass total expected losses by 0.4 per cent of capital. The quantiles of the loss distributions show a pattern similar to the other simulations with the exception of market risk: with higher quantiles, the impact of the stress test in terms of losses relative to capital decreases and at the 99.9 per cent quantile the market risk loss is even slightly less than in the baseline scenario.

None of the crisis scenarios shows a major impact on contagion risk in the interbank market. Furthermore, the capital ratio of the Austrian banking system remains clearly above the regulatory minimum requirement of 8 per cent in both stress scenarios.

---

[44] Let A be the 'event that the stress scenario occurs' and B the 'event that causes the loss to exceed the 99 per cent quantile of the loss distribution'. That is $P(A \cap B) = P(B|A) * P(A)$.

12.7.2 Contagion analysis of foreign currency loan defaults

In contrast to other countries joining the euro area, Austrian banks have a relatively high volume of outstanding foreign currency loans, mostly denominated in Swiss francs.[45] This raises the question of how indirect credit risk induced by foreign-exchange-rate risk of these loans might affect the overall stability of the Austrian banking system. Though indirect credit risk of foreign-currency loans is not explicitly modelled within the framework of the SRM, the issue can be addressed through a stress test that directly shocks banks' capital before clearing as described in section 12.5.2.

The stress test presented in this example analyses potential fundamental and contagious bank defaults as a consequence of the loss of a fixed share of each bank's outstanding foreign currency loans, where the share ranges from 0.5 to 100 per cent and for simplicity a loss given default of 100 per cent is assumed. The respective amount is deducted from each bank's capital before clearing and through clearing the interbank market domino effects in the system that emerge through bank defaults driven by the initial shock can be analysed.

As can be seen in Figure 12.3, all banks would be able to lose up to 15 per cent of their foreign currency loan portfolio without defaulting. However, up to 50 per cent of each bank's foreign currency loans could be written off without causing any contagious defaults or a significant number of fundamental defaults. Below this threshold only a very few banks with very limited market share in terms of Austrian banks' total assets would be affected. A first significant increase in contagious defaults in up to thirty banks can be observed at 55 per cent of lost foreign-currency loans, though the respective market share is limited. By increasing the share the number of contagious defaults decreases as the concerned banks are defaulting fundamentally, i.e., through the initial shock. The next significant increase in contagion can be observed at around 60 per cent of lost foreign currency loans with more than 40 contagious defaults corresponding to a market share of around 7 per cent. At 65 per cent, the number of contagious defaults increases dramatically to almost 100, though the respective increase in market share remains moderate. A further increase of the share up to the total loss of each bank's foreign currency loan portfolio does not lead to significant additional contagious bank defaults, though in total the number of defaults increases by up to 200, corresponding to almost one-third of the Austrian banking system's assets.

---

[45] The share of foreign currency lending in total lending to domestic customers stood at 16 per cent in December 2007, representing a volume of €46.7 bn in outstanding loans.

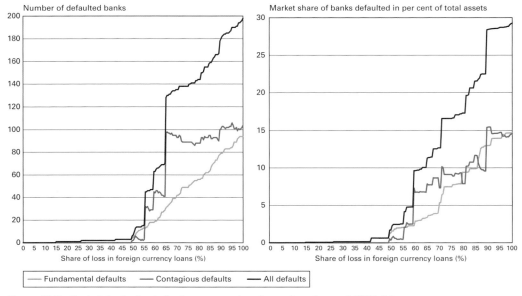

Number of defaulted banks

Market share of banks defaulted in per cent of total assets

Share of loss in foreign currency loans (%)

Share of loss in foreign currency loans (%)

——— Fundamental defaults   ——— Contagious defaults   ——— All defaults

Figure 12.3   Bank defaults due to foreign currency loan losses based on end-2007 data
Source: OeNB.

What can be learnt from this exercise? First of all, only a very serious and unrealistic shock to the foreign currency loan portfolio of Austrian banks would be necessary to put strain on the stability of the banking system. However, given the extreme scenarios, with more than 50 per cent of the foreign-currency portfolio defaulting, fundamental bank defaults would on average roughly be doubled in terms of market share through contagious defaults. Second, the results clearly reflect the sectoral and regional structure of the Austrian banking system as well as the regional distribution of foreign-currency lending. In the western part of Austria foreign-currency lending is significantly more widespread than in the rest of the country. Consequently, these banks have a higher share of foreign-currency lending in total lending and are affected at an earlier stage of the stress test. The sharp increase in the number of contagious defaults at the thresholds described above can be traced back to the three tier structure of one specific sub-sector of the Austrian banking system. At the thresholds, the respective regional apex institutions default leading to contagious defaults of many, if not all, banks within the same banking sector and province. As these are typically very small banks, the respective increases in terms of market share are less significant and mostly driven by the apex institutions' defaults. Other major increases in market share of affected banks can be traced back to medium-sized banks with large foreign currency loan portfolios belonging to other sub-sectors. Overall one can conclude from this exercise that foreign-currency lending does not put a threat on the overall stability of the Austrian banking system for realistic scenarios. A systemic impact could be observed at most at the regional level, though still under very serious and rather implausible scenarios only.

12.7.3 FSAP stress tests

The SRM was also used to perform stress tests in the course of the FSAP-2007. Besides being used for sensitivity stress tests, the SRM was also adopted to assess the impact of a macroeconomic stress scenario over a three-year horizon. The scenario was constructed to estimate the impact of an enduring global recession on the Austrian banking system starting in the third quarter of 2007 and lasting for three years. The OeNB's quarterly forecast model was used to implement the scenario in terms of macroeconomic variables, which resulted in a two-year period of zero or slightly negative GDP growth rates corresponding to the most prolonged recession Austria experienced since the Second World War.[46]

As the global downturn scenario was constructed for a three-year time horizon with quarterly frequency, some changes to the original framework were necessary to use the SRM in the context of multi-period stress-testing. First, market risk was not considered in the calculations, as this would have demanded for additional assumptions regarding banks' reactions to changes in the economic environment, in particular market risk factors. Second, to reduce simulation time, macroeconomic risk factors were not simulated; instead, PDs were shocked directly according to the impact of the scenario on the domestic PDs described above. However, econometric modelling analogous to the model described in section 12.3.3 was used to estimate the impact of the unfavourable macroeconomic condition on domestic credit risk. For the overall Austrian economy the global downturn scenario led to an increase in PDs of up to 71 per cent relative to the baseline. Third, to assess contagion risk within the Austrian interbank market in a multi-period environment, the interbank market was cleared after each quarter. If a bank

---

[46] For further details see Boss *et al.* (2008) and IMF (2008). Please note that for the sake of comparison these publications mostly refer to results that do not take into account contagion risk, while Table 12.3 does. For the second scenario that assumed a regional shock in CESEE affecting Austrian banks through their strong engagement in the region, the SRM could not be used due to data limitations. This will change, however, in the future as respective data is now available under the new reporting scheme that became effective at the beginning of 2008.

Table 12.3 Impact of the global downturn scenario of the Austrian FSAP update in 2007

Global downturn: impact on CAR with contagion[a]

	CAR 2007/06	Quarterly CAR from 2007/09 to 2010/06												Overall impact[b]
		Q1	Q2	Q3	Q4	Q5	Q6	Q7	Q8	Q9	Q10	Q11	Q12	
Total system	12.6	12.6	12.6	12.6	12.6	12.6	12.6	12.6	12.5	12.5	12.5	12.4	12.4	−0.22
Aggregates by size[c]														
Big banks (6)	11.5	11.5	11.5	11.5	11.5	11.5	11.5	11.5	11.5	11.5	11.5	11.5	11.5	−0.06
Large banks (22)	13.3	13.3	13.3	13.2	13.2	13.2	13.2	13.1	13.1	13.0	12.9	12.7	12.6	−0.66
Medium-sized banks (39)	18.2	18.2	18.2	18.2	18.2	18.2	18.2	18.1	18.0	18.0	17.8	17.7	17.5	−0.70
Small banks (635)	16.2	16.1	16.1	16.1	16.1	16.0	16.0	15.9	15.8	15.6	15.5	15.2	15.0	−1.18
Aggregates by sector[d]														
Joint stock banks (34)	13.6	13.6	13.6	13.6	13.6	13.6	13.6	13.6	13.6	13.5	13.5	13.5	13.4	−0.16
Savings banks (8)	10.9	10.9	10.9	10.9	10.9	10.9	10.9	10.9	10.9	10.9	10.8	10.8	10.8	−0.03
State mortage banks (5)	10.5	10.5	10.5	10.5	10.5	10.5	10.5	10.5	10.5	10.5	10.5	10.5	10.4	−0.10
Raiffeisen banks (561)	13.1	13.1	13.1	13.1	13.0	13.0	13.0	13.0	12.9	12.9	12.8	12.7	12.6	−0.50
Volksbanken (64)	12.3	12.3	12.3	12.3	12.3	12.3	12.2	12.2	12.2	12.1	12.1	12.0	11.9	−0.38
Special purpose banks (30)	16.2	16.0	16.0	15.8	15.8	15.6	15.5	15.2	15.1	14.7	14.5	14.0	13.7	−2.45
Distribution of banks' CAR according to share in total number of banks														
Over 12 per cent	75.6	75.2	75.2	75.2	75.1	74.9	74.4	73.2	72.4	71.2	70.2	68.7	67.0	−8.69
10 to 12 per cent	16.7	16.8	16.8	16.7	16.4	16.2	16.5	17.2	16.8	17.7	17.8	16.4	16.4	−0.28
8 to 10 per cent	7.7	7.8	7.7	7.8	8.3	8.4	8.7	8.5	9.5	8.8	9.5	11.1	11.1	3.42
4 to 8 per cent	0.0	0.0	0.1	0.1	0.1	0.3	0.3	0.7	1.0	1.9	1.9	3.3	4.8	4.84
Under 4 per cent	0.0	0.1	0.1	0.1	0.1	0.1	0.1	0.3	0.3	0.4	0.6	0.6	0.7	0.71

Table 12.3 (cont.)

Global downturn: impact on CAR with contagion[a]

	CAR 2007/06	Quarterly CAR from 2007/09 to 2010/06												Overall impact[b]
		Q1	Q2	Q3	Q4	Q5	Q6	Q7	Q8	Q9	Q10	Q11	Q12	
Distribution of banks' CAR according to share in total assets														
Over 12 per cent	41.5	41.2	41.2	41.2	41.1	41.1	41.0	40.4	40.3	40.1	40.0	39.9	39.7	−1.78
10 to 12 per cent	52.5	52.6	52.6	52.6	52.6	52.6	52.4	53.0	53.0	53.1	53.2	52.4	51.1	−1.43
8 to 10 per cent	6.0	6.0	6.0	6.0	6.0	6.0	6.2	6.2	6.3	6.2	6.3	6.9	7.4	1.43
4 to 8 per cent	0.0	0.0	0.1	0.1	0.1	0.1	0.1	0.1	0.1	0.2	0.2	0.5	1.4	1.41
Under 4 per cent	0.0	0.3	0.3	0.3	0.3	0.3	0.3	0.3	0.3	0.3	0.3	0.3	0.4	0.37

Notes:
[a] Figures in per cent if not stated otherwise;
[b] Change of Capital Adequacy Ratios (CARs) in percentage points relative to baseline;
[c] Number of banks in brackets, see section 12.2.1 for the definition of the breakdown by size;
[d] Number of banks in brackets, see section 12.2.1 for the definition of the breakdown by sectors.

Source: OeNB

defaulted in some period, its interbank exposure was ignored in subsequent quarters to avoid double counting contagion effects. As a default criterion, a CAR below a 4 per cent threshold was assumed. Finally, in contrast to the actual standard implementation of the SRM, in this stress test banks' profits were taken into account, assuming a path of decreasing profits relative to the baseline profits in June 2007, where quarterly profits decreased by up to 17 per cent relative to the baseline profits. It was assumed that expected losses are fully covered by existing loan loss provisions, and that additional expected losses due to increased PDs and potential losses in the interbank market in consequence of other banks' defaults would affect profits in first line. Only in cases where profits were not sufficient to cover these losses was capital eaten up. On the contrary, capital could not grow through profits, assuming that they were distributed among shareholders after each period.

Table 12.3 shows results of the global downturn scenario of the FSAP-2007 for the Austrian banking system in terms of the impact on the CAR for the aggregated banking system, various sub-aggregates and the respective distribution according to the number of banks and their share in total assets. Due to the fact that some banks could not cover the additional expected credit risk losses, the overall CAR dropped by about 0.22 percentage points, although aggregate profits were still sufficient to cover the additional losses. The largest impact on the aggregated level struck small banks, which showed a 1.18 percentage point reduction of their aggregate CAR to 15 per cent at the end of the three-year horizon. For the six largest banks, however, the impact on the aggregate CAR was a mere 0.06 percentage points as most of them could cover additional credit risk losses through profits. Regarding sector aggregates, special purpose banks were affected most with a decrease in CAR of 2.45 percentage points, resulting in a CAR of 13.7.

Some very small banks fell below the 8 per cent level (undercapitalised), and even fewer fell below the 4 per cent threshold (insolvent). However, the undercapitalised banks accounted for only about 1.4 per cent of total assets of the Austrian banking system, and the insolvent ones for less than 0.4 per cent, which confirms that only very small banks were affected severely by the stress scenario. These severely hit banks typically show a weak capital base and low or negative profits. In addition, virtually all of them are organised in one of the tiered sectors of the Austrian banking system and would most likely benefit from a solution within their sector thus preventing actual defaults.[47]

---

[47] This would typically imply a merger or a capital injection organised within the sector.

These implicit guarantees within the sectors were not taken into account so that all banks falling below the 4 percent CAR threshold potentially could cause domino effects. Nevertheless results including interbank contagion risk showed an impact only slightly higher compared to simulations that did not account for contagion. This can be traced back to the fact that none of the systemically important banks is severely affected by the scenario – in fact most of them could absorb additional credit risk losses through projected profits.

The use of the SRM in the FSAP-2007 exercise pointed out some important directions for its further development. Besides the integration of Austrian banks' subsidiaries in CESEE into the network model, which is crucial from the OeNB's perspective given their strong engagement in the region, this would in particular demand for extending the current time horizon of the SRM to a longer period, which will be discussed in the following concluding remarks.

12.8 Conclusions

The SRM is a new framework for the risk assessment of a banking system. Its first innovation concerns the analytical focus on the entire banking system rather than individual institutions. Conceptually it is possible to take this perspective by measuring the impact of a set of risk factors on banks in combination with a network model of mutual credit relations, the second innovation of the SRM. Most important, though, is the SRM's combination of the two. As shown in this chapter, this kind of framework can be easily applied as the input data is readily available at regulatory authorities, the kind of institutions for which a model as suggested here is of crucial interest. In addition, it was shown how the SRM can be used for stress-testing. As a stress-testing tool it allows for a consistent treatment of stress scenarios by using a simulation from the conditional risk factor distribution given the stressed values of some risk factors. By its modular structure the SRM, however, also allows for more traditional approaches to stress-testing, such as sensitivity analyses. These methods are nested in the SRM.

Of course in an attempt to develop good quantitative models for systemic risk assessment the SRM is only a first step. The model has some advantages as well as some limitations. Looking at the limitations, perhaps the most relevant one is, at the same time, the main advantage: the mechanical nature of the SRM. In a way the SRM could be seen as a form of balance sheet mechanics. Throughout the analysis it is assumed that portfolio positions (balance sheets) are given and their values are entirely determined by the risk factors. While this mechanical perspective is useful for a short-term analysis of risks that can be observed in the available data of the banking system, clearly it would be desirable to have some aspects of behaviour of the major players in the model.[48] This need not necessarily be (in a first step) a fully-fledged model of optimising behaviour. Some empirically founded hypotheses about bank behaviour might already be a big step forward. Looking at the current international debt crisis, the liquidity problems in many different segments of the international capital markets, including interbank markets, are playing a key role. These behavioural aspects, such as banks being reluctant to roll over debt because they cannot value assets and risks, cannot be described in a mechanical model of clearing a system of debts.

The second limitation is that the model does not take into account the interaction between behaviour, balance sheet mechanics and asset prices that play a key role in the risks borne by the banking system. The biggest challenge for future developments is the question of whether these aspects can be taken into account in a tractable and traceable way. Such an extension would be a big step forward because it would not only give a richer and more realistic picture of risk exposure of the banking system, it would also open the possibility to look at longer (and perhaps more meaningful) time horizons.

With these limitations in mind consider the main advantages of the model. The system perspective can uncover exposures to aggregate risks that are invisible for traditional banking supervision which relies on the assessment of single institutions only. The biggest limitation of the SRM also features among its main advantages: the model does not rely on a sophisticated theory of economic behaviour. In fact, the model is simply a tool to interpret available data in a novel way. The consequences of a given liability and asset structure in combination with realistic shock scenarios are uncovered in terms of implied technical insolvencies of institutions. Its mechanical nature allows the direct combination with banking data and is the reason for its applicability. The model is designed to exploit existing data sources. Although these sources are not perfect, the SRM shows that despite the daunting complexity of the subject the quantification of financial stability at the system level is possible.

We hope that the SRM is interesting for other researchers at central banks and international institutions that look for quantitative models of systemic risk. We believe that our ideas and results should be encouraging because they show that useful things can be done. We also hope that the limitations of our

---

[48] See also Chapter 3.

model are a challenge for future research. Among the many challenges, the step beyond the pure balance sheet mechanics while keeping tractability is perhaps the major one.

REFERENCES

Alessandri, P., P. Gai, S. Kapadia, N. Mora and C. Puhr (2007), *A Framework for Quantifying Systemic Stability*, Bank of England, mimeo.

Blien, U. and F. Graef (1997), 'Entropy Optimising Methods for the Estimation of Tables', *Classification, Data Analysis, and Data Highways*, Springer.

Boss, M. (2002), 'A Macroeconomic Credit Risk Model for Stress Testing the Austrian Credit Portfolio', *OeNB Financial Stability Report*, 4.

Boss, M., T. Breuer, H. Elsinger, G. Krenn, A. Lehar, C. Puhr and M. Summer (2006), 'Systemic Risk Monitor: Risk Assessment and Stress Testing for the Austrian Banking System', *OeNB technical document*, available upon request from the authors.

Boss, M., G. Fenz, G. Krenn, J. Pann, C. Puhr, T. Scheiber, S. W. Schmitz, M. Schneider and E. Ubl (2008), 'Stress Tests for the Austrian FSAP Update 2007: Methodology, Scenarios and Results', *OeNB Financial Stability Report*, 15.

Boss, M., G. Krenn, C. Puhr and M. Summer (2006), 'Systemic Risk Monitor: A Model for Systemic Risk Analysis and Stress Testing of Banking Systems', *OeNB Financial Stability Report*, 11.

Credit Suisse (1997), *CreditRisk+. A Credit Risk Management Framework*, Credit Suisse Financial Products.

Daul, S., E. De Giorgi, F. Lindskog and A. McNeil (2003), 'The Grouped t-copula with an Application to Credit Risk', *Risk*, 16, November.

DeRaaij, G. and B. Raunig (2002), 'Evaluating Density Forecasts with an Application to Stock Market Returns', *OeNB Working Paper*, 59.

Eisenberg, L. and T. Noe (2001), 'Systemic Risk in Financial Systems', *Management Science*, 47, February.

Elsinger, H. (2007), *Financial Networks, Cross Holdings, and Limited Liability*, OeNB, mimeo.

Elsinger, H., A. Lehar and M. Summer (2006), 'Risk Assessment for Banking Systems', *Management Science*, 52, September.

International Monetary Fund (2008), 'Austria: Financial Sector Assessment Program Technical Note – Stress Testing and Short-Term Vulnerabilities', *IMF Country Report*, 08/204, July.

McNeil, A. and R. Frey (2000), 'Estimation of Tail-related Risk Measures for Heteroscedastic Financial Time Series: an Extreme Value Approach', *Journal of Empirical Finance*, 7, November.

Nelsen, R. B. (2006), *An Introduction to Copulas*, Springer.

OeNB/FMA (2005), *Off-site Analysis Framework of Austrian Banking Supervision – Austrian Banking Business Analysis*, Vienna.

Papke, L. and J. Wooldridge (1996), 'Econometric Methods for Fractional Response Variables with an Application to 401(k) Plan Participation Rates', *Journal of Applied Econometrics*, 11, November.

13 From macro to micro: the French experience on credit risk stress-testing

Muriel Tiesset and Clément Martin[*]

13.1 Main features and objectives of the French stress-testing framework

The stress-testing approach adopted by the Commission Bancaire – Banque de France is based on a reduced form credit risk model, where the capacity of a borrowing agent to repay his debt is determined by the difference between the value of his assets and the nominal value of his debt. Hence, the link with stress-testing exercises can be easily made through two complementary steps. First, the asset is modelled as a variable that adjusts over time under the realisation of random shocks, which can either be idiosyncratic (agent-specific) or systemic (macroeconomic) in nature. In that context, our stress test will implicitly consist of quantifying the impact of these shocks – or risk factors – to the asset value of the borrower. Second, according to Merton (1974), the comparison of the asset value to the nominal debt value determines the default of the borrower. The default occurs when the value of the debt exceeds the value of the assets. Therefore, the measure of credit risk, over a one-year horizon, is the probability of default (PD). The Basel 2 regulatory framework – namely the Internal Ratings Based (IRB) approach for credit risk – provides us with an appropriate structure for stress-testing. Compliant with Vasicek (2002), our stress-testing exercises will aim at assessing how systemic and/or idiosyncratic risk factors may affect the dynamic of PDs in banks' loan portfolios.

In the Basel 2 IRB approach, the minimum capital requirement is determined through the distribution of losses occurring because of default events in banks' loan portfolios. The emphasis is put on unexpected losses, determined by the 99.9 per cent confidence level of the loss distribution. In turn, the expected losses (the average loss over the distribution) are taken into account

[*] Banque de France – French Banking Commission. This chapter expresses the opinions of the authors and does not necessarily reflect the views of the French Banking Commission and the Banque de France.

through depreciations in the banking book. Hence, the computation of Basel 2 regulatory capital depends on four essential different factors: the PD, the loss given default (LGD), the exposure at default (EAD), and the correlation to systematic risk (the link between the default of two borrowers, depending on idiosyncratic – credit quality – but also on a common systematic factor, usually identified as the macroeconomic conditions under which these two borrowers operate). In principle, stress-testing exercises may focus on each of the parameters of the credit risk model. In practice though, supervisors generally consider some of these parameters to be more sensitive to economic and financial fluctuations than others, namely PDs and LGDs. Moreover, the most recent works on stress-testing have opened the field and provided some insight in the understanding of changes in the 'correlation to the systematic factor' under stress conditions.[1]

Hence, the genesis of the French stress-testing toolbox has clearly been inspired by Basel 2 but was also led by some important data issues. Interestingly, the Banque de France has recently obtained an agreement as External Credit Assessment Institution (ECAI) under Basel 2 for its internal rating system of French companies. In parallel, the French central bank holds and regularly updates a Credit Register for all corporate loans above €25,000, granted by French resident banks. Put together, these two sources of information help with capturing the entire loss distribution of the corporate portfolios of French banks and analysing the distortion of that distribution under stress conditions. At this stage, it is then possible to analyse the migration of credit volumes towards higher-risk buckets, and estimate additional potential losses due to this migration, both in terms of expected losses (EL) and unexpected losses (UL). In that sense, we do not restrict ourselves to PD analysis but make use of the whole distribution of losses. Consequently, this stress-testing framework may convey information on losses due to a shock, then on additional risk weighted assets (RWA), but also on the amount of regulatory capital needed under Basel 2.

In order to measure additional capital requirements following the occurrence of a stress event, it is also incumbent to infer how the numerator of the implicit solvency ratio will change after the shock. Though our framework does not yet address the issue of banks' provisioning policy with respect to potential risks arising, we have developed an analysis on how banks' revenues may be affected by macro or financial shocks. In a first approximation, it is indeed possible to consider that losses arising from an unexpected stress event

---

[1] See Avesani *et al.* (2006) or Goodhart *et al.* (2004).

may directly affect the level of Tier-1 capital at banks. Eventually, our global assessment can be done on the basis of a 'stressed' solvency ratio such as a Basel 2-compliant Tier-1 ratio.

As regards the nature and explanation of shocks, a clear option was taken – in line with the International Monetary Fund (IMF) Financial Sector Assessment Program (FSAP) exercise carried out in 2004 – towards a scenario-based analysis in the first place, which does not exclude, in a second round, the possibility to implement micro-based stress tests and sensitivity analyses of the banking sector's resilience.[2] In most cases, the stress-testing procedure starts with the most general information (macro or financial risk factors) and ends with looking at the resilience of the banking sector as a whole but also of individual banks. In addition, some specific tools have been developed in order to support offsite supervisors' examinations, and namely provide them with a micro-based assessment of individual banks' expected losses according to the structure of their balance sheet.[3]

Finally, but most importantly, we need to consider what would be the accurate interpretation of the results obtained through the simulation of stress tests. The key is to examine stress-testing results in the context of a crisis such as the financial turmoil that started in mid-2007. This kind of 'benchmarking exercise' has the purpose of better identifying what a stress test exercise of this art is about and what it is not about. The 2007–8 financial crisis is a good example of a severe shock that can be used for benchmarking purposes. It started with a strong increase in delinquencies rates on the much-delimited US market for sub prime loans, and ended up rapidly in a crisis of the whole securitisation market. Due to a lack of transparency, from complex products based on underlying depreciated sub-prime assets, the crisis broadened to most of the credit derivatives, including all types of asset-backed securities (ABSs), collateralised debt obligations (CDOs), asset-backed commercial papers (ABCPs) and special investment vehicles (SIVs). At a certain stage of the crisis, namely three or four months after its initial surge, a relatively large proportion of analysts considered that it essentially was a financial crisis, the impact of which was to be measured through depreciations on the trading books of banks. Certainly, when looking at the depreciations that were disclosed by large international banks, it seems impossible to consider this crisis is anecdotal. Back to our stress-testing framework, though, it is also obvious that it is useless to analyse the first round effects of the crisis.

---

[2] See De Bandt and Oung (2004).   [3] Système d'Aide à l'Analyse Bancaire, 2nd version (SAABA2).

Since then, the story has been developing. The initial assumption of a permanent decoupling of the credit and business cycles has been progressively left out. Different channels of contagion – outside of the direct recessionary effect of the 2007 financial crisis on the US economy – are at stake. In particular, deleveraging and re-intermediation of assets of low quality in banks' balance sheets may have triggered new conditions on the loans market that can be summed up as higher cost of refinancing and lower quality in banks' counterparties. Moreover, outside of credit, other financial markets have been hit. Hence, the macroeconomic and macrofinancial risks now appear to be the most plausible. Undoubtedly, our stress-testing framework may obtain some interesting results as regards the impact of lower growth perspective, higher refinancing rates, lower asset prices on financial markets, lower credit supply (credit crunch) or lower quality of counterparts on banks' balance sheets and profit and loss accounts. In that sense, potential second round effects of a financial crisis on the banking sector, such as the recent one, may be captured by our macro stress tests.

We present the different stress-testing tools developed and used at the French Banking Commission in the following way. Section 13.2 addresses the structure of our macro stress-testing framework and provides developments on scenario analysis. Section 13.3 revisits the issue of *ad hoc* shocks regarding the quality of corporate loans, more in line with credit risk analysis in banks. Section 13.4 refers to micro-based stress-testing and potential links with macro shocks. Section 13.5 concludes.

13.2 Stress-testing the French banking sector through macroeconomic scenarios

The heart of our macro stress-testing framework is based upon a credit risk model that encompasses the links between macroeconomic factors and banking sector resilience, through the analysis of the migration of corporate credit ratings. Thus, the metric used for the quantification of the capacity of the French banking sector to resist an adverse macro shock can be based on the whole migration of the loss distribution and, in turn, on the estimation of *stressed* RWA. As a consequence, in addition to losses, it is possible to develop a metric based on a solvency ratio.

We propose to test the resilience of the French banking system via the impact on the Tier-1 ratio.[4] Two simultaneous effects from a macroeconomic

---

[4] The French banking system is proxied by an aggregation of the eight largest banking groups.

shock may indeed affect the Tier-1 ratio of the banking system: on the denominator side, the deterioration of the credit quality of banks' counterparts, due to the macro shock, increases the banks' RWA; on the numerator side, equity is going to be lower because of a drop in banks' profitability. The stressed Tier-1 ratio (*indexed by s*) is then compared to the actual ratio (from the baseline scenario) of the French banking sector.

The global impact γ_t^s of the defined macroeconomic shock(s) at time t, compared to the initial level of the baseline scenario *(indexed by 0)* is such as:

$$\gamma_t^s = Tier1_t^0/RWA_t^0 - Tier1_t^s/RWA_t^s \tag{1}$$

As a result, one of the strengths of our framework resides in its comprehensiveness and explicit relationship between macro scenario designs (with a satellite macroeconomic model) and their impact on bank-specific data, using a single metric to report on the stress-testing results, a stressed Tier-1 ratio (Figure 13.1).

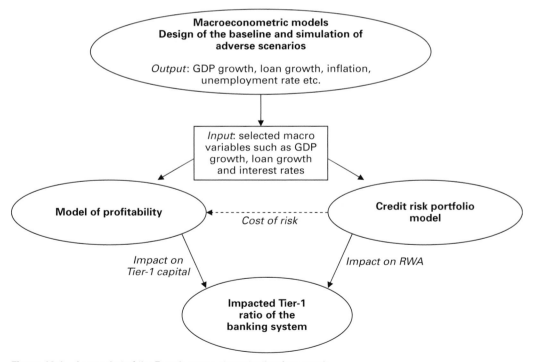

Figure 13.1   A snapshot of the French macro stress-testing framework

13.2.1 The corporate credit risk model: impact of stress scenarios on RWAs

In different risk models, credit risk migration matrixes are often assumed to be invariant over time, but as credit risks may change with the business cycle, the structure of banks' credit portfolios can be distorted (Box 13.1).

We examine how far the impact of macro risk factors is observable both in the shift (towards the right) and the distortion (including a potentially larger tail) of the loss distribution. This is what makes our approach of credit risk

---

Box 13.1 A migration model for credit risk

Estimates of future risk-weighted assets are computed using the probability of migration from one rating class to another, in banks' corporate portfolios. These probabilities are summed up in a 'migration matrix'. The historical transition matrixes are obtained using the scoring systems developed at the Banque de France ('the score').[5]

We make the assumption that the migration of corporates from one rating class to another between two periods may be related to either the phase of the business cycle or changes in interest rates.

Before any analysis can be carried out, each element of the migration matrixes (M_t) has to be 'linearised'. Hence, adopting a Markovian approach, it is possible to transform each element of the system according to the following *logit*-type model:

$$M_t = [P(rating_t = j | rating_{t-1} = i)]_{ij}$$

$$z_{i,t} = \log \left[\frac{P(rating_t \leq j | rating_{t-1} = i)}{P(rating_t < j | rating_{t-1} = i)} \right]$$

$$z_{ij,t} = \theta_{ij} z_{ij,t-1} + \alpha_{ij} + \beta_{ij} X_t + \varepsilon_{ij,t}$$

$$X_t = macroeconomic\ variables\ (GDP\ growth\ and\ interest\ rates)$$

The z_{ijt} are then econometrically estimated using macroeconomic factors such as GDP growth, short-term and long-term interest rates as regressors. Hence, using stressed macro factors, we can use a reverse engineering process to recompose 'stressed' transition Matrices M^S.

Thus, a stressed loan portfolio P^S can be obtained, using the initial known portfolio P_{t-1}, computed from the scoring system combined with banks' corporate exposures reported in the Credit Register): $P_t^S = M_t^S \cdot P_{t-1}$.

Hence, knowing the entire risk composition of the stressed portfolio, it is possible to measure what would be the additional capital requirements, based on the increase in EL and UL combined in a Basel 2 formula (see Appendix 1).

---

[5] See Appendix 1 for a short description of the Banque de France 'Score'.

more comprehensive than the traditional ones, which usually look only at the event of default. Using this type of framework – though more complex to interpret – opens the view on how credit risk globally changes in the wake of a shock to the economy and/or to financial markets.

This first step provides us with an estimate of the potential increase (or decrease) of RWA during stressed periods (see section 13.2.3 below for a description of the stress scenarios tested) on the banking sector, with a distinction between two different effects. First, there may be a 'volume effect' after a recessionary shock, due to a downward adjustment of the size of the loans' portfolio. This may decrease the amount of risk borne by banks and, as a consequence, reduce the amount of RWA. This would then, other things equal, increase banks' Tier-1 ratio. On the contrary, the subsequent 'risk effect' would reduce banks' Tier-1 ratio, through the decline in credit quality of corporate counterparties. The latter effect would indeed mechanically raise the total RWA. As a result, the interpretation of the macro stress-testing exercises will consist of identifying which of these two effects may dominate the other one over a certain period of time after the occurrence of the stress.

In that context, we consider that this approach is rather dynamic and partly integrates what could be the reactions of non-financial actors as well as banks (in terms of credit demand and supply, though not explicitly expressed in this framework) in the occurrence of a macro or financial shock with a recessive impact on the economy.

13.2.2 The determinants of bank profitability

The model developed by De Bandt and Oung (2004) and used for the French IMF FSAP exercise looked at the net interest margin as a *proxy* of banking profitability. Though, as the ECB already pointed out, the trend towards disintermediation reveals an increasing share of non-interest income in banks' revenue. The share of commissions and fees and trading revenues in the net banking income of French banks have clearly increased over the past few years, namely due to important changes in banks' business mix (Box 13.2).

Given these recent changes, it sounds preferable to estimate the main determinants of banking profitability, in order to account for the main transmission channels of a macro or financial shock on banks' profit and loss accounts. In particular, Lehmann and Manz (2006) and Rouabah (2006), focusing respectively on the Switzerland and Luxembourg banking systems, look at macro and bank-specific drivers of income sources such as interest margins, commissions and fees, profit and loss from trading activities, etc.

Box 13.2 A steady decline in the share of interest income in France

In recent years, large French banking groups have sought to increase the proportion of non-interest income in order to maintain satisfactory profitability in times of low interest rates and keen competition on the domestic market. These factors have led to a lasting contraction of lending margins. Consequently, the share of interest income included in net banking income has shrunk substantially. On the other hand, the share of commission income has increased. In particular, the provision of financial services, including managing payment instruments, along with commissions on customer transactions, accounts for the bulk. Also, the share of trading income has increased, with a more volatile profile and a large contribution from transactions in forward financial instruments.

The increase in non-interest income can be explained by different factors relating to the general macroeconomic environment and by other factors that are specific to the banking industry in France. Factors explaining the growth of non-interest banking income in many countries include technological progress, deregulation of financial markets, consolidation of the industry and a downward trend in intermediation income stemming from keen competition. Under French regulations, it is possible to adopt a universal banking model for highly diversified business activities, including asset management, which further boosts commission income. At the same time, competition in intermediation is particularly keen in France, where lending margins are considerably thinner than European averages. This competition also explains much of the increasing geographical diversification of intermediation income, as French banks expand into areas with higher potential for growth both in terms of margins and business volume.

French banks, like other major international banks, have drawn inspiration from the 'originate and distribute' model, where business activity stemming from intermediation is transformed into products that are negotiable on financial markets.

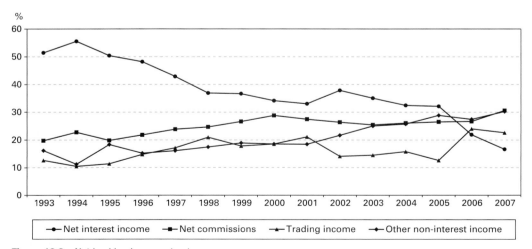

Figure 13.2 Net banking income structure
Source: Commission Bancaire.

To identify the main determinants of French banks' profitability, and thus the main potential channels of transmission of shocks on banks' revenues, we regress banking profitability (in terms of return on assets, ROA) on macroeconomic and financial factors, as well as on bank-specific factors. Using ROA as the endogenous variable allows us to implicitly take into account fluctuations of both non-interest (retail and financial services fees, trading revenues, etc.) and net interest income (intermediation revenues).[6] The main determinants identified are gross domestic product (GDP) growth (or, alternatively, the stock index return), the growth of loans to the private sector adjusted by the spread on short- versus long-term interest rates (proxy for the interest margin), and the idiosyncratic credit risk (proxied by the loan losses to provision ratio of banks).

Not surprisingly, the regression results suggest that a higher GDP growth or higher stock returns – an alternative explanatory variable to GDP growth in the equation – increase banking profits. The growth of credit to the private sector adjusted by the interest rate spread (proxy of the interest margin) also has a positive impact on banking incomes through the intermediation activities (retail fees and loans rates). Alternative estimations also suggest that yield curve volatility is rather harmful to banks' profitability. This result is consistent with the economic intuition that French banks mainly offer fixed-rate retail loans (real estate sector) and are then exposed to interest rate fluctuations on their balance sheets. Finally, loan loss provisions (as a proxy of credit risk) have a strong negative effect on banks' profit.

13.2.3 Scenario analysis and stress impact measurement

The simulations of selected macro and financial scenarios are based on the macroeconometric models (Mascotte and Nigem) developed and/or used by the Banque de France for the purpose of the 'Broad Macroeconomic Projection Exercise' carried out at the Eurosystem level.[7] First, these models simulate the baseline scenario defined as the forecast of the French economy over a period of two years. In particular, the Nigem model estimates the feedback effects of macroeconomic shocks through an international multi-country approach.

---

[6] See Appendix 2 for a description of the methodology and results of the estimations.
[7] Mascotte is a macroeconometric model for France, see Baghli *et al.* (2004). Nigem is an international new Keynesian macroeconometric model developed by the National Institute of Economics and Social Research (*NIESR*), London.

Macro models have the advantage of providing an analytical framework which makes different transmission mechanisms consistent with macroeconomic behaviours. However, these kinds of model do not incorporate any assumption as regards financial constraints in the economy, which means for example that households obtain as much credit as they need, even in situations where it does not economically make sense. This is indeed a serious limitation, which we usually try to smooth by adding additional assumptions in the macroeconomic model.

The macro stress test exercise is then based on a multi-step procedure. The choice of scenarios is particularly important. Relating to the baseline scenario, stress scenarios are defined as being sufficiently adverse but plausible, reflecting the experts' points of view of the current risk environment.[8] Most of the impacts of the stress scenarios are measured at the banking system level, represented by the eight largest banking groups.[9] One of the first objectives of the macro stress-testing exercise is indeed to have a view on potential systemic risk. Bearing in mind some potential limitations, it is also possible to simulate the impact of the stress scenarios at the individual bank level.[10]

Two types of macro shocks are simulated.

Transitory shocks are implemented progressively over the period. After a few quarters (two to four, depending on the strength and persistence of the shock), stressed variables start jumping back to their initial level, which is reached at the end of the two-year horizon of the stress-testing exercise. Against this backdrop, the maximum impact of the shock is essentially observable within the first year after the occurrence of the shock (Table 13.1).

These types of shocks can usually be qualified as demand shocks, coming through a correction in external or internal demand. The most recent stress-testing exercises include both an external demand shock (a 20 per cent decline in the global foreign demand addressed to France) and an internal demand shock (a combined slowdown in resident consumption and investment) such that the French economy plunges into recession.

- As of January 2008, we observe that a 20 per cent decline in the global demand addressed to France leads to negative GDP growth for the next two

[8] Stress scenarios are discussed with economists at the Banque de France economics department.

[9] These represent about 85 per cent of the banking sector's assets.

[10] Most of the estimations are done at the banking system level, even if they include some idiosyncratic factors (namely in the ROA estimates). As a result, we have to infer that all the resulting relationships found at the system level also yield for each bank taken separately. Nevertheless, given that in France the eight largest banking groups are all very diversified, and in a sense have (at the group level) a relatively similar business mix, this extrapolation may give some insight on individual banks' capacity of resilience, as a first approximation.

Table 13.1 Stress impact of transitory 'demand' shocks *

	Macroeconomic impact						Impact on the banking sector					
	Impact on GDP growth (ppt)		Impact on loan growth to the private sector (ppt)		Impact on after-tax net profit growth (%)		Change in the growth rate of RWA (ppt)				Change in Tier-1 ratio (bp)	
							Volume effect (ppt)	Risk effect (ppt)	Volume effect (ppt)	Risk effect (ppt)		
Scenarios	2008	2009	2008	2009	2008	2009	2008	2008	2009	2009	2008	2009
Transitory shocks												
−20% drop of the world demand for French goods	−1.2	−0.4	−0.6	−1.2	−30.5%	−11.4%	3.9	4.2	−3.7	−2.4	−55	−17
Shock on consumption and investment	−1.2	−0.6	−3.0	−3.4	−27.7%	−9.8%	2.6	5.3	−7.5	−4.1	−46	18

* Differences to the baseline scenario

quarters. The French activity is impacted (drop in consumption and investment, deficit in the balance of trade, etc.) resulting in a sharp contraction in internal global demand and, with a certain delay, in the loan growth. This in turn leads to an important decline in banks' profits (−30.5 per cent in 2008, −11.4 per cent in 2009). The degradation of counterparties' credit quality, due to the recession, increases the growth rate of RWA, the risk effect being clearly dominant during the period of the stress (first year). As a result, the solvency Tier-1 ratio is negatively impacted.

- A recession caused by an internal demand shock has similar effects on the Tier-1 ratio, but with a different mix between volume and risk effects.

Permanent shocks are entirely taken into account at the occurrence of the stress period and maintained throughout the whole period. These shocks are more often referred to as market or monetary policy shocks. The most recent stress-testing exercises simulate three types of these shocks (Table 13.2).

- A 20 per cent depreciation of the dollar against the euro. This scenario leads to a decline in the competitiveness of French goods. The impact on the activity is marginal, the international trade of French goods being mainly carried out in the euro area. However, French banks have foreign exchange trading activities and a sudden depreciation of the dollar may have a significant impact on their portfolios. These are usually hedged but the depreciation may have indirect consequences on financial markets with the decline of some specific asset prices such as interest rates, and may potentially spread out through financial markets contagion. Eventually, banks' profits are impacted but the RWA decrease because of a downward adjustment of the size of banks' balance sheets as regards loans (volume effect) dominates.

- A parallel shift upwards of 200 basis points of the whole euro yield curve. This stress scenario has a significant impact on the solvency ratio, even more after two years. The rising interest rates lead to a deterioration of the credit quality of banks' counterparts; the increase of risk impacts significantly the dynamics of RWA (+10.6 percentage points on the growth rate of RWA compared to the baseline, on the portfolio risk profile) which triggers a sharp drop in the Tier-1 ratio of more than a half of a percentage point.

- Further inversion of the yield curve (an increase of 200 basis points in the Euribor 3-month rate, an increase of 100 basis points in the 10-year government bond yield). This scenario has a similar global effect on banks' solvency to the parallel shift of the yield curve. Nevertheless, this

Table 13.2 Stress impact of permanent market or policy shocks*

	Macroeconomic impact						Impact on the banking sector					
	Impact on GDP growth (ppt)		Impact on loan growth to the private sector (ppt)		Impact on after-tax net profit growth (%)		Impact on the growth rate of RWA (ppt)				Change in Tier-1 ratio (bp)	
							Volume effect (ppt)	Risk effect (ppt)	Volume effect (ppt)	Risk effect (ppt)		
Scenarios	2008	2009	2008	2009	2008	2009	2008	2008	2009	2009	2008	2009
20% depreciation of the dollar against the euro	−0.3	−0.1	−1.0	−0.6	−6.8%	−4.5%	0.1	1.1	−1.1	−0.5	−11	−0.3
Parallel shift of the euro yield curve (+200 bp)	−0.2	−0.3	−1.3	−1.3	−7.8%	−13.3%	−3.3	−1.8	9.7	10.6	16	−54
Increase of 200 bp of the Euribor-3M and 100 bp of the OAT-10yrs	−0.1	−0.1	−0.9	−0.8	−16.5%	−31.8%	−3.0	−2.0	7.3	7.8	6	−46

Permanent shocks

* Differences to the baseline scenario

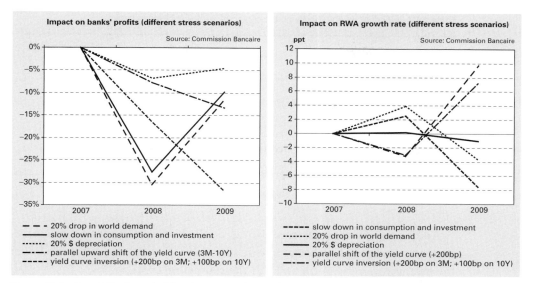

Figure 13.3   Cumulative impact of the stress scenarios on the dynamics of banks' profitability and RWA.

result occurs with a different mix between numerator effects (more pronounced in that scenario) and denominator effects (less pronounced). Figure 13.3 summarises the impact of different scenarios.

13.3 Stress-testing corporate credit portfolios through *ad hoc* credit shocks: analysing banks' concentration risk on business sectors

Taking a more micro-oriented perspective, the French Banking Commission also conducts uniform 'downgrading' stress exercises, in order to detect potential vulnerabilities directly at corporate portfolio level, such as sector concentration risk. The stress is applied on the whole French banking system and separately for each of the eight major French banking groups.[11]

This sensitivity analysis relies upon the simulation of a downgrade of one to two notches in the average credit quality of banks' loan portfolios, using the Banque de France's rating scale as a benchmark (Table 13.3). The impact of the shock translates into an instantaneous increase in the PD of the portfolio and, other things equal, an instantaneous drop in the banks' Tier-1 ratio.

[11] In the chapter, we only publish *ad hoc* credit shock results of the whole banking system.

Table 13.3 Impact of *ad hoc* shocks on the corporate portfolio of French banks

Credit shock	Impact on the probability of default (%)	Impact on the Tier-1 ratio (bp)
Downgrade by one notch in the credit quality of French corporate counterparties	57%	−87
Downgrade by one notch in the credit quality of French commercial real estate counterparties	15%	−29
Downgrade by two notches in the credit quality of French commercial real estate counterparties	23%	−42

Source: Banque de France (SCR), Commission Bancaire estimates

Additional downgrades can also be applied on sector-specific exposures such as commercial real estate, which has been particularly scrutinised over the past few months in the wake of the sub-prime crisis.

The one notch credit quality shock on the banks' corporate portfolio credit quality is significant with an average PD increase of almost 57 per cent.[12] The one notch (two-notch) credit quality shock on banks' commercial real estate exposures leads to a 15 per cent (23 per cent) rise in the PD of the whole corporate exposure. Even for extreme stress scenarios, the results of the simulations suggest that the impact on the solvency ratio remains absorbable for the French banking sector, but has a non-negligible cost in terms of capital. When sector-specific scenarios show a particular concentration risk at one or several banks, it may lead to a particular monitoring of these banks' exposures on that sector.

13.4 Micro surveillance of French banks' credit portfolio risk profile and potential micro/macro links

Since 2006, the French Banking Commission has been using a 'Support System for Banking Analysis', SAABA2, in which the approach of credit risk has been adapted to fulfil the new regulatory environment (the Basel 2 Accord), focusing on the potential futures losses (EL and UL) in French banks' credit portfolios. The results of this exercise are also mainly devoted to support on-site and off-site supervisors in their daily monitoring of individual banks.

---

[12] The portfolio structure is taken at the end of March 2008.

13.4.1 The methodology of SAABA2: measuring the credit risk profile at the individual level

Based on the premise that credit risk is the banks' major risk, the SAABA2 system is designed to undertake a detailed credit portfolio analysis of each banking institution. Then, an *ad hoc* credit shock is simulated, calibrated according to a scaling factor of the computed amount of EL. Hence, the system computes a stressed Basel 2 ratio, and concludes on the capacity of individual banks to absorb losses (Box 13.3).

13.4.2 A fictive example

Table 13.4 presents the SAABA2-based credit portfolio of a fictive French large banking group. The bank is significantly involved in different segments of the domestic market, granting credits to corporates, households or public administrations. The bank is also active on the money market. Most of the loan losses stem from retail and corporate portfolios.

The *ad hoc* credit shock is simulated using a scaling factor $[\lambda = 3]$ on the amount of expected losses of the bank's credit portfolio.[13] This calibration fits the 95 per cent confidence level regarding the IRB approach. As a result, the adjusted Tier-1 ratio falls by almost 40 per cent. The impact is quite impor-

Table 13.4 Credit portfolio of a fictive bank (million)

	Exposures	PD	LGD	EL	Non-performing exposures	Non-performing losses	Total exposures	Total losses
Domestic								
Interbank lending	70,000	0.18%	24.0%	30.2	35	8.4	70,035	38.6
Retail	200,000	2.15%	25.8%	1,111.9	1,550	400.2	201,550	1,512.0
Public administrations	11,000	0.10%	10.0%	1.1	45	4.5	11,045	5.6
Corporate	250,000	1.23%	50.0%	1,538.5	13,000	6,500.0	263,000	8,038.5
Total domestic	**531,000**			**2,681.7**	**14,630**	**6,913.1**	**545,630**	**9,594.8**
Foreign	200,000	0.43%	50.0%	429.8	3,308	1,654.0	203,308	2,083.8
Total	**731,000**			**3,111.5**	**17,938**	**8,567.1**	**748,938**	**11,678.6**

Source: SAABA2 – Commission Bancaire

---

[13] The insufficient loan loss provisions of the studied bank impacts its Tier-1 ratio of 20 basis points.

Box 13.3 The SAABA2 system: a measure of credit risk at individual bank level

The methodology of the system involves banks' Tier-1 solvency ratio and all outstanding individual credit counterparts of each bank. It integrated the Basel 2 IRB key parameters of the portfolio structure (PD, EAD, LGD).[14] The process can be summed up in three stages:

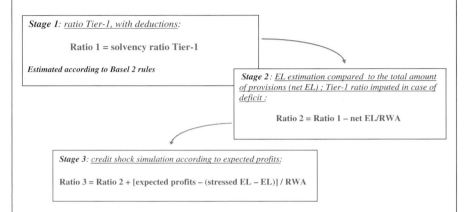

Stage 1: *ratio Tier-1, with deductions*:

Ratio 1 = solvency ratio Tier-1

Estimated according to Basel 2 rules

Stage 2: *EL estimation compared to the total amount of provisions (net EL) ; Tier-1 ratio imputed in case of deficit*:

Ratio 2 = Ratio 1 – net EL/RWA

Stage 3: *credit shock simulation according to expected profits*:

Ratio 3 = Ratio 2 + [expected profits – (stressed EL – EL)] / RWA

First, the initial Basel 2 Tier-1 ratio is calculated. A conservative approach is adopted in the sense that the Tier-1 ratio is impacted in case of insufficient loan loss provisions.

The EL of a given portfolio (retail, corporate, interbank etc.) is then estimated; this step is the heart of the SAABA2 system and makes consistent in a single framework different types of data from complementary databases.

Eventually, a credit risk shock is simulated and banks' solvency levels are impacted due to the occurrence of a shock, represented by 'stressed EL' or equivalently, 'unexpected losses' (UL). Here, UL are not estimated through the simulation of a scenario, but calibrated according to the level of EL: $UL = \lambda EL$.

Initially, the scaling factor λ *has been* settled to 3, as it was consistent with the findings of Basel 2 QIS5 conducted by the Basel Committee of Banking Supervision. Nevertheless, this factor is a parameter of the system and can be easily changed.

The SAABA2 analysis tool is micro-based, but some macro/micro extensions are feasible. In particular, the simulated credit stress is purely *ad hoc* (the exogenous shock is calibrated on the basis of expected losses) and is not defined in the context of wider macroeconomic scenarios. Bearing in mind some potential limitations as regards the extrapolation of macroeconomic estimated relationships to individual banks' analysis, the calibration of the shock (UL) could relatively easily be related to our macro stress-testing framework described above.

---

[14] SAABA2 uses several sources of internal and external information. These include data of the Banque de France (corporate exposures and default rate estimations) and the Banking Commission (prudential data from the database 'BAFI') as well as some additional results from on-site supervisory inspections or impact studies such as the recent Basel Committee of Banking Supervision (BCBS) quantitative impact study (QIS5) The external sources also include S&P's country risk data (sovereign and corporate default rates from foreign exposures).

Table 13.5 SAABA2 solvency analysis

Solvency analysis	
Tier-1 ratio	7.2%
Adjusted Tier-1 ratio	7.0%
Stressed adjusted Tier-1 ratio	4.2%
Global regulatory solvency ratio	10.7%

Source: SAABA2 – Commission Bancaire

tant, however the stressed Tier-1 ratio remains just above the 4 per cent prudential threshold (Table 13.5).

13.5 Conclusions

So far, our objective as regards stress-testing has been to develop a toolbox, putting most of our efforts in both top-down integrated macro stress-testing exercises, looking essentially at systemic risk, and in *ad hoc* sensitivity analyses that may have more direct applications as regards individual banks' risk monitoring. The principle of a toolbox has also been guided by the necessity to diversify the methodologies, in order to identify and curtail potential model risk. Model risk can indeed have two dimensions. First, mis-specifications of risk factors can arise from the estimations. Second, some models may not be completely resilient to tail events as regards their capacity of risk prediction.

In addition, the question of how a delayed impact of a shock is taken into account in a 'stressed' solvency ratio is crucial. In particular, if the right timing of the impact is not well captured by the model, it may be the case that the adjustment of the 'stressed' numerator and 'stressed' denominator, observed at a certain period of time after the shock, is not guaranteed, and that this may bias the estimation of banks' solvency resulting from that stress.

Our further research will be targeted at diversifying our views and methodologies and providing additional insight on existing tools.

For instance, the question of how asset correlations change under a stress event is crucial to estimate what would be the relevant amount of additional regulatory capital that would be necessary for a bank to withstand the shock, without suffering too much from its occurrence.

Moreover, it is also necessary to find interesting ways to benchmark our models. A first possibility would be to go to banks and run bottom-up exercises on the same types of scenarios. A second complementary approach would be to draw lessons from the severe past crises, such as the sub-prime turmoil of 2007, and derive from our observation historical or hypothetical scenarios that would be relevant for banks' risk assessments, and diversify the panel of risks addressed in stress-testing exercises, including for instance liquidity or interest rate risk.

In the same vein, one of the obvious interests of further developing our current tools would be to put more emphasis on macro/micro links in the stress-testing exercises, and find ways to better assess potential macro effects on individual banks, taking into account their own specificities.

Finally, one of the main challenges of macro stress-testing frameworks currently in use, together with ours, is to address the question of feedback effects, from the financial to the real sector, including the question of the (pro) cyclicality of credit, the financial sector and financial sector regulation.

Appendix 1 The credit risk migration model

The rating is estimated with the Banque de France's 'Score'.[15] The score summarises the information contained in factors that affect the default probability. The Banque de France collects default information and uses firm-specific variables from their balance sheet for default prediction (business ratios, profitability, margins, debt structure, etc.). The firms' ratings are then compiled to calculate transition matrixes based on a cohort approach. The model follows the approach of Wei (2003) and Wilson (1997a, b).

1.1 Modelling business cycle effects on transition matrixes

We consider a transition matrix $M_t = (P_{ijt})_{1 \leq i,j \leq D, 0 \leq t \leq T}$, where at time t $P_{ijt} = P(S_t = i | S_{t-1} = i)$ is the probability to change from rating i to j between t and $t - 1$. S_t is the rating class at time t ($S_t = 1,...,7, D$).[16] $P(S_t)$ is the default probability at time t according to the risk rating S_t (estimated by the score). The rating scale presents a satisfactory granularity. The score has been recalibrated with six risk classes, since 2002.

We estimate the model with quarterly data from 1989 to 2002. The length of the time series is long enough to ensure robust results. Three representative

---

[15] For more details, see Bardos (2006).

[16] 7 is the highest quality rating (i.e., Standard & Poor's (S&P's) AAA rating), 1 is the poorest one (S&P's CCC rating).

sectors (industry, services and transport, 51 per cent of the total French corporate exposures) are used to calculate the credit migration matrixes.

We estimate the *logit*-transformed migration risk and the risk of state of default D with economic variables as follows:

$$z_{ijt} = \log\left(\frac{P(S_t \leq j | S_t = i)}{P(S_t > j | S_t = i)}\right) = \log\left(\frac{\sum_{k=1}^{j} P_{ikt}}{\sum_{k=j+1}^{7} P_{ikt}}\right)$$

$$= \alpha_{ij} + \mu_{ij}z_{ijt-1} + \beta'X_t + \varepsilon_{ijt}$$

$$z_{iDt} = \log\left(\frac{P(S_t)}{1 - P(S_t)}\right) = \alpha_{iD} + \mu_{iD}z_{iDt-1} + \beta'X_t + \varepsilon_{iDt}$$

X_t is the vector of macroeconomic factors, provided as an input (baseline and stress scenarios) by the Mascotte model (GDP growth, interest rates). In the stationary state (without macro factors' influences), credit migrations are driven by idiosyncratic risk ($\alpha_{ij} + \varepsilon_{ijt}$). The dynamic specification of the model captures the persistence and contagion effect of credit rating changes, showing the heterogeneity of the corporate portfolio. Firms react differently to an external shock, and the adjustment speed may also differ significantly.

The estimations consist of regressing each z_{ijt} on macroeconomic variables (GDP growth, interest rates). The results are not always significant, due to sometimes (1) weak explanatory power of the model, and (2) insignificant estimates. A part of the variance may certainly be captured by idiosyncratic variables (firm-specific), which are not taken into account in such a framework. To offset some of the limitations of this estimation, we adopt a conservative approach and assume that the α per cent quartile of the estimator $\beta_{1-\alpha}$ is 5 per cent. The estimated coefficients are adjusted with the corresponding standard deviation.

The credit migration model is then stressed. For instance, assuming the GDP growth as macroeconomic factor , we have:

$$\mu = \begin{pmatrix} 0.04 & 0.07 & 0.09 & 0.26 & 0.35 & 0.20 \\ 0.44 & 0.37 & -0.01 & -0.03 & 0.11 & 0.14 \\ 0.28 & 0.42 & 0.27 & 0.45 & 0.59 & 0.56 \\ 0.10 & 0.19 & 0.30 & 0.45 & 0.83 & 0.73 \\ -0.08 & 0.08 & 0.35 & 0.25 & 0.47 & 0.62 \\ 0.04 & 0.02 & 0.34 & 0.38 & 0.25 & 0.20 \\ 0.10 & 0.17 & 0.31 & 0.51 & 0.51 & 0.52 \end{pmatrix}$$

$$\alpha = \begin{pmatrix} -0.46 & 0.80 & 1.65 & 1.85 & 2.07 & 3.21 \\ -1.34 & 0.02 & 1.71 & 2.98 & 3.50 & 4.48 \\ -3.09 & -1.14 & 0.39 & 1.02 & 1.40 & 2.45 \\ -5.06 & -2.71 & -0.81 & 0.36 & 0.40 & 1.28 \\ -7.08 & -4.30 & -1.64 & -0.88 & 0.57 & 1.46 \\ -7.24 & -5.72 & -2.51 & -1.67 & -0.94 & 1.41 \\ -6.68 & -5.20 & -3.61 & -1.99 & -1.46 & -0.63 \end{pmatrix}$$

$$\beta_{95\%}^{GDP} = \begin{pmatrix} -12.08 & -11.00 & -11.57 & -13.02 & -14.16 & -15.27 \\ -11.84 & -7.65 & -13.56 & -22.86 & -22.02 & -26.01 \\ -19.12 & -7.61 & -6.89 & -7.03 & -9.17 & -19.83 \\ -14.70 & -10.95 & -8.48 & -5.48 & -4.85 & -15.75 \\ -25.56 & -18.84 & -8.90 & -8.86 & -4.89 & -12.07 \\ -15.25 & -11.31 & -9.69 & -7.98 & -6.21 & -6.10 \\ -17.28 & -8.41 & -7.85 & -6.64 & -5.40 & -2.63 \end{pmatrix}$$

The coefficient of the matrix is consistent with the economic intuition as GDP growth reduces the downgrading to upgrading probability ratio.

1.2 The capital requirements under a stress credit portfolio

Given an initial credit portfolio $B_{l_0}\left[(S_0)_{i=1,\dots,7,D}\right]$ with the initial risk structure $(S_0)_{i=1,\dots,7,D}$ regarding the baseline scenario l_0, we simulate the T horizon portfolio credit quality deformation as for a given stress scenario l as follows:[17]

$$B_l\left[(S_T)_i\right] = B_l\left[(S_{T-1})_i\right]M_T^{(l)} = B_l\left[(S_{T-2})_i\right]M_T^{(l)}M_{T-1}^{(l)} = \dots$$
$$= B_{l_0}\left[(S_0)_i\right]\prod_{k=0}^{T}M_{T-k}^{(l)}$$

Where $M_{T-k}^{(l)}$ is the transition matrix at time $T\text{-}k$ for a given scenario l.
We obtain the capital requirements by estimating the unexpected losses (UL) for each $t=1\dots,T$, assuming that $LGD = 45\%$ (Basel 2 standard approach):

$$EL\left[(S_t)_i\right] = LGD \cdot B\left[(S_t)_i\right]$$
$$UL\left[(S_t)_i\right] = CreditVaR_{99.9\%,t} - EL\left[(S_t)_i\right] = B\left[(S_t)_i\right] \cdot IRB[P(S_t)]$$

The IRB formula assumes that counterparties' asset return follows a Merton–Vasicek process:[18]

---

[17] Under the non-time homogeneity Markov chain assumption, we assume no new credit allocation.
[18] For a detailed development of the IRB formula using the one-factor Gaussian copula model, see Vasicek (2002).

$$IRB[P(S_t)] = \left[LGD \cdot \Phi\left[[.1 - \gamma[P(S_t)]]^{-1/2} \cdot \Phi^{-1}[P(S_t)] + \left(\frac{\gamma[P(S_t)]}{1 - \gamma[P(S_t)]} \right)^{1/2} \right. \right.$$

$$\left. \left. \cdot\Phi^{-1}(99.9\%) \right] - P(S_t) \cdot LGD \right]$$

with the following Basel 2 *IRB* corporate correlation:

$$\gamma[P(S_t)] = 0.12 \cdot \frac{1 - \exp[-50 \cdot P(S_t)]}{1 - \exp(-50)} + 0.24 \cdot \frac{\exp[-50 \cdot P(S_t)]}{1 - \exp(-50)}$$

Appendix 2 The model of bank profitability

Estimation: methodology and results for the equation used for stress-testing

We regress global banking profitability (in terms of return on asset, ROA) on macroeconomic and financial factors, as well as on bank-specific factors. Using ROA as the endogenous variable allows us to implicitly take into account fluctuations of both non-interest (retail and financial services fees, trading revenues, etc.) and net interest income (intermediation revenues). The model of profitability follows a dynamic panel estimation approach. We extract the data from the 'BAFI' database (French supervisory database), on an annual basis, unconsolidated, for the period 1993–2006. The Arellano and Bond estimator is simulated (generalised method of moments (GMM) estimates), using lagged endogenous and exogenous variables as instruments to get rid of residuals' autocorrelation.

$$\pi_{it} = \underset{(3.03)}{0.16}\,\pi_{it-1} + \underset{(3.19)}{0.083}\,\Delta GDP_t + \underset{(3.47)}{0.01}\,s_t \cdot \Delta L_t - \underset{(-5.22)}{0.15}\,\kappa_{it} + \varepsilon_{it}$$

Student statistic in parentheses
π_{it} is the annual ROA of the bank i at time t;
ΔGDP_t is the annual growth of the GDP at time t;
s_t is the annual risk-free interest rate spread: Obligations Assimilables du Tresor (OAT) 10 years–Euribor 3 months at time t;
ΔL_t is the annual growth of credits to the private sector at time t;
κ_{it} is the annual cost of risk of the bank i at time t;
ε_{it} is the disturbance of the model.

Some additional control variables are added, which do not alter the stability of the estimated equation.

For the stress-testing exercise (both for the central and stress scenarios), expected realisations of exogenous macro variables (GDP and loan growth, interest rate spread, etc.) are simulated with the macroeconomic model of the Banque de France (Mascotte).

The credit risk born by banks is proxied by the loan losses to provision ratio. The expected additional risk, stemming from the stress scenarios, is directly drawn from the credit risk model (migration matrix).

REFERENCES

Avesani, R., A. García Pascual and J. Li (2006), 'A New Risk Indicator and Stress Testing Tool: a Multifactor Nth-to-Default CDS Basket', *IMF Working Paper*, 105.

Baghli, M., V. Brunhes-Lesage, O. De Bandt, H. Fraisse and J. P. Villetel (2004), 'Modèle d'Analyse et de Prevision de la COnjoncture TrimesTriellE – Mascotte', *Banque de France Working Paper*, 5.

Bardos, M. (2006), 'Banque de France Scores: Developments, Applications and Maintenances', *Banque de France Monthly Bulletin Digest*, 151.

De Bandt, O. and V. Oung (2004), 'Assessment of Stress-tests Conducted on the French Banking System', *Banque de France Financial Stability Review*, 5.

Fabi, F., S. Laviola and P. Marullo Reedtz (2004), 'The Treatment of SMEs Loans in the New Basel Capital Accord: Some Evaluations', *BNL Quarterly Review*, 228, March.

Goodhart, C. A. E., P. Sunirand and D. P. Tsomocos (2004), 'A Model to Analyse Financial Fragility: Applications', *Journal of Financial Stability*, 1, 1–30.

Lehmann, H. and M. Manz (2006), 'The Exposure of Swiss Banks to Macroeconomic Shocks: an Empirical Investigation', *Swiss National Banks Working Papers*, 4.

Merton, R. C. (1974), 'On the Pricing of Corporate Debt: the Risk Structure of Interest Rates', *Journal of Finance*, 29 (2), 449–70.

Rouabah, A. (2006), 'La Sensibilité de l'Activité Bancaire aux chocs Macroéconomiques: une Analyse en Panel sur des Données des Banques Luxembourgeoises', *Banque Centrale du Luxembourg Cahier d'études*, 21.

Vasicek, O. (2002), 'Loan Portfolio Value', *Risk*, December, 160–2.

Virolainen, K. (2004), 'Macro Stress Testing with a Macroeconomic Credit Risk Model for Finland', *Bank of Finland Discussion Papers*, 18.

Wei, J. Z. (2003), 'A Multi-factor Credit Migration Model for Sovereign and Corporate Debts', *Journal of International Money and Finance*, 22, 709–35.

Wilson, T. C. (1997a), 'Portfolio Credit Risk I', *Risk*, 10 (9), 111–17.

(1997b), 'Portfolio Credit Risk 2', *Risk*, 10 (10), 56–61.

14 Stress-testing in the EU new member states

Adam Głogowski[*]

14.1 Introduction

There are several important common features of Central and Eastern Europe (CEE) financial systems that influence the analysis of financial stability, including the design of stress tests. Financial systems in European Union (EU) new member states (NMS) are bank-dominated, making banks the focal point of financial stability analysis. Therefore macro stress-testing rarely includes non-bank financial institutions.[1]

The CEE banking systems have a relatively short history of functioning in a market economy and they went through deep-reaching processes of structural change. These included privatisation, development of local financial markets and a broadening of the product range. Perhaps the biggest changes took place in the ownership structure. Most state-owned banks in the region were privatised and taken over by foreign investors, who introduced their skills and corporate culture, significantly changing the market behaviour of many banks. The picture of banking systems found in historical time series is also influenced by important one-off events. The restructuring programmes in the Czech Republic and Slovakia, after their banking systems experienced problems in the late 1990s, are examples of such structural breaks. These developments mean that time series consistent with the current shape of the financial system are quite short.

As mentioned, NMS banks are typically owned by international banking groups, mostly from EU-15 countries.[2] This influences the policy of NMS banks, making them put more emphasis on local market operations. More

---

[*] National Bank of Poland, Financial System Department. The views expressed herein are those of the author only and should not be construed to represent the official viewpoint of the National Bank of Poland. The author is indebted to Marta Gołajewska for valuable comments on a draft version.

[1] This is however also common in other countries (see Chapter 2). An exception is the approach of the Czech National Bank (CNB, 2007), where the macro stress test includes insurers and pension funds.

[2] See e.g., Mérő and Valentinyi (2003).

importantly, this also raises the question of whether and how parent company support or spillover effects should be factored in to stress-testing exercises. As international banking groups typically operate in NMS through subsidiaries, which take part in host country deposit guarantee schemes (as opposed to branches), local authorities are interested in the health of subsidiaries on a stand-alone basis.[3]

The rapid development of financial intermediation in NMS since the second half of the 1990s, in mostly benign economic conditions, means that the performance of certain financial products, such as mortgages, is not tested yet through a full economic cycle. This again reduces the usefulness of aggregate historical time series for forward-looking analysis. Consequently, the use of alternative data (such as surveys, or micro level data) is needed to form forward-looking judgments.

In some countries, interest rate differentials between the local currency and the markets of highly developed economies have spurred lending in foreign exchange (especially the Swiss franc) to unhedged borrowers, such as households. This adds another dimension to the analysis of credit risk. From the group of countries with flexible exchange-rate regimes, foreign exchange (FX) lending is most prominent in Hungary and Poland, accounting for 60 per cent and 25 per cent of outstanding loans to non-financial entities, respectively. Foreign exchange mortgage loans are most often identified as a risk to financial stability.[4]

Data availability problems are a general issue in CEE countries. Some sources of data which have a relatively long history of functioning in the developed economies (e.g., credit registers) have been functioning in the CEE for a short period of time only. Real-estate price data are also of limited coverage and quality.

This chapter presents the stress-testing experience of EU new member states (NMS) from Central and Eastern Europe (CEE). Special focus is given to Poland but the discussion also includes the experience of other countries. The chapter describes the stress-testing approaches employed by NMS central banks for credit risk, market risk and liquidity risk as well as for contagion through the interbank market. The final part of the chapter offers some thoughts on stress-testing challenges for NMS in the future.

---

[3] In each of the eight CEE NMS the subsidiaries of foreign banks have a much larger share in the banking market than branches. For detailed data see e.g., European Central Bank (ECB) (2007).

[4] Even if FX loans account only for 25 per cent of loans to non-financial entities in Poland, FX mortgage loans account for 57 per cent of mortgage loans (as of March 2008).

14.2 Credit risk stress-testing

Credit risk stress-testing in NMS is evolving from the use of simple simulations, which formed the backbone of early Financial Sector Assessment Program (FSAP) exercises, towards increasingly complex macroeconomic credit risk models. These often take as inputs stress scenarios generated using macroeconometric forecasting models. To address the shortcomings of historical aggregate data for the analysis of credit risk (indicated above), some central banks use micro level data (such as household finance surveys) to gauge credit risk and perform stress tests. In this chapter, examples of all three types of stress tests are reviewed.

The simulations based on *ad hoc* assumptions about the development of credit risk indicators were widely used during initial FSAP exercises in the early 2000s. A typical stress scenario was based on large historical moves in loan quality.[5] Some of them were adopted by CEE central banks as their first approach to stress-testing financial systems, and remain in use today. Examples of such simulations are presented in Table 14.1.

The common feature of these simulations is the attempt to express banks' capital buffers in terms of the ability to absorb losses from current or potential impaired loans. They can be interpreted as measures of the banks' ability to withstand large macroeconomic shocks, without specifying the exact nature or the probability of shocks. In some cases (e.g., Czech Republic) the scale of the shocks is based on large historical changes. The results of these stress tests, carried out periodically under similar assumptions, can be regarded as additional financial soundness indicators published as part of financial stability analysis.[6] While they may be criticised for being arbitrary (i.e., they are not attached to macroeconomic scenarios), their value-added lies in the ability to track over time the changing capacity of the banks to absorb the impact of similar shocks.

An intermediate step between *ad hoc* simulations and model-based stress tests is the use of sensitivity analyses carried out using estimated elasticities of credit risk indicators with respect to macroeconomic variables. This approach is used by the Bank of Lithuania (2007). They investigate the effects of several scenarios of interest rate increases and real estate price falls on non-performing loans and capital adequacy of banks. The impact is calculated

[5] For an example see e.g., International Monetary Fund (IMF) (2001).
[6] See Chapter 6.

Table 14.1 Stress tests for credit risk

Country	Description
Czech Republic	• An increase in non-performing loans (NPLs) by 30 per cent • An increase in NPL ratio by 3 percentage points • Between 10 per cent and 40 per cent of loans to households or loans to corporations become non-performing
Latvia	• Calculation of the capital adequacy ratio under the assumption that 20 per cent of loans from selected portfolios (loans to export industries, loans to domestic market industries, real-estate loans, housing loans) become non-performing • Bank-by-bank calculation of an increase in NPLs that would decrease the capital adequacy ratio to 8 per cent
Poland	• Calculation of credit losses incurred in the event of a bankruptcy of three largest corporate (non-financial) borrowers and their impact on capital adequacy • Bank-by-bank calculation of an increase in impaired loans that would decrease the capital adequacy ratio to 8 per cent • Calculation of the capital adequacy ratio under the assumption that impairment provisions increase to cover the whole unsecured part of impaired loans; additional decreases in collateral value of 25 per cent and 50 per cent
Slovakia	• Largest historical monthly increases in NPLs happen for 2 or 5 months in succession • A 4 per cent increase in non-performing household loans combined with a drop in prices of real-estate collateral of 30 per cent or 50 per cent

Source: CNB (2007), Bank of Latvia (2007), NBP (2008), NBS (2007)

using mutual elasticities of interest rates, non-performing loans (NPLs), value-added in real-estate sector and real-estate prices.

A different approach to modelling credit risk is used by the Bank of Slovenia. Kavčič *et al.* (2005) use data on credit quality at the level of individual corporate borrowers. They use a random effect panel ordered probit model to assign to each borrower probabilities of being assigned to one of five supervisory loan quality categories. Their model focuses on financial indicators at the level of the company (short-term debt as percentage of assets, free cash flow generation and sales), rather than macroeconomic indicators. Consequently, the model is used in stress test scenarios defined in terms of changes of indicators of corporate financial health. The stress test results presented by Kavčič *et al.* (2005) assume shocks in the form of an increase in short-term debt ratio and a decrease in cash flow generation. The shocks were chosen on the basis of the historical distributions, the size of the shocks was chosen to be two standard deviations. Their results indicate that an increase in short-term debt ratios of companies can increase by 200 per cent of the share of bad loans in the banks' portfolio, while a deterioration in cash flow generation has a less pronounced effect.

Econometric analysis of credit risk in the CEEs is hampered by data issues. However, the accumulation of experience in financial stability analysis in CEE central banks, as well as longer available time series, meant that since around 2005 some central banks in the region have started to augment their analysis with stress tests based on econometric models of credit risk.

Jurča and Zeman (2008) discuss the challenges related to data availability and quality in the context of Slovakia. Their experience is fairly typical of the CEE countries. They use aggregate data on the share of NPLs in the loan portfolio between 1995 and 2006 as their credit risk indicator. The short-comings of the data include: regulatory changes in the definitions of NPLs, including the adoption of International Financial Reporting Standards (IFRS), difficulties in interpreting declining NPL ratios in a period of strong credit growth and lack of information on the sales of NPLs.[7,8]

To circumvent these difficulties, they also consider using alternative measures of credit risk, such as default rates calculated using the National Bank of Slovakia's credit register. They find, however, that data quality is insufficient, especially in the early period of the credit register's operation. Moreover, these statistics are also distorted by regulatory changes, as loan quality in the credit register is defined using the criteria set in the regulations. Changes in regulations in turn induce large flows of borrowers between loan quality categories, distorting the picture of transition frequencies.

Jurča and Zeman (2008) encounter another problem in their analysis, as they find the NPL ratio series to be non-stationary in their sample. This is due

---

[7] During the transition period in the early 1990s, in many CEE countries the definitions of NPLs were set by regulators, often with minimum ratios of coverage by specific provisions. This prescriptive approach was motivated by lack of expertise in credit risk assessment and loan valuation in the banking system. For example, the National Bank of Poland introduced a regulation in 1992 defining four categories of loan quality: regular, sub-standard, doubtful and loss, with minimum coverage by provisions set at 0, 20, 50 and 100 per cent of unsecured part of exposures in each category. The categories were defined on the basis of amount of days past due, as well as assessment of the financial condition of the borrower. Between 1992 and 2006 the regulations were substantially amended three times. The last change allowed the banks to identify impaired loans and calculate impairment charges using IFRS.

[8] Secondary loan markets started to develop fairly recently in the CEEs – in Poland this market came to life only in around 2004–5, when legal and tax impediments discouraging banks from the sale of loans were partly lifted. The lack of secondary loan markets in some CEEs meant that NPLs were accumulating on the balance sheets of banks, creating somewhat artificially high NPL ratios. In the case of Poland, this was exacerbated by legal uncertainties regarding the possibility of moving old, unrecoverable, fully provisioned NPLs off the balance sheet and posting them as memo items. When the secondary market for loans started functioning, some banks took this opportunity to clean up their balance sheets, significantly reducing NPL ratios. For further analysis of the Polish case see e.g., National Bank of Poland (NBP, 2007b, Box 4).

to high NPL ratios at the beginning of their sample period, when banks' balance sheets still showed significant effects of the economic transition. The NPL ratio declined in the following years due to strong credit growth and cleanup operations, thus forming a trend.[9] Using both ordinary regressions and a vector error correction model (VECM) approach, they find significant influence of gross domestic product (GDP) growth, interest rates and the exchange rate on loan quality. Their model is used by the National Bank of Slovakia (2007) to perform stress tests based on shocks to macroeconomic variables. The stress test uses scenarios based on maximum adverse changes of relevant macroeconomic factors over a ten-year period. The results of the stress test indicate that Slovakian banks are most vulnerable to an appreciation of the exchange rate and a slowdown in economic growth.

Another step in the complexity of stress-testing approaches is the use of macroeconomic scenarios calibrated using macroeconometric models. This approach is used by the National Bank of Poland (NBP, 2008). The stress-testing framework of the NBP includes credit risk costs as well as net interest income. Both are modelled using panel models on individual bank data, to maximise available information and to take into account differences across banks. Credit risk is modelled separately for corporate and household loans, using the ratio of impairment provisions to loans as the dependent variable.

In the stress test exercise, a stress scenario is simulated using the NBP's main monetary policy model. A three-year stress scenario of stagflation in the world economy is defined using variables exogenous to the model to ensure internal consistency of the scenario.[10] The outputs from the macroeconometric model serve as inputs to model credit risk and net interest income, which together with assumptions about credit growth allow projection of net income, credit losses and capital adequacy ratios throughout the scenario. The stress test indicates that banks will be able to absorb increased loan losses through their income.

Jakubík and Heřmánek (2008) present a relatively complex stress-testing framework for the Czech Republic. Their approach uses outputs from the Czech National Bank's macroeconometric model as inputs to models of default rates and credit growth, estimated separately for households and

[9] This problem can also be encountered when available data do not span a full business cycle. Non-stationarity is not typical for measures of realised credit risk (such as the share of NPLs in a loan portfolio) observed over a longer time period, as these measures typically exhibit a cyclical pattern, following the economic cycle with a lag.

[10] Macroeconomic shock scenarios used in earlier NBP macro stress tests included an oil price shock and a scenario of market turbulence resulting in local currency depreciation as well as a slowdown in highly developed economies (NBP, 2007b).

corporations. Credit growth is modelled using a VECM approach, while default rates – calculated on the basis of changes in the volume of NPLs – are modelled using one-factor Merton models. In its stress-testing exercise, the Czech National Bank (2007) uses this framework to consider three scenarios: external and domestic demand shock, as well as an exchange rate appreciation. The shocks have a more prominent impact on credit growth than on NPLs. In all cases, banks are able to absorb losses without significant decreases in their capital adequacy ratios.

Some aspects of credit risk modelling in CEE countries are difficult to take into account if aggregate time series are the only available data source. This is the case with mortgage loans which are a relatively new product in CEE countries (in relation to their maturities). In the case of Poland, their share started to increase quickly only in around 2002.[11] As mortgages are extended with maturities exceeding twenty years, most of the loans are quite 'young'. Moreover, macroeconomic conditions in the region have been generally benign during that time. Thus, the data available to gauge the performance of mortgage loans cover neither the full lifecycle of this product, nor a full business cycle. Their usefulness for judging credit losses in an economic downturn is limited.

There are also problems with the assessment of the link between exchange rate moves and the credit risk of loans in foreign currencies. In the case of Poland, where mortgages in foreign currencies are widespread, this category of loans has consistently shown better (and more stable) performance than mortgages in the local currency (see NBP, 2007a). This is to some extent due to exchange rate developments during the period when foreign exchange loans became popular: lack of long-lasting depreciation shocks and a long-term local currency appreciation trend. In such conditions, historical data show little sensitivity to the quality of FX loans, and loan losses to exchange rate moves.[12] This situation calls for the use of stress-testing tools that are less dependent on historical time series data.

A possible approach that allows capture of risks from FX lending and loans untested through the business cycle involves the use of micro level data, such as household finance surveys. This approach is used, for example, in Hungary and Poland. For Poland, Zajączkowski and Żochowski (2007) use data from a household finance survey conducted yearly by the Polish Central Statistical Office. The data contains information on incomes and expenditures of around

---

[11] The share of housing loans in loans to households in Poland increased from 17.7 per cent in 2001 to 47.7 per cent in March 2008.

[12] See e.g., Głogowski (2008).

thirty thousand households. They use the data to calculate the financial margin of indebted households.[13] As their data do not contain much information about the structure of household debt, they are forced to rely upon aggregate data to formulate assumptions regarding interest rates, loan maturities and currency composition of household debt. Nevertheless, they are able to conduct simulations to investigate the impact of increases in interest rates and a depreciation of the exchange rate on financial margins of households.[14] Negative financial margins are not synonymous with default, but they can be expected to be closely correlated.[15] Their results indicate that, while households with mortgage debt are relatively in the best financial condition, they are the most sensitive to shocks in interest rates.[16,17]

The model of Zajączkowski and Żochowski (2007) is used by the NBP (2007b) to capture the impact of exchange rate depreciation (resulting from a macroeconomic scenario of turbulence on world markets) on loan losses. This is due to the fact that the credit risk models employed in the stress-testing exercise do not identify a statistically significant link between exchange rate moves and loan losses. The result of the simulation – an increase in the percentage of households with negative margins, and an associated increase in loan losses – is added to the output of the basic credit risk model (see Figure 14.1).

A similar approach, based on a smaller but richer dataset of indebted households, is used by Holló and Papp (2007). They use data collected in a survey of household finances commissioned by the Central Bank of Hungary. Their data include information on household incomes and debt characteristics as well as repayment problems. This allows them not only to analyse financial margins but also estimate models of default probability based on household characteristics as well as financial margins. They investigate the impact of a set of financial shocks (changes in interest rates and exchange rates) and unemployment shocks on the debt-at-risk.[18] With additional

---

[13] The margin is usually defined as the part of household income that is left after paying debt service expenditures and basic living costs.

[14] A later piece of research based on this dataset, presented in NBP (2008), conducts a simulation of an increase in unemployment.

[15] The assumptions about the expenditures related to basic living costs almost always constitute an educated guess, as it is hard to judge the ability of households to adjust their spending patterns when faced with financial difficulties. This means that income margins are an approximation. Moreover, when faced with default, some households can raise additional funds by selling some of their assets or by borrowing from outside the financial system (e.g., from family members). In the case of Poland, the household finance survey does not contain information on the value of assets owned by households.

[16] I.e., the proportion of households with negative financial margins is lowest in this group.

[17] This is also due to the fact that practically all mortgages are extended with floating interest rates.

[18] Defined as the relation of probability of default (PD)-weighted value of loans to nominal value of loans.

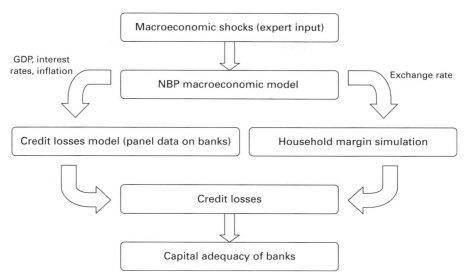

Figure 14.1   An example of a credit risk stress test combining aggregate and microlevel models. The approach of the National Bank of Poland (NBP)
Source: Based on NBP (2007b).

assumptions about recovery rates, they are also able to investigate the impact of increased PDs on the capital adequacy of the Hungarian banking system. They find that due to the prevalence of loans in foreign currencies (mostly the Swiss franc) in Hungary, the sensitivity to changes in foreign interest rates and exchange rates is larger than for changes in domestic interest rates. This is true even when shocks applied to domestic interest rates are larger than the ones used for foreign interest rates. Their results are used by Magyar Nemzeti Bank (MNB, 2008) as one of the tools used to assess the impact of a macroeconomic stress scenario on the Hungarian banking system.

14.3 Market risk stress-testing

The financial markets of NMS are quite simple in comparison to the markets of highly developed economies, reducing the scope of market risk-taking. The most developed markets, besides the money market, are usually foreign exchange and government bond markets, as well as FX and interest rate derivatives. While the capitalisation of equity markets has increased, the exposures of banks to equities tend to be marginal.[19] This is due to low importance of investment banking activities for CEE banks. Their exposures to world markets seem to be limited, as typically their role in international financial groups is to focus on domestic markets.

The most important types of market risk faced by CEE banks are interest rate risk (stemming mainly from loans, deposits and government bonds) and exchange rate risk. Stress tests conducted by authorities in the CEE countries broadly reflect this structure of market risk-taking by banks, as the examples in Table 14.2 demonstrate.

Stress tests indicate low sensitivity of CEE banks to market risk. The exposure of banks to banking book interest rate risk is limited as large proportions of loans carry floating interest rates. Foreign exchange positions are usually almost square, even in countries where banks hold large portfolios of loans in foreign currencies. Interest rate changes can have an impact on profits and capital, but in most of the stress scenarios mentioned above, the shocks do not cause the banks to fall below minimum capital adequacy requirements.

In Poland and Hungary, where foreign exchange lending is an important asset category for some banks, gross foreign exchange positions are quite large. Banks typically have large long balance sheet positions offset by short derivative positions. The most popular instruments used to close the foreign exchange positions are FX swaps and cross-currency interest rate swaps.[20] While these instruments allow the banks to hedge against FX risk and book the margins on FX loans, they are subject to rollover risk.[21,22] This risk is hard to quantify in stress tests, as it is difficult to identify precisely what circumstances would be needed for local banks not to be able to renew their hedges. Consequently, no stress tests so far take into account this risk.

---

[19] In Poland, the ratio of stock market capitalisation to GDP (taking into account only domestic companies) increased from 16.6 per cent in 2003 to 43.8 per cent in 2007.

[20] Or, more precisely, synthetic forwards. An FX swap transaction combined with a spot FX transaction replicates an FX forward transaction.

[21] From an economic point of view, the local banks lend the funds in local currency to non-residents, receiving the local interbank rate and simultaneously borrow funds in foreign currency, paying the relevant LIBOR rate (plus a premium). The local bank offsets the LIBOR payments against interest received on foreign currency loans, which almost universally carry floating rates tied to LIBOR rates. The ability of CEE banks to hedge their FX loan portfolios to some extent depends on the demand for CEE currencies (e.g., for financing investment in CEE government bonds) on the part of non-residents.

[22] Cross-currency interest rate swaps used by CEE banks to hedge positions arising from their portfolios of FX mortgages typically have maturities of three or five years, while mortgage maturities exceed twenty years. FX swap transactions have even shorter maturities (typically three months).

Table 14.2 Stress tests for market risk

Country	Interest rate risk stress test	Foreign exchange risk stress test
Czech Republic	• Yield curve moves up 100 or 200 basis points • Calculation of maximum yield curve shift under which the banking system maintains a capital adequacy ratio of above 8 per cent • Impact on net interest income and market value of debt securities	• Depreciation of the koruna by 15 per cent or 20 per cent
Hungary	• Yield curve moves up by 200 basis points for foreign currencies and 500 basis points for the forint • Impact on profits evaluated using repricing gap data	• Depreciation of the forint by 30 per cent
Poland	• Yield curves in zloty, euro, US dollar and Swiss franc move twice more than the expected rate changes (as inferred from forward rate agreement (FRA) quotes) • Impact on net interest income over a one-year horizon evaluated using repricing gap data	• No stress tests on open FX position conducted (only value-at-risk (VaR) analysis published)
Slovakia	• Yield curve moves up by 200 basis points or 500 basis points, impact on banks (change in economic value) evaluated using repricing gap data • NBS base rate moves up by 200 basis points, changes of interest rates on loans and deposits estimated using pass-through models; evaluation of impact on net interest income over one year	• Depreciation and appreciation of the koruna by 15 per cent versus the euro, changes of exchange rates *vis à vis* other currencies estimated on the basis of historical covariances • Most adverse (from the point of view of individual banks) historical monthly changes of exchange rates

Source: CNB (2007), MNB (2007), NBP (2007b), NBS (2007)

14.4 Liquidity risk stress-testing

Liquidity risk is rarely considered, mainly because of problems with data availability. Published stress tests usually depend on assumptions concerning the behaviour of assets and liabilities in the event of a crisis of confidence towards an individual bank.

An example of such a stress test is presented by Balazs and More (2007) for the Hungarian banking system. They propose a 'stress liquidity indicator' which is defined as the percentage of customer deposits that a bank is able to pay out within a set period if it loses its interbank market funding and has no external sources of liquidity other than its portfolio of marketable securities. The indicator shows the share of customer deposits that can be covered by a bank's liquid assets and cash inflows generated through normal business. They find that average 'stress liquidity indicators' for Hungarian banks fluctuated in the range of 20–30 per cent in 2004–7, but with substantial dispersion between banks. No clear trend has been observed, despite rapid growth in lending. The authors indicate that banks actively sought to bolster their liquidity position by seeking long maturity funding. They explicitly omit from their analysis any possibility of parent bank support. The rationale is that they want to investigate the shock absorption capacity of Hungarian banks on a stand-alone basis, but they also point out that liquidity shocks for subsidiaries could be triggered by financial problems of parent banks. Their scenario can be thus interpreted as a stylised example of spillover of shocks from parent companies to subsidiaries.

As discussed in previous chapters, liquidity risk also has a network dimension. The interbank deposit market is a crucial tool for banks in their day-to-day liquidity management. A default by a bank on its interbank obligations may cause losses which are not large enough to bring the creditor bank into insolvency, but it can exhaust its liquidity buffer. This in turn can lead to a domino effect of illiquidity-induced defaults on the interbank market. A preliminary analysis of this type of risk, based on data from Poland, is conducted by Hałaj (2007). He adopts a network model in the spirit of Elsinger *et al.* (2003) to investigate the potential of liquidity domino effects on the Polish interbank market. In his model, a bank can default on its interbank obligations if it cannot cover the net outflows arising from operations with the non-bank sector (which are random in the model) and from interbank placements with money raised from selling liquid Treasury securities. The model assumption is that a bank can only sell the securities to another domestic bank which has a surplus of liquidity after fulfilling all of its obligations. Using a Monte Carlo simulation with parameters determined on the basis of historical data available at the National Bank of Poland, Hałaj (2007) shows that the risk of liquidity contagion is quite rare. This is due to many banks holding significant portfolios of Treasury securities. Average liquidity injections that would be needed to prevent contagion amount to around 0.05 per cent of bank sector assets.[23]

---

[23] Conditional on the occurrence of contagion.

The results are subject to some uncertainty, especially in the area of parameter choice for probability distributions of flows generated by operations with non-bank customers.

The rapid growth of lending in the second half of the 2000s, which increases the relevance of market funding for some banks, suggests that the importance of liquidity stress tests to financial stability will grow in years to come.

14.5 Interbank contagion in stress tests

The ability to conduct the analysis of interbank contagion in stress tests is very much dependent on data availability. Nevertheless, in countries where central banks have data on interbank exposures, this type of analysis is included in stress tests. The examples below focus on the impact that interbank exposures can inflict on creditor banks in terms of credit losses and their capital position (contagion due to credit risk).

The National Bank of Slovakia (2007) uses data on interbank loans and deposits to investigate the results of failure ('primary default') of a single bank. Due to the relatively small share of interbank transactions in the balance sheet of the Slovakian banking system, the impact is limited, with only a small number of banks falling below minimum capital adequacy requirements.

The Czech National Bank (CNB, 2006) augments a similar situation with a worst case scenario, where the default of the largest debtor banks for each bank is assumed. Another modification used by the CNB is the integration of the interbank contagion exercise into the stress test based on a macroeconomic scenario. The probability of primary default of each bank depends on its capital adequacy ratio after taking the results of credit and market risk shocks into account. The average impact of interbank contagion on capital adequacy is small, accounting for around 10 per cent of the total decrease in capital adequacy ratios.

A similar approach is used by the National Bank of Poland (2008) to estimate the scale of interbank contagion risk. In the simulation, the probability of primary default for each individual bank depends on its capital adequacy ratio. The scale of interbank contagion is assessed looking at the size of banks which are subject to 'secondary default' as well as the value of interbank liabilities that these banks are unable to repay. A probability distribution of losses due to interbank contagion is constructed using a Monte Carlo simulation. The scale of possible interbank contagion is low, as banks at risk of secondary default have a share of around 6 per cent in the Polish banking sector, and losses due to secondary defaults are less than 0.1 per cent of assets. An important caveat is that exposures to foreign banks are not investigated in this framework due to lack of detailed data.

Stress tests of interbank contagion generally do not indicate that this type of risk is a serious problem in CEEs. The accuracy of this analysis is limited, however, as interbank exposures can shift quickly and the authorities often have only 'snapshot' month-end data.

14.6 Challenges for the future

One of the main challenges for stress-testing NMS banking systems concerns the risks stemming from current rapid credit growth and the general increase in financial intermediation (especially in the case of households) seen in some of the countries. This has several consequences. The increase in aggregate indicators of debt burden (such as ratios of household debt to disposable income) is not synonymous with an increase in the debt burden measured at the level of individual borrowers.[24] While increasing intermediation can to some extent involve increased lending to customers from the lower end of the creditworthiness spectrum, the aggregate debt burden ratios are generally poor predictors of credit risk. The use of microdata can relieve some of the problems, but their quality, timeliness and coverage are typically worse than is the case with aggregate data.

Another aspect of the rapid credit growth in the household sector is the increasing role of products untested through the business cycle in the banks' risk profile. This is a challenge for regulators interested in macro stress-testing. The same features of the credit market are also a challenge for banks in many areas of their risk management such as internal capital adequacy assessment, risk-sensitive product pricing for customers or developing risk-sensitive internal transfer-pricing mechanisms.

A significant part of the growth in lending comes from mortgage loans. This increases the importance of real-estate prices as a risk factor for CEE banking systems. A quantitative understanding of the interplay between mortgage lending, economic growth and real-estate prices will become more and more crucial in assessing the credit risk related to mortgages in an economic downturn. So far, the quality and quantity of data on real-estate prices make it difficult to form quantitative conclusions in this regard. Even where these

---

[24] For an analysis of this divergence see e.g., NBP (2007a).

data are available, it is difficult to disentangle price moves due to convergence processes from developments related to lending and other fundamental factors. Improving this capability is an important challenge for CEE authorities.

Another challenge will be to quantify the consequences of foreign funding of credit growth, especially where the funding comes from foreign parent companies of local banks. Foreign funding increases the exposure of CEE banks to developments on world markets, both in terms of funding costs and funding availability. Until the sub-prime turmoil of 2007–8 it could have been reasonable to assume that as long as local banks remain in robust financial condition, they can obtain necessary funding on world markets. The crisis has demonstrated that, contrary to expectations of market participants, markets of highly developed economies are not immune to liquidity breakdowns and confidence crises. Such highly non-linear events are difficult to incorporate in stress tests as they amount to a significant regime shift. Authorities wishing to incorporate them in stress tests will have to work closely with banks to obtain market intelligence.

Parent companies acting as a funding source present another analytical challenge for financial stability analysis and stress tests. Under normal market conditions, funding obtained from the parent company can be relatively cheap (due to higher ratings of parent companies) and stable, contributing to smooth functioning of the host country financial system. In times of financial crisis this stays true as long as the crisis is contained in the host country. If the source of the crisis is to be found in the home economy of the parent company, then its ability to support its subsidiaries can be undermined. The sub-prime turmoil has shown that the possibility of internationally active banks experiencing difficulties should not be discounted. Financial problems of parent companies may then have a negative impact on fundamentally sound subsidiaries, for example through reputation risk.

The challenges listed in the previous paragraph are examples of the so-called home-host problem in financial system supervision. International financial groups which own an important part of the CEE banking systems can in some cases be a source of support for the host country financial system and in other cases a transmission channel for shocks occurring in the world economy. In stress-testing exercises the CEE authorities usually investigate the robustness of locally incorporated banks on a standalone basis, regardless of their ownership, effectively assuming no parent support. This helps to avoid excessively optimistic conclusions based on assumptions about support from the parent companies. The spillover effects (problems at the parent company influencing the standing of the subsidiary) are more difficult to capture. The outcome of parent company problems can be dependent on the policy of the parent company in a crisis situation (e.g., what sort of support can be extended by the subsidiaries to the parent company), the scale of intragroup transactions and the degree of independence that the subsidiary enjoys. The inclusion of these effects in stress tests is very limited at present.

Macro stress-testing in NMS is increasing in sophistication, despite limitations caused mostly by data problems. The combination of rapid financial system development, an ownership structure dominated by foreign investors and increasing importance of foreign funding means that it will continue to be a challenging task for many years to come.

REFERENCES

Balazs, T. and C. More (2007), 'How Resilient are Hungarian Banks to Liquidity Shocks?', *MNB Bulletin*, June.

Bank of Latvia (2007), *Financial Stability Report, 2006*.

Bank of Lithuania (2007), *Financial Stability Review, 2006*, June.

Czech National Bank (2006), *Financial Stability Report, 2005*.

(2007), *Financial Stability Report, 2006*.

Elsinger, H., A. Lehar and M. Summer (2003), 'Risk Assessment for Banking Systems', *Vienna University Working Paper*.

European Central Bank (2007), *EU Banking Structures*.

Głogowski, A. (2008), 'Macroeconomic Determinants of Polish Banks' Loan Losses – Results of a Panel Data Study', *NBP Working Paper*, 53.

Hałaj, G. (2007), 'Assessing Liquidity Risk in Banking System', paper presented at *2008 Campus for Finance Research Conference*, Vallendar.

Holló, D. and M. Papp (2007), 'Assessing Household Credit Risk: Evidence from a Household Survey', *MNB Occasional Paper*, 70, December.

International Monetary Fund (2001), 'Republic of Poland: Financial System Stability Assessment', IMF Country Report, 01/67, June.

Jakubík, P., and J. Heřmánek (2008), 'Stress Testing of the Czech Banking Sector', *IES Charles University Prague Working Paper*, 2.

Jurča, P. and P. Zeman (2008), 'Macro Stress Testing of the Slovak Banking Sector', *NBS Working Paper*, 1.

Kavčič, M., T. Košak, F. Ramšak and T. Šuler (2005), 'Macro Stress Tests for the Slovenian Banking System', *Bank of Slovenia Financial Stability Report*, June.

Magyar Nemzeti Bank (2007), *Report on Financial Stability*, April.

(2008), *Report on Financial Stability*, April.

Mérő, K. and M. Valentinyi (2003), 'The Role of Foreign Banks in Five Central and Eastern European Countries', *MNB Working Paper*, 10.

National Bank of Poland (2007a), *Financial Stability Report, 2006.*
    (2007b), *Financial Stability Review, first half of 2007.*
    (2008), *Financial Stability Report, 2008, June.*
National Bank of Slovakia (2007), *Financial Stability Report, 2006.*
Zajączkowski, S. and D. Żochowski (2007), 'Loan Service Burden of Households – Distributions and Stress Tests', *National Bank of Poland Financial Stability Report.*

15 Cross-border macro stress-testing: progress and future challenges for the EU

Olli Castrén, John Fell and Nico Valckx[*]

15.1 Introduction

As seen in the previous chapters, macro stress-testing has become an integral part of the financial stability assessment work being carried out by many central banks around the world. Within the European Union (EU), the process of financial integration, particularly intense within the euro area, is leading to a greater degree of interconnectedness between national financial systems. Although this interconnectedness creates a strong case for conducting macro stress tests which take account of cross-border dimensions, progress in this area has been relatively slow for at least two main reasons. The first reason is practical: there is a paucity of harmonised data across countries with sufficient time spans to allow for quantitative assessment of the relevant sources of risk and exposures.[1] The second reason is institutional: the national responsibility for financial supervision in the EU means that the scope for sharing information across institutions and on a cross-border basis may be limited by national practices and legal restrictions.

Undoubtedly the greatest methodological advances in macro stress-testing have been made in the area of quantification of credit risk. An important reason for this is that effective management of credit risk is paramount for commercial banks. As concerns cross-border linkages across banking sectors, two main channels for credit risk can be distinguished: common exposures to the same (or systemic) sources of risk and balance sheet linkages between institutions. Common credit risk exposures can be a source of contagion across national banking sectors if widespread

---

[*] European Central Bank (ECB). The opinions expressed herein are those of the author and do not necessarily reflect those of the ECB.

[1] See also Chapter 6.

or systemic shocks affect institutions in a number of different countries simultaneously or if individual banks have exposures in multiple countries. Balance sheet linkages can be a source of contagion across national banking sectors, both for systemic and idiosyncratic shocks. With such linkages, shocks can, and often are, propagated between financial institutions located in different countries through the interbank money and repo markets.

This chapter begins with a general and non-exhaustive discussion of the progress that has been made by central banks in building quantitative frameworks for stress-testing cross-border credit risk exposures. It then goes on to distinguish between progress that has been made in modelling the credit risk that arises from lending to non-financial sectors in the economy and credit risk that emerges from interbank lending. Indirect ways of measuring cross-border contagion of stress, such as those based on market prices, are not covered in this context.[2] In the second half of the chapter, the particular challenges for cross-border stress-testing at the European level are discussed, mostly drawing on work that has been recently carried out under the aegis of the European System of Central Bank (ESCB) Banking Supervision Committee.

15.2 Accounting for the cross-border dimension in credit risk stress-testing

Cross-border credit risk stress typically arises as a result of systemic shocks that affect either several borrowers in different countries simultaneously, or a single large borrower to which banks residing in several countries have common exposures. In addition, due to the increasing role of wholesale markets as a source of bank financing, credit risk in the interbank market, where problems can arise if distress in a single institution that faced an idiosyncratic shock spreads in the system, has become a relevant issue from the systemic risk perspective.

---

[2] Approaches based on market data can be used if interbank relationships and correlations between credit portfolios are difficult to measure. For example, Hartmann *et al.* (2005) use the interdependencies of (excess returns) equity prices to estimate spill-overs among banks (i.e., systemic risk) and also to assess their sensitivity to common shocks (i.e., systematic risk). Gropp *et al.* (2006) and Čihák and Ong (2007) indirectly measure cross-border contagion by estimating the interdependencies of banks' distance to default.

15.2.1 Analysing the cross-country implications of systemic shocks

Identifying and stress-testing large common exposures

Exposures to single-name corporates experiencing distress can threaten an individual bank's financial health, or its ability to maintain core operations. In cases where several banks are directly and simultaneously exposed to a large single borrower – either via syndicated loans, or via separate credit lines extended independently to a single borrower – such joint concentration risk may also pose direct systemic risks.

The fact that large exposures to single-name firms carry an element of contagion risk explains why authorities responsible for monitoring financial stability typically advocate that large exposures to individual firms should be identified, monitored and managed in an adequate way.[3] For individual institutions, stress-testing large exposures has received plenty of attention in the economic capital calculations that form a part of the Basel 2 Accord. In particular, banks that choose to use their own models in the context of the Internal Ratings Based (IRB) approach as opposed to the Standardised Approach are required to stress test their capital calculations.[4] Research carried out by the Basel Committee suggests that the impact of increased borrower concentration (i.e., a larger share of individual borrowers in banks' loan books) on economic capital tends to be substantial.

Regarding the cross-border stress dimension that may arise from joint large exposures by several banks, the nature of the joint lending exposures is an important determinant as to how the banks can manage and stress test such risks. If the joint exposures are in the form of syndicated loans, banks are typically aware of the size of each other's exposures and can take these into account in their own stress tests. On the other hand, should the banks be lending to a large firm on an individual basis, they are not necessarily aware of all of the credit commitments the firm has undertaken with other financial counterparties, particularly if the firm is active in borrowing in several countries. In the latter cases, the cross-border dimension of the exposures is far more difficult to gauge, and it would require exchange of information among the authorities that are responsible for supervising the

---

[3] In this vein, the ESCB Banking Supervision Committee undertook a survey in 2005 to assess whether the idiosyncratic risk of large exposures to single-name corporates would be a concern from the perspective of the stability of large EU banks. For a summary of the findings, see ECB (2006c).

[4] See also Chapters 2 and 5.

relevant institutions. Given the importance of such common exposures as a potential channel of contagion across banks domiciling in different countries, sharing information on common large exposures and individual bank level stress test results would contribute to the prevention of financial stress on a cross-border basis.

Analysing the impact of systemic shocks using cross-section models

When information on bank or banking system level credit quality indicators is available, econometric techniques can be used to gauge the cross-section dimension of financial stress. A common way of modelling cross-border stress in this context is to use some relatively homogenous variable that characterises the evolution of the credit quality of the loan books either at a single bank or single country level. The cyclical dynamics of these variables can then be explained using a set of macro financial risk factors which can also be subjected to various stress scenarios.

The choice of the dependent variable used in these regression estimations seems to follow two main avenues. One is to exploit the data generated in numerous banking crisis studies, which mostly gives a strict binomial dichotomy in time series: crisis vs. non-crisis event. The other uses ordinary statistical time series such as banks' non-performing lending, loan losses, firm bankruptcies, or some proxies for those, such as loan loss provisions. However, the empirical cross-country studies often suffer from the fact that the countrywide samples are rather heterogeneous. Hence, the dependent variable is usually chosen to be some discrete one-off crisis data. Probit/logit estimation techniques can be used if the samples are sufficiently large to allow statistically sufficient variation in the binomial data for testing purposes. Regarding the explanatory variables, it is typically found that the gross domestic product (GDP), or GDP innovations and interest rates are among the most important factors in explaining loan losses and provisions. The importance of GDP and interest rates can also be seen in the recent work on procyclicality inspired by the new Basel Accord and International Accounting Standards (IAS) regulation on banks' loan loss provisioning behaviour. A further group of important explanatory variables are measures of banks' lending and asset prices.

Using these approaches, there is quite a rich literature on the relationships between the business cycle and banking stability, particularly at a single-country level. These studies have often been developed in connection with the International Monetary Fund's (IMF's) Financial Sector Assessment

Programs (FSAPs).[5] To capture the cross-border dimension, a cross-section or panel approach is typically used in such estimations.[6]

Analysing the impact of common shocks on large and complex institutions

An alternative way of analysing cross-border linkages is to apply single-bank credit risk stress-testing methods on institutions which are likely to be important for the functioning of the financial system as determined by some agreed metrics. Statistical methods, such as cluster analysis, can provide a robust identification of institutions which, according to some prespecified criteria, can be seen as most relevant for periodic analysis of financial system stability.

As an example, the ECB uses such a methodology to identify a set of large and complex banking groups (LCBGs) which are closely monitored in the periodic financial stability assessment work.[7] It should be emphasised that these institutions are not necessarily those that are often called 'systemically relevant institutions'. Rather, they are banking groups whose size and nature of business is such that their failure and inability to operate would most likely have adverse – albeit not necessarily severe – implications for various forms of financial intermediation, the smooth functioning of financial markets or other financial institutions operating within the system. Cross-border stress-testing can then be carried out on these institutions with the assumption that problems in individual institutions belonging to this group are likely to have implications for the rest of the cross-border financial system, in this case the euro area, given their size and importance in a number of banking activities.

---

[5] In Europe, Salas and Saurina (2002) analyse the relationship between problem loans and the economic cycle for a sample of Spanish commercial and saving banks in the period 1985–97. For the UK, Austria and Italy, respectively, Pain (2003), Arpa *et al.* (2001) and Quagliariello (2007) investigate the influence of business cycle on loan loss provisions. Using vector autoregression (VAR), Marcucci and Quagliariello (2008) analyse the cyclical pattern of Italian default rates. For French banks, Demuynck (2004) and Martin (2005) study the relationship between a non-perfoming loan (NPL) indicator and interest rate, credit and GDP growth. Using large panel datasets, Głogowski (2006) and Bethlendi (2006) analysed the link between macroeconomic processes and loan loss provisions in Poland and Hungary. For the Netherlands, Van den End *et al.* (2006) use a breakdown of retail and wholesale exposures to analyse the impact of macro financial risk on the credit risk model for banks' loan portfolios. On the IMF experience with stress-testing, see Chapter 16.

[6] As an example of empirical analysis in a multi-country context, Pesola (2005) studies the role of macroeconomic shocks in explaining the ratio of banks' loan losses to lending for nine European countries (Belgium, Denmark, Finland, Germany, Greece, Norway, Spain, Sweden and the UK). For EU banks, Valckx (2003) considers loan loss provisioning policy using a sample of fifteen European banking systems between 1979 and 2001. In ECB (2005), an empirical model is estimated using data for fifteen mature countries over the period 1980–2001. The analysis suggests that low economic activity, high domestic credit growth and rapid growth in property prices, as well as low profitability and low liquidity in the banking sector, have good properties as leading indicators of financial distress.

[7] See ECB (2006d; 2007a).

Stress-testing of the LCBGs' loan portfolios provides a first step for assessing the potential for systemic banking risk in the euro area. This task is alleviated by the fact that information on banks' credit exposures is in many cases publicly available in a relatively granular form. To assess how the individual LCBGs' credit portfolio risk changes in response to scenarios which involve shocks to a set of relevant macro financial variables, changes to the implied default probabilities of the banks' individual borrowers, or sectors of borrowers, can be estimated as an intermediate step.[8] These conditional default probabilities can then be used as inputs in bank-level credit portfolio models to calculate the impact of the shocks on individual LCBGs' credit risk measures.[9] The cross-border dimension of such analysis comes from two distinct sources: the design of the scenario, which typically aims at capturing cross-border elements, and, as mentioned above, the fact that the solvency of the institutions in question is judged to be important for the stability of the entire cross-border financial system. Common lending exposures, should they exist, would typically imply that several LCBGs would face stress simultaneously.

To more explicitly analyse the extent of spill-over of distress among a group of banks, such as the LCBGs, methods such as the banking stability index can be used.[10] This approach allows for a time-varying correlation of probabilities of bank default, i.e., it provides a measure of the likelihood of other banks facing distress given that one bank is in distress (for example, as a result of an idiosyncratic shock to its credit portfolio). Taking into account in this way the joint probability of default of the large and complex banks improves the information content of the stress tests by capturing the dynamic correlation structure of a given stress scenario.

15.2.2 Balance sheet approach: cross-country stress-testing using network models

In an integrated financial system, such as the euro area, cross-border banking flows are an important source of funding for financial institutions as well as for private sector borrowers. At the same time, however, in times of financial stress a network of cross-border banking flows could provide a channel through which problems in one institution may propagate wider throughout the financial system via interbank credit exposures. Therefore, stress-testing

---

[8] See ECB (2007b).   [9] See ECB (2007c).
[10] See Segoviano *et al.* (2006) and Goodhart and Segoviano (2008).

such interconnections provides an important part of a cross-border stress-testing framework.

There are two main steps that need to be carried out when analysing contagion in banking flows networks. The first step is to determine the bilateral exposures between involved banks. The second step is to develop a suitable algorithm that simulates how a stress event at one bank or at a certain set of banks is propagated through the system along the paths of bilateral exposures.

A common problem with this approach is that the matrix of bilateral exposures, which constitutes a crucial input, is generally not available, at least on a cross-border basis. Three approaches have been devised in the literature to circumvent this problem and infer a matrix of bilateral exposures.[11]

First, the matrix of bilateral exposures can be estimated using the maximum entropy technique.[12] This approach has been applied to banking systems in several countries (see section 15.3.3). Since this approach takes account of the interbank exposures in all maturities it is a particularly suitable method to assess how the insolvency of a given bank would impact the solvency of its counterparts.

Second, methods developed for payment system analysis can be applied.[13] Although these methods can be very accurate in identifying overnight operations in payments system data, they cannot be used to identify operations with longer maturities. The approaches could thus be more suitable for assessing interbank contagion linked to the very short-term interbank market, and in particular to estimate how a short-term liquidity shock could propagate.

Third, to specifically analyse cross-border exposures at the country level, a cross-border banking flows network can be constructed using consolidated claims of cross-border transactions as reported by the Bank for International Settlements (BIS). Figure 15.1 illustrates such a network for a number of EU countries, plus the US.[14]

---

[11] See Chapters 11 and 12.   [12] See Upper and Worms (2004).

[13] See Furfine (1999). Using this approach, Beyeler et al. (2006) analysed the topology of the interbank payment flows within the US Fedwire real-time settlement system. They found that the network is characterised by a relatively small number of 'strong' flows so that on a daily basis, 75 per cent of the payment flows involved less than 0.1 per cent of the institutions in the system. Moreover, most banks have only a few connections while a small number of 'hub banks' can have thousands of connections. Obviously, in terms of preventing systemic crises whereby disturbances can quickly spread within the network of institutions, identifying such systemically relevant hub institutions and closely monitoring their liquidity and solvency situation would be particularly relevant.

[14] See ECB (2008).

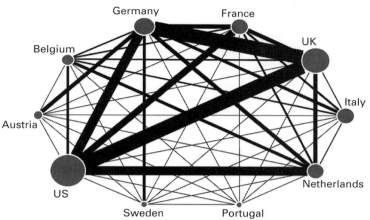

Figure 15.1   Gross cross-border banking flows across selected EU countries and the US (claims plus debts)
Note: The size of the circles and the thickness of the lines are proportional to the volume of the claims
and debts for each country.
Sources: BIS and ECB calculations.

By looking at the total net debt and claim flows in the system, it could be
seen that the UK would have only a rather small net debt position while, in
terms of gross flows, which are shown in the figure, it is a very large player,
reflecting its position as a centre for financial transactions in the EU. Germany
and, to a lesser extent, France and the Netherlands, are also important hubs in
the EU banking system in that they process a large amount of gross debt and
claims flows. The figure also shows the importance of the US as global
financial counterparty to many EU countries in gross terms; however, this
hides the fact that the US has a large net debt position *vis à vis* many European
countries.

Once the bilateral cross-border exposures have been identified using some
of the above-mentioned techniques, stress-testing can be performed using a
simulation procedure. A typical simulation algorithm in this context would
assume the default of one bank in the network, which possibly causes erosion
of capital in other banks.[15] The process would then be repeated until there is a
round with no new bank failures.

Figure 15.2 summarises the result of a stress test applied to the 'extended'
euro area cross-border banking flow network.

---

[15]   More specifically, contagion would occur if the loss given default (LGD) times the exposure of the other
banks towards the failed bank exceeds the capital (or the capital buffer) of the other banks. Information
on the bank's capital buffers can be relatively easily obtained from publicly available databases.

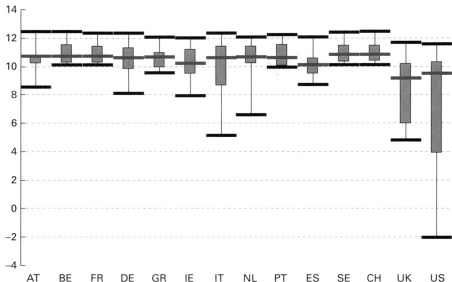

Figure 15.2   Banking system regulatory capital ratios after a failure of a national banking system in the cross-border banking flows network (overall capital ratios, %; regulatory minimum = 8%)
Sources: BIS, IMF and ECB calculations.

More specifically, the figure shows the distributions of the estimated impacts on the overall solvency ratios of individual euro area countries' banking systems when a country on the horizontal axis fails to honour its commitments to its counterparties.[16]

Two main conclusions arise from this stylised exercise. First, abstracting from any confidence effects, the results suggest that a 'failure' of any one of the euro area countries could be mostly manageable for the rest of the cross-border system in the sense that there are only very few cases where the capital ratios might fall below the 8 per cent minimum regulatory threshold. On the other hand, the figure confirms the importance of the largest international financial centres for the euro area financial system. Problems in the UK and, in particular, the US can contribute to extreme losses for some individual

---

[16] In the simulation, it was assumed that a large part of the cross-border exposures are collateralised so that the maximum loss suffered by all other countries due to the failure of any one counterparty is limited to 40 per cent of the total cross-border exposure. In addition, second round effects are incorporated which means that an endogenous failure of some countries in the network as a result of the initial exogenous failure of one country may trigger further endogenous failures in the system. It was further assumed that interbank credit losses directly affect the capital of the banking system, i.e., there are no profit buffers which could absorb part of the impact.

banking systems although the median capital ratios remain above the regulatory minimum also in these cases.

15.3 European challenges to cross-border stress-testing

15.3.1 What is the extent of cross-border activity in the European context?

Interlinkages across financial institutions and financial systems can arise from a number of different sources. Previous studies that analyse cross-border banking in Europe usually focus on the empirical relevance of cross-border banking. This is done through analysing either the 'outward reach' (cross-border activities through foreign branches or subsidiaries) or the 'inward attraction' (the extent of foreign bank presence in the host country) of banks. See for example the EU Banking Structures Report (ECB, 2006a) and Schoenmaker and Oosterloo (2005). The Banking Structures Report utilises bank level data to reveal a sustained increase in internationalisation within the EU banking sector.[17] Between 2003 and 2005 the average percentage of reporting banks' assets in branches and subsidiaries abroad (outward reach) relative to total assets rose from 24 per cent to 38 per cent. From data on foreign assets, revenues and employees of the thirty largest EU banking groups, Schoenmaker and Oosterloo (2005) come to the same conclusion. However, there are large differences in outward reach across countries. Internationally active banks from large countries tend to have greater outward orientation in terms of assets. In addition to this, 'inward attraction' has also grown. The average market share of foreign branches and subsidiaries in the EU as a whole stood at 26 per cent at the end of 2005 (ECB, 2006a). Large variations across countries are evident. New Member states' (NMS) banking sectors are typically characterised by high levels of foreign bank ownership (67 per cent on average in 2005).

The two studies previously mentioned present cross-border breakdowns by type of activity. ECB (2006a) illustrates that the share of cross-border

---

[17] Bank level data are collected for forty-six major EU banking groups (representing around 57 per cent of total EU banking sector assets) through a regular mapping exercise. In addition, the EU Banking Structures Report publishes country level aggregates, which are collected through national central banks. The latter dataset is more complete in its coverage of banks, however the data only show assets of subsidiaries and branches of banks from foreign countries. Hence, only inward attraction and not outward reach.

interbank loans and deposits within the euro area has increased since 1999 to nearly 35 per cent of the total outstanding in 2005. Based on less recent data series, Schoenmaker and Oosterloo (2005) find a marked difference in cross-border activities for the interbank market across EU countries. They assert that this difference can be explained by the size of the domestic interbank market within a given country (larger markets have lower cross-border shares because more local counterparties are available). According to ECB (2006a), the cross-border component of non-bank debt securities has doubled from 25 per cent to over 50 per cent.

15.3.2 Current practices and institutional obstacles to modelling interlinkages

In several EU countries, the interbank contagion model of Upper and Worms (2004) has been tested and generally yielded reassuring results, although contagion indicators proved to be somewhat important in some countries. Simulations of the worst case scenarios show that banks representing less than 5 per cent of total balance sheet assets would be affected by contagion on the Belgian interbank market, while for the German system the failure of a single bank could lead to the breakdown of up to 15 per cent of the banking sector in terms of assets. Generally, the degree of contagion depends on the size of failing banks' losses that affect creditor banks in the system. Besides Germany (Upper and Worms, 2004), the model has been applied in Belgium (Degryse and Nguyen, 2004), Austria (Boss et al. 2004), the UK (Wells, 2004), Portugal (Cocco et al. 2005), the Netherlands (Van Lelyveld and Liedorp, 2006), Italy (Mistrulli, 2007) and Poland (Halaj, 2007). Some of these studies also incorporated large exposures data (Wells, 2004 and Degryse and Nguyen, 2004), foreign exposures of domestic banks (Degryse and Nguyen, 2004 and Van Lelyveld and Liedorp, 2006) and compared actual data with estimated data (Mistrulli, 2007).

Furthermore, anecdotal evidence confirms that national central banks of Austria, Belgium, Denmark, Germany, Italy, the Netherlands, Portugal and the UK have some experience with studies using payment data, as in Furfine (1999). For example, for the netting system in Italy, Angelini et al. (1996) found that only about 4 per cent of participants were large enough to trigger systemic crises using data from January 1992 and the average monetary loss was less than 3 per cent of the daily flow of funds through the clearing system. For the UK, for the period March 2002–March 2003, Millard and Polenghi (2004) showed that most of the unsecured overnight loans transactions are exchanged among four settlement members out of a total of thirteen but that operational failures would not greatly affect the overnight interbank loan market. For Portugal, Farinha and Gaspar (2007) found that since 1999 operations with other Portuguese banks have been a small and decreasing proportion of total operations in the overnight market. Their study also found no evidence of hierarchical relations between large and small banks, and documented that large banks have a richer set of cross-border counterparts and are more active in the market.

Unfortunately, however, a comprehensive modelling of cross-border inter-linkages still appears to be lacking, due to data restrictions and institutional obstacles. Research prospects would be greatly enhanced if it was possible to use interbank and/or payments data for a representative sample of EU banks. However, data restrictions and modelling challenges – even at the national level – make explicit consideration of bank-to-bank linkages in a cross-border context prohibitively costly or impossible. Upper (2007) argues that only with credit register data interbank linkages can be estimated accurately. However, even then, several caveats should be in place, as these data may only cover exposures exceeding a threshold, report credit lines instead of actual exposures or exclude off-balance sheet items.[18] When using aggregate interbank lending and borrowing data, exposures will be biased towards a complete structure of claims, whereas in reality, small exposures may be non-existent, due to fixed costs for screening, and market concentration higher, due to relationship lending – limiting the number of counterparties. In fact, Mistrulli (2007) shows that for the Italian banking system the use of maximum entropy techniques, as in Upper and Worms (2004), underestimates contagion risk relative to an approach that uses information on actual bilateral exposures. Furthermore, much of the existing empirical literature on interbank linkages focuses on the consequences of a shock to a single bank when tracing through the consequences of that shock for other banks in the system, whereas in reality, shocks may be correlated and interplay with interbank contagion.

Several institutional factors also hamper the in-depth examination of cross-border linkages between EU banks. These have partly to do with the differing supervisory, regulatory and accounting frameworks across EU member states. For example, several national central banks as well as the ECB do not have access to prudential information or credit registers and thus cannot compile detailed statistics on interbank lending and/or payments at the individual bank level. More specifically, to operationalise the model by Upper and Worms (2004) in a cross-border context, one would need information from

---

[18] Also, not all central credit registers include data on interbank exposures. See Chapter 6.

banks on their aggregate domestic and cross-border interbank assets and liabilities by country and counterparty. These data are generally not available or their use is hampered by confidentiality limitations. Indeed, as noted by Fonteyne and van der Vossen (2007), information about cross-border financial groups is dispersed among various national agencies involved in the supervision of the group and may leave no single supervisor with a complete overview of all risks within and between financial groups. However, the recent introduction in the EU of colleges of supervisors for the major cross-border banking groups is expected to enhance the availability of information for the relevant supervisors on the group as a whole. One approximation could be to use ECB statistics on monetary and financial institutions' (MFIs') cross-border loans to other MFIs to derive banks' cross-border exposures. However, such aggregate information imposes the assumption that individual banks in a given country have the same level of geographic diversification, which clearly yields inaccurate results. Also in the case of the Furfine (1999) approach, data constraints and confidentiality issues impede the use of domestic and cross-border payment system data.

15.3.3 The changing banking landscape and propagation of stress

Major changes have taken place in the European banking landscape over the past years thanks to increased financial integration, relating mainly to money market integration, integration of settlement systems (TARGET and TARGET-2) and cross-border banking consolidation, in the wake of European monetary unification and the introduction of the euro. In the second half of the 1980s, significant financial liberalisation and modernisation took place. This process was triggered by the single European market programme which allowed for the free provision of services, including financial services, and the free flow of capital among EU member states. This led to a rise in the number of cross-border mergers and acquisitions (M&As) in the financial sector and in the cross-border provision of financial services. For instance, until the late 1990s, only around 10 per cent of M&As in the banking sector were cross-border. By 2005, this percentage increased to about 25 per cent. External assets held by EU residents have increased markedly, from around 40 per cent of GDP in 1993 to around 80 per cent in 2006. After a strong expansion over the past years, the cross-border euro area component in banks' bond holdings is now slightly above 50 per cent. Also, interbank activity has an important cross-border share, around 30 per cent and with a clearly increasing trend, although this may partly reflect the growing importance of intragroup transactions.

These developments have changed the possibilities for propagation of stress within the European financial system. For instance, cross-border M&As change the ways in which banks are interlinked and, as banks expand into new geographical areas, can change their longer term risk profiles. More uniform pricing strategies across EU member states and greater financial integration may become apparent if cross-border banking groups continue to grow and establishments of the same banking group in different countries adopt similar standards and strategies. Eventually, the segmentation of banking markets along national markets may become more blurred and change the nature of risks banks are facing. In particular, common and sectoral exposures as opposed to country-wide shocks may become more prevalent in a similar fashion as common factors increasingly drive national EU stock markets and determine EU member states' business cycles. Furthermore, the predominance of large cross-border banks may increase the EU's vulnerability to contagion and regulatory arbitrage. Moreover, centralisation by banks of key business functions such as liquidity and risk management, as well as managerial control, may make separate assessments of subsidiaries and branches more difficult.

In this context, recent studies find that EU-wide macroeconomic and banking-specific shocks are significant and suggest that some risks have increased since unification and may have led to greater contagion risks. Decressin (2006), for instance, found that developments in balance sheet and profitability indicators of Europe's 100 largest banks do not cluster naturally around countries. Also ECB studies found evidence of significant cross-border contagion, which may have increased since the introduction of the euro (Gropp *et al.*, 2006).

15.3.4 Recent ESCB work on modelling challenges

As mentioned in the introduction to this chapter, two types of cross-border linkages can be identified: balance sheet linkages and common exposures to systemic shocks. Cross-border balance sheet linkages can cause direct contagion across EU banking sectors, if idiosyncratic shocks are transmitted between financial institutions of different EU member states, most notably through the interbank money and repo market (see section 15.2). In addition, cross-border ownership links can be a cause of contagion as they entail intragroup exposures. For instance, foreign branches and subsidiaries may depend on the parent bank for capital and liquidity provision, while the parent bank can suffer losses through its participations in other EU member states.

Cross-border common exposures can cause indirect contagion across EU banking sectors, if widespread or systemic shocks affect institutions in different EU member states alike.

The ESCB Banking Supervision Committee recently explored the challenges of modelling cross-border contagion from an empirical and modelling perspective (ECB, 2006b). From these perspectives, the most important challenge is the lack of comparable data across all EU member states with a sufficient time span and granularity.

Cross-border ownership links can be derived from banks' annual reports, external data providers such as Bureau van Dijk (BvD) Bankscope (banks' subsidiary structures) and merger data. As mentioned in section 15.3.1, the ECB undertakes bi-annually a mapping of the activities of large internationally active EU banks (ECB, 2007a). One way in which such information could be used is to identify country pairs that are more closely linked and hence more likely to be subject to contagion from distress in each other's banking sector. The information could also be used to quantify the potential spill-over effects of bank or country-specific shocks on banks or banking sectors of other EU countries.

Cross-border common exposures can be stress-tested relatively easily, for instance by computing banks' or entire banking sectors' credit exposure toward borrowers in relevant foreign countries. One way of modelling is by using credit exposure-weighted GDP growth rates as an input in a model of bank or banking sector loan loss provisions, default rate or level of non-performing loans. As mentioned in section 15.2.1, many studies identified the business cycle as having a negative and significant impact on bad loans and loss provisions. The use of foreign exposure-weighted macroeconomic indicators allows taking account of foreign risk drivers in explaining loan losses or other indicators of credit risk, which is still considered the main source of risk for EU banks. To illustrate, consider a model of loan loss provisions (LLP) estimated using panel regression techniques for banking sectors in the EU (EU-25 except Luxembourg):

$$LLP = F(LLP_{-1}, WGDP, \text{interest rate}, \Delta \text{credit})$$

where WGDP denotes the weighted GDP growth, interest rate is a short-term interest rate, and Δ credit is aggregate credit growth calculated on a domestically incorporated basis.

Table 15.1 shows that in the long-term, a 1 per cent decrease of GDP makes the LLP ratio increase by 0.4 percentage points. The (lagged) change

Table 15.1 LLP dynamic panel estimation

LLP_{-1}	0.39 (5.77)
WGDP	−0.15 (−3.37)
$WGDP_{-1}$	−0.24 (−3.49)
Δ credit	0.12 (2.94)
Interest rate (lagged)	0.14 (2.96)
Autocorrelation order 1	z = −1.41
Autocorrelation order 2	z = −0.42
Sargan test [prob= 0.68]	$\chi^2_{(22)} = 18.44$

Note: The model uses the Arellano–Bond fixed-effect estimator and is based on 119 annual observations, from 24 EU countries, spanning data between 1993 and 2005.

Table 15.2 Sensitivity test of a decline in WGDP

% profit	− 1%	−2%	− 3%
Weighted	11.3	22.7	34.0
Minimum	2.0	4.0	6.0
Maximum	16.2	32.3	48.5
% capital			
Weighted	3.5	7.0	10.6
Minimum	0.3	0.7	1.0
Maximum	4.8	9.6	14.4

Note: The impact of extra provisions under WGDP stress is calculated as a percentage of gross profit before provisions and capital.

of short-term interest rate is also significant and reveals that increases in interest rates reduce borrowers' ability to repay their loans. Based on this outcome, one can undertake a simple stress test of the impact of a one-year slowdown in GDP growth by 1, 2 or 3 per cent. In the worst case, the impact would on average amount to 34 per cent of profits and 11 per cent of total capital (Table 15.2).

This exercise allows us to draw some conclusions concerning the stance of macro stress-testing for EU countries based on country data. First, the availability of even relatively straightforward and comparable data on an EU-wide level is non-trivial. For most countries, data series on LLP start in the mid-1990s and for new EU member states generally only after 2000. Aggregate NPL data are non-existent on an EU-wide level. The short time span also implies that potentially different structures cannot easily be taken into account. Doing so, e.g., by splitting the sample, would render the results less reliable. Data frequency is another issue, since around one-third of EU countries provide LLP data only on an annual basis. For real-time financial stability monitoring, one would need higher frequency information.

Finally, stress-testing or scenario analysis under this approach is a very partial equilibrium exercise. It relies on the *ceteris paribus* assumption, independently from other variables. However, this concern can be addressed, e.g., by adding a satellite macro model onto the LLP model.

15.4 Conclusions

This chapter provides an overview of the methods and practices that have been developed for stress-testing practices on the cross-border level. Given its importance for banks' operations, stress-testing credit risk has attracted most attention over the past years while, at the same time, the financial contagion literature has yielded important contributions to analysing the international spill-over of market risk. However, it should be highlighted that despite this focus on a few main risk factors, plenty of work remains to be done in analysing the cross-border dimension in other risk factors, most notably liquidity risk and counterparty risk. However, the pertinent data problems continue to hamper the advances in all fields of cross-border stress-testing. Greater access to quantitative and qualitative supervisory information – especially about large and complex EU banking groups – may overcome the obstacles to analysing cross-border exposures, documented in this chapter. While the Pillar III disclosure rules of the Basel 2 Accord will improve the situation somewhat at the individual institution level, a proper understanding of the common lending and network exposures requires cooperation at the level of relevant authorities. As argued by Fonteyne and van der Vossen (2007), current national confidentiality regimes could be replaced by a European confidentiality regime, covering all prudential authorities and the ECB and allowing appropriate data protection and a free flow of information among the agencies involved. It would also allow the exploitation of the data for cross-border stress-testing, financial stability monitoring at the EU level, and eventually form a basis for crisis management and resolution.

REFERENCES

Angelini, P., G. Maresca and D. Russo (1996), 'Systemic Risk in the Netting System', *Journal of Banking and Finance*, 20 (5), 853–68.

Arpa, M., I. Giulini, A. Ittner and F. Pauer (2001), 'The Influence of Macroeconomic Developments on Austrian Banks: Implications for Banking Supervision', *BIS Paper*, 1.

Bethlendi, A. (2006), 'Provisioning Practice of Hungarian banks', *MNB Occasional Paper*, 56.

Beyeler, W., R. Glass, M. Bech and K. Soramaki (2006), 'Congestion and Cascades in Payment Systems', *FRB of New York Staff Report*, 259.

Boss, M., H. Elsinger, S. Thurner and M. Summer (2004), 'Network Topology of the Interbank Market', *Quantitative Finance*, 4, 1–8.

Čihák, M. and L. Ong (2007), 'Estimating Spillover Risk Among Large EU banks', *IMF Working Paper*, 267.

Cocco, J., F. Gomes and N. Martins (2005), 'Lending Relationships in the Interbank Market', *London Business School Working Paper*.

Decressin, J. (2006), 'A Bank Business Correlation Perspective on Pan-European Supervision', *Euro Area Policies – Selected Issues, IMF Country Report*, 288.

Degryse, H. and G. Nguyen (2004), 'Interbank Exposures: an Empirical Examination of Systemic Risk in the Belgian Interbank Market', *NBB Working Paper*, 43.

Demuynck, J. (2004), *Un Modèle d'Évolution des Créances Douteuses dans le Cadre du FSAP-FMI*, Secrétariat Général de la Commission Bancaire – Banque de France mimeo.

ECB (2005), 'Indicators of Financial Distress in Mature Economies', *Financial Stability Review*, June, 126–31.

(2006a), *EU Banking Structures*, October.

(2006b), 'Country-level Macro Stress Testing Practices', *Financial Stability Review*, June, 147–54.

(2006c), 'Survey on EU Banks' Large Exposures on Single-name Corporates', *Financial Stability Review*, June, 102–4.

(2006d), 'Identifying Large and Complex Banking Groups for Financial System Stability', *Financial Stability Review*, December, 131–9.

(2007a), 'Identifying Large and Complex Banking Groups for Financial System Stability', *Financial Stability Review*, December, 98–9.

(2007b), 'Global Macro-financial Developments and Expected Corporate Sector Default Frequencies in the Euro Area', *Financial Stability Review*, June, 152–8.

(2007c), 'Assessing Portfolio Credit Risk in a Sample of EU Large and Complex Banking Groups', *Financial Stability Review*, June, 159–65.

(2008), 'Analysing the Topology of the EU Cross-border Banking Flows Network', *Financial Stability Review*, June, 108–9.

Farinha, L. and V. Gaspar (2007), 'Portuguese Banks in the Euro Area Market for Daily Funds', *Bank of Portugal Economic Bulletin*, 13 (1), 65–78.

Fonteyne, W. and W. van der Vossen (2007), 'Financial Integration and Stability', in J. Decressin, H. Faruqee and W. Fonteyne (eds.), *Integrating Europe's Financial Markets*, International Monetary Fund, 199–237.

Furfine, C. (1999), 'The Microstructure of the Federal Funds Market', *Financial Markets, Institutions and Instruments*, 8, 24–44.

Głogowski, A. (2006), *Determinants of Polish Banks' Loan Losses – a Panel Investigation*, National Bank of Poland, mimeo.

Goodhart, C. and M. Segoviano (2008), 'Banking Stability Index', *IMF Working Paper*, forthcoming.

Gropp, R., M. Lo Duca and J. Vesala (2006), 'Cross-border Bank Contagion in Europe', *ECB Working Paper*, 662.

Halaj, G. (2007), 'Contagion Effect in Banking System – Measures Based on Randomised Loss Scenarios', *Financial Markets and Institutions*, 6, 69–80.

Hartmann, P., S. Straetmans and C. de Vries (2005), 'Banking System Stability: a Cross-Atlantic Perspective', in M. Carey and R. Stulz (eds.), *Risks of Financial Institutions*, National Bureau of Economic Research Conference Report, University of Chicago Press, XI, 655.

Marcucci, J. and M. Quagliariello (2008), 'Is Bank Portfolio Riskiness Procyclical? Evidence from Italy using a Vector Autoregression', *Journal of International Financial Market, Institutions & Money*, 18, 46–63.

Martin, C. (2005), *A NPL's Model for Stress-tests on the French Banking System*, Secrétariat Général de la Commission Bancaire – Banque de France mimeo.

Millard, S. and M. Polenghi (2004), 'The Relationship Between the Overnight Interbank Unsecured Loan Market and the CHAPS Sterling System', *Bank of England Quarterly Bulletin*, Spring, 42–7.

Mistrulli, P. (2007), 'Interbank Lending Patterns and Financial Contagion', *Bank of Italy Working Paper*, 641.

Pain, D. (2003), 'The Provisioning Experience of the Major UK Banks: a Small Panel Investigation', *Bank of England Working Paper*, 177.

Pesola, J. (2005), 'Banking Fragility and Distress: an Econometric Study of Macroeconomic Determinants', *Bank of Finland Discussion Paper*, 13.

Quagliariello, M. (2007), 'Banks' Riskiness over the Business Cycle: a Panel Analysis on Italian Intermediaries', *Applied Financial Economics*, 17 (2).

Salas, V. and J. Saurina (2002), 'Credit Risk in Two Institutional Settings: Spanish Commercial and Saving Banks', *Journal of Financial Services Research*, 22, 3.

Schoenmaker D. and S. Oosterloo (2005), 'Financial Supervision in an Integrating Europe: Measuring Cross-border Externalities', *International Finance*, 8 (1), 1–27.

Segoviano, M., B. Hofmann and C. Goodhart (2006), 'Default, Credit Growth, and Asset Prices', *IMF Working Paper*, 223.

Upper, C. (2007), 'Using Counterfactual Simulations to Assess the Danger of Contagion in Interbank Markets', *BIS Working Paper*, 234.

Upper, C. and A. Worms (2004), 'Estimating Bilateral Exposures in the German Interbank Market: Is There a Danger of Contagion?', *European Economic Review*, 48 (4), 827–49.

Valckx, N. (2003), *What Determines Loan Loss Provisioning in the EU?* ECB mimeo.

Van den End, J. W., M. Hoeberichts and M. Tabbae (2006), 'Modelling Scenario Analysis and Macro Stress-testing', *DNB Working Paper*, 119.

Van Lelyveld, I. and F. Liedorp (2006), 'Interbank Contagion in the Dutch Banking Sector: A Sensitivity Analysis', *International Journal of Central Banking*, 2 (2), 99–133.

Wells, S. (2004), 'Financial Interlinkages in the United Kingdom's Interbank Market and the Risk of Contagion', *Bank of England Working Paper*, 230.

16 Stress-testing at the IMF

Marina Moretti, Stéphanie Stolz and Mark Swinburne[*]

16.1 Introduction

For almost a decade, the IMF has been using stress tests to identify vulnerabilities across institutions that could undermine the stability of a country's financial system. Stress tests are typically performed as part of the Financial Sector Assessment Program (FSAP) – a joint effort by the IMF and the World Bank. Since the program's inception in 1999, the FSAP has become an essential element of the Fund's engagement on financial issues with its member countries. FSAPs have been or are being carried out for over 120 countries – two-thirds of Fund membership. FSAP re-assessments (that is, updates of the original, first assessment) are also taking place, with more than forty FSAP updates completed or underway. Some form of stress-testing has been universal in these assessments, ranging from very simple to more sophisticated exercises with associated macromodelling.

Reflecting the growing integration of financial sector work into Fund surveillance, Article IV teams have also started experimenting with stress-testing as part of regular consultations.[1] It is very early days yet, and such exercises will probably be done on only a sub-set of countries and in a more limited fashion than what could be undertaken in an FSAP, given the broader scope of Article IV surveillance. But the direction of movement over time seems clear. It is in turn facilitated by the rapid expansion of interest in, and capacity for, macro stress-testing among the authorities in an increasingly wide range of countries.

---

[*] International Monetary Fund (IMF). The views expressed in this chapter are those of the authors and do not necessarily represent those of the IMF or IMF policy.

[1] Under Article IV of the IMF Articles of Agreement, member countries undertake to collaborate to promote the stability of the global system of exchange rates and, in particular, commit to run their domestic and external policies in keeping with an agreed code of conduct. Article IV also sets forth an obligation for the IMF to 'oversee the compliance of each member with its obligations under Article IV', which it does through (typically annual) Article IV consultations and reports.

Technical assistance on stress-testing is another area of the Fund's work that has been expanding in recent years. Authorities often request technical assistance following FSAPs, with a view to improving their stress-testing approaches and receiving assistance in applying the techniques. The IMF also cooperates with a number of central banks and supervisory agencies in less formal ways, such as joint projects on stress-testing related issues – projects are ongoing for instance with the European Central Bank (ECB) and the Deutsche Bundesbank on innovative stress-testing methodologies.

Parallel to concrete applications is methodological work on the development of stress-testing techniques. This work program aims at enhancing the quality of stress tests being performed in-house as well as by country authorities. The thrust of much of this work is to take better account of macrofinancial linkages, using a range of different analytical perspectives and, where feasible, using their results as cross-checks. Feedback on the different methodologies from inside and outside the Fund is critical in identifying the more promising approaches for the IMF to develop and apply further.

Last but not least, the IMF has been serving as a hub for promoting macro stress tests and for fostering cooperation in this field among central banks. One example is the Expert Forum on Advanced Stress Testing Techniques, launched by the IMF in 2006. It meets approximately every year and a half with the participation of supervisory agencies and central banks that are leading the work on stress-testing.[2]

This chapter focuses on the IMF's experience with the more comprehensive form of stress-testing in FSAPs. Section 16.2 provides background on the nature of an FSAP and the role of macro stress-testing within it. Section 16.3 describes how the methodology of stress-testing in FSAPs has been evolving and what are fairly common approaches now being used, at least for more advanced economies. Finally, section 16.4 discusses the main strengths and challenges for future development of macro stress-testing in FSAPs. The Annex provides an overview of stress-testing practice in European FSAPs.

---

[2] The first Expert Forum took place in May 2006 at IMF headquarters; the second in November 2007 hosted by the Nederlandsche Bank; and the third in May 2009 hosted by the Deutsche Bundesbank in Berlin. The IMF also participates in external working groups and programs that are active in this area, such as the Basel Committee for Banking Supervision, the Electronic Platform on Stress Testing of the Deutsche Bundesbank, and the Regulation and Financial Stability Program of the Financial Markets Group Research Centre at the London School of Economics.

16.2 Background: overview of the FSAP

The broad objective of the FSAP is to help strengthen and deepen financial systems and enhance their resilience to potential financial crises. Supported by experts from a range of national agencies and standard-setting bodies, work under the program seeks to identify the strengths and vulnerabilities of a country's financial system; determine how key sources of risk are being managed; ascertain the sector's developmental and technical assistance needs; and help prioritise policy responses. The program is designed to assess the stability of financial systems as a whole, rather than individual institutions, and to emphasise prevention and mitigation rather than crisis resolution.

A key feature of the FSAP – perhaps the defining feature – is that it endeavours to take a relatively broad, holistic view of system-level risks and vulnerabilities. This means not only the main structural, institutional and market features and activities of the financial sector, but also the financial policy framework within which the financial sector operates, in particular the strengths and weaknesses of arrangements to prevent or manage financial sector crises, and how these in turn affect financial sector behaviour.[3]

It also means applying a range of both quantitative and qualitative tools and methodologies to get at the important issues. Formal assessments of international standards and codes relevant for the financial sector, for example, are one important tool on the qualitative side, but are not always the most suitable (or cost effective) way of addressing policy issues.

Likewise, stress-testing is a key quantitative tool in FSAPs but not the only one. A number of indicators are also used as a basis for analysing the health and stability of the financial system. Among them are financial soundness indicators (FSIs) – that is, aggregated data on individual banking institutions and their non-bank clients, and indicators that are representative of the markets in which these institutions operate – and, where feasible and available, market-based data drawn from price and volatility measures of various capital market instruments.[4] Analyses of aggregate balance sheets (macro, sectoral) and (supervisory or other) early warning systems are also used in the FSAP context.

---

[3] See IMF–World Bank (2005).   [4] See Chapter 6.

16.3 Stress-testing in FSAPs[5]

There is an important point of principle underlying this rather eclectic approach, under which – to re-iterate – stress-testing is a key tool in FSAPs, but one that is supplemented by both qualitative analysis and other forms of quantitative analysis. As stated succinctly by Bunn *et al.* (2005):

[N]o single model is ever likely to capture fully the diverse channels through which shocks may affect the financial system. Stress testing models will, therefore, remain a complement to, rather than a substitute for broader macroprudential analysis of potential threats to financial stability. (p. 117)

Thus, FSAP stress-testing is not interpreted as providing numerical estimates that are in themselves very precise. Rather, the benefit lies as much in the analytical process undertaken by the FSAP team and the authorities in constructing the stress-testing as a means to explore potential vulnerabilities in the financial system. Stress tests are an instrument for a useful dialogue on these issues, and often too a useful learning experience.

It is also fair to say that the FSAP stress-testing process has often had a longer lasting effect on countries, quite apart from helping assess financial stability at the time of the FSAP. In particular, it has encouraged policy-makers to further develop their own capacities in this area, as part of the broader process of building a more specific financial stability assessment function and capacity.[6] At times this has been directly supported by Fund technical assistance, notably with a view to putting models and procedures in place which could then be used both for FSAP stress-testing and by the authorities on a more frequent, regular basis.

FSAP stress tests are tailored to country-specific circumstances, both as to the different types of potential vulnerabilities to be subjected to stress-testing, and the exact nature, coverage, and size of the shocks applied to the various risk factors. In combination with the ongoing evolution of stress-testing methodologies, this has therefore resulted in quite a wide range of approaches.[7] Within this, some basic principles of 'good practice' in FSAP stress-testing have developed over time and are continuing to evolve.

---

[5] This section draws especially on Blaschke *et al.* (2001), Jones *et al.* (2004) and Čihák (2007).
[6] See also on this the report of the IMF's Independent Evaluation Office (2006).
[7] See the Annex to this chapter for a summary of practices for FSAP stress-testing in European countries. The focus is on Europe as the region with most extensive FSAP coverage to date.

16.3.1 Stress-testing approaches

Stress tests in FSAPs come in several broad varieties, but are all aimed at examining the potential vulnerabilities at the system level.[8]

On one dimension, they may either be in the form of a range of sensitivity tests addressing the impact of shocks to single risk factors in each test, possibly in a rather *ad hoc* and a theoretic fashion; or they may be tests focusing on scenarios in which multiple risk factors change in a fashion that is intended to be internally consistent.

On a second dimension, FSAP stress tests can be either bottom-up, run by individual financial institutions, or top-down, run by an organisation with a focus on the stability of the whole financial system. Such an organisation is typically the central bank, the financial supervisor, or the IMF.

On a third dimension, and notwithstanding the ultimate focus on the system level, FSAP stress tests can be either bank-by-bank, run on the portfolios of individual financial institutions, or at the aggregate level, based on an aggregate system-wide model.

First, given the IMF's focus and comparative advantage, it is perhaps not surprising that FSAP stress tests have increasingly emphasised the design of adverse macroeconomic scenarios, and the impact of these scenarios on the creditworthiness of financial institutions and the stability of the financial system as a whole. The construction of such macro scenarios – and more generally the identification of the macro-level risk factors to be shocked – is a critical exercise in the FSAP stress-testing process, whether the scenarios are applied in a bank-by-bank exercise, or only at the aggregate level.

Second, since FSAP stress tests are fundamentally intended to address the risks that arise from common shocks, the essence of FSAP stress-testing is that the same shocks are applied uniformly to all institutions, again, whether the methodology follows a bank-by-bank or an aggregate approach.[9]

Third, no careful analysis of system-level stability can afford to look only at the system-level aggregates and averages. Some attempt also needs to be made to understand the nature of the dispersion underneath the aggregates and averages, since concentrations of exposures and vulnerabilities that may be important for the system can be hidden beneath more benign-looking aggregates. Some form of bank-by-bank testing is therefore critical in FSAPs, whether or not this is informed by well-integrated and internally consistent

---

[8] See Chapter 2.
[9] That is, the same shocks are applied to a given set of institutions covered within a given stress test.

macro scenarios. Indeed, for FSAPs the merit of purely aggregate tests lies mainly in providing supplementary analysis, especially – in the spirit of the principle of not relying too heavily on any one model – as a means of partially cross-checking the results of bank-by-bank tests.

In terms of the calibration of the scenarios and shocks, the basic underlying principle for FSAP stress-testing is that the shocks should be 'extreme but plausible'. What that translates to in any particular case can vary quite widely depending on circumstances.[10]

16.3.2 Stress-testing experience

As already noted, stress-testing processes and methodologies in FSAPs have evolved quite significantly since the early days of the program, and in a number of ways, as summarised in Table 16.1.[11]

The following main points are to be highlighted.

First of all, most FSAPs conduct single-factor sensitivity analyses, but these have evolved from being central to the analysis to being more supplementary, for instance as a means of obtaining some sense of the partial derivatives that may be associated with a broader, multi-factor scenario. In contrast, more recent FSAPs have increasingly involved explicit macroeconomic scenario analyses, of varying natures and degrees of complexity.

The testing increasingly involves national authorities directly at all levels, from the design of the methodology and selection of scenarios and shocks in agreement with the FSAP team, to the implementation or coordination of the tests, and the analysis of test results (Table 16.A2). It also increasingly involves

Table 16.1 Evolution of stress-testing methodologies in European FSAPs (% of all FSAPs initiated in the period)

	2000–2	2003–5	2006–7[b]
Scenario analysis	64	95	82
Contagion analysis [a]	11	38	55
Insurance sector stress testing	25	37	9

[a] Includes cross-border and interbank contagion
[b] Includes a high proportion of less advanced countries
Source: Čihák (2007); and IMF staff calculations

[10] See Chapter 4.
[11] Table 16.A1 in the Annex lists the European countries whose FSAPs are covered in this survey. The survey focuses on European FSAPs, as Europe is the continent with the most complete coverage of FSAPs.

financial institutions directly, at least in relatively advanced systems. Institution-by-institution implementation uses the banks' own models, analyses and judgments about the impact of the given scenarios and shocks.

In terms of risks to be considered, interbank contagion is becoming more commonly integrated into the stress-testing to examine further, indirect effects of the common shocks. Typically this has been based around a matrix of mutual exposures in the domestic interbank money market.

Finally, non-bank financial institutions are also increasingly covered in FSAP stress-testing, mainly insurance companies and to a lesser degree pension funds (Table 16.A3). Most commonly, non-banks are tested separately from the banking sector, but in a number of cases, cross-sectoral conglomerates have been tested at the overall group level.

16.3.3 Risks addressed in FSAP stress tests

FSAPs have addressed a range of different risks in stress tests, within the broad categories of credit risk; market risk (interest rate, exchange rate, volatility, equity, real estate and other asset price risks); liquidity risk; and contagion risk.

Credit risk

Credit risk has been a key focus of FSAPs, reflecting the fact that in many countries it remains the main overall source of risk for banks, as typically re-confirmed by the stress tests themselves. At the same time, both in the FSAP context and more generally, it is also a risk area in need of enhanced assessment and management tools.

A fairly typical approach in the early days of the FSAP and still common in less-developed systems or as part of single-factor sensitivity tests are mechanical exercises (Table 16.A4). In these simple tests, banks' balance sheets are shocked directly, i.e., shocks are directly applied to nonperforming loans (NPLs) or provisions and a link to the macroeconomy is not modelled explicitly. Typical tests assess what would happen if banks raise their provisioning to reflect loan quality deterioration either overall or in particular parts of their portfolio, or if their largest borrowers default (concentration risk). The NPL migration and loan reclassification analysis is still an essential part of most FSAPs as part of the single-factor sensitivity tests.

Increasingly, more advanced approaches have been used that are based on loan performance data and regressions (single equation, structural and vector autoregression). A typical stress test in this category models NPLs or loan-loss provisions as a function of various macroeconomic variables.[12] Increasingly, this has also been undertaken through more sophisticated analyses of probabilities of default (PDs) and loss given default (LGD). For example, the Austria FSAP modelled default rates as a function of macro variables (see Table 16.A4). Stressed default rates can then be used by the FSAP team and/or the authorities to conduct top-down stress tests using off-site supervisory data; or can be provided as inputs to the banks, for them to calculate (un)expected losses bottom-up using their internal models. It is also useful to analyse and discuss differences between the outcomes of the bottom-up and top-down approaches.

In this category of more advanced approaches, two methodologies the IMF has been working on are worth highlighting.

The first methodology is a portfolio credit risk model based on CreditRisk+ that has been complemented with models of PDs and LGDs with specific links to macrofinancial factors.[13] The model can be applied with obligor-level or more aggregate supervisory data. Because it uses as basic input the same data required by the Basel 2 Internal Ratings Based (IRB) approach, it provides a valuable tool for financial supervisors to benchmark their credit risk evaluations. This model has been applied in several FSAPs (e.g., within Europe, Greece), and in the context of technical assistance; it has also been shared with various authorities, including the European Central Bank, the central banks of Argentina, Iceland and Portugal, and the bank superintendencies of China, Costa Rica, Colombia and Morocco.

The second approach uses non-parametric techniques to address two major constraints faced by standard macro stress-testing: short time series of risk variables and lack of default dependence information. It combines three quantitative tools: (1) the conditional probability of default (CoPoD), which measures default risk through time with short time series; (2) the consistent information multi-variate density optimisation (CIMDO), which measures portfolio credit risk; and (3) the CIMDO-copula, which measures default dependence under data-constrained environments.[14] This framework for macro stress-testing can be used to look at the effects of shocks on individual banks as well as at the system level.[15] In particular, this approach allows to better quantify the impact of macroeconomic shocks on individual banks' economic capital and on the banking system's economic capital, despite short

---

[12] Household and corporate portfolios are sometimes modelled separately or, data permitting, the corporate sector is disaggregated further. Chapter 9 provides an example.

[13] See Avesani et al. (2006).   [14] See Segoviano (2006a, 2006b, 2008).

[15] See Segoviano and Padilla (2006) and Segoviano and Goodhart (2008). The framework also allows to calculate a stability measure of the banking system and to measure liquidity risk and counterparty risk.

time series of default probabilities and accounting for changes in correlations among banks' assets through the economic cycle. This model was used, for instance, in the Denmark and Lithuania FSAPs. Input data is also in line with the Basel 2 IRB approach.

Loan performance could also be linked to macro variables using corporate sector data (e.g., leverage and interest coverage) and possibly household data. Such approaches consider explicitly borrower characteristics that have a bearing on the ability of corporates and households to pay down their loans. Yet this requires series of microeconomic data that are often not available. Working with micro data is also time-consuming. Hence, these approaches have not been used yet in FSAPs.

The credit risk scenarios used in FSAPs have depended crucially on country circumstances and data availability. For the mechanical approaches, shocks to NPLs or provisions are typically *ad hoc* or based on historical banking system data or on cross-country evidence. For the more advanced approaches, scenarios are common and cover a set of macro variables such as GDP, interest rates and exchange rates. Depending on country circumstances, the scenarios are calibrated using macroeconomic models (mostly those of central banks), the IMF's macroeconomic framework, or historical data for the country or for comparable countries. The scenarios typically range from less severe to crisis-type scenarios and include both domestic downturns and external shocks. Other specific issues have been examined where they were particularly relevant, such as cross-border lending (e.g., Austria, Spain), foreign currency lending (e.g., Croatia), country exposure (e.g., Luxembourg), or loan concentrations in general (e.g., the Netherlands, Russia) or to specific sectors (e.g., agriculture in Belarus, information and communication technologies in Finland).

Market risk

Market risk has tended to show smaller effects in FSAPs, partly due to the shorter horizon but also presumably reflecting the fact that it is often an area better managed by banks. The analysis of market risks has used a range of different approaches. For interest rate risk analysis, some FSAPs have looked at repricing and maturity gaps, others have looked at duration and others at value-at-risk (VaR) (Table 16.A5). For exchange rate risk analysis, tests focused on net open positions in some cases and on VaR measures in other cases (Table 16.A6).

Market risk shocks have been built on *ad hoc*, hypothetical, or historical movements in the relevant variables. In the case of interest rates, this may involve a parallel shift in the yield curve or a steepening or flattening of the yield curve (Table 16.A7). For exchange rate shocks, it may involve *ad hoc* devaluations or historically large depreciations and/or appreciations (Table 16.A8). Some other risks have been tested where relevant, including equity and real estate price risk, commodity price risk, credit spread risk, and the impact on interest margins of competition risk (Table 16.A9).

Liquidity risk

Stress tests for liquidity risk have become an essential part of the most recent FSAPs (Table 16.A10). These stress tests have assumed shocks to deposits and wholesale funding and often include a cross-border scenario in which foreign investors and parent banks stop funding the domestic banks. In addition to funding liquidity, a few FSAPs have also stressed market liquidity by assuming haircuts on quasi-liquid assets. The shocks have been calibrated based on historical data (e.g., Croatia, France), but often had to be assumed *ad hoc* (e.g., Austria) as the available time series did not include significant liquidity shortages. The results of the stress tests have most often been reported in terms of changes to a liquidity ratio measure, which has been the regulatory ratio or defined *ad hoc*. Some FSAPs reported the days until the banks become illiquid. Those FSAPs that looked at market liquidity also sometimes quantified the effect of shocks to liquidity on the banks' capital adequacy ratio (CAR).

Contagion risk

Stress-testing contagion risk is an important complement to stress tests of individual institutions faced with common shocks. As noted earlier, stress-testing contagion risk is becoming more common in FSAPs (see Table 16.A10). These tests often focus on 'pure' contagion, i.e., they assess whether the (random) failure of a bank causes a substantial deterioration in the capital adequacy in other banks. They are typically run in several iterations, as the contagion-induced failures can in turn induce failures in other banks, which can again lead to further failures, and so on. The channel of contagion that is mostly examined is through net domestic, uncollateralised interbank exposures (e.g., Belgium, Croatia).

While this 'pure' contagion analysis is useful, it does not look at the likelihood of the failures that trigger the contagion. Hence, some FSAPs analyse interbank contagion triggered by factors influencing the whole system at the same time. To do so, outcomes of stress tests are typically used as inputs into the contagion exercise, which then quantifies the knock-on effects. The mechanics of such a macro-linked contagion analysis are similar to the simple contagion test, but it takes place in a weakened system and takes into account the likelihood of the failures that trigger the contagion. This approach was used for instance in Poland, Russia and Austria.[16]

16.4 FSAP stress-testing going forward

As the FSAP continues and is increasingly dominated by reassessments (or FSAP updates), a range of issues arise on how its stress-testing component might or should evolve further. Some of these are narrower issues about how the underlying analytical methodologies could evolve, and some are broader issues having more to do with the stress-testing process in FSAPs.

16.4.1 Methodological agenda

Looking at the methodologies first, it seems clear that the IMF, like other macro stress-testers, will want to continue to work on the further development of credit risk modelling. This would include specific modelling of distributions of PDs and LGDs, as well as correlations between banks and between portfolios to better reflect credit risk at the system level. But there is also a range of other specific areas for further development, or at least consideration in light of the challenges they may pose to stress-testing.[17]

On risk types, further work on liquidity risk is warranted, expanding existing work on funding and market (asset) liquidity risk as well as to incorporate off-balance sheet concentration risk (e.g., excessive committed and uncommitted credit lines to a single counterparty). In addition, the joint analysis of market, credit and liquidity risk requires strengthening. Typically, the impact on bank capital of different types of risk is assessed separately and then, if anything, added up, which may be technically incorrect since VaR measures are not additive. The correlations between credit, market and liquidity risks could be examined at several levels. First, the joint analysis of indirect credit risk (banking book effects arising from changes in key market prices) alongside the associated market risk (trading book) effects could be strengthened. Second, wider ranging scenarios could be considered that directly include funding or market liquidity stresses (a liquidity run) as well as the more normal macro effects (so that the shocks represent more of a 'perfect storm').

---

[16] See also Chapter 12.   [17] See also Chapter 3.

Also, contagion stress-testing needs further development. One form that could be explored, in line with the analysis undertaken by some central banks, would be to examine mutual exposures in payment and settlement systems. Another would be to consider possible liquidity contagion, especially where there is experience from past runs. Yet another component that could be considered is the scope to use extreme value theory (EVT) to explore correlations between institutions as the basis for a contagion stress test.[18] Cross-border transmission channels also need more consistent coverage in FSAP stress-testing, including cross-border contagion between financial institutions.[19]

Scenario analysis could be conducted using the contingent claims approach (CCA). The CCA methodology combines balance sheet and market information with widely used finance techniques to construct risk-adjusted balance sheets that better reflect credit risk. By using a factor model to determine which key domestic and international factors drive changes in the financial institution's assets, it is possible to link macro shocks to credit risk indicators. This approach can be applied to a wide range of financial institutions (provided they issue securities in sufficiently deep markets). This approach is particularly useful when detailed obligor-level data are not available. The CCA was implemented in a working paper on Chile, and its use is envisaged for future FSAPs.[20]

While stress-testing of insurance companies and financial conglomerates will likely continue to become more common, an open question to be considered is how far FSAP stress tests should go towards including other non-bank financial institutions directly in the quantitative stress-testing analysis.

There are also challenges to model the behavioural responses of different players under stress events. While monetary policy reaction functions are sometimes built into the formulation of macro stress-testing, what should be done, if anything, about the reaction functions of the financial institutions? On the one hand, these may mitigate the effects of shocks on individual institutions, but if they allow for common reactions, herding behaviour, fire-sales and the like, the opposite may well be true at the system level.

From a pure modelling perspective, the potential presence of non-linearities and structural breaks in behavioural relationships can seriously reduce the

---

[18] This would examine correlations between extreme negative movements in institutions' distances to default, and result in an interinstitutional matrix that might be able to be used in a fashion analogous to an interbank exposures matrix. For a recent EVT analysis, though not linked to a stress test, see Chan-Lau *et al.* (2007) and Čihák and Ong (2007).

[19] On this issue, see Chapter 7.   [20] See Gray and Walsh (2008).

reliability of the stress test.[21] This issue arises in virtually all stress tests we do, but appreciating the potential implications is crucial. One quite common example in an FSAP context is modelling the impact of a major devaluation in a hard currency peg country. Past time series for such a country may be of very limited use given a lack of past exchange rate volatility. However experience from other countries and expert judgment can often play a key role in calibrating such a test. Various authors have tried to model non-linearities more explicitly, though this is still largely uncharted territory.

Finally, as mentioned in other chapters, there is an increasing need to take into account second-round feedback effects – from the financial sector back to the macroeconomic environment – in quantitative modelling. The modelling here typically gets complex quite quickly. This literature is relatively new, but there are already a number of papers that look into possible feedback loops.[22]

16.4.2 Other aspects on the agenda

At the level of FSAP processes more generally, there are also a couple of important broader points. First, FSAPs need to further improve the integration of stress-testing and other modes of quantitative analysis. This includes continuing to improve the availability of FSIs, an ongoing medium-term work plan in the IMF that builds on the recent 'coordinated compilation exercise'. And, relatedly, further 'benchmarking' of FSIs, not in any mechanistic sense, but built around a growing understanding of how different countries' FSIs need to be interpreted. Finally, it also means more widespread use of market-based indicators and analysis thereof, both as modes that are complementary to stress test analysis and also, where feasible, actually reflected directly in the stress test analysis.

Second, the rather wide range of practice to date raises a question: should FSAP stress-testing be more standardised? More precisely, what is the appropriate balance between cross-country uniformity of stress tests versus continuation of the case by case approach? The consensus among FSAP stress-testers is that, while more uniformity would have its attractions, standardising the shocks and their sizes across countries would not in fact achieve much real uniformity because of the different natures, activities and

---

[21] See also CGFS (2000, 2005) and Sorge (2004) for further discussion on this and other challenges.
[22] See for instance Aspachs *et al.* (2006), Segoviano *et al.* (2006), Goodhart *et al.* (2008a, 2008b), Gonzalez-Hermosillo and Segoviano (2008), Maechler and Tieman (2008).

potential vulnerabilities of different countries' systems: what might look like standardisation could be quite misleading. That said, there may be scope to standardise FSAP stress-testing more at the level of broader good practices, within a flexible overall framework. Initial steps have been taken in this direction, and an adaptable 'template' for smaller and less complex financial systems has been made publicly available.[23]

In seeing how much further there is to go in this direction, we also have to keep in mind that macro stress-testing is still a new field which will continue to evolve. In this context, there is a basic trade-off to be struck between the general desirability of greater analytical rigor and accuracy, including through the use of multiple approaches as consistency checks; and the non-negligible resource costs, computational burden and data availability issues.

Some of those costs are more in the nature of startup, rather than on-going, costs, and the trade-off has been eased as an increasingly wide fraternity of macro stress-testers has invested time and effort in pushing out the boundaries of the feasible. But the trade-off has not gone away and FSAP stress-testers in particular will continue to face it. In managing this over time, we will want to continue to have close dialogue with stress-testing counterparts among policy-makers and academics.

Annex   Stress-testing in European FSAPs[24]

Table 16.A1 FSAPs covered in this survey

	FSAP	Update
Austria	2003	2007
Belarus	2004	
Belgium	2004	
Bosnia and Herzegovina	2005	
Bulgaria	2001	
Croatia	2001	2007
Czech Republic	2000	
Denmark	2005	
Estonia	2000	

[23] See IMF-World Bank (2005) and Čihák (2007).
[24] This annex updates Čihák (2007), Appendix III. It covers FSAPs initiated between 2000 and 2007.

Table 16.A1 (cont.)

	FSAP	Update
Finland	2001	
France	2004	
Germany	2003	
Greece	2005	
Hungary	2000	2005
Iceland	2000	
Ireland	2000	2006
Israel	2000	
Italy	2004	
Latvia	2001	2007
Lithuania	2001	2007
Luxembourg	2001	
Macedonia, Former Yugoslav Republic of	2003	
Malta	2002	
Moldova	2004	2007
Montenegro	2006	
Netherlands	2003	
Norway	2004	
Poland	2000	2006
Portugal	2005	
Romania	2003	
Russian Federation	2002	2007
Serbia	2005	
Slovak Republic	2002	2006
Slovenia	2000	2003
Spain	2005	
Sweden	2001	
Switzerland	2001	2006
Ukraine	2002	
United Kingdom	2002	

Table 16.A2 Who did the calculations in European FSAP stress tests?

	FSAP
Supervisory agency/ central bank	Austria (2003, 2007), Belgium (2004), Denmark (2005), Estonia (2000), Finland (2004), Germany (2003), Hungary (2005), Ireland (2000, 2006), Israel (2000), Italy (2004), Latvia (2007), Lithuania (2007), Malta (2002), Moldova (2007), Netherlands (2003), Norway (2004), Portugal (2005), Russia (2007), Slovakia (2007), Spain (2005), Sweden (2001), Switzerland (2001, 2006), United Kingdom (2002)

Table 16.A2 (cont.)

	FSAP
FSAP team	Belarus (2004), Belgium (2004), Bosnia and Herzegovina (2005), Croatia (2001, 2007), Czech Republic (2000), Denmark (2005), Estonia (2000), Hungary (2000), Iceland (2000), Ireland (2000), Israel (2000), Latvia (2001, 2007), Lithuania (2001, 2007), Macedonia (2003), Moldova (2004, 2007), Montenegro (2006), Norway (2004), Poland (2000, 2006), Portugal (2005), Romania (2003), Russia (2002), Serbia (2005), Slovakia (2002, 2007), Slovenia (2000), Spain (2005), Ukraine (2002), United Kingdom (2002)
Financial institutions	Austria (2007), Belgium (2004), Denmark (2005), Estonia (2000), Finland (2004), Germany (2003), Greece (2005), Ireland (2000, 2006), Israel (2000), Italy (2004), Lithuania (2007), Luxembourg (2001), Malta (2002), Netherlands (2003), Norway (2004), Portugal (2005), Russia (2007), Spain (2005), Switzerland (2006), United Kingdom (2002)

Note: In some FSAPs, calculations were done by several parties, as indicated in the table.

Table 16.A3 Institutions covered in European FSAP stress tests

Institutions covered	FSAP
All banks (bank by bank)	Belarus (2004), Belgium (2004), Croatia (2007), Italy (2004), Latvia (2007), Lithuania (2001), Moldova (2004, 2007), Montenegro (2006), Poland (2006), Russia (2007), Slovakia (2007), Slovenia (2003), Switzerland (2006), Ukraine (2002)
Large/systemically important banks (bank by bank)	Austria (2003, 2007), Belgium (2004), Bosnia and Herzegovina (2005), Croatia (2001), Czech Republic (2000), Denmark (2005), Estonia (2000), Finland (2001), France (2004), Germany (2003), Greece (2005), Hungary (2005), Iceland (2000), Ireland (2000, 2006), Israel (2000), Italy (2004[a]), Latvia (2001), Lithuania (2007), Luxembourg (2001), Malta (2002), Netherlands (2003), Norway (2004), Poland (2000), Romania (2003), Russia (2002, 2007[b]), Serbia (2005), Slovakia (2002), Slovenia (2000), Spain (2005), Sweden (2001), Switzerland (2001, 2007[b]), United Kingdom (2002)
Insurance companies	Belgium (2004), Denmark (2005), Finland (2001), France (2004), Italy (2004), Netherlands (2003), Norway (2004), Portugal (2005), Spain (2005), Sweden (2001), Switzerland (2006), United Kingdom (2002)
Pension funds	Netherlands (2003), United Kingdom (2002)
Mortgage banks	Ireland (2006)

Notes:
[a] For part of the top-down stress tests
[b] For bottom-up stress tests

Table 16.A4 Approaches to credit risk modelling in European FSAPs

Approach to credit risk modelling	FSAP
NPLs, provisions: historical or macro-regressions	Austria (2003), Czech Republic (2000), France (2004), Iceland (2000), Ireland (2006), Israel (2000), Romania (2003), Russia (2002), Sweden (2001)
NPLs, provisions: *ad hoc* approaches	Belarus (2004), Bosnia and Herzegovina (2005), Bulgaria (2001), Croatia (2001, 2007), France (2004), Hungary (2000, 2005), Ireland (2000), Israel (2000), Latvia (2001, 2007), Lithuania (2001), Macedonia (2003), Malta (2002), Moldova (2004, 2007), Montenegro (2006), Poland (2000, 2006), Russia (2007), Serbia (2005), Slovakia (2002, 2007), Slovenia (2000, 2003), Switzerland (2001), Ukraine (2002)
Shocks to probabilities of default based on historical observations or regressions	Austria (2003, 2007), Belgium (2004), Denmark (2005), Greece (2005), Lithuania (2007), Luxembourg (2001), Russia (2002), Spain (2005)
Shocks to probabilities of default (*ad hoc*)	Germany (2003), Italy (2004), Netherlands (2003), Norway (2004), United Kingdom (2002)
Shocks to profits based on regressions	Switzerland (2006)
Explicit analysis of cross-border lending	Austria (2003, 2007), Spain (2005)
Explicit analysis of foreign exchange lending	Austria (2003, 2007), Croatia (2001, 2007)
Explicit analysis of loan concentration	Greece (2005), Latvia (2007), Malta (2002), Moldova (2007), Montenegro (2006), Netherlands (2003), Poland (2006), Russia (2002, 2007), Serbia (2005)
Explicit analysis of sectoral shocks	Belarus (2004), Finland (2001), Greece (2005), Latvia (2007), Moldova (2007)
Analysis of LTV ratios, mortgage PDs	Croatia (2001), Sweden (2001)

Table 16.A5 Approaches to interest rate risk modelling in European FSAPs

Approach to interest rate risk modelling	FSAP
Repricing or maturity gap analysis	Austria (2003, 2007), Belarus (2004), Belgium (2004), Croatia (2001, 2007), Czech Republic (2000), Greece (2005), Hungary (2000, 2005), Ireland (2006), Italy (2004), Latvia (2007), Lithuania (2001, 2007), Macedonia (2003), Malta (2002), Moldova (2004, 2007), Montenegro (2006), Poland (2000, 2006), Romania (2003), Russia (2002, 2007), Serbia (2005), Ukraine (2002)
Duration	Belgium (2004), Greece (2005), Iceland (2000), Ireland (2006), Israel (2000), Italy (2004), Latvia (2001, 2007), Norway (2004), Poland (2006), Slovakia (2002, 2007), Switzerland (2001)

Table 16.A5 (cont.)

Approach to interest rate risk modelling	FSAP
Value-at-risk	Denmark (2005), Finland (2004), Germany (2003), Israel (2000), Italy (2004), Netherlands (2003), Switzerland (2006), United Kingdom (2002)
Others (e.g., Δ NPV of balance sheet, Δ market value of bank capital, regressions, simulations)	Austria (2007), Norway (2004), Sweden (2001)

Table 16.A6　Approaches to exchange rate risk modelling in European FSAPs

Approach to exchange rate risk modelling	FSAP
Sensitivity analysis on the net open position	Austria (2003, 2007), Belarus (2004), Belgium (2004), Bulgaria (2001), Croatia (2001, 2007), Czech Republic (2000), Hungary (2000, 2005), Iceland (2000), Ireland (2006), Latvia (2001, 2007), Lithuania (2001, 2007), Macedonia (2003), Malta (2002), Moldova (2004, 2007), Montenegro (2006), Norway (2004), Poland (2000, 2006), Romania (2003), Russia (2002, 2007), Serbia (2005), Slovakia (2002, 2007), Slovenia (2000, 2003), Sweden (2001), Switzerland (2001), Ukraine (2002)
Value-at-risk	France (2004), Germany (2003), Israel (2000), Netherlands (2003), Switzerland (2006), United Kingdom (2002)

Table 16.A7　Interest rate shocks in European FSAPs

Interest rate scenarios used	Examples of Shock Sizes
• *ad hoc* or hypothetical interest rate increase	• 3 standard deviations of 3-month changes
• Parallel shift in yield curve	• 50%–100% increase
• Flattening/steepening of yield curve	• three-fold increase in nominal rate
• Historical interest rate increase	• 100 basis point shock to interest rates
• Basel Committee Amendment to Capital Accord to incorporate market risk	• 100 basis point shock to dollar interest rates and a concomitant 300 basis point shock to local currency interest rates
	• 300 basis point increase
	• +500, +200, +0 (+0, +200, +500) basis point increase in interest rates for 3-month, 3-month to 1-year, and over 1-year

Table 16.A8 Exchange rate shocks in European FSAPs

Exchange rate scenarios used	Examples of shock sizes
• *ad hoc* or hypothetical devaluation • Historical large exchange rate changes	• 20%–50% devaluation • 30% devaluation • 10% depreciation • 20% depreciation/appreciation • 40% depreciation/appreciation of euro/dollar exchange rate

Table 16.A9 Approaches to modelling other market risks in European FSAPs

Risk modelling approaches	FSAP
Shock to main stock market index	Austria (2003, 2007), Belgium (2004), Croatia (2007), Finland (2001), France (2004), Germany (2003), Greece (2005), Israel (2000), Italy (2004), Latvia (2001, 2007), Lithuania (2001, 2007), Malta (2002), Netherlands (2003), Norway (2004), Russia (2007), Slovakia (2002), Switzerland (2006), United Kingdom (2002)
Spread risk	Greece (2005), Russia (2007), Switzerland (2006)
Implied volatility of options risk	Austria (2007)
Housing price shock	Ireland (2006), Lithuania (2007), Netherlands (2003), Norway (2004), Slovakia (2007), Ukraine (2002), United Kingdom (2002)
Commodity price	Finland (2001)
Competition risk (interest rate margin)	Lithuania (2001), Slovenia (2000, 2003)

Table 16.A10 Approaches to liquidity and contagion risk modelling in European FSAPs

Risk modelling approaches	FSAP
Liquidity risk (*ad hoc* decline in liquidity)	Austria (2003, 2007), Belarus (2004), Belgium (2004), Bosnia and Herzegovina (2005), Croatia (2007), Germany (2003), Greece (2005), Ireland (2006), Italy (2004), Latvia (2007), Lithuania (2001), Montenegro (2006), Netherlands (2003), Poland (2006), Russia (2002, 2007), Slovakia (2007), Spain (2005), Switzerland (2006), Ukraine (2002), United Kingdom (2002)
Liquidity risk (historical shock)	Croatia (2001), France (2004), Lithuania (2007), Moldova (2007)
Interbank contagion	Austria (2003, 2007), Belgium (2004), Croatia (2007), Greece (2005), Luxembourg (2001), Netherlands (2003), Romania (2003), United Kingdom (2002)

REFERENCES

Aspachs, O., C. A. E. Goodhart, M. Segoviano Basurto, D. Tsomocos and L. Zicchino (2006), 'Searching for a Metric for Financial Stability', *LSE Financial Markets Group Special Paper Series*, 167.

Avesani, R., K. Liu, A. Mirestean and J. Salvati (2006), 'Review and Implementation of Credit Risk Models of the Financial Sector Assessment Program (FSAP)', *IMF Working Paper*, 06/134.

Blaschke, W., M. Jones, G. Majnoni and S. Martinez Peria (2001), 'Stress Testing of Financial Systems: An Overview of Issues, Methodologies, and FSAP Experiences', *IMF Working Paper*, 01/88.

Bunn, P., A. Cunningham and M. Drehmann (2005), 'Stress Testing as a Tool for Assessing Systemic Risks', *Bank of England Financial Stability Review*, June, 116–26.

Chan-Lau, J. A., M. Srobona and L. L. Ong (2007), 'Contagion Risk in the International Banking System and Implications for London as a Global Financial Center', *IMF Working Paper*, 07/74.

Čihák, M. (2006), 'How do Central Banks Write on Financial Stability?', *IMF Working Paper*, 06/163.

 (2007), 'Introduction to Applied Stress Testing', *IMF Working Paper*, 07/59.

Čihák, M. and L. L. Ong (2007), 'Estimating Spillover Risk among Large EU Banks', *IMF Working Paper*, 07/267.

Committee on the Global Financial System (2000), *Stress Testing by Large Financial Institutions: Current Practice and Aggregation Issues*, Basel.

 (2005), *Stress Testing at Major Financial Institutions: Survey Results and Practice*, Basel.

Drehmann, M. (2005), 'A Market Based Macro Stress Test for the Corporate Credit Exposures of UK Banks', Paper presented at the *Basel Committee Workshop on Banking and Financial Stability*, Vienna, April.

Gonzalez-Hermosillo, B. and M. Segoviano Basurto (2008), 'Global Financial Stability and Macro-Financial Linkages', *IMF Working Paper*, forthcoming.

Goodhart, C. A. E., B. Hofmann and M. Segoviano Basurto (2008a), 'Bank Regulation and Macroeconomic Fluctuations', in X. Freixas, P. Hartmann and C. Mayer (eds.), *Handbook of European Financial Markets and Institutions*, 690–720.

Goodhart, C. A. E., M. Segoviano Basurto and D. Tsomocos (2008b), 'Measuring Financial Stability', *IMF Working Paper*, forthcoming.

Gray, D. and J. P. Walsh (2008), 'Model for Stress-testing with a Contingent Claims Model of the Chilean Banking System', *IMF Working Paper*, 08/89.

Independent Evaluation Office (2006), *Report on the Evaluation of the Financial Sector Assessment Program*, IMF, Washington DC.

International Monetary Fund and the World Bank (2005), *Financial Sector Assessment – A Handbook*, Washington DC.

Jones, M., P. Hilbers and G. Slack (2004), 'Stress Testing Financial Systems: What to Do when the Governor Calls', *IMF Working Paper*, 04/127.

Maechler, A. and A. Tieman (2008), 'The Real Effects of Financial Sector Risk', *IMF Working Paper*, forthcoming.

Segoviano Basurto, M. (2006a), 'The Conditional Probability of Default Methodology', *LSE Financial Markets Group Discussion Paper*, 558.

(2006b), 'The Consistent Information Multivariate Density Optimising Methodology', *LSE Financial Markets Group Discussion Paper*, 557.

(2008), 'CIMDO-Copula: Robust Estimation of Default Dependence with Data Restrictions', *IMF Working Paper*, forthcoming.

Segoviano Basurto, M. and C. A. E. Goodhart (2008), 'Banking Stability Index', *IMF Working Paper*, forthcoming.

Segoviano Basurto, M., C. A. E. Goodhart and B. Hofmann (2006), 'Default, Credit Growth, and Asset Prices', *IMF Working Paper*, 06/223.

Segoviano Basurto, M. and P. Padilla (2006), 'Portfolio Credit Risk and Macroeconomic Shocks: Applications to Stress Testing under Data-restricted Environments', *IMF Working Paper*, 06/283.

Sorge, M. (2004), 'Stress-testing Financial Systems: an Overview of Current Methodologies', *BIS Working Paper*, 165.

Conclusions

Mario Quagliariello[*]

If this same story has given the reader any pleasure, he must thank the anonymous author, and, in some measure, his reviser, for the gratification. But if, instead, we have only succeeded in wearying him, he may rest assured that we did not do so on purpose.

A. Manzoni, The Betrothed, 1840–2

Macroeconomic stress tests have constantly improved over the years, becoming a crucial component of the toolkit of banking supervisors and central banks for assessing financial stability. As shown in the second part of the book, the implementation of comprehensive stress-testing programs and the development of quantitative methodologies have allowed public authorities to make significant progress in this field.

Notwithstanding the remarkable advances and the encouraging state of the art, there are still major challenges to be addressed. They concern the methodological side, as well as data constraints and the practical use of stress test results. In these concluding remarks, I will not list all the issues that remain open. They have already – and with much more competence – been discussed in the previous chapters. I would rather recall those shortcomings that are, in my view, the top priorities for future work.

As far as methodology is concerned, a first area for improvements is clearly the calibration of the shocks and the design of macroeconomic scenarios. While it is unquestionable that they should be extreme but plausible, it is not at all obvious what 'extreme and plausible' means. The definition of stress scenarios remains largely at the discretion of the analyst and, perhaps, this is neither surprising nor unreasonable. After all, estimating the probability of a catastrophic event involves some human judgment being made on the basis of a limited set of information. However, objectivity and credibility are critical for well-founded stress-testing, particularly when results are to be reported either to political authorities or to the general public. In such situations, the

[*] Bank of Italy. The opinions expressed herein are those of the author and do not necessarily reflect those of the Bank of Italy.

introduction of some standards of plausibility or, at least, the identification of thresholds at which plausibility of a stress scenario can be assured, may be advisable. As described in various chapters, advanced statistical methods can be of some help.

Also, there is undoubtedly a need for longer time horizons in scenario design, since the impact of a specific shock may require time to emerge and the turbulence ignited by the shock may be long-lasting, particularly for some risks. However, the extension of the time horizons makes any *ceteris paribus* assumption less reasonable. In particular, the hypothesis that market players do not respond to the shock becomes problematic. In principle, stress tests should properly model the reactions of other intermediaries, depositors and public authorities when the shock materialises. Some stress tests already include the response of the monetary authorities; in some cases, attempts are made to model the reactions of other market participants, but this remains an area where enhancements are needed. This requires, on the other hand, some degree of pragmatism in order to avoid excessively ambitious modelling strategies, which would end up in over-complex models. Sophistication may certainly make the model more robust, but it would limit its accessibility and, thus, its practical usefulness. A sensible approach is to improve the ability of the models to describe the dynamics of risks, avoiding disproportionate complications. Remaining limitations can be easily dealt with by careful presentation of the results and transparent communication of the underlying assumptions.

Another crucial point to be considered is the relationship across risk types. Most stress tests, with a few notable exceptions, tend either to analyse risks separately or assume that they are independent. But risks are not uncorrelated and tend to interact, particularly in stress situations. In 2007–8, the financial crisis has revealed the strength of such interactions: credit, market and liquidity risks re-inforce each other and, in turn, are likely to hit the whole economy.

The book provides some excellent examples of stress-testing methodologies that take into account the simultaneous impact of different risk types. However, also in this field there is room for improvement. While the interactions between credit and interest rate risks are more easily modelled, liquidity risk is seldom integrated in a more comprehensive framework. This is hard to model since it would imply some sort of behavioural response of – for instance – depositors and other intermediaries. Incorporating the possibility of a bank run conditional to a macroeconomic shock would increase the illustrative power of such an exercise, however it is all but straightforward. In addition, correlations across risks are not stable in stress times and are difficult to measure.

Stress tests should also take into account the cross-country dimension of financial stability. Shocks in a specific country can easily and suddenly affect other jurisdictions, the role of global players in financial markets has dramatically increased in recent years. Ideally, stress tests should not disregard these connections and possible cross-border contagion, even though spillover effects across intermediaries, countries and markets remain difficult to capture.

The different applications presented in the book made it clear that data are also a key element in stress-testing. These simulations are typically data-intensive and rely on a wide variety of information, ranging from aggregate financial and monetary aggregates to market indicators, from bank-specific to structural variables.

A first challenge with data availability arises from the – perhaps abused but very incisive – black swan problem. Extreme shocks – like black swans – are rare and thus not easy to observe or predict. The lack of data on the behaviour of key variables in times of stress is probably the most serious obstacle to truly robust statistical inference. Scarcity of data on past crises also entails that the econometric models are very often estimated assuming 'normal-times' linear relationships, which are unlikely to hold in crisis times.

Second, stress tests assume that the relationships among variables remain constant over time, which implies a considerable consistency of the time series used in the analysis. Unfortunately, most of the time series do present structural breaks, which may undermine the reliability of the whole simulation, regardless of the sophistication of the model and the talent of the analyst.

Third, data problems come out for some risks that are rather new or whose quantification requires new inputs. For instance, credit risk – the most traditional risk banks deal with – is increasingly measured in terms of probabilities of default, loss-given default and exposures at default, for which long time series are not yet available. Furthermore, while macroeconomic variables are generally reliable, micro data tend to be much more prone to uncertain quality, inadequate timeliness and unsatisfactory coverage.

Despite some existing challenges, stress tests represent a valuable device for assessing financial stability and effectively complement more backward-looking tools. As the book has tried to illustrate, authorities that regularly perform such exercises are better able to identify the main threats to financial stability, assess their likely impact on the banking sector and, possibly, define pre-emptive actions.

In addition, disclosing the outcome of stress tests increases accountability and makes market participants more aware of major risks. However, authorities should carefully trade-off between the need to adequately inform the public and the willingness to avoid panic. While there is an undeniable beneficial effect deriving from the disclosure of financial stability analyses carried out by public authorities, there is some – understandable – debate on what they should do when stress test results are not good. In fact, concerns regarding existing vulnerabilities and possible shocks can induce self-fulfilling consequences, due to the reaction of market participants.

This risk can be avoided with thoughtful communication strategies, which should include easy-to-understand explanations and precise caveats on the function of stress tests. While the methods used for getting a given set of results should be transparent, reproducible and robust, the recipient of external communication should be aware that such simulations represent probabilistic worst cases and they should not be intended as forecasts of future disasters.

Another issue with communication is linked to the credibility of the stress-testing program in terms of economic assumptions, statistical methodologies, qualitative judgment and reporting framework. Indeed, the final goal of stress-testing is to persuade the different players to adopt countermeasures that reduce either the probability or the impact of a crisis. This requires that the results are seen as realistic and plausible. If stress test results are considered as highly unlikely, the warnings they provide may be ignored. This means that no countermeasure is adopted until it is too late.

A final remark is that stress tests always imply subjectivity. While model risk can be controlled and poor-data problems managed, subjectivity risk is unavoidable. In that sense, I agree with those arguing that stress tests are more an art than a science. Still, I would not over-emphasise this characterisation. What the final user should avoid is the illusion of precision: a range of results is typically more informative than spurious accuracy.

Since stress tests are imperfect, they provide the best contribution to financial stability assessment when those in charge of implementing and interpreting them are conscious of both their potential and inherent weakness. Although their output should not be considered as an infallible prediction, stress tests do contribute to a deeper understanding of possible threats to financial systems and to ensuring financial stability.

Index